THE TRANSFORMATIVE VISION

The
Transformative
Vision

Reflections on the Nature

and History of Human Expression

by José A. Argüelles

SHAMBHALA

Boulder & London

1975

SHAMBHALA PUBLICATIONS, INC.
1920 13th Street
Boulder, Colorado 80302

© 1975 by José A. Argüelles
ISBN 0-87773-055-5
LCC 74-75096

Designed by Hal Hershey
Frontispiece by Armando Busick

Distributed in the United States by *Random House*
and in Canada by *Random House of Canada Ltd.*

Distributed in the Commonwealth
by *Routledge & Kegan Paul Ltd.*
London and Henley-on-Thames

Printed in the United States of America

This book is dedicated
to my children,
Joshua and Tara

Contents

A NOTE ABOUT ILLUSTRATIONS

This is essentially a book about inner vision. In order not to detract from, and even to enhance this focus of attention, it was finally decided not to reproduce any of the works of art which are described and spoken of throughout the text. In cases where the reader may wish to become more familiar with certain of the works described, I have provided an ample bibliography which includes numerous illustrative texts.

Introduction

WHAT YOU are about to read is the product of an adventure that has been years in the making. Since I was a child art has been my vocation and my love. As a young man in the late 1950's, I painted vigorously in the manner of the then-popular abstract expressionists. It seemed natural to me to fling out my energies in blazing swirls across the canvas. I thought that this was what art was about: to express one's deepest feelings with ardor. Besides energy I apparently exhibited some talent and was placed in the advanced painting class in my last year as an undergraduate student. With me was one other student who had also been painting in the manner of the abstract expressionists. One day, to my very great surprise, my fellow student came in with a canvas not at all like those he was accustomed to painting. This canvas was painted in simple flat colors arranged in a few quasi-geometric forms. "What is *that*?" I asked him, somewhat amazed at his sudden change. "It's hard-edge," he replied. "Haven't you heard? It's the latest style." I was dimly aware of "hard-edge" from the art journals, but I was stunned by the notion that art might be simply style, like clothes to be taken off or put on without the slightest regard to the inner feelings. If this was what the art-game was about, I wanted nothing to do with it. But since art had been the center of my existence, I was reluctant to give it up. I was left with the basic problem of how to reconcile art and life.

I reached this impasse in 1960, and for the next six years I produced little as a painter except an occasional morose self-portrait and a lot of absent-minded doodling. But the problem that had confronted me in that advanced painting class would not leave me, and I vowed to resolve it. Since I could not paint in full conscience without first understanding myself and the problem of art in greater perspective, I enrolled as a graduate student in the history of art. The rote procedure of graduate training was redeemed for me by a deep and abiding feeling that somehow it was *the way*. What mattered to me was not the memorization of categories and the cataloging of information, which were easy enough, but the occasional glimpses I received of the tortuous route of the spirit as it manifested in artifact, and the intuition of certain thinkers whose writing I was fortunate enough to become acquainted with.

The problem of art, I slowly discovered, was inextricably involved with the problem of history, and the problem of history with the unfathomed depths of man's own nature. A rare art historian like Wilhelm Worringer revealed to me that art was generated by spiritual forces, and that art history properly understood was a "history of the human psyche and its forms of expression." In the chapter to his book *Form in Gothic* entitled

"The Science of Art as Human Psychology," Worringer advanced the idea of shifting the emphasis of art history from the objects of perception to perception itself. The study of art would then be a study of the psychic categories or possibilities expressed by the spirit as it passes through human form. Worringer concludes this chapter by observing,

> The variability of these psychical categories, which have found their formal expression in the development of style, progresses by mutations, the orderliness of which is regulated by the fundamental process governing all development in human history: the checkered fateful adjustment of man to the outer world. This ceaseless shifting in man's relation to the impressions crowding in upon him from the surrounding world forms the starting point for all psychology on the grand scale, and no historical, cultural, or artistic phenomenon is within reach of our understanding until it has been set in the perspective of this determining point of view.[1]

When I became aware of Worringer's viewpoint, toward the end of my graduate training, it confirmed a deep, as yet inexpressible intuition of mine that my orthodox historical training was misleading and arbitrary—that whereas I should have been learning more about human nature, I had been taught only about its effects. And these effects were increasingly disastrous or absurd for the simple reason that learning about human nature—psychology on the grand scale—had been ignored, and this ignorance had been institutionalized. As a result, the study of history had become a narrowly circumscribed and totally intellectual endeavor entirely removed from the actual experience of human expression. The realm of contemporary art, too, had been circumscribed and subverted until it served only a blind self-interest. I had advanced a bit closer to an understanding of my problem.

I left school to experience the world, which in the mid-1960's was a strange and chaotic place that bore little resemblance to what I had known inside the university. It was a world characterized by war, civil riots, seething unrest, an electronic culture gone mad, the strange enchantment of drugs, of occult murmurings, of sciences and literatures never touched upon in the classroom. Through a total letting-go and immersion in this *other* world, I finally began to *see*. History was no longer a meaningless façade of facts and artifacts, but an alchemical formula, a symbolic calculus, a mystery play enacted by the collective human psyche on the planetary stage. At the same time the divisions between mind and body, intellect and creativity—divisions I had always accepted as rigid and absolute—suddenly seemed flimsy, fluctuating, and arbitrary. There was nothing to stop me from going beyond them.

In a state of exaltation I began painting again, this time from a deep and seemingly timeless space. As my painting progressed, I slowly began to consolidate my thoughts and feelings about history. It now seemed clear to me that our present era is one of transition. In the spring of 1968 I wrote, in a fit of enthusiasm, a brief paper entitled "Art in a Period of Transition: The Dawn of New Magic." This paper announced the central themes of *The Transformative Vision*: history as a mythic cycle, the transcendence of reason, and the visionary role of the artist. But these ideas needed further experience before they could come to full maturity.

My work as a scholar took me into the realm of psychophysics, whose unitive aesthetic, I came to realize, provided the basis of Worringer's viewpoint. My work as a painter led me into the realm of the perennial philosophy, whose primary artistic manifestation is the mandala. Gradually, over a three-year period, I was finally able to unite these two currents of thought—the psychophysical aesthetic and the perennial philosophy. Their marriage was the resolution I had been seeking, and it is the guiding principle of this book.

I must say a word about my method. My purpose is primarily to present a "history of the human psyche and its forms of expression" in the critical period from the European Renaissance to the present. Since this period is marked by a tremendous surge of European thought and activity, much of the book focuses on Europe. But I have tried to place the development of the European psyche within the larger context of the nature of the human organism and its planetary environment, and within the context of non-European cosmological systems, namely the ancient Mexican and the Hindu-Buddhist, in order to achieve a more global perspective. At the same time I am painfully aware of the limitations in my choice of material; though I have dwelled on the visual arts and to a slightly lesser degree on literature, I may be faulted for my general neglect of music and the dramatic arts. I do believe, however, that my presentation will permit those more knowledgeable in these areas to draw the obvious conclusions. In any case I have by no means intended to suggest that any area of human expression should be slighted.

I am also aware that even in the areas of the visual arts and literature, there is much that I have undoubtedly left out. The aesthetic ideas of Gurdjieff, the Pre-Raphaelites, and the contemporary renaissance of popular Chicano mural art in the United States are several examples that immediately spring to mind. Again, I hope that my presentation will enable readers to draw their own conclusions. The transformative vision is a thread passing through countless individuals, famous and infamous, known and unknown. I have not attempted to give a complete account of its workings but through sufficient example to demonstrate its reality and universality as well as its permutations in the context of historical developments.

It also seems appropriate to comment on two key terms that are used in this book—*psyche* and *techne*. Of course, the former term has been long and variously used in our culture, generally to mean soul, spirit, or the subtle essence that animates our thoughts and actions. I have used *psyche* more specifically to refer to the aspect of human behavior that relates to the right cerebral hemispere; psyche in this sense is the innate human ability to intuit or to perceive as a whole, that underlies the primary human impulse toward expression. By *techne* I mean the mutually defining counter-aspect of psyche, which is specifically related to the left-cerebral-hemisphere functions of logic, analysis, language, and mathematics. It is techne that physically actualizes the impulses emanating from psyche. Whereas psyche is primary and relates man to nature as such, techne is secondary and accounts for the artificial, structuring side of human being. Though these two aspects of human nature can function independently of each other, the degree of their independence defines the degree of human imbalance, sickness, or insanity. In actuality they cannot be understood separately. Being a whole, their mutual self-definition comprises the basis of the psychophysical point of view. This is a unitive understanding synonymous with the perennial philosophy, whose dynamic I have defined as *the transformative vision*. The harmonious essence of this vision is the transcendence of the conflicts we call history.

Should the ideology and mentality of history prevail, then the transformative vision may have to continue as a strange underground development. But I do not think that this shall be the case. A rhythm more powerful and inexorable than the rhythm of human reason is sweeping through the human race, a rhythm that springs from deep within the bowels of the earth and resonates with the most distant reaches of stellar space. This rhythm is the heartbeat of the transformative vision.

Such, then, is the background to the pages that follow. The basic problem posed to me in the studio some fourteen years ago has finally been resolved. Art is the perfect marriage of psychic impulse and technical implementation. Since the fullness of life is defined no differently, the resolution is not a conclusion but a beginning. May the reader join with me in this adventure.

CHAPTER ONE

The Dialectical Setting: Human Hemispheres
and Planetary Poles

OUR SHIMMERING blue planet, seen from afar, is bisected by two planes: the equatorial, or horizontal, plane and the vertical plane of the polar axis. The equatorial plane splits the world into two inversely symmetrical hemispheres, the Northern and Southern, capped by the two polar regions. The north polar region is essentially water, the Arctic Ocean, around which are grouped various land masses, all pointing generally southward: the peninsular regions of Greenland, Scandinavia, Spain, Italy, and Greece; the continent of Africa; the subcontinents of Arabia, India, and Malaysia; the peninsulas of Baja California and Florida; and the continent of South America. Even the island continent of Australia bends generally southward at both ends. The south polar region, on the other hand, is a major land mass surrounded by the confluence of the world's great oceans: the Atlantic, the Pacific, and the Indian. Most of the world's land masses are in the Northern Hemisphere; the Southern Hemisphere is largely water. Yet the polar center of the North is water, and that of the South is land.

The vertical polar plane, characterized by the rhythmic fluctuations of day and night, similarly divides the world into two hemispheres, commonly known as the Eastern and Western, or, respectively, the Old World and the New. Like the Northern and Southern hemispheres, the Eastern and Western represent a dynamic balance of inverse symmetry: the Old world of Eurasia and Africa is a significantly greater land mass than the New World of the Americas. The latter, however, if one is to follow the not altogether arbitrary prime meridian of Greenwich, contains the greater part of the world's large oceans, the Atlantic and the Pacific. Corresponding to the rationally imposed prime meridian is the natural meridian of the Mid-Atlantic Ridge, a sinuous backbone that runs suboceanically from polar zone to polar zone. This submerged spinal cord has its terrestrial counterpart in the New World mountain range of the Rockies-Sierras-Cordilleras, also running from polar zone to polar zone. The New World vertical mountain range is complemented in the Old World by the horizontal zone of the Atlas, Alpine, Caucasus, and Himalaya ranges.

The inverse symmetry of the globe provides the guiding frame of reference for the dialectical process of human events since the peak of the last glaciation some twelve thousand years ago, when the world assumed its present configuration. During this period, geologically known as the Holocene ("most recent age"), the human race emerged as a significant factor in the evolution of the globe. Correspondingly, human history and culture may be viewed as the attempt to achieve a dynamic integration of a motivating set of polar but complementary archetypes: on the one hand, the feminine archetype of the giver-receiver, the great mother/goddess/ muse; and on the other, the masculine archetype of the power-acquiring shaman/technocrat/artist.* In its simplest essence, the feminine archetype is psyche, the inherent capacity to know or to realize, and the masculine archetype is techne, the innate ability to achieve or to put into practice. To the former belong the qualities of mind, intuition, and spirit; to the latter, body, intellect, and matter. Psyche is primary and techne secondary, for realization precedes actualization. Psyche literally means breath, while techne means skill or art, insofar as art is any kind of external accomplishment. In more civilized societies where art, artifice, and artifact prevail as a form of technology, psyche tends to be considered secondary; in extreme cases, techne may completely dominate psyche. In certain kinds of tribal societies techne may be submerged under psyche. But there is always some kind of psychic life, no matter how perverted or repressed, just as there is always some kind of technical expression, no matter how basic or crude. Otherwise human being would simply not be human.

The interplay of these two fundamental tendencies in all of their manifestations gives rise to the dialectic of evolution in every phase of human culture. In addition to being archetypes of primary organic and sexual differentiation, psyche and techne are expressions of the two primary aspects of consciousness, whose complementary dynamics determine the very destiny of our planet. Consciousness of such a destiny cannot exist without a conscience. In fact, the words consciousness and conscience stem from the same meaning: to know well, to know thoroughly, to know all together. Though knowing all together is an inherent capacity synonymous with being itself, it is a capacity that few people exercise in all its fullness. To know all together is to be in complete communion with psyche and in complete command of techne. Most people live arbitrary, mechanical existences in which error and aberration succeed each other unendingly, while the mind is plagued with sundry neuroses and the body with various diseases. This dis-integrated life process consists of a series of momentary experiences held together by a minimal awareness sufficient to pull the organism through its round of existence. Psyche is totally unconscious and techne totally mechanical, for there is no recognized relation between the two. But this is the life of the waking dead, and it is no real life at all. An integration of the two modes of being, psyche and techne, gives rise to and defines a mythic or cosmic state of consciousness, a harmonization of opposites in which war and strife have become transformed into a conscious

---

*I am using "archetype" not in the Jungian sense but in a mythic-poetic sense to mean a primal tendency or quality latent in consciousness and capable of being expressed in an infinite number of ways.

interplay of energies, and the human organism itself is in a dynamic balance with the primal forces of the earth and the radiant forces of the heavens. Lack of integration—the tendency to polarization—of the two archetypes accounts for the process known as history, which more and more becomes a conflict, rather than an interplay, between one mode of consciousness and the other. The present world conflict stems from a major polarization of consciousness that parodies the geographical division of the hemispheres. Accordingly, the contemporary convulsions, like those on the geological scale, may be necessary equilibrating events which precede the appearance of new life forms and the disappearance of old ones.

Perhaps the simplest and most concise—not to mention the oldest—symbol of the integrated interplay of the two modes of consciousness is the ancient *t'ai-chi* symbol of the Chinese. It symbolizes not only the synergistic totality of the two modes of consciousness and of the global hemispheres, but also the interaction of day and night, life and death, masculine and feminine, existence and nonexistence. The dot of light appearing in the dark *(yin)* side and the dot of dark in the light *(yang)* side show that each side contains the potential of becoming the other. The dark and the light—yin and yang—do not represent two absolutes but the two major aspects of a dynamic unity, and the components of a process which is self-transforming. Because the opposite aspects define and change into each other, they are vitally—and innately—interdependent. In its utter simplicity, the t'ai-chi model makes clearer the totality of processes that are both global and mental; and it relates both of these processes into one psychoglobal whole.

In order to understand the workings of the larger whole within the human realm, we must first recognize that the masculine archetype, techne, represented historically by the rise of Europe as a world power in the sixteenth century, has come to dominate all present psychoglobal processes. The European world conquest was built upon a particular perceptual model that crystallizes the technical mode of being, while casting psyche aside to atrophy. Carlos Castaneda has contrasted the European's pre-eminently intellectual way of experiencing reality with the sorcerer's intuitive way:

In European membership the world is built largely from what the eyes report to the mind. In sorcery the total body is used as a perceptor. As Europeans we see a world out there and talk to ourselves about it. We are here and the world is there. Our eyes feed our reason and we have no direct knowledge of things. According to sorcery this burden on the eyes is unnecessary. We know with the total body.[1]

The consequences of the clash between the European technocrat and the non-European sorcerer—the shaman, the medicine man, and the yogi—over the past four centuries reveal the drama of human consciousness in direct conflict with itself. This drama has resulted in the *apparent* triumph of techne over psyche. But, in view of the present chaos in which the human race finds itself, the triumph is ever more illusory, especially since the victory of the technocrat over the shaman merely represents the victory of one male power-seeking archetype over the other. This only underscores the tremendous imbalance that has developed over millennia within our collective nature—an imbalance so deep and pervasive that it generally cannot be discerned. Even when perceived, as in Castaneda's observation, it is difficult to communicate the entirety, much less the nature of the imbalance, since the intellectual aspect of consciousness has pre-empted the rights to all forms of expression. That is, no communication regarding world affairs is taken seriously unless it is firmly based on prevailing intellectual, power-seeking, assumptions, regardless of how one-sided these assumptions are.

A further dimension to the entire polarized situation is revealed by the fact that not only is the human species divided into masculine and feminine, techne and psyche, but the human brain itself is divided into two distinct spheres, each with its separate functions and attributes. Following the principle of inverse symmetry, each cerebral hemisphere controls the opposite side of the body: the right hemisphere controls the left side of the body; the left hemisphere, the right. Robert Ornstein has recently summed up the cerebral functions:

Both the structure and the function of these two "half-brains" in some part underlie the two modes of consciousness which simultaneously co-exist within each one of us. Although each hemisphere shares the potential for many functions, and both sides participate in most activities, in the normal person the two hemispheres tend to specialize. The left hemisphere (connected to the right side of the body) is predominantly involved with analytic, logical thinking, especially in verbal and mathematical functions. Its mode of operation is primarily linear. This hemisphere seems to process information sequentially. This mode of operation of necessity must underlie logical thought, since logic depends on sequence and order. Language and mathematics, both left-hemisphere activities, also depend predominantly on linear time.

If the left hemisphere is specialized for analysis, the right hemisphere (again, remember, connected to the left side of the body) seems specialized for holistic mentation. Its language ability is quite limited. This hemisphere is primarily responsible for our orientation in space, artistic endeavor, crafts, body image, recognition of faces. It processes information more diffusely than does the left hemisphere, and its responsibilities demand a ready integration of inputs at once. If the left hemisphere can be termed predominantly analytic and sequential in its operation, then the right hemisphere is more holistic and relational, and more simultaneous in its mode of operation.[2]

In terms of the t'ai-chi symbol, the left is the dark, or yin side of the body, but it is animated by the light yang dot, which may be said to represent the right cerebral hemisphere. The right is the light, or yang, side of the body, animated by the dark yin dot, represeting in this analogy the left cerebral hemisphere. In archetypal terms psyche is represented by the right cerebral hemisphere and the left side of the body, and techne by the left cerebral hemisphere and the right side of the body. More commonly speaking, our present cultural values are determined by a tendency to right-handedness (techne) as opposed to left-handedness (psyche). As a right-handed culture we believe in law and order, reason, the supremacy of technique, and in "Might makes right"—instead of rite. It is interesting, too, that "right" etymologically means "straight" or "not curved," whereas left means "sky," "that which is curved." Health may correspondingly be defined as a dynamic interplay of the two sides of the brain and of the related nervous systems and modes of consciousness. Sickness results when one side is impaired or exerts undue control over the other, or when both sides are disconnected. Ornstein continues:

In hundreds of clinical cases, it has been found that damage to the left hemisphere very often interferes with, and can in some cases completely destroy, language ability. Often patients cannot speak after such left-hemisphere lesions, a condition known as "aphasia." An injury to the right hemisphere may not interfere with language performance at all, but may cause severe disturbance in spatial awareness, in musical ability, in recognition of other people, or in awareness of one's own body. Some patients with right-hemisphere damage cannot dress themselves adequately, although their speech and reason remain unimpaired.[3]

As Ornstein further notes, "There exists a tendencey to term the left and right hemispheres the 'major' and 'minor' respectively."[4] This tendency in neurological parlance betrays a much deeper and more serious prejudice symptomatic of a profound psychocultural *dis-ease*. It implies that the world of the European—for all intents and purposes, the entire "modern" world—is a *split-brain culture* so dominated by the left hemisphere that it has lost contact with its own innate bodily responses by reducing all experience to logical, linear functions. Because the curve-denying, right-handed European has conquered the world, the problems we face and the solutions offered are oriented almost exclusively to the left hemisphere. Given the extremity of the situation, this imbalance must be understood and treated like any other pathology.

Despite its division into hemispheres and polar zones, the world is a unity. Likewise, a healthy person or culture is a conscious, psychotechnical, yin/yang totality, recognizing the interplay of opposites within each other—the dots of opposite value within each side of the t'ai-chi symbol. To live by this principle ensures transformability and duration; it is the basis of sanity and integration. A nonintegrated point of view, by contrast, is necessarily dualistic, denying the interplay of opposites and precluding the transformation of either side. The consequence is eternal conflict between two unresolvable opposites. This is the legacy of the modern European world view, with its highly evolved structure of mutually exclusive, antagonistic opposites—right and left (in politics), mind and body, capitalism and communism, science and art, man and woman, civilization and nature, to name some obvious examples.

Clearly we live in a time when by some unknown authority, techne wields invincible power over psyche. Consequently psyche itself is perverted and polluted, and the fulfillment of cosmic purpose seems threatened. There would be ceaseless struggle were there not a third, synergistic force at work, a force greater than the sum of the two primary modes of being. This is the force of an awakened and expanded consciousness, which inspires the reconciliation of opposites; it is the energy of the spirit of the whole. In *Fantasia of the Unconscious* D. H. Lawrence wrote, "Existence is truly a matter of propagation between two infinites. . . . Midway between the two cosmic infinites lies the third, which is more than infinite. This is the Holy Ghost Life, individual life."[5] This third-force thread of holy consciousness—the spirit of the whole—imperceptibly weaves the disasters of the body and the errors of the mind into a meaningful pattern. It is the essence of the transformative vision, through which history is transcended and the mythic whole of cosmos—the order of the universe—is once more regained.

To a deep extent the events of what we call history reflect the continual fluctuations of our own psychophysiological makeup. The psychosomatic nature of the current world impasse has been described in different ways by some recent thinkers, including Norman O. Brown, in *Life Against Death* and *Love's Body*, and Arthur Koestler, in *The Ghost in the Machine*, a study of human "urge to self-destruction." Koestler writes: "We must search for a cure for the *schizophysiology* inherent in man's nature, and the resulting split in our minds which led to the situation in which we find ourselves."[6] In searching for a "cure" it will be helpful to describe and define the most recent developmental phase of human consciousness as an integral aspect of a transformative process which is both psychological and global, pertaining to the mind as well as the body, the individual as well as the collective whole, man as well as nature. Because of the pathology inherent in human consciousness—inherent even in the very notion of an evolutionary process—an excruciating dilemma on the global scale has developed. To untangle the mammoth Gordian knot that now wraps the world in a puzzling technological maze demands a return of psyche to the throne of human wisdom. Should some Alexander with his sword attempt to slice through this knot, he would also slice through the world. In the meantime learned men debate over the amount of time remaining not only for survival of the human race but perhaps even for the entire earth.

As I have already indicated, the pathology of our modern world has its root in the present technical, left-hemisphere tyranny, which is European in origin. I do not mean to single the Europeans out for censure; they are a part of a drama in which all the protagonists—conqueror and conquered—must play their roles. The fact of the matter is that the Europeans were most ripe to be the active carriers of the left-hemisphere *disease* that developed and spread with startling swiftness and acuity toward the beginning of the sixteenth century. This is the time known, of course, as the Renaissance. With the exception of certain aspects of Greco-Roman thought and culture, which modern Europeans tend to view as their true spiritual source, the pre-Renaissance development of human cultures generally represents a dynamic balance of the two sides of the brain—language, astronomy, mathematics, commerce, and agriculture balanced by poetry, music, architecture, and the various arts and crafts, all wedded into one mythic whole, fed by the tributaries of some profoundly religious intuition. Thus, among the most notable monuments expressing the unitive, interdependent functioning of both sides of the human brain are the great cathedrals of Europe, dedicated to the Madonna feminine archetype, constructed scarcely a few centuries before the climactic cerebral split began to manifest itself externally.

Globally, the Europeans occupy a promontory of the Eurasian land mass—the westernmost portion of the eastern or *left* hemisphere of the globe (if one is standing in Greenwich facing the sun), in the Old World. From the fall of Rome until the Renaissance, the Europeans were not so much Europeans as they were tribes of Christians. It was only after the split in the Christian Church took place, early in the sixteenth century, that the seafaring Europeans quite dramatically became themselves—conquerors of the Cross. Prior to that time they had been warriors of the Cross, both among themselves and in opposition to the Muslims. As conquerors the Europeans' first mission was the conquest of the New World—globally speaking, the western or right hemisphere, the land of the "noble savage."

One of the strongest clues indicating the operation of a transformative process inaugurating the left-hemisphere tyranny at the critical early-sixteenth-century juncture is the coincidence of Cortés' amazing conquest of Mexico with Martin Luther's divisive Reformation of the Christian Church. Conquest and Reformation were both completed in 1521. The price for conquering and repressing the right hemisphere—globally and neurophysiologically—was the splitting of the left. The greatest historical irony is encompassed by the fact that it was on April 21, 1519, Good Friday, that Hernando Cortés set the flag of the Cross on Mexican soil, at a site that was to become the Spanish city Vera Cruz (True Cross); at the very same time, Martin Luther was writing his epoch-making tract, *Concerning Christian Liberty*. Even more awesome is the fact that Good Friday, April 21, 1519, corresponded in the Mexican calendar to the day Ce

Acatl (One Reed), dedicated to the principal god/hero of the ancient Mexicans, Quetzalcoatl. Furthermore, the ancient Mexican seers had prophesied that this particular day would mark the end of a "heaven" period consisting of thirteen 52-year cycles and the beginning of a major "hell" period consisting of nine 52-year cycles, or 468 years.[7] Knowing this full well, the Aztec emperor, Moctezuma, in actuality an adversary and conqueror of the forces of Quetzalcoatl, hoped that Cortés himself would be none other than the vanquished Quetzalcoatl, the god returned, for at least, according to tradition, Quetzalcoatl was not a vengeful god. Moctezuma and the Mexicans soon learned that he represented something much worse: Cortés was their own god of war disguised by the banner of the "Prince of Peace." Well versed in the ancient philosophy of the ceaseless transformation of opposites, the Mexicans acquiesced.

The meeting of Cortés and Moctezuma has been considered one of the more dramatic curiosities of world history. But what it signaled was nothing less than the triumphant ascent of the left cerebral hemisphere over the right, and ultimately, of techne over psyche. What was an entry into Hell for the cultures of the New World and ultimately for all non-European peoples, was concurrently the high point of a Renaissance or rebirth among the Europeans. But if the reign of Pope Leo X from 1513 to 1521 was the high point of the Renaissance, it also culminated, as we have already noted, in a momentous split within the Christian Church. Externally over the past four centuries since then, the Europeans appear to have dominated the non-Europeans and correspondingly, the functions of the left cerebral hemisphere appear to have subjugated and repressed those of the right. But at the same time, the technical, left-hemisphere culture of the Europeans, as if in a fever, has released more and more energy through a process of continual sublimation and division within itself. This energy, much like the energy released by the splitting atom, has tended to be exploitative and violent in nature. Corresponding to the repression, exploitation, or even extermination of the non-European races, among the Europeans themselves there has been, since the Reformation, a continual round of religious and civil wars, inquisitions, revolutions, and struggles against inimical and heretical social elements within the body politic. At a more subtle level, accompanying the rise of science in the post-Reformation period and the consequent rise of rationalist/materialist philosophy with its strict mind-matter dualism, there has been a growing civil war of the mind: an unceasing skepticism toward, repression of, and often, open battle against what have come to be termed the irrational elements of the human psyche—the neglected right-hemisphere functions. As of the nineteenth century these "irrational" elements began their own incessant agitation against the dominant rationalist culture in the form of "underground," quasi-artistic, counterculture "movements." And finally, there appeared in the nineteenth century the divisive doctrine of dialectical materialism, which was to provide the breeding ground of the twentieth-century "holy war" between capitalism and communism, a war that is merely the host for a hundred lesser wars, cold and hot, physical and psychic, each waged against the background of the most insidious war—man against himself.

Clearly, the 468-year hell period that began in 1519 for the Mexicans and other non-European peoples pertains to the Europeans as well. Left-hemisphere mastery has been paid for, in the end, by the mindless, terroristic, and overwhelming rebellion of the right-hemisphere functions—manifested both by actual "third world" rebellion and terrorism, and by disintegrative and irrational technocratic social behavior. To the Europeans these dimensions of hell were not at all evident at the time of the first great world voyages and explorations. Not only were there the New World discoveries, but by the end of the fifteenth century, there were wonders like the printing press and gunpowder. In Italy these technological accomplishments were accompanied by a sense of *renasciaminto*, a cultural feeling that seemed to augur a return of the Golden Age of Mediterranean antiquity. But what was interpreted as a rebirth of the ancient world was in actuality an upheaval of the Age of Iron. That the European intelligentsia should have developed a nostalgia for the distant reaches of the Golden Age just when technological and political world domination by their own culture was swiftly coming into focus is of the greatest psychological and historical significance, for in traditional terms, the Renaissance, an expression of the Age of Iron, or Fourth Age, was the "beginning of the end."

In order to obtain a broader perspective, let us make a slight calendrical digression. In both East and West there persists the theory of the four ages as a kind of metahistorical framework of cosmic development. The first and longest of these is the Golden Age, or in the Hindu tradition, Sattya Yuga. Then, in descending order, come the Silver, the Bronze, and finally, the Iron Age—respectively, Treta, Dvarpa, and Kali Yuga in the Hindu tradition. In the Golden Age things change very slowly over a vast period of time, for the simple reason that there is little need for "progress"; it is the era of the gods, of felicity and peace and cosmic harmony. Through the successive ages, however, time becomes more crowded, and as activity and conflict increase, reality becomes more and more demythologized. According to the Hindu reckoning, the ratio of the length of the ages is 4:3:2:1. The last age, the Iron Age or Kali Yuga, may be the briefest in duration, but it is also the one in which there is the greatest amount of activity; the gods no longer manifest in this age, at least not as gods, and man attains, through his perfecting of tools forged from the metals of the earth— symbolized by iron, whose color is black—mastery over the planet. Or so it would seem. In any case the scheme is cyclic and endless: the conclusion of the last age is the beginning of the first. But whether or not it heralds the beginning of the millennium envisioned by the nineteenth-century positivists is another matter. See Appendix A, page 297.

A similar progression of ages formed the cosmological framework of the ancient Mexicans, symbolically depicted on the famous Aztec Calendar Stone. In addition to the traditional four ages, however, the Mexicans perceived a fifth age or sun, ruled by the Sun of Movement, which may be viewed as the culminating aspect of the Kali Yuga or Age of Iron. The symbol for this fifth age, Ollin, means "Earth-Shaking," change or movement. It spans at the most a little more than a millennium, consisting of thirteen 52-year heaven cycles, from 843 to 1519, and nine 52-year hell cycles, from 1519 to 1987.

According to this reckoning the heaven period between 843 and 1519 was the age of the last great pretechnological renaissance: cultures of the Christians in Europe; the Muslims in North Africa and the Near East; the peoples of Ghana and Kenya in West and East Africa respectively; the Hindus in India; the Buddhists of Khmer, Java, Tibet, China, and Japan; the Incas in the Andes, the Mayans in Central America, and the Toltecs and Aztecs in Mexico; the so-called mound-builders of the greater Mississippi valley and the cliff-dwellers of the American Southwest; and the Polynesians of the Pacific all attest to a vital global flowering, a dynamic and diverse expression of a deeply unitive—religious in the fullest meaning of the word—sense of being. But scattered among these Iron Age expressions of cultural unity were equally many signs of decay; nearly all of these cultures were built upon much older civilizations and teachings whose inner significance no longer accorded in many cases with their outward cultural expression. Conflict values tended to dominate, giving rise, for instance, to militarism among the Christians and Muslims, and imperialism among the Incas and Aztecs; in the Far East, the warrior class of Japan remained powerful, while the Mongol invaders swept across the entire Eurasian land mass.

In the contrast between the spiritual dynamism and the growing militaristic imperialism of these pretechnological cultures, the split in favor of the left cerebral hemisphere, which was overtly to come in the sixteenth century, was already latent. Thus the period around 843 marked the inception of a climactic age in human history, one in which the inherent "schizophysiology" of the human organism was to produce mounting confusion, until the critical point in 1519 when the mental condition of the human race slipped out of balance. In a sense the events following this point mark the most drastic change in human and global events since the dawn of what we call history. The changes that have occurred since then have been so dramatic that, in accordance with the Mexican notion of the Fifth Sun, the Sun of Movement, the last four and one-half centuries must be viewed as a period of increasing *movement* at all levels, of evolutionary transformation so spectacular and swift that its outcome can only be a climax of unimaginable consequences.

Though the Age of Iron or Kali Yuga, is characterized by "negative" attributes—black, dark, without virtue, degenerate, materialistic, confused, and so forth—which have resulted in increasing pathology, repression, mental illness, and confusion, it is equally a period of transition and opportunity. To look back to an idealized Golden Age, as was common among the Humanists of Renaissance Europe, or among the "primitivists" of the past two centuries, only compounds the difficulty of our present situation by skirting the responsibility of accepting and appreciating its reality. A "final" age is also an age of transformation: its guiding lights are the heretics and the visionaries who, seizing the opportunity, maintain a middle ground between futile revolution and blind materialism. These people are agents of conscious change vivifying the mass movements of humanity that come to characterize this period in the great cycle of ages. Through them the present situation is articulated and the groundwork of the future is laid. They are the few who retain a relatively healthy balance between psyche and techne and who are thus able to create a vision of the direction of human events that responds to the deepest aspirations of our being.

The balance maintained by the "transformative visionaries" is nothing less than a dialog between the two hemispheres. And this dialog itself is the unifying thread of a process that is *transcendental* through and through, moving in patterns that encompass spheres of consciousness infinitely greater than what any individual can perceive. What is transcendental is the attainment of consciousness itself, for consciousness as *knowing all together* goes beyond—literally, transcends—the struggle of opposites, achieving their reconciliation. As this age draws to a close, we return to the primacy of psychic knowledge and ability. Though this may mean the effacement of technology as we now know it, through the integration of our past experience it also implies the rediscovery of the basis for a technique which is neither art nor science, but both, and more than both. Such a technique will be founded on the laws of the mind in tune with the laws governing the order of the universe. The mental horizon is no different than the global/historical; what governs the mind is no different than the law of planetary development, and vice versa. The only error is the belief in absolute exclusion, the error of nonacceptance. In 1519 the priests and seers of ancient Mexico were put to death; the entire world slowly began to accept "European membership"; reason appropriated the organ of vision and the rest of the sense-body shrank in proportion. Yet today, from pole to pole the world shakes; a presence long silent moves once again: a form unseen, but not unfelt; a name unvoiced, but not unknown.

CHAPTER TWO

Art and Consciousness: From Cosmic Myth

to Single Vision

THOUGH THEIR lives are rooted in both cerebral hemispheres, the transformative visionaries tend to stand out as being artistically inclined simply because of the analytical bias of the techne-oriented European civilization. Indeed, one of the outstanding features of this civilization is the antagonism that develops between what comes to be called science and art. The former term literally means "knowledge"; the latter, "a way of doing things." If wisdom is the union of these two, their separation implies a loss of meaning, a fall into absurdity. The scientist becomes the exemplar of left-hemisphere functions: cold, logical, dispassionate, objective, verbal and highly literate, the proponent of value as quantity. The artist becomes the scientist's polar opposite: emotional, often inarticulate, intuitive, irrational, passionately involved in life, often political in an overt way (whereas the scientist, because of the coolness demanded of his vocation, tends to remain silent), the proponent of value as quality. These are stereotypes describing two specialized modes of human behavior and knowledge. Insofar as each is rooted in only one side of the human brain—the scientist in the left, the artist in the right—each is an incomplete being. In our present stage of cultural development, these stereotypes reflect very real social utilitarian values: just as the neurologist tends to describe the left hemisphere as the "major" and the right as the "minor," in our technological survival value system the artist is by far a more dispensable creature than the scientist. Of course, the value system is loaded, being a function of an almost exclusively left-hemisphere approach to reality that discredits the validity of right-hemisphere knowledge. In political and financial terms, this means that the scientist is assured of success; the artist, at best, is assured of a hard struggle.

The artist who learns how to survive in contemporary left-hemisphere culture is often the one who adopts its values. But in so doing he unwittingly cuts himself off from the right-hemisphere source, and hence defeating himself *to the extent that as an artist he is supposed to be representing and expressing right-hemisphere functions.* Thus, as the culture develops along profit-making lines that stress novelty, gadgetry, and innovation for the sake of innovation, the artist consciously or unconsciously is swept along. But because of inherent social bias, even adopting these values brings him no assurance of success. The problem lies in society's unquestioning acceptance of the roles of artist and scientist as absolutely distinct. The very creation of these roles is a technical, left-hemisphere fiction, a socially fixed distortion of innately interdependent neurocerebral responses to reality. In an integrated neurocerebral circuit there would be no such roles as artist and scientist, certainly not in an absolute sense.

In the Golden Age, when existence was most basic and nonspecialized, an individual could assume any number of different roles—hunter, gatherer, sorcerer, craftsman, parent—and every member of the group could share these roles more or less equally, with a minimum burden to the psyche. The greatest specialization at this stage was probably that of sexual differentiation and reproduction. Insofar as the expressive functions of what we now call art are concerned, there was no necessary specialization, either into stereotyped roles or by sex. Claude Levi-Strauss reports that in a certain Brazilian tribe it is the women who do the more physically demanding sculpture and the men who do the painting and body-design, indicating the fluidity of the expressive functions regardless of sex. But most important, at this primordial, mythic stage of development *everyone* expresses himself or herself through some medium.

Ironically, as the species has become more highly developed—that is, involved in its technical capacity *as an end in itself*—the unique evolutionary capacity of human being for nonspecialization has become more and more abused. But the problem of specialization did not become globally critical until the development of a mechanistic technology in Europe during the late Iron Age. Accompanying this development was the split of cerebral functions, leading to the creation of the two archetypal roles of artist and scientist. Through the Bronze Age and into the mid-Iron Age, what we now would call the arts had achieved a high level of technical virtuosity and symbolically expressive sophistication. Yet, generally speaking, there was no such thing as the practice of art for its own sake; nor was the role of artist regarded with special favor or, more important, as a person's sole occupation. This held true even through the greater part of the Iron Age. In the Yuan Dynasty of China (13th–14th century A.D.), for instance, the arts reached a technical and expressive level unsurpassed in any other culture. But the artisans who created these works were not strictly professional artists in the way we would understand the term today. Among other things, these men and women painted, made pottery and sculpture, and wrote poetry; yet making art was rarely ever their sole or even chief occupation. In their society the refined practice of some art or craft was expected of anyone who aspired to be a cultivated human being. In the words of Lun Yü,

> A man should stir himself with poetry
> Stand firm in ritual
> Complete himself in music. [1]

In a late observance of this tradition, the Emperor Hirohito annually composed a poem to be read to his subjects—a curious and touching contrast during the Second World War to the direction his country had taken as a military power.

In Christian Europe through the Middle Ages the various arts were practiced as crafts, none necessarily more important than the others, with the possible exception of architecture. Though the practice of a given art was the trade of a particular craftsman for his lifetime, "there is no evidence for the existence of any of the mystique of the Great Artist in the Middle Ages,"[2] as Andrew Martindale comments in a recent book, *The Rise of the Artist in the Middle Ages and Early Renaissance*. However, Martindale's assumptions are projections of our own post-Renaissance culture, as statements like the following reveal: "There is, in fact, little evidence for an informed interest in the arts by non-artists at all. Nothing is indeed more striking than the apparent apathy towards art."[3] Martindale is operating on the assumption, commonly held among European membership, that there is a thing called *art* created by a particular psychogenetic type, the supreme ideal of whom is the "Great Artist." What he interprets as apathy toward art, in the Christian Middle Ages may simply reflect the fact that the specific concept "art" was nonexistent at the time. Without the specialized notion of art there was, in the Middle Ages, no need either for the mystique of the Great Artist, or for the glorification of art. There was, on the contrary, a vital and participatory appreciation for the practice of the various crafts, especially as they could be combined into the unified expression of the most profound spiritual truths animating and uniting the populace. Would the inhabitants of any small town in America today not only contribute their money but their own time to construct a major religious monument? Because there was a genuine involvement of the people in a creative project, craftsmen were expected to do their best according to the canon of collective belief, and so there was no reason to ostentatiously proclaim or criticize their accomplishments.

The criticism of today, which defines art and on which art thrives, is the result of aesthetic confusion consequent to the breakdown of collective spiritual tradition. Aesthetic confusion is what makes art as a specialized notion possible; it is what happens when the psychotechnical balance has been greatly disturbed. Such a disturbance occurred at the end of the Middle Ages; Marshall McLuhan attributes it largely to the invention of the printing press, with its overemphasis on the visual mode, a theory corroborated by Castaneda's statement that "in European membership the world is built largely from what the eyes report to the body." Whatever the cause, the disruption of the relatively balanced interplay of the mind and the senses in favor of a single sensory mode, the visual, has created the atmosphere that makes possible the specialized concept of art distinct from the practice of a craft.

Art is a critical—hence ultimately undefinable—term developed in Renaissance Europe to denote activity that is primarily right-hemisphere in origin. The terms of critical definition, however, are left-hemisphere. The paradox of psychic function defined by technical terms is apparent in the idea of the Great Artist, created by those Renaissance individuals who, in their pride and desire to be considered distinct from craftsmen and the equal of philosophers—masters of the word—implicitly created their polar opposite, the scientist. In practice, art came to mean fine art, which is ultimately art for art's sake. Fine art created its opposite in applied art; the former is considered more significant or valuable than the latter, primarily because the practice of fine art becomes inextricably involved with the printed word. In contradistinction, the applied arts have no voice, and cut off from the religious traditions that imbued them with meaning in the Middle Ages, they have suffered an atrophy compounded by the fatal impact of mechanization.

It is interesting that although the modern European culture developed as a left-hemisphere civilization, through the role of the artist, it was the right hemisphere that consciously split from the left in the early sixteenth century. This separation really allowed the left-hemisphere functions to develop freely, and in the literary, sequential, mechanistic Gutenberg culture that began to form by the end of the fifteenth century, it was finally the left hemisphere that predominated. The irony is that once the means of human expression—common to all in the psychocultural phases we have designated as the Gold, Silver, and Bronze ages—were specialized and usurped by the artist of the late Iron Age, the majority of European membership became nonexpressive agents of left-hemisphere functions. This situation set the stage for a left-hemisphere technological take-over, which in the end condemned all psychic, expressive means (except certain forms of political propaganda art and advertising) and even the artist to be considered *secondary* survival characteristics. Thus the creation of art as a distinct category of human behavior had the effect of downgrading the universal urge to expression. The repression of the human expressive urge makes way for a race of robots—and ultimately it means death to the species.

In one of his most provocative statements, William Blake declared, "Art Degraded, Imagination Denied, War Govern'd the Nations."[4] This is an accurate description of modern conditions, if consciousness is seen as an integrated circuit: art (as innate expressive means) is degraded in the educative process and looked upon as an essentially noncontributive social nicety; imagination, the intuitive function of the right hemisphere, is denied and condemned as being irrational; as a consequence, humanity lacks broad-scale positive expressive means, and war does govern the nations. The important insight in Blake's aphorism is the relationship between art (as innate expressive means) and war—the negative expression of the repressed imbalance of human energy. Though war is the thread of history, in a split-brain culture it pre-empts all other forces in gathering and focusing the power of the collective imagination. Right-hemisphere energy, denied its natural outlet, seeks release in bizarre and unexpected—irrational—behavior. The degraded art Blake protested against is the creation of specialists who, since the Renaissance, have only aggravated the psychocultural imbalance by appropriating for themselves the expressive means and investing them with the alienating fine-arts values that have ensured their general social uselessness. In a fundamental sense, art and war in the modern world are functions of the same problem; as a specialized and compensatory role function, art will exist as long as war does, for both are symptoms of the same neurocerebral disease. When war truly ceases, then *art as an end in itself* will cease. But for this to occur, the artist who totally identifies with his particular role, like the career army general and the laboratory scientist, would have to be "therapized" and introduced to other ways of being human.

In a memorable line from the Graham Greene–Carol Reed thriller, *The Third Man* (1946), the sinister Harry Lime (Orson Welles), riding a ferris wheel high over war-torn Vienna, philosophizes to his baffled companion, a writer of Western fiction à la Zane Grey (Joseph Cotton): "In Italy in a brief period of fifty years under the bloody rule of the Borgias and the Medici you have Leonardo, Raphael, Michelangelo! In Switzerland you have one thousand years of democracy, and what do you get? The cuckoo clock!" Harry Lime's witty remarks express the common view that artistic genius—the Great Artist—appears only in times of strife, and that without high tension there can be no great works of art. The close relationship between "great art" and war sheds light on a major aspect of the modern European psyche, which had its birth in Renaissance Italy. The core of this relationship lies in the idea of the *artist as a unique ego*. In this respect the Renaissance artist was a precursor of the egotism which became the glorified cultural ideal of nineteenth-century European and American laissez-faire individualism. More interesting, the Renaissance artist's identity set the stage for that of his polar opposite, the scientist, whose image often is not that of the rugged individualist (there are exceptions) but that of the self-effacing servant. It should be remembered that at the time the modern-artist archetype was born in the late fifteenth century, there existed no scientists as such, though there were alchemical experimenters. If Copernicus exemplified in 1543 the birth of the new scientific world view, it was not until a century later that his methods were distilled sufficiently to create both science and the scientist. But toward 1500 it was the Great Artist himself who combined both the artist and scientist types in one personality: this very interesting and significant phenomenon can be seen in Albrecht Dürer, for one, but nowhere more dramatically than in the case of Leonardo da Vinci.

The personality and achievement of Leonardo da Vinci (1452–1519) have enthralled numerous European scholars, poets, artists, and psychologists. Often Leonardo is referred to as the epitome of the "Renaissance Man," the universal genius who combined the ideal of the artist and the scientist in one personality. In view of his uniqueness, however, it would seem that Leonardo blazed forth as a mutant, androgynous model of psychotechnical, right- and left-hemisphere integration. He passed on before he could be fully comprehended—even by himself. What followed after him, culturally speaking, was not integration but the steady development of the seemingly antagonistic artist and scientist archetypes—the war between psyche and techne. Leonardo da Vinci is an exception in human development, and since the Renaissance few have approached his combination of artist and scientist. One may recall Goethe, perhaps; or the painter George Seurat, who declared, "Some say they see poetry in my painting; I see only science"; or Albert Einstein, who played the violin and said of his own scientific discoveries, "There is no logical way to the discovery of these elementary laws; there is only the way of intuition." But by and large, Leonardo and his achievement stand alone.

Leonardo looms at the pinnacle of the European Renaissance—a troubled, puzzling giant whose left-handed, backward writing, which can be read only with the aid of a mirror, dramatically reveals the degree of neurocerebral integration he had experienced. Yet, in the *visual* character of the ideas he articulated, there is a strong left-hemisphere bias that is uniquely European—the Gutenberg touch. Justifying Castaneda's description of European membership—"Our eyes feed our reason and we have no direct knowledge of things"—Leonardo, echoing Aristotle on the five senses, wrote: "The sense which is nearest to the organ of perception functions most quickly; and this is the eye, the chief, the leader of all others (senses); of this only will we treat in order not to be too long."[5] Here Leonardo set forth the basic left-hemisphere visual bias of the European world view, giving greater weight to the eye as an instrument of knowledge than to the other organs of sense and the body as a whole. There is a mystical truth to the symbolic function of the eye as the organ of divine light. However, Leonardo confounded this truth with an inherited Platonic-Christian prejudice that denigrates the body and elevates the eye, whose medium of information is *light*, symbolic of the spirit, above all other senses and modes of knowing.[6] Ignoring that heliotropy (literally, "turning toward the sun") is a fundamental property of *all* life, regardless of whether, for instance, a flower has *eyes*, Leonardo wrote:

The eye, which is the window of the soul, is the chief organ whereby the understanding can have the most complete and magnificent view of the infinite works of nature.

Now do you not see that the eye embraces the beauty of the whole world? . . . It counsels and corrects all the arts of mankind. . . . It is the prince of mathematics, and the sciences founded on it are absolutely certain. It has measured the distances and sizes of the stars; it has discovered the elements and their location. . . . It has given birth to architecture and to perspective and the divine art of painting.

Oh, excellent thing, superior to all others created by God! What praises can do justice to your nobility? What peoples, what tongues will fully describe your function? The eye is the window of the human body through which it feels its way and enjoys the beauty of the world. Owing to the eye *the soul is content to stay in its bodily prison, for without it such bodily prison is torture.*

O marvelous, O stupendous necessity, thou with supreme reason compellest all effects to be the direct result of their causes; and by a supreme and irrevocable law every natural action obeys thee by the shortest process possible. Who would believe that so small a space could contain all the images of the universe. . . .

The eye whereby the beauty of the world is reflected is of such excellence that whoso consents to its loss deprives himself of the representation of all the works of nature. *The soul is content to stay imprisoned in the human body because thanks to our eyes we can see these things;* for through the eyes all the various things of nature are represented to the soul. *Whoso loses his eyes leaves his soul in a dark prison without hope of ever again seeing the sun, light of all the world;* How many are there to whom the darkness of night is hateful though it is but of short duration; what would they do if such darkness were to be their companion for life?[7]

It is not a big step from Leonardo's reflections on the significance and importance of the eye—and his implicit denial of anything but visual knowledge—to the thought of Descartes, who in 1637 published both his classic study on optics and his famous *Discourse on Method,* with its world-shaking declaration: "I think, therefore I am." The body-negating and visual, reason-affirming dualism hinted at by Leonardo was more emphatically expressed by Descartes, who denuded Leonardo's premise of *all* sensory input:

From the very fact that I doubted the truth of other things, it followed very evidently and very certainly that I existed. On the other hand, if I had ceased to think while all the rest of what I had ever imagined remained true, I would have no reason to believe that I existed; therefore I concluded that I was a substance whose whole essence or nature was only to think, and which to exist has no need of space nor of any material thing. Thus it follows that this ego, this soul, by which I am what I am, is entirely distinct from the body and is easier to know than the latter, and that even if the body were not, the soul would not cease to be all that it now is.[8]

The irony of the emphasis on visual knowledge is that beginning as an assertion that the eye is the window of the soul, and hence that the soul exists absolutely distinct from the body, it generates a dualism that creates a belief in matter which, under the banner of triumphant materialism, finally all but eliminates the doctrine of the transcendent soul—while retaining a belief in a nontranscendent individual ego. The point here is that Descartes' absolutely dualistic statement was possible only because of the already existing cultural tendency—exemplified in Leonardo's comments—to view the body as at best a *prison* for the soul. Visual knowledge alienates the psyche and degrades the body, which comes to be equated with the world of matter. In contrast to the soul or ego, matter is considered dead and inert. Hence the body and the entire material realm come to be viewed as something that can be willfully manipulated; and since the world of matter is without "feeling," there is a tendency in dealing with it to dispense with the morality that supposedly obtains in human relations.

This dualism of body and soul, matter and mind, gives rise to the two extremes of human behavior, asceticism and libertinism. The ascetic is motivated by feelings of fear and disgust toward his body and a desire to maintain what he takes to be the purity of his eternal element, mind or spirit. In denying his body the ascetic also denies his emotions, which seem related to body responses. He will employ the most drastic means—mortification, torture, war—to preserve the purity of what to him is eternally true, and to negate or destroy what to him is "dirty." The ultimate end of asceticism is the destruction of the body in order to save the spirit that inhabits it.

At the other end of the spectrum is the libertine. Dismissing the body altogether as a frivolity, and the world as useless and vain, the libertine indulges completely in a maelstrom of passion. In a fundamental sense the body and the world are so evil for the libertine that he can save himself only by reckless acts of violence. The ascetic and the libertine share a negativism based on a profoundly dualistic attitude; essentially they illustrate two different ways of responding to bodily discomfort. If the ascetic feels he must destroy in order to save, the libertine glories in the rising body count.

Corresponding to these two extremes of behavior are the archetypes of the scientist and the artist. The former is the self-effacing ascetic, cool and objective, purging himself of human emotion, at least insofar as his work is concerned; at the extreme he becomes a faceless, soulless zombie, sacrificing all to the demands of the technocratic state. It was the scientist who created the atom bomb, the ultimate weapon of those who would destroy in order to save. The artist, on the other hand, is the libertine, careless with his own emotions and body to the point of self-destruction, drowning in a whirlpool of passion, crucified by the "evil" desires of his own flesh; such has been the lot of Baudelaire, Rimbaud, and van Gogh, to name a few. These two extremes came into their own with Frankenstein (the scientist) and the Marquis de Sade (the artist) in the late eighteenth and early nineteenth centuries. Related to the ascetic/scientist archetype, on the one hand, are the general/conqueror, the politician/priest, and the merchant/entrepreneur. Related to the artist are the female archetypes—muse, housewife, sex object—the revolutionary, and the socially maladjusted, whether they be criminals and lunatics or the self-alienated madmen Colin Wilson describes as the "outsiders." Essentially, however, all of these modern types are imbalanced personalities whose behavior reflects repressed, sublimated, or poorly understood elements of the neglected hemisphere.

Taking the dualism back to its Renaissance source, we may say that the scientist and artist are really the same person split into two bodies. As specializations of a universal type, their personalities actually suffer from a loss of individuality. Leonardo was the exception; he was able to wear the masks of both, but not without difficulty. It is interesting that just before his death in 1519 he developed partial paralysis of the right hand. Kenneth Clark, in his admirable study of Leonardo, notes the internal conflicts within the Master's art. One of these is "the conflict between his aesthetic and his scientific approach to painting, the former deeply, even extravagantly romantic, comparable to such later painters as El Greco and Turner; the other, found in the composition of the *Last Supper*, forming the foundation of later academicism."[9] It is interesting that not only does Leonardo embody the later archetypes of artist and scientist, but as an artist he embodies both the later academic and antiacademic trends; his art is both "classic" and "romantic." The world of art reflects the same psychotechnical split that affects society as a whole. Clark continues:

Even more bewildering is the contrast between his drawings and his notebooks. In all his writings—one of the most voluminous and complete records of a mind at work which has come down to us—there is hardly a trace of human emotion. Of his affections, his tastes, his health, his opinions on current events we know nothing. Yet if we turn from his writings to his drawings, we find a subtle and tender understanding of human feelings which is not solely due to the efficiency of the optic nerve.[10]

Clearly, according to Clark's observations, the scientist archetype expressed itself through Leonardo's notebooks, the artist archetype through his drawings. In the end, Clark concludes, Leonardo, through his study of nature, became more and more convinced of man's impotence, until finally, "The intellect is no longer supreme, and human beings cease to be the center of nature . . . or when they appear as St. Anne or St. John, they are no longer human but symbols of force and mystery, messengers from a world which Leonardo da Vinci, the disciple of experience, has not explored, though he has earned the right to proclaim its existence."[11]

This concluding reflection on Leonardo underlines the essential modern inability to match left-hemisphere articulation with right-hemisphere feeling, with Leonardo himself not fully bridging the chasm between the two. One of his last paintings, for instance, the enigmatically pointing *St. John* (1515), does nothing more than deepen the mystery of the nature of things; it presents the vague, almost sentimental image and atmosphere that later generations of bourgeois, left-hemisphere insensitives would come to expect from art: a comforting, misty, emotional, or patriotic image that satisfies the psychic gnawing in the right-hemisphere cavity without trying to tell them anything or demanding any real thinking.

It is interesting that in his late paintings Leonardo abandoned the earlier mode of linear perspective for his own innovation of atmospheric perspective and *sfumato*—the smoky, soft-edge treatment of forms. In fact, the *St. John*, in contrast to the *Last Supper* (1495-97), really has no perspective at all; instead, the figure of St. John obtrudes from a dense fog. Linear perspective, developed by fifteenth-century artists like Uccello and Piero della Francesca, and used with utter perfection by Leonardo in his *Adoration of the Kings* (1481) and *Last Supper,* is the embodied source of the rational/mechanistic point of view. Leonardo's abandonment of it can be seen as a retreat into the right hemisphere, or at least a retreat away from the left, for the one-point perspective system, which dominates all later fifteenth- and sixteenth-century Italian painting, is a remarkable left-hemisphere contrivance. It is the sword of techne, by which psyche is subdued. The one-point, linear perspective is an intellectual, rationalistic, and above all purely mechanistic way of dividing space, a development synchronous with Gutenberg's press. Along with the printed word, it is the single most powerful agent for standardizing the perceptions of the collective mind of Europe over the next few centuries. If the printed word promotes mental uniformity, one-print perspective enforces that uniformity at the visual-sensory level. The grid system employed by one-point perspective is the forerunner of refined cartography and of the Cartesian system of coordinates, the source of all later scientific systems using graphs. Essentially, the one-point perspective is just that—a graph applied to the eye for the purpose of mechanizing vision, and thus mind.

Though the standardization of vision through one-point perspective provided a powerful means of focusing the mind, as exemplified in the subsequent invention of the telescope (1590) and the microscope (1610), as a knowledge base it also entailed severe limitations. A knowledge system so narrowly visual in its orientation, and so philosophically dichotomizing between soul (perceiver) and matter (perceived), physiologically limits the primary realm of experienced reality to a narrow band of radiation that falls between red light, with a wave length of .00007 centimeters, and violet light, with a wave length of .00004 centimeters. Though Leonardo declared that the eye "is the chief organ whereby the understanding can have the most complete and magnificent view of the infinite works of nature," the last one hundred years of physical research have amply demonstrated, as Lincoln Barnett points out, that "the human eye fails to respond to most 'lights' in the world and that what man can perceive of the reality around him is distorted and enfeebled by the limitations of his organ of vision. The world would appear far different if his eye were sensitive, for example, to

X-rays."[12] Besides relegating the right-hemisphere knowledge of psyche to the realm of "irrational" mystery, the psychological effect of a predominantly visual knowledge system directed by the analytical and technical priorities of the left hemisphere is to *entitize* the ego. When the visual process is mechanized into a static checkerboard, the perceiving ego is also mechanized into a series of compartmentalized and rigidly determined *I*'s. Like the external world, the internal world of the self comes to be conceived as a sequentially ordered universe of discrete, quantifiable units flowing irreversibly away in one direction, the vanishing point of the past. Space and time are now separate "physical" categories susceptible of left-hemisphere analysis and measurement. The mythic world with its fluid correspondences between opposites, between greater and lesser things held together at the center by an ego-transcending mystery, which being a mystery is no less real, has ceased to exist at the collective level.

As a distinct conglomerate of discrete categories, the ego corresponds precisely to the orthodox Christian doctrine of permanent, unchanging souls destined for either heaven or hell. This psychological attitude, more than anything else, prepared the way for the totally mechanistic world view of the seventeenth century, so eloquently summed up in Newton's laws of gravity and the development of "celestial mechanics." Since the ego perceives the world as a static entity, there naturally developed the powerful philosophy of materialism—the notion that phenomena, being stable and inert, may be grasped and appropriated in whatever way and by whatever means for whatever human needs. Despite the breakthrough of the Einsteinian world view, in which space and time are viewed as interrelated intuitive functions rather than as the separate quantifiable entities of mechanistic science, the collective mind is still in the grip of what Blake so beautifully described as "single vision and Newton's Sleep." A correspondingly Einsteinian psychological base for disentitizing the ego has yet to be developed—or, at least, understood and applied.

I have spoken earlier of the uniquely human attribute of nonspecialization; it is also easy for the human being to fill the "void" of his uniqueness, simply in order to avoid the responsibility it entails. Human history is the struggle to remain open. Time and again human consciousness fixates, and slams the door on its greatest gift, the open-endedness of infinite possibility. As a result we do not experience reality but merely our *concept* of it. The most difficult trials in the development of consciousness are involved in the dissolution of what William Burroughs has described as the "image-fix." The Newtonian idea, for instance, that the universe is like a perfect machine—celestial mechanics—is one currently widespread image-fix. So pervasive is this idea that all of our attitudes are tainted with it. Even the human body is thought of as a machine, and behaviorism has developed as the corresponding mechanistic approach to psychology. Whatever validity the Newtonian idea might originally have had is completely offset by the dreadful need to believe in it—and nothing else. The tendency for human consciousness to freeze itself, to strive for greater material "proof" of itself, attests to the power of insecurity in the face of constant change. However, this insecurity is but the reverse side of adaptability. Confronted with mounting complexity, the species tends to forego adaptability in favor of a "reliable" guide. An image of the universe is developed and sunk into consciousness, where it remains, a bedrock image-fix, a final resort or proof that the world is "really" the way we want it to be.

The one-point perspective system—"single vision and Newton's Sleep"—is one of the most powerful means of image-fixing yet conceived. Created by the late-fifteenth-century artistic avant-garde, it gave European man the leverage to fix the world according to his will. The interplay of art and science in this process is awe-inspiring testimony to the subtle and irrevocable forces of evolving consciousness.

CHAPTER THREE

The High Renaissance Vision: The Formation
of a Literary Artistic Elite

BESIDES EXEMPLIFYING the two archetypes of the scientist and the artist, Leonardo displayed within his own art the dichotomous tendencies of all later European art: the dominant, academic "classicism" and the subdominant, antiacademic "romanticism." As an individual artist, no one more than Raphael epitomizes the dominant left-hemisphere approach that provided the basis of academic art until its demise late in the nineteenth century. Even twentieth-century "modernism," though no longer Raphaelesque in appearance, continues to be motivated by the same technical attitude that sustained the classical art academies. In this respect Raphael's vision proved to be the most powerful molding force of the European consciousness through its dramatic Faustian surge. On the one hand, it fixed the world in a particular image; and on the other, it played the vital role of anesthetizing the right hemisphere, rendering psyche suspect.

Raphael's life and work do contain sentimental elements expressing the right-hemisphere, feminine/artistic libertine archetype, reflected especially in the sweet and tender paintings of Madonna and Child and in his last, unfinished work, the *Transfiguration*. But the prime works of his career, and the paintings that more than any others epitomize the High Renaissance, are the two large frescoes in the Vatican's Stanza della Segnatura executed for Pope Julius II and Pope Leo X: the *School of Athens* and the *Dispute Concerning the Blessed Sacrament* (the *Disputà*). Painted between 1509 and 1512, these works powerfully reflect the theme of the room: the human intellect. Thus they are the culminating expression of the essentially technical, left-hemisphere conception of art that began with Leon Battista Alberti's neo-Pythagorean notion that mathematics is the common ground between science and art.* Emphasizing the curious yin-yang crossover of functions that occurred in the Renaissance, Arnold Hauser comments that the mathematical perspective in painting in the fifteenth century "is a scientific conception, whereas the Universum of Kepler and Galileo is a fundamentally aesthetic vision."[1] However this may be, what happened in the Renaissance was a left-hemisphere development. In the *School of Athens* and the *Disputà*, the glorification of the human intellect attains a precision and a grandiose beauty that announce in no uncertain

---

*Though this notion is intrinsically valid, it degenerated when number ceased to have a symbolic value and was conceived solely in arithmetical terms.

terms the coming triumph of technical, split-brain European culture in world affairs.

In terms of the split nature of consciousness, the themes reflect left-hemisphere philosophy and right-hemisphere theology—though here theology is essentially a left-hemisphere intellectual conception. The *Disputà*, ironically presaging the more powerful Protestant dispute Martin Luther was to provoke within a few years, presents very clearly the dichotomy between spirit and matter, heaven and earth. The rising crescent form of the heavenly aspect and the contrasting downward forms of the earthly have a disconcerting effect, unconsciously echoing the contemporary European mind. Raphael's image of heaven above and earth below is a powerful archetype that appears in the Chinese *Book of Changes* as the image P'i (Standstill or Stagnation): "Heaven and earth do not unite, and all beings fail to achieve union. Upper and lower do not unite, and in the world, states go down to ruin."[2] The ominous meaning attributed to this symbol is borne out by the tremendous social and political chaos generated by the single-pointed and powerfully advancing European vision. In Raphael's painting the heavenly creatures are already a totally anthropomorphized group of individuals whose sacred nature is rather artificially conveyed by the jarringly nonnaturalistic late Medieval device of rays of light and the halo about Christ. By this time in Europe the sacred had departed from worldly affairs; despite the overwhelming *political* presence of the Church, European culture was rapidly becoming secular and materialistic. Thus the donor became an important presence in many a sacred painting from this period. The static nature of religion and the consequent emptiness of sacred forms, though handsome and well proportioned, are quite evident in the *Disputà*, while the painting's structure emphasizes the imprisonment of intuitive functions in the intellectual net of the one-point perspective system. Above all, the *Disputà* reveals the disparity between the secular visual conception of Renaissance art and the sacred vision of Medieval art. The very choice of the theme, glorifying Church history (rather than timeless myth) in terms of a theological dispute, emphasizes the mundane, political nature of Renaissance culture.

Though Raphael was undoubtedly a great and powerful artist, owing to his own personal ambitions he could not help but reflect in his art the political consciousness of the Renaissance. The basic notion of the Great Artist is political in nature, since its very definition implies an aspiration for recognition among the princes and rulers of *this* world. It is this psychological factor, more than any other, that accounts for the lack of sacred presence in the art of many of the great artists, and which contributed to the growing secular elitism of the fine arts. By contrast, the ideal of the craftsman/artisan was not to be considered great by the rulers of the world—though the desire for fame and worldly pride are snares artisans may fall into no less than anyone else—but to attain through the practice of his craft an inner mastery and a sense of spiritual freedom. The psychologist A. Reza Arasteh, in describing the classical Persian craftsman, speaks as well for the Medieval Christian:

No matter what media he worked in, the artist painstakingly strove to achieve the aim he had set for himself. In his desire to express his deepest feelings he transformed simple materials into works of art. His mind, heart and hands worked harmoniously together. Ultimately the ideal became fused with the object at hand to form one lasting design. This unified motive explains the presence of such symbols of Nature as the sun, stars, moon, and heavens, which are so majestically recreated. . . . In the process of giving permanence to his idea, the artist internalized it, which helped ward off the anxiety resulting from man's alienation from Nature.[3]

Like the classical alchemist, the pre-Renaissance artist was motivated by the ideal of realizing internally that with which he was working externally. Like the post-Renaissance culture it prefigured, the Great Artist ideal was primarily geared to an external technical virtuosity tied to the goal of ego aggrandizement, often conceived of as political or social recognition. At the age of 26, for instance, Raphael had become a success as one of the leading artists for Pope Julius II and later Pope Leo X. This accounts for his being considered a Great Artist as much as the quality of his art. Mass media having replaced the influence of the Pope, today's Raphael is an artist like Picasso. Seeking external power and recognition, the craftsman-alchemist dies and the Great Artist is born: whereas the former worked for the transformation and transcendence of his ego through identification with the cosmic elements, the latter works for the temporal recognition and fixation of his ego. It is the artist's purpose that makes the difference between the creation of a sacred art moved by a spiritual force and the creation of a worldly art, which, technically powerful as it may be, most often remains tied in its meaning to specific worldly motivations and conditions. For this reason the secular art of the post-Renaissance period necessitates critics, literary interpreters, and finally art historians to help explain the artist's motives and intentions to the masses. In its style and intent, the art developed in the Renaissance is exclusive: it is meant for a literate, self-interested clientele of politicians and humanists. Arnold Hauser describes the situation in the following way:

The art of the early Renaissance could still be understood by the broad masses; even the poor and uneducated could find some points of contact with it, although they were on the periphery of its real artistic influence; the masses have no contact at all with the new art. What possible meaning could Raphael's *School of Athens* and Michelangelo's *Sybils* have for them, even if they had ever been able to see these works?[4]

A curious phenomenon occurred in the Renaissance: *culture,* meaning the broad spectrum of artifacts and manners manifested by a particular group, ceased to be the integral expression of the beliefs binding European society and was replaced by an elitist *cult of culture.* Such a cult can be formed only when the integral, mythic unity of a group or race has been disturbed. Thus in Europe the yin-yang, psychotechnical balance was upset early in the sixteenth century not by outside factors but by internal contradictions, which had become so great that they could no longer be held together as a whole. As a direct result of the cultural disintegration, the momentum of the European people as a totality continued to accelerate tremendously. The previously unifying Medieval craft culture slowly became transformed into poular and folk-art culture, which steadily grew less effective and was all but destroyed with the onset of industrialism in the mid-eighteenth century. The culture of the ruling classes, however, taking off from late Medieval prototypes, was transformed into a cult of culture. For this reason, the work that is considered the masterpiece in the Stanza della Segnatura is not the one dealing with a religious theme but the *School of Athens,* which expresses in one comprehensive whole the new elitist cult of culture.

The *School of Athens* is the foundation stone of the Western vision up until the twentieth century; it is a crystallization of both the perceptual process that determines the quality of European consciousness and the guiding inspirational spirit of modern European elitist culture—nostalgia for and consequently idealization of the "classical" Greco-Roman Mediterranean past. Perceptually the *School of Athens* is a full-blown hallucination carefully constructed upon the principle of one-point perspective, with its unique use of the horizon line, a receding geometrical grid, beautifully worked out in the illusion of floor and barrel-vaulted ceiling, into which the various figures are proportionally located. The vanishing point—the *sine qua non of* "single vision"—is perfectly placed between Aristotle and Plato, the officially sanctioned fountainheads of Western intellectual endeavor. Depicted around them is a fantasy world in which the leading philosophical and literary figures of the ancient Mediterranean culture are assembled.

Passing through the vanishing point, which symbolizes the flow toward the past, Western poetic and literary consciousness became utterly preoccupied with the gods, myths, philosophy, and history of the ancient Mediterranean culture, to the point of a tragic and fatalistic identification that began to disintegrate only in the later nineteenth century. In the nostalgia of the *School of Athens* there is already something inherently decadent, no matter how brilliantly presented. Reverence for ancestors is an integral aspect of human culture, and at one level the *School of Athens* represents an unusual form of ancestor worship. But when culture begins to pattern itself upon models of the past, regardless of change, or when present deviations are disguised as a form of reverence for the past, then decadence has set in. An example of the former kind of decadence is a blind, unquestioning allegiance to precedent or ritual; an example of the latter is the practice common in America until quite recently of designing banks as if they were the entrances to Roman or Greek temples.

Ironically, the *School of Athens*, like the *Disputá*, announces the coming split within the Church by ideally depicting pre- and non-Christian symbols within the heart of the Christian establishment—the Vatican. This was an officially approved, if inherently heretical, act foreboding the eclipse of the mythology and iconography of Christ by the gods and the derivative scientific and philosophical systems known as humanism. Although the Church would muster up her own Counter-Reformation following the fatal schism promulgated by Martin Luther and the Northern Europeans in general, it was to be more in the nature of a last-ditch stand, a feeling of underlying remorse spearheaded by St. Ignatius Loyola and ignited by St. Theresa. But the mysticism of the sixteenth- and seventeenth-century Catholic Church was no match for what was heralded by the *School of Athens*. By the eighteenth century the Mediterranean world that gave birth to humanism and to the Counter-Reformation was in a state of profound decline, already a ruin to be visited by curious and well-informed Northerners like Johann Winckelmann and Gavin Hamilton. The neo-Platonism that spawned the *School of Athens* in the early sixteenth century was like a viper nourishing itself at the breast of the Church, which was never really to recover her dignity, authority, and power. If there was to be successful art representing the Church in the seventeenth century, it was the result of intensive propaganda efforts, and not a universal—which is the meaning of "Catholic"—spontaneous response. The classical monuments of Bernini, the triumphs of St. Peter's and the Vatican, are the glorious emblems of an ideology attempting to consolidate itself, and not the vigorous achievement of a new doctrine sure of itself. In this respect the Baroque Catholic culture of the seventeenth century is a virtuoso backwater in the history of European civilization.

A more significant sign of the times was the appearance of the *School of Athens* as the apotheosis of contemporary European neo-Platonism and the crisis within the Christian belief system itself. No matter how much contemporary thinkers might have rationalized to accommodate ancient Greek philosophy within the Christian world view, their position marks a complete 180-degree turn from that taken by the Church in the centuries immediately following the fall of Rome. This compromising attitude buried whatever living quality the classical tradition carried, so that as it was reinstated, it already partook of the Christian mind/body split, and its real meanings were thereby distorted.

The question arises to what extent the teaching of Christ, representing an essentially Near Eastern or Oriental point of view, was really absorbed by the West. The fact that the Northern Europeans almost unanimously rejected any depiction of Christ or even of biblical teachings in their art following the Reformation is most unusual. Though one might hearken to a similar edict in the Islamic faith, there is really no parallel. Post-Reformation Northern European art reflects a distinctively secular and profane world view, whereas the Muslim aesthetic, though abjuring the visualization of its Prophet, tended to remain highly symbolic and sacred in its overall attitude. The depths of the crisis that the *School of Athens* so calmly heralded is further emphasized by its iconographical contrast with the Christian art of the preceding centuries. The imitation of Christ once produced in stained glass and illuminated manuscripts had become an effort too great to sustain, and Christ had to become decentralized and desacralized. What was an eternally living mythic truth to the Medieval Christian became transformed through the eyes of the Renaissance artist into an allegorical fable or historical account. With Christ no longer central, the mystery of His being vanished in the pursuit of personal power and glory. History appears where mystery disappears. The *School of Athens* presented a fantasy window through which the literate princes of latter-day Rome, disregarding the example and teaching of Christ, might read their intellectual pedigree in aristocratic solitude.

Though the painting's architectural structure echoes the barrel-vaulted architecture of the Stanza, it also negates that architecture in search of a supreme illusion. And what is this illusion? It is that of one moment condensed from eternity, frozen into the spectacle of a stage set of antiquity cast in sixteenth-century trappings. Both the presage and the perfection of the Cartesian mode of perception visually applied, it is a massive rupture of the sacred. The *School of Athens* is not a sacred image. It is a highly centered image, but the centering is achieved by a mechanical process—the one-point perspective system. Though there is still a felicitous concordance between symbol and perspectival system, this system does not inspire a spiritual, transpersonal vision, but a mechanical and individualistic one. The painting "works" from only one particular angle of vision, mechanically freezing the viewer into one particular space. By contrast, though a work based on transcendental symbolic code may be centered and fixed in one place, its very fixity obliterates individuality and invites the presence of eternity.

Marshall McLuhan has remarked rather lightly that "schizophrenia may be a necessary consequence of literacy."[5] What he failed to point out is that schizophrenia is hell. The consequence of literacy, mechanization, and the one-point perspective system was nothing less than a collective falling away from a sacred to a profane state of being. What was profaned by this fall was the imagination and soul of man—the psyche itself. In his book *Sacred Art in East and West*, Titus Burckhardt comments:

The science of perspective became a real mental passion, a cold passion perhaps, and one not far removed from intellectual research, but destructive of pictorial symbolism: through perspective the picture becomes an imaginary world, and at the same time the world becomes a closed system, opaque to every gleam of the supernatural. In mural painting a mathematical perspective is in reality absurd, for it not only destroys the architectural unity of the wall, but it also obliges the spectator to place himself on the imaginary visual axis, on pain of subjecting all the forms to a false foreshortening. In much the same way architecture is stripped of its most subtle qualities when the purely geometrical proportions of medieval art are replaced by arithmetical, and therefore relatively quantitative, proportions; in this respect the prescriptions of Vitruvius did much harm. These things serve incidentally to show up the pedantic character of the Renaissance: in losing its attachment to Heaven, it loses also its link with the earth, that is to say, with the people and with the true tradition of the crafts.[6]

In the mechanical, rigidly perspectival visual system of the post-Renaissance West, the center is in the individual ego outside of the window frame, and not within the work of art itself; this amounts to saying that there is no longer any sacred center, for visual art itself no longer functions as a divine symbol but simply as the picture of an imaginary world. The glamorous, refined movie sets of Hollywood have their antecedents in Renaissance Rome. But if the center depends upon the individual, the individual himself tends to be without a center, for his senses inevitably lose their integral coherence as the life processes are mechanized and segmented, and his sense of divine participation is slowly sapped away.

Raphael's *School of Athens* is a compendium of what was to dominate the West for the next three or four centuries: its perceptual system found its ultimate conclusion in the perfection of photography in the nineteenth century; its subject matter and attitude remain the core of what in our colleges and universities is called the humanities—the great dialogue of a predominantly European, secular, intellectual, and literary world view in which the mechanically applied intellect deriving from distorted snips of Aristotle has replaced the transcendental vision of Christ. The latent sterility of this artistic point of view was further emphasized by the decline of the Catholic/humanist culture through the seventeenth century and the simultaneous separation of perceptual structure from subject matter that occurred in the art and culture of Northern Europe.

In the art of Vermeer, for instance, the pristine purity of the optical perception is really the subject matter of the painting. By contrast, the art of Rembrandt is a flood of emotion that becomes the perceptual medium itself and even obscures the subject matter. Vermeer painted no self-portraits; Rembrandt exemplifies the modern Western artist obsessed with himself—the pinnacle of self-doubting individualism. Vermeer perfected the illusion so grandiosely announced in the *School of Athens*. Rembrandt developed its nostalgic content to a subjective ultimate. The art of both Vermeer and Rembrandt, however, is highly anecdotal in a narrative sense, reflecting the triumph of a literary culture. The anecdote is simply the literary unit of measure. According to literary humanist values there is no visual art that cannot be verbally translated to an exact degree. But in the shadows of Rembrandt, as in the later work of Leonardo, there lurks a trace of that which defies verbal conceptualization. They are shadows that lengthen and deepen with every application of Descartes' coordinates, for they symbolize those psychic processes driven by the mechanical process of technological civilization into what one day would be called the unconscious.

Though mythic, collective time is still apparent in the *School of Athens*, the painting is dominated by the individual point of view, which provides the basis of techno-fantasy: each individual is wrapped up in his or her own private fantasy, apart from the whole. Vermeer's image of a young lady privately reading a letter in her home is a paradigm of the fall from a mythic time/space into a personal one. The scene is perfect for the perspectival grid system—an isolated member of the new, literate, bourgeoisie "stealing a moment of time" from the clearly articulated flow of Protestant life, while the viewer is left to fill in the profound solitude with his own imagination. There are no gods here, only an industrious people building a world of material comfort.

By contrast, Rembrandt's energy was massed against a perceptual system that fundamentally denies the mythic and the sacred. Thus in his art mystery could be maintained only by the predominance of shadow—at best a negative and tragic mystery, not a life-redeeming one. With the eclipse of Christ from the mythic center of Western consciousness, tragedy became the prevailing mode. The ultimate tragic view is the inability to conceive of redemption—and this is what haunts the work of Rembrandt, for redemption can occur only in a mythic, sacred time/space, one in which the individual ceases to exist, having become transfigured through realizing his participation in the divine process. Rembrandt's Christ is an exact inversion of this sacred principle. He is utterly human, that is to say, pathetic and wretched, a projection of the existential/Protestant bourgeois vision of man: an isolated individual trapped in a meaningless universe, cast down to earth from a paradise that more and more is rationalized into being but a dream, a fantasy, a wish for escape from the hard necessities of mercantile life. No wonder that Rembrandt's work has acquired such immense popularity in a time of absurd and mechanically ruthless war: how easy it is to identify with this downtrodden beggar, this Christ who is not Christ but simply man without God, beseeching an entire civilization for its redemption.

Rembrandt himself typifies the artist who bears within him a burning sensitivity to this cruel situation, a sensitivity that society has managed to drum out of most of its other members. Already the monumental figures in Renaissance art—Leonardo, Raphael, and Michelangelo—had found it necessary to carve out their own dominion from the hide of a society that cared less and less for the creations of the arts as it moved farther and farther away from the true wellsprings of the spirit. As Titus Burckhardt notes, "The Renaissance was promoted by nobles who had become merchants and merchants who had become princes."[7] If the artist of the Baroque period was fortunate, he was able to find a patron who would support him in style. Yet part of the blame for the artist's being thrown into such a ruthless situation was his own. It was men like Leonardo and Michelangelo who sought to proclaim painting and the visual arts in general as a branch of the humanities on an equal footing with the literary arts. This already reflected the supreme value placed on the printed word as the criterion of judgment, as well as the artist's sense of inferiority before the might of the printed word. In later times this sense of inferiority became a prideful spite; or, as in the case of Rembrandt, it became an almost self-pitying preoccupation with the artist's own fate—a nihilistic individualism that extended from Caravaggio and Rembrandt, through Kierkegaard and Dostoevsky, to the Dadaists and Surrealists of the twentieth century. Most significant, by the seventeenth century there emerged a unique pathological type, the isolated urban artist: he who must live by his wits.

Raphael's stately urban vision of Aristotle and Plato* descending the marble steps is but a dream portraying one of the Western mind's most powerful illusions: that the world is essentially *other*, distinct from oneself, embodied in the ultimate reality of matter, comprehensible only through a materialistic science and depictable only through a materialistic art that regards only the visible as real and only the real as visible. The sacred, the numinous, the ineffable and intangible experiences of psyche are banished to the "irrational" realm of the mystical, and the mystical itself is one day proclaimed only a branch of the insane and the unconscious—a realm left for the visionaries alone to decipher. The Renaissance marked the beginning of the dictatorship of reason, and the suppression of that which reason cannot define, much less circumscribe. It marked the beginning of the subjugation of psyche to the ruthless might of techne.

Though I have spoken at length of Raphael's masterpiece as the paradigm of the rationalized vision of Western consciousness, there is a famous and distinct counter-paradigm in the *Garden of Earthly Delights*,

---

*It is interesting that it is these two, who committed to the written word what Socrates spoke, who are deified, and not Socrates himself, the summation of an *oral* culture.

painted in 1500 by the enigmatic Hieronymous Bosch. It is a testament to the normative left-hemisphere values created by artists like Raphael that the noted art historian H. W. Janson, in his popular and monumental but one-sided *History of Art*, should describe this work by Bosch as "full of weird and seemingly irrational imagery."[8] Because our civilization has pursued so diligently the path of mundane reason, the paradigm presented in the central panel of Bosch's great work is no longer understood.

The vision offered by Raphael has come to represent the forces of modern culture almost completely. It is the way of technical intellect, which rationalizes experience into a materialism that simultaneously denies and blindly exploits both body and mind, and sets the senses, which might otherwise be guided, against each other. In this process, to use Henry Adams's metaphor, the Virgin is transformed into the dynamo; the mystery of the Mother becomes the science of matter. In contrast to the coldly intellectual and highly civilized order of the *School of Athens*, the *Garden of Earthly Delights* depicts in vivid organic imagery the fundamental truths of the wisdom of body-and-mind—truths that when denied, suppressed, or exploited, undermine the intellectual processes themselves. No matter how it is rationalized, the body remains the "ground of being" to which the intellect must cling, like fire to a piece of wood.

In characteristic late Medieval fashion, Bosch's work is divided into three parts—hence tryptich—and is immense, measuring some seven feet high and almost thirteen feet wide. The left-panel foreground depicts the creation of Adam and Eve, Man and Woman—natural creatures in a natural setting; in the center is the Fountain of Life; and in the background, mountains or rocks exemplifying organic architectural forms. The motif of organic architecture, which extends to the background of the central panel, contrasts profoundly with the grandiose architecture depicted by Raphael in the *School of Athens*. Raphael's Athens is a humanist monument to the triumph of man's intellect over nature. This theme, the product of a marriage between the classical tradition of improving on nature by depicting the ideal rather than the real and the predominant Medieval Christian belief in man's superiority over nature, resulted in the antiecological forces of Renaissance humanism and modern science. Bosch's vision, like the heretical vision of St. Francis in the thirteenth century, presents the ecological alternative.

In his essay "On the Historical Roots of Our Ecological Crisis," Lynn White suggests that "St. Francis tried to depose man from his monarchy and set up a democracy of all God's creatures";[9] in so doing, St. Francis posed an alternative Christianity. I would suggest that the vision of this alternative Christianity, a "democracy of all God's creatures," is precisely what Bosch has presented in the major central panel of his masterpiece. In this vision there is a total interfusion not only of man and animal but of man and vegetable nature—indeed, a union of man and all of the natural elements. In the farther background of the central panel, the Fountain of Life appears again, now the center of the organic city of a true planetary democracy.* Bosch's vision appears as a dream only from within the technical confines of the urbanizing intellect. Raphael's *School of Athens* is a completely urban vision: not a single blade of grass shows through the stones, and only in the background and through the cupola does one catch a glimpse of sky or clouds; in a curious way this work prefigures our modern rectilinear and indoor computerized environments, into which scarcely a ray of sunshine can penetrate. Humanism is the creator of the beautiful tomb of the senses. The presumed superiority of man's intellect has caused a devastating cleavage in the natural order, a cleavage experienced as the never-ending war waged by classical artists and technologists alike in their effort to perfect, redeem, and purify nature. It is also the war the humanist wages against other human beings in an effort to convert them to the "higher" truths, based on the inner war each humanist wages against his own body and mind to maintain the supremacy of reason.

For "civilized" man, Bosch's vision is a bitter pill to swallow; like that of St. Francis it expresses the necessity of human humility, the need to realize that man is fundamentally no better or greater than an ant or a strawberry; if man excels it is only in his conscious ability and ingenuity in praising the Creator. Bosch's vision was shared by Blake, who wrote, "The notion that man has a body distinct from his soul is to be expunged."[10] In the central panel of the *Garden of Earthly Delights*, humanity experiences directly the miracle of being. The ability to experience reality directly increases in direct proportion as our own self-importance diminishes. In the *School of Athens* man is the most important creature in the universe; no longer even a part of the natural process: the painting shows no other living creatures, but only inert artifacts—statues of over-sized male figures. Lynn White writes, "Despite Copernicus, all the cosmos rotates around our little globe. Despite Darwin we are not in our hearts, part of the natural process. We are superior to nature, contemptuous of it, willing to use it for our slightest whim."[11] It is not that humankind is not a glorious and unique evolutionary phenomenon, but that we have abused our uniqueness by denying our natural commonality.

Thus, in the right panel of the *Garden of Earthly Delights*, Bosch presents a vision of the hell of human pride, greed, and ignorance, a hell created by the separation of the senses—symbolized by the knife shown cutting through the ears—as well as by man's effort to enhance and

---

*The central panel may represent the precivilized, antediluvian world, as E. H. Gombrich has recently suggested ("Bosch's 'Garden of Earthly Delights': A Progress Report," *Journal of the Warburg and Courtauld Institute*, 32 [1969], 162–70). Specifically, Gombrich's thesis relates to the biblical descriptions of Paradise and the "licentious" world of the time of Noah—licentious, however, only in the eyes of the orthodox Christian moralist.

amplify sensory experience through artistic or artful contrivances. Addicted to our sensory experiences rather than accepting experience with detachment through the senses, we become *artful;* that is, we acquire a certain sensory greed springing from a dissatisfaction with the natural mode. But our addiction is hell because it remains purely sensory and can never be totally satisfied. The right panel illustrates a truth that contradicts our most basic notions of art and its cherished place in culture, for in Bosch's vision the instruments of art become instruments of torture. However, it is not sensory experience in itself that is negative, but the artificial cultivation of sensory experience divorced from the psychic wellsprings. When we need art to soothe or amplify our senses, it is only because we are already at war; there has already been a conscious split from nature and within our own nature. The right-panel vision prophetically describes the European mental condition following the Renaissance—the suffering of Great Artists and the creation of artificial sensory needs, all under the shadows of cities bombed and burning in the night. It is precisely this relationship that Thomas Mann explored in his novel *Dr. Faustus:* war is hell only because art is hell.

Bosch's vision of art-as-hell recalls the wisdom of the Chinese sage Chuang-Tzu:

If the rules of the sages were entirely set aside in the world, a beginning might be made of reasoning with the people. If the six musical accords were reduced to a state of utter confusion, organs and lutes all burned and the ears of the musicians like the blind Khwang stopped up, all men would begin to possess and employ their natural power of hearing. If elegant ornaments were abolished, the five embellishing colors disused, and the eyes of men like Li Ku glued up, all men would begin to possess and employ their natural power of vision. If the hook and the line were destroyed, the compass and square thrown away, and the fingers of men like the artful Khui smashed, all men would begin to possess and employ their natural skill;—as it is said, "The greatest art is like stupidity." . . . When men possessed and employed their natural faculty of knowledge, there would be no delusions in the world. When they possessed and employed their natural virtue, there would be no depravity in the world. Men like Tzang (Shan), Shih (Khiu), Yang (Ku), Mo (Ti), Shih Khwang (the musician), the artist Khui and Li Ku, all displayed their qualities outwardly, and set the world in a blaze of admiration and confounded it—a method which is of no use![12]

What Chuang Tzu and Bosch both perceived was not so much the inutility of the arts as a fundamental problem that confronts humankind in its evolution: art—the variety of responses to reality—encoded as culture becomes a beautiful snare that ultimately serves only to deceive the individual by keeping him enslaved in a particular perceptual "gloss." The tragedy of all human collectivities has been their failure to pass beyond their own cultural/perceptual glosses. When art, or any of the means of knowing and expressing ceases to be a rung on the ladder of greater evolutionary development and instead becomes an end in itself, the individual becomes a parody of his labors: how much more so for entire cultures? When culture becomes a refinement rather than an integral expression of internal necessity, it blinds and dulls the senses rather than educating them; when the senses are sundered from the wholeness of innate experience, when the cumulative power of culture distorts perception more than it aids it, and distracts attention more than it serves it, when knowledge deludes rather than enlightens, and when social mores are used to rationalize rather than uplift, then it is inevitable that war should become civilization's most distinguishing feature—that activity, finally, to which all other modes of knowing and artistic practice must be subordinated.

In advanced civilized—*citified*—conditions, order exists only on a rational, intellectual level as a blueprint or a work of fine art; the reality of the social/planetary whole remains a seething chaos. The ingenuity and refinement of art is surpassed finally by the ingenuity and ultra-refinement of technology, with its avant-garde, the armaments industry; the cultivation of sense desires is outstripped only by the holy awe of cities enflamed by war. The psychological relationship between art and war, which Bosch prophetically realized in the right panel of the *Garden of Earthly Delights*, was exemplified some four hundred years later in the personality of Adolf Hitler. Young Hitler, enamored of the less popular and more "irrational" social role of the artist, aspired to become one of the Great Artists. For four bitter years in Vienna between 1909 and 1913, even after having been rejected by the Academy of Fine Arts and the School of Architecture, he stubbornly pursued the goal of becoming a famous painter. The pathways to expression, already culturally distorted, were closed off to Hitler forever without any hope of his being acclaimed an artist when the blind and futile effort of World War I burst upon Europe in 1914. Following the war, frustrated creativity in Hitler turned to a messianic fury stoked by the unconscious urges of centuries of repressed feelings, and exacerbated and divided senses.

The culture that produced Hitler was not Bosch's but Raphael's. For four centuries the mental glories of the academic vision cloaked the essential disorder of existence. The vision of St. Francis and Bosch was already but a dream in 1500, for European civilization had already embarked upon an age of technology: the left hemisphere had already usurped right-hemisphere expressive means; technical ability had already replaced the primacy of psychic knowledge. The stage was set for the disordered order of modern technological civilization. Behind the plinths and orders of Vitruvian proportion and the sequence of linear perspective lay the evolutionary snare of culture, confounding, dividing, and limiting the *senses* and consciousness of man.

CHAPTER FOUR

The Academization of Single Vision

IF THE *School of Athens* sums up the artistic beginning of the reign of reason, then Rembrandt's famous print, the so-called *Faustus*, exemplifies the intuitive realm confounded by reason. Rembrandt's dense, smoky style is an attempted negation of the pre-Cartesian clarity of the *School of Athens*. In making the leap to what we today call science, Faustus, the legendary sixteenth-century alchemist, left behind the mystery of the spirit that once animated both the arts and the sciences of pre-Renaissance Europe. In his study Faustus contemplated the mystery that is simply the indissoluble unity of life and death, a unity Faustus himself, because of his pact with the Devil, had come to doubt. Of this doubt was born science, which separates life from death, body from mind, spirit from matter. Romance was also born from this doubt, for it represents the struggle to regain the unitive vision. From the Aristotelian mirror of Doctor Faustus emerged not one man but two: the scientist and the artist, Descartes and Rembrandt, the schizophrenic twins of modern Western culture.

But within the world of art itself, Rembrandt, the self-doubting artist, was already deviating from the contemporary seventeenth-century academic model. In this respect he was the forerunner of the romantic, counter-cultural antihero of the nineteenth century. By contrast, the academy of art, which began to predominate in Rembrandt's time, was actually a stopgap cultural measure giving a sense of coherence and structure to a realm of knowing that by unconscious social agreement had already been abandoned. Subordinated to the perceptual system and literary philosophy that developed in the Renaissance, the visual arts needed an institutional framework to help them remain "pure"—to preserve the distinction between fine or "high" and applied or "low" arts and crafts. Even within the realm of fine arts there appeared the distinction between theory and practice. With the world itself divided into objective and subjective realms, the function of fine art became to objectify what is essentially subjective. When the one-point perspective system was established as an official academic mode in the seventeenth century, it very clearly became the function of the artist to rationalize what originally was a subjective mode of feeling and seeing. The inherent contradictoriness of this situation manifested itself in a variety of ways, until it finally brought about the disintegration of the academic system late in the nineteenth century.

The academy's formation as an institution may be traced to the competitive reaction of the artist confronted with the power of the printed word. Proclaiming the freedom of his imagination and the loftiness of his inspiration, the Renaissance artist undid the collective association of the Medieval guild system. At the same time, feeling insecure without the guild, the artist demanded a recognition he felt would place him on an equal basis with the philosopher and the scientist. The sense of inferiority behind this demand became a new source of internal conflict. The artist acquired the potential of evolving into an antisocial force, if only in the sense that he was no longer organized in a coherent social form. He therefore developed an ambiguous status, both in the eyes of society and in his own.

The formation of the various Italian academies in the sixteenth century, and the perfection of the academic model in the formation of the French Academy of the seventeenth century, satisfied the artist's longing for a new kind of prestige, symbolized by the very term *academy*, the name of Plato's school. The *School of Athens* literally materialized as the academy. The academization of art made a social institution of the one-point perspective system and the entire "backward"-looking school of humanism in general, thus inaugurating a profoundly conservative and authoritarian attitude within the arts and the creative process as a whole. Not only did the distinction arise between "high" art and "low" or folk art, but art itself came to be regarded as a decorative frill almost entirely devoid of any social, environmental, or psychological utility. The artist developed into a distinct professional in a society of professionals. For several centuries professionalization was aided by the academy system, which was also able to give a majority of artists practicing according to the new perceptual canon of the Renaissance a certain amount of social prestige and economic protection, much in the manner of the Medieval guild system.

Most significant, until its breakdown in the nineteenth century, the academy was the basic conditioning factor of visual perception in the Western world. Its influence spread especially into the conquered realms of the New World, where its grip gave firm assurance that pre-European conventions would be totally extinguished. It is not surprising, then, that the academic values lingered longer in colonialized countries like Mexico than in Europe itself. The noted muralist José Clemente Orozco's description of the academy in Mexico in 1910 gives a true picture of the academic dogma and the profound servility it demanded: "Academic criteria held sway: 'The ancients long ago reached perfection, they did everything that could be done, and nothing is left for us except to bow down to them and humbly imitate them. Florentine drawing with Venetian coloring. . . .'"[1] In other words, the academy was a tyrannical institution whose main function was to suppress authentic feeling and intuition—psyche—and to standardize values and perceptions. The intimidation of the imagination was further reinforced by the belief that in sculpture and architecture the Greeks and Romans were without peer, and that in painting Raphael had attained the pinnacle of human creativity. As the academy took hold, an elaborate system was developed whereby an artist could choose, so to speak, the best elements of the past masters in a kind of assembly line of the imagination, and put them together into a prescribed form. What some have described as the eclecticism of the academy was in reality the regimentation of creative thought; it was the triumph of technique over the human spirit in the very realm where the primacy of psyche might have been expected to hold forth.

Many of the peculiarities of the Western consciousness as they emerged across the entire world in the nineteenth century can be traced to the formation and structure of the academy. Because of the academic concept—a basically authoritarian and institutional approach to reality—the rules of art, like a system of political laws, were assembled into a distinct, literary code. Consequently visual perception was narrowed into a single, precise mode, in which deviations were not given recognition. The academic tendency was always to seek as precise a visual equivalent for the verbal as possible. The study of perspective and *disegno*—contour drawing—was the technical staple of this perceptual mode. Despite the efforts of the Rubenistes to defend the virtues of color against its adversaries, the Poussinistes, who championed the cause of line, color lost its intrinsic symbolic value in the Renaissance, and it was not until the breakthrough of Impressionism that color began to come into its own again.

The general subordination of color to more complex formal/literary values in the academic tradition is of immense psychological interest, for it parallels the general suppression of the psyche as a predominant feature of modern Western culture. According to the French psychophysiologist Charles Henry, visual sensation may be broken down into three components of increasing complexity: light, color, and form. The supremacy of form in the academic tradition is also the supremacy of the least immediate psychovisual component, the one that is already subject to the greatest influence from preconceived—cultural—data. In a fundamental sense the Western eye and brain, under the influence of the academy, was educated away from what the eye is primarily concerned with seeing: light and color. Form is fundamentally a preconceived, mental construction projected outward through the eye; as such, it is intimately related to name or idea. The world of form in classical Indian philosophy is called *namarupa*, literally "name/form," indicating the essentially mental nature of this world. Titus Burckhardt comments on this general topic:

A rigorous perspective in painting inevitably involves a loss of chromatic symbolism, since color is called upon to represent an illumination indispensable to the production of an illusion of space, and so loses its direct nature. A medieval painting is luminous, not because it suggests a source of light situated in the world depicted, but because its colours directly manifest qualities inherent in light; they are touches of the primordial light that is present in the heart. The development of chiaroscuro, on the contrary, turns colour into nothing more than the play of an imaginary light; the magic of lighting carries painting into a sort of intermediate world analogous to a dream, a dream sometimes grandiose, but one that envelops the spirit instead of liberating it.[2]

Not only did color lose its symbolic and psychological significance in the academic vision, but its use never fully corresponded to the new science of color developed through seventeenth-century optics and Newton's classical research. The color of Rubens in the seventeenth, Watteau in the eighteenth, and Delacroix in the nineteenth century was intuitively scientific, but these artists, great as they were, tended to be exceptions, for the academy's heavy emphasis on literary classicism was inherently anticolor, reinforcing the innate formalism of the perspectival mode. Thus Poussin's color was based on a literary rather than a psychophysiological interpretation of ancient color theory. By demanding strict adherence to its rules, the academy insulated the artist from experiencing for himself the fundamental psychovisual phenomena with which he was dealing. The experiential example of Leonardo was never fully appreciated; instead his work became part of the standardized mental furniture of the academic artist.

Another factor powerfully affecting academic emphasis on form was the humanist concept underlying the practice of the arts through the Renaissance and Baroque periods: *ut pictura poesis*, "as in painting, so in poetry." Though painting is given precedence in this famous quotation from Horace, the implications are that the painter—the highest of the visual artists, according to Leonardo—is guided by the word. Image and word must be one; all else is mental caprice. This idea profoundly affected the hierarchy of the arts within the academic system itself, and further supported the elitist, literary concept of the arts as opposed to a crafts tradition. According to the canon *ut pictura poesis*, the highest art was the painting of "history" taken from ancient literature and focusing on a precise, dramatic moment. In this notion there was a fundamental conceit: happy the educated prince who could choose a suitable moment from a particular myth and suggest it to his favorite artist, or who could, seeing a painting for the first time, trace its exact literary origin. This astonishingly elitist approach contained the seed of the nineteenth-century concept of art for art's sake, with its complex relationship between literary critic and artist. Such literary esotericism calls of necessity for some kind of mediating interpreter— the critic, the historian of art, the aesthetician.

The literary nature of the arts was spelled out in the institution of the "conferences" begun by Le Brun in the seventeenth-century French Academy, and epitomized by Reynold's famous *Discourses*, addressed to the English Academy in the eighteenth century. These lectures emphasize the essentially mental world of concepts that defined the visual arts. Reliance upon concept, rather than upon the inherently visual, is what makes much of post-Renaissance Western art so difficult to comprehend without art history and criticism. Indeed, academic art is art-historical art; that is, it is a tradition of art defined and acquiring meaning only by virtue of its own past. By contrast, the arts of most of the pretechnological traditions derived their meaning not from the previous work done in that tradition but from a spiritual philosophy. More explicitly, the Western academic tradition in the seventeenth and eighteenth centuries standardized the external form epitomized by Raphael or Michelangelo or even Rubens, at the expense of the spirit that had given birth to that form. But then, this process was inevitable, since Western culture after the Renaissance became ever more spiritually arid. If there was any "spiritual" philosophy transmitted at the time of Joshua Reynolds in the 1770's, it was the philosophy of literary humanism, itself devoid of transcendental intent and techniques. Literary humanism was essentially the printed transmission of an allegiance to a time so distantly past that to truly approach it the science of archaeology had to be invented.

The fundamental value of the humanist/academic tradition was the supremacy of man, separate from nature and essentially bound to no god but his own fate. This was the ideal of Michelangelo and Rembrandt, of Caravaggio and Rubens, of Velazquez and Watteau, and in literature, of Shakespeare and Cervantes. If some of these artists portrayed Christ, the Son of God, it was essentially in the image of the particular artist—man himself, individualized, atomized, and set adrift. Arnold Hauser writes of the artist during this period:

The spiritual existence of the artist is always in danger; neither an authoritarian nor a liberal order of society is entirely free from peril for him; the one gives him less freedom, the other less security. There are artists who feel safe only when they are free, but there are also such as can breathe freely only when they are secure. The seventeenth century was, at any rate, one of the periods furthest removed from the ideal of a synthesis of freedom and security.[3]

This may also be taken as a critique of the academy, which could accommodate only the most restricted artistic impulses.

If the academy provided shelter, it was of the competitive variety, reflecting the open market values of a secular bourgeois society. Competition was ultimately dictated by the humanist/classical concept of man's supremacy over nature. It was this concept that placed history painting at the top of the academic hierarchy, for in history painting the subject was exclusively man and his passions. This value system extended downward through the lesser genres, so that a landscape without figures was considered inferior to a landscape with figures; and of course, a landscape of a contemporary locale was considered quite inferior to a historical landscape. The great prizes, the Prix de Rome for instance, were to be won in the realm of history painting. If an artist like Watteau exhibited genius in other areas, new genres such as the *fête galante* might be created, but they remained at a lower level than history painting. This emphasizes the academy's conservatism, which made more than one artist wretched and kept the practice of "high art" in the hands of the remaining aristocracy and moneyed bourgeoisie of Europe. By the eighteenth century the craftsman had been all but driven into social oblivion, the final death blow to be given by the rise of the machine. The crafts that could survive did so only at the expense of becoming an adjunct of the academy, as in the case of the Gobelin tapestry works in France. Even there, more often than not, the craftsman's task was to duplicate a current marvel of history painting.

With the supremacy of man as the highest value of humanist culture, the study of man as a mechanistic physiological system became another basic function of art. Through the late Medieval period the image of man as a microcosm had been a common motif. There are many Medieval and early Renaissance drawings and engravings in which man is depicted as the literal center of a confluence of energies symbolizing the zodiacal signs or the basic alchemical elements. In this view each man is a symbol, a complete reflection of the forces that operate through the universe. It is a mistake to view this image of man as anthropocentric; rather it shows man as an intermediary focusing forces of the macrocosmos and the microcosmos. Today this view is once more coming into its own. Lincoln Barnett writes: "It is perhaps significant to man that in terms of magnitude he is the mean between macrocosm and microcosm. Stated crudely this means that super-giant red star (the largest material body in the universe) is just as much bigger than man as an electron (one of the tiniest of physical entities) is smaller."[4]

This view has been the basis of a particular kind of psychology in which man's self-knowledge and internal harmony are the prerequisites of social and environmental harmony. Leonardo's famous drawing belongs to this ideological family, though it is interesting that in the drawing the man is slightly off center, and the circle and square are not perfectly conjoint. With the rise of the Copernican worldview came a fallacy that displaced the microcosmic view of man with the existential one. Since it had been proven that the earth was not the center of the solar system but seemingly a small, arbitrarily placed sphere in an infinite universe, man's position was seen as equally arbitrary and absurd. This conclusion, however, did nothing to lessen, and even magnified, the egocentricity of the humanist point of view. Although the microcosmic, symbolic, and Copernican viewpoints are not mutually exclusive, the microcosmic viewpoint was emphatically displaced by the new Cartesian concept of man: a physiological system of various mechanical functions in which no soul could be discovered and which existed apart from nature because of its reasoning faculty—*cogito ergo sum!*

No longer admitting of the microcosmic, symbolic view, man became an alien on the planet earth. In academic art this new attitude carried over, and perhaps almost in embarrassment over its spiritual poverty, painters began to idealize man in their work. In history painting this was simple, since none of the characters depicted existed any longer, and the idealization of man was easily part and parcel of the overall idealization of the classical past, the "golden age" when somehow men were nobler. Yet since humanism contained no inherent spirituality, the idealization of the human form in academic art tended to produce overmuscled caricatures of real men, based to varying degrees upon the remnants of ancient Greco-Roman statuary. The Christian iconographical scheme was subordinated to this point of view as well; what had been sacred dramas to the Medieval mind became "histories" in the academic period, intrinsically no different than the Greco-Roman histories that were the staple of high art. By the eighteenth century there ceased to be, for all practical purposes, a vital tradition of sacred art in Europe.

Collectively, post-Renaissance European man had entered a phase of increasingly unrelated activity dominated by a competitive mercantile ethic and a dichotomous philosophy of materialism. Reflecting the overall dominance of techne, the expressive outlets became the property of state institutions, and knowledge itself became splintered into various seemingly autonomous intellectual pursuits, each with its own ethic of self-interest, protected by its own academy, or today, by its own university department. The doctrine of art for art's sake, which arose in the court and academy of Louis XIV, mirrored similar attitudes in other human endeavors, which Adam Smith rationalized as "enlightened self-interest." The role given art by the academy in the eighteenth century was critical, for when the wellsprings of human expression are channeled away from the process of life itself, then the human community is diminished and impoverished. In the fifteenth century Alberti had declared: "The arts are learnt by reason and method; they are mastered by practice." The expressive function of art has its sources in the deep "irrational" levels of being; when art is thought to be the exclusive property of reason, it no longer serves its true purpose—to inform and inspire as the very breath of life itself. Academic art became a parade of mental constructions and moral sophistries through which man was supposedly ennobled and nature improved upon. Inspiration, which in the Socratic view is the very origin of art, became a problem for Joshua Reynolds to moralize upon: what is its place in the training of the artist? The very question indicates how far the creative process had been separated from its psychic origins. What Socrates had called the "divine madness" was rationalized into the anthropomorphic muses of eighteenth-century culture, faintly disguised dramatizations of society ladies who posed for the painter in a bid for a kind of immortality, what Thackeray called "vanity fair."

By the middle of the eighteenth century European culture was experiencing a curious bankruptcy. Whereas the traditional culture—the "world of the arts" that had replaced the spiritual culture of Medieval Europe—though incredibly refined, especially in the realm of music, was running aground on its own rules, the actual material prosperity of European civilization was expanding, owing as much to successful, if ruthless, colonization policies throughout the world as to the intrinsically aggressive materialistic philosophy that had become the mainstay of the European peoples themselves. But the aridity and sense of bankruptcy that even the French Academy was feeling in the mid-eighteenth century was symptomatic of something much larger and more far-reaching that was just then occurring: the transition from an essentially pretechnological to a technological culture, an unprecedented move in the development of the human species.

Actually, as Lewis Mumford pointed out in *Technics and Civilization*, Europe had entered an eotechnic phase sometime around the tenth century with the invention of the mechanical clock, the technological innovation that finally made possible the mechanical attitude of "single vision." With the discarding of the sacred cultural models in the sixteenth century following the invention of perspective and movable type, and the codification of the system known as modern science in the seventeenth century, Europe was totally prepared in the eighteenth century to embark upon the first widespread standardization of human society through the process known as the first Industrial Revolution. The standardized nature of the academic art of the mid-eighteenth century dramatically reflects the European sensibility on the eve of the Industrial Revolution.

The creation of an academic painting was an almost totally devitalized process. A mental stage was established according to the rigorous perspective system, and puppets were placed on it corresponding to a preconceived literary idea: this was the structural studio-set of Poussin's "classicism." The stylistic reaction to this ideal was the phase known as Rococo, culminating in the work of Fragonard and certain churches built in Austria and Bavaria during the early eighteenth century. Rococo, like the preceding stylistic phase, Baroque, was a vital expression, however diluted, that managed to survive the hard rationalism of the academy: a spontaneous, "decorative" outburst negating the geometric rigor of Cartesian logic. But Rococo was also the art of an effete aristocracy whose pleasure, no longer contained by a spiritual regimen, only ended in debauchery. Baroque and Rococo may be viewed as native European expressions futilely maintaining the organic tradition of the Gothic. In 1750, however, Christ was no longer the redeemer, and rational, "enlightened" man had usurped the world stage for himself.

In terms of organic cultural processes, the establishment of the academy as the official state organ of culture, capable of overriding and even integrating such fundamentally irrational phenomena as the Rococo style into its own practices, is symptomatic of an already advanced state of cultural degeneration. Culture, in this sense, is the universally understood means of expression of a given social organism; the more highly integrated the culture, the more conscious and universally shared are the means and meaning of expression. The great craftsmen and builders of Gothic Europe were able to bring about a high level of cultural integration by the construction of cathedrals. The process of erecting these great edifices offered an opportunity for universal participation, uniting all of the arts, beliefs, and spiritual practices of the society in one tangible whole. The case of mid-eighteenth-century Europe is quite the reverse: the arts were no longer coalesced into one work but fragmented into easel painting, chamber music, novels, and secular architecture. Furthermore, the craft/guild system was under fatal attack from two sides—the usurpation of the arts by the academies, and the mechanization of life that was about to become universal, thus dispensing with the need for "handicrafts," as they were to be called in the nineteenth century. That the means of culture were now left in the hands of a few privileged people only shows that the rest of the people, the "masses" as they came to be called, were culturally deprived. Not only would the masses become desensitized and brutalized as a result, but the very meaning of life could no longer be coherently expressed and transmitted. This, then, is the bane of mechanized civilization.

Cultural disintegration, which manifests socially in increasing modes of specialization—professionalism—has been aggravated by universal sensory fragmentation. Again, the Gothic cathedral provides an example of an aesthetic process whose end is achieved when a participant is able to experience a state of psychosensorial interfusion. The effect of different sensory agents acting upon the participant simultaneously transfuses and uplifts the whole being, evoking a transcendent experience. With the onset of the Renaissance this total experience became much more the exception than the rule. One may recall certain multimedia events, such as the synchronization of water sculpture, lights, and music by the great Baroque artist Gianlorenzo Bernini, who, it should be added, was quite familiar with the nature of the mystical experience. But by and large, from the sixteenth century onward Europeans suffered increasing sensorial fragmentation, an inevitable result of the mechanization of consciousness, which naturally limits the organism to a splintered, sequential point of view. By the mid-eighteenth century even the idea of the psychotechnic experience of wholeness had become either heresy or an exotic oddity, almost beyond the belief of the "civilized" mind. In acceding to the power of Faust's quest, Europe had ceased to be a cultural whole, and became instead the breeding ground of desperate, schizophrenic half-men.

Of course, the cultural disintegration caused by mechanized consciousness was supported by the academies and rationalized into a new belief system that was born out of but finally supplanted Christianity. Siegfried Giedion has described this new system as "the creed of progress." Giedion writes:

Once more the contrast should be stressed between the ancient and the modern outlook. The ancients perceived the world as eternally existing and self-renewing, whereas we perceive it as *created* and existing within temporal limits; that is, the world is determined to a specific goal and purpose. Closely bound up with this belief that the world has a definite purpose is the outlook of rationalism. Rationalism, whether retaining its belief in God or not, reaches its ideological peak in the thinkers of the latter half of the eighteenth century. Rationalism goes hand in hand with the idea of progress. The eighteenth century all but identifies the advance of science with social progress and the perfectability of man.

In the nineteenth century the creed of progress was raised into a dogma given various interpretations in the course of the century.[5]

Academic art completely supported the new belief system, for it represented the standardization of the senses. In 1771 the first *Encyclopedia Britannica* defined art as "a system of rules serving to facilitate the performance of certain actions," and painting as "the art of representing natural bodies, and giving them an appearance of life, by turn of lines and the degrees of colours"—rational, externally oriented definitions leaving little to the imagination. Not only was art rational, but in the art of history painting, the noblest visual art conceivable, lay the basis for the creed of progress itself: history, the unique propulsion of human events. The very notion of history contains the assumption that man has a development apart from the general development of nature. This is what is meant by the perfectability of man in the creed of progress—as if man could be perfected at the expense of nature, or at least with little regard to nature, which is seen by rationalism as devoid of consciousness, intelligence, and feeling. In this belief lies the fatal seed of both the European's success and his ultimate downfall. This sense of history, we have seen, began at the time of the Renaissance and was peculiarly focused upon the ancient Mediterranean civilizations of Greece and Rome. The raising of history painting— originally meaning merely the telling of a story taken from a writer of the past—to the highest level of academic art established that particular sense of aloofness and confidence in human control over events that is necessary for the ideological notion of history to take root. By the late eighteenth century the ideology of history had borne its first fruit in the form of the American and French revolutions. What had been the direct optical perception of Leonardo, literally embellished by Raphael, became transformed through the academies into the relentless ideology of history.

CHAPTER FIVE

The Birth of History

WHEN WE speak of history, we are really speaking of a way of rationalizing time. There is perhaps nothing more profoundly subjective than the experience of time; it is the medium of consciousness itself. As such, it is indissoluble and inseparable from consciousness. To understand time is to understand the laws governing the unfoldment of our own mind. These are laws intuitively arrived at and expressible through the simplest and most natural images—the transformation of seed into plant and of plant into seed, sunrise and sunset, the turning of the seasons, the procession of the equinoxes, the cycles of the heavenly bodies. There is something inexplicably "round" about time, round and unfathomably deep.

In view of time's enigmatic nature, it is no surprise that the first efforts toward mechanization involved "straightening" time out. The invention of the clock set in motion the illusion that time flows in a particular direction through rationally determinable standard units. The values created by this process of temporal regulation eventually evolved into the modern psychomechanistic complex known as history.

In his memorable work *Cosmos and History*, Mircea Eliade describes modern man as "consciously and voluntarily historical," in contrast to traditional, pretechnological man, who negates history. "Whether he abolishes it periodically, whether he devalues it by perpetually finding transhistorical models and archetypes for it, whether, finally, he gives it a metahistorical meaning . . . the man of the traditional civilizations accorded the historical event no value in itself; in other words he did not regard it as a specific category of his own mode of existence."[1] By the mid-eighteenth century European man, the child of Christianity, had voluntarily accepted history, thus making a distinct break with his own past and with almost all of the other world cultures. Man's acceptance of the absolute uniqueness of historical events is itself a unique event. The consequences are enormous, for they ultimately imply a denial of divine intervention; a negation of archetypes, replaced by the inalienable uniqueness of the individual ego; and a suppression of any consideration other than the cause-and-effect relationships underlying events. It is this insistence on seeing everything as a linear progression of causes and effects that gives a false order to history, just as the invention of the clock imposed a false regimentation on time itself.

The first edition of the *Encyclopaedia Britannica* pointedly defined human history as distinct from the history of nature: "History, a description or recital of things as they are, or have been, in a continued orderly narration of the principal facts and circumstances thereof. History with regard to its subject is divided into the history of Nature, and the history of Actions. The history of Actions is a continued relation of a series of memorable events."[2] Those periods in which there seem to be no memorable events, or at least no records, tend to be devalued by the historical attitude—hence the term Dark Ages. Like the moments ticked off by the clock, each historical event is irreversible, and in a sense unredeemable. Even if Hegel spoke of the ever more perfect manifestations of the Universal Spirit, and Marx of the classless state, to the average person these are but abstractions that hardly justify the terror of everyday events. By the twentieth century, Eliade comments, a philosopher like Heidegger "has gone to the trouble of showing that the historicity of human existence forbids all hope of transcending time and history."[3] This is the final, bleak point of view inaugurated by the philosophers of the eighteenth-century Enlightenment. For history, which began as an "ennobling" narrative of past events, has become transformed through academic artistic values into an ideology shaping human events in the present, and providing the exclusive basis for predicting and controlling the future. As such this ideology masks a fear of change that is contemptuous of criticism and holds dogmatically to its own "progressive" assumptions. K. R. Popper, in his remarkable study *The Poverty of Historicism*, concludes: "It almost looks as if the historicists were trying to compensate themselves for the loss of an unchanging world by clinging to the faith that change can be foreseen because it is ruled by an unchanging law."[4] This "unchanging law" is historicism, or progress itself.

We can view the period from around 1750 to the present as *the age of history*, and we may regard history as an acute form of self-consciousness that cuts the present moment off from all relationship and meaning save the causal, thereby inhibiting the capacity for integrative action. In the form of the doctrine of progress, history is mechanics applied to the ordering of human events and life-styles, regardless of their idiosyncrasies. This accounts for the various "tragic events" of recent history—the massacres, the uprootings, the rape of certain states and peoples, the mass bombings—for mechanics is the infinitely repeatable extension of power-as-order over the seeming randomness of events. To *make history* is to exert power. Earlier times had seen great migrations of people, "barbaric invasions," and even the resort to war by religious movements as a means of dispensing their teachings. But only in modern Europe (and, by extension, America) did men begin to make history—that is, exert power over others—as the only means of redeeming or justifying their own lives. The history of the modern world from the late eighteenth century to the present—the age of history—is the record of shifting balances of power, characterized by three broad areas of change: 1) The mechanization of consciousness, the materialization of values, and the industrialization of human society with its consequent disruption of planetary ecosystems; 2) accelerated social and political change in the form of upheavals, revolution, and world warfare, accompanied by the triumph of democracy, whether of the capitalistic or of the socialistic variety; 3) cultural disintegration, the stratification of knowledge by academic institutions and the continuing counter-development of visionary renegades who combine social and political critique with essentially mystical aspiration.

In terms of human development, the age of self-conscious historicism is brief, violent, and chaotic. It epitomizes, on the one hand, the triumph of techne, and on the other, the disintegration of the human spirit's capacity to express itself as an integral function of nature. But according to dialectical process, every phase of development contains the seed of its opposite. As Mao Tse-tung has said, "The fundamental cause of the development of a thing is not external but internal; it lies in the contradictoriness within the thing. This internal contradiction exists in every single thing, hence its motion and development."[5] The contradictoriness inherent in the age of history is the persistence of the transformative vision, the redemption of history through the return of consciousness to its root source, exemplifying what Eliade has called the Eternal Return: the primordial process by which man receives cosmic consecration through identification with transcendent forces, whether these forces be "spiritual" or related to the cycles of the earth and the heavens.

Time, distinguished from space, sequentialized into history, intellectualized into units of hours, minutes, and seconds, and further abstracted into money, loses its psychobiological significance. The source of this misunderstanding is to be found in the orthodox Christian doctrine of the uniqueness of the event of Christ, which alone gives meaning to all other events. From the Christ-event to the Second Coming, in the Christian view, all human activity takes place in unrepeatable units, redemption being possible only by relation to the unique Christ-event. This doctrine is absolutist and terrifyingly single-minded. It breaks from the traditional view, common to most world cultures, that time is cyclic and that the meaning of human existence is related to certain recurring cosmic patterns. The antiecological force of the Christian view lies in its assertion of a significance for humans separate from that for nature; man alone is redeemable, and nature by implication is corrupt, lacking either soul or intelligence. By contrast, the Mahayana Buddhists, for example, believe that all sentient creatures down to the least blade of grass are to be redeemed or enlightened.* Theories of reincarnation that would strongly support a cyclic view of time were supplanted early in the formation of

---

*Mahayana Buddhism is the form of Buddhism dominant in China, Korea, and Japan. Its most prominent school is Ch'an or Zen.

Christian dogma by the doctrine of the unique soul-event, implying the monadic permanence of each individual human entity; once a soul comes into bodily existence, it exists eternally as that particular "personality" in which it was embodied during its time on earth. However illogical this view may be, it reinforces the idea of time as a series of unrepeatable events occurring in a single line of development, as well as the idea expressed in the original *Encyclopedia Britannica* that there is a human history distinct from the history of nature.

The cyclic doctrine of the Golden Age was resuscitated briefly during the Renaissance, but only on a piecemeal basis that sprang chiefly from literary nostalgia rather than intellectual commitment. With the outstanding exception of Giambattista Vico's cyclical ideas, the linear doctrine of strictly human history took hold after the Renaissance, a notable heresy in the evolution of human culture. The present historical view of the significance of human events is itself but a manifestation of the ideological separation of human affairs from the natural processes. In actuality it does not deny the persistence of larger processes, as the standard historical preoccupation with the rise and fall of cultures shows, but merely exhibits a fundamental ignorance regarding their full extent. Contemporary intellectual pride, compounded by scientific bias, is unwilling to acknowledge a valid insight in the myths, hymns, and creations of prescientific cultures. The notion of cyclical time as a vital, palpable medium affecting even the course of human events is generally regarded as a mythic view that has little bearing upon our present situation.

The traditional procreative and cyclic view of time is expressed in the *Atharva Veda*:

> On Time is laid the overflowing vessel
> Which we behold in many places appearing.
> He carries from us all the worlds of creatures.
> They call him KALA in the highest Heaven.
> For he made the worlds of Life,
> And gathered all living things together.
> Their son did he become, who was their Father:
> No other higher power than he existeth. [6]

From this point of view we are children who have forgotten that it is we who begat ourselves and are the authors of our own situation. In so doing we plunge ourselves into history, which is the playground of our forgetfulness. The cyclical point of view does not maintain that events are mechanically repeated but that there is an inescapable law of periodicity to which all things are subject. Spring occurs annually, but it is not always the same flower that blooms. Nature renews herself, but only by dying to herself. This notion is inimical to the ideology of history, or more precisely, to the ideology of progress spawned by eighteenth-century history. Though the New Year is regularly celebrated in our society, with the exception of hangovers it has little effect on the collective behavior, and little implication of renewal. The idea of renewal through a collectively agreed upon "destruction" or stopping of all life functions is one that monetary work-a-day values have long since scrapped—and along with it the socially accepted dispersal of accumulated negative energy, now released sporadically through antisocial crime and rebelliousness. In ancient Mexico, by contrast, at the end of a 52-year cycle there were thirteen "accumulated" days, corresponding to the thirteen leap years occurring during that cycle. During these thirteen days the houses and temples were cleaned and many artifacts destroyed; there was a general fast and penance, and all the fires were put out. On the fourteenth morning a new fire was lit, and a new 52-year period of socially agreed upon reality began. Customs like this are a human collective's way of dying to itself in order that, like nature, it may be renewed. They also indicate an open acceptance of the "decreasing," negative element in nature, an element that today is deliberately avoided at all costs, much as any coming to terms with the meaning of death is avoided. Our myth of progress is summed up in the concept of a continually increasing Gross National Product, and funeral homes and cemeteries that function as if they were pleasure palaces.

These observations aside, it should be evident that progress and history are as stern and demanding as any other deities produced by the human imagination. The period of ideological historicism, of modern Christianity and technological development, has its own organic process of evolution. It is first of all a function of the Iron Age or Kali Yuga, and even more precisely, of the so-called Fifth Sun of the Mexican calendar, the age of change and transition ruled by the sign Ollin. Technological development is a fulfillment of this symbol for change and movement, for technology is based upon the notion of endless change mechanized into movement in a single prescribed direction. Its immediate roots, as Lynn White, and more comprehensively, Lewis Mumford have indicated, lie in the invention of the water clock, possibly as early as about A.D. 800. This event marked the beginning of what Mumford calls the eotechnic period.[7] The next seven hundred years, until about 1519, which may be distinguished as the early eotechnic period, were a most remarkable time in terms of world civilization, as I have earlier indicated. On the one hand, premechanistic cultural development and expansion on a global scale reached their peak, signaling the triumph of the great world religions as orthodoxy. On the other hand, militarism increased notably.

The combination of militarism with the rich cultural manifestations of the early eotechnic suggest that technology developed in a global context of tremendous ferment and achievement. But it was through the Western

European Christian culture that the many early manifestations of the new technology first took hold: the regimentation of monasticism; the development of the water clock, and later the first mechanical clock; a growing militarism, requiring a high degree of regimentation; the development of movable type and one-point perspective; and the perfection of guns and gunpowder, marking the culmination of early eotechnic culture by 1519.

The late phase of the eotechnic, from 1519 to 1727, corresponds to the first four hell periods of the Mexican calendar system. The entire hell period may be called "The Ascent of the Jaguar," a symbol of materialism, or the passage of the sun through the underworld. This period marks the overt rise of a militaristic psychology of dominance as the primary motivating power in world events. The neurocerebral imbalance that became so pronounced after 1519 was paralleled in philosophy by the development of strict subject-object dualism, in which techne reigns, at least overtly, over psyche. This development in philosophy began before 1519 as an aspect of a religious militarism in which hostility became an intransigent feature of certain orthodox belief systems, especially Islam, Christianity, and the Aztec and Inca social and religious systems. In the psychology of dominance, hostility is the compelling force used to gain power over others. Before hostility degenerates into physical war, it may masquerade as a compassionate, all-knowing superiority. In this case the urge to conquer appears as a kind of possessive love that invites a false feeling of dependence on the conquering agent. This process is precisely what was taking place during the emergence in 1519 of Western Christianity (both Protestant and Catholic) as the dominant ideological force in world affairs. The conqueror's possessive love can be seen in the phenomenon of colonialism, which was so strongly buttressed by the Christian missionaries. The same psychology of dominance also underlies the belief in the supreme power of technology—the logic of technique.

Symbolically, we may speak of the period between approximately 800 and 1519 as the "dimming of the radiant light," which refers to the first movement toward the developing split into subject and object; from 1519 to 1727 as the period of the "diffused glow," indicating the growing dependence upon the object following the split; and the paleotechnic and neotechnic periods, from 1727 to the present as the period of the "settled gloom," which marked the final loss of collective intrinsic awareness (of psychotechnical unity) and the utter triumph of "objective" knowledge— that is, complete reliance on the "objective" material world.[8]

The chief historical features of the late phase of the eotechnic—1519–1727—include the rise of Protestantism and the Catholic consolidation; the first great wave of European colonization; the development and triumph of science as ideology and technique; the consequent eclipse of the mystical "schools" of thought, either through Inquisition or through intellectual banishment; the academization of knowledge and the arts; the steady decline of India, China, and Islam; and the equally steady growth of sequentialized clock/print/money consciousness. The paleotechnic period, from 1727 to 1883, which comprises the fifth, sixth, and seventh hell periods of the Mexican age of change, spans the time from Newton's death to the beginning electrification of technology. This was the period of intense industrialization and the consequent transformation of the world into a field for materialist imperialism and technological conquest.

During the paleotechnic period history and the kindred doctrine of progress emerged as the supporting ideological system of European world dominance. Thereafter all of history was made to read as if it were a linear prelude to the exclusive development of modern European thought and culture: the Egyptian pyramids led directly to the dynamo; all other cultural achievements were considered subsidiary. By 1883, with the sole exception of Tibet, no major world culture had survived the direct imprint of European power. At the same time in Europe (and America) counter-cultural struggles and political revolutions were beginning to appear. By 1779, the beginning of the sixth hell period, the American Revolution and the counter-force toward romanticism had set in motion a powerful wave of change. By 1831, the beginning of the seventh hell period, industrialism had become an obviously irresistible force, and materialism had made a triumphant sweep over all other ideological forces in Europe and the world. This accounts for the rise during this 52-year period—from 1831 to 1883—of dialectical materialism, communism, socialism, and anarchism, and for the integration of the thrust of romanticism into the culture as a whole.

The neotechnic period began in 1883, and according to the Mexican calendar, it will culminate in 1987. It comprises the last two hell periods and is characterized by the emergence of an increasingly nonmaterialistic science, phenomenally manifested first by electricity, then by relativity, quantum physics, and the development of nuclear energy. It is also characterized by full-scale world conflict, the two world wars being thus far only the peak periods of turmoil in an age continually marked by internal conflict, civil war, and terrorism, as well as sporadic external conflicts between various sovereign states, and marked as well by a heightened state of psychic, i.e., propaganda, warfare. By 1959 the last integral pretechnological civilization, the Tibetan, was destroyed, and the world was uniformly convulsed in psychotechnological warfare. At the same time, however minute by comparison, there have been various transcendent impulses, from Theosophy, which began in 1875, to the more recent thought of Teilhard de Chardin and the current and often covert efforts of various groups working for a transformation of consciousness and the emergence of a harmonious and unified global civilization.*

From the point of view of technological development, the ideology of history was a paleotechnic necessity. The development of the steam engine and the birth of archaeology went hand in hand. The scientific study of the past, inaugurated in the mid-eighteenth century as the science of archaeology, marked the beginning of the detached and rootless (and often ruthless) consciousness known as historicism. The effect of archaeology was immediately noticeable in the arts in the 1760's, for a new exactitude was demanded in history painting. Architecture, costume, pose, more than ever had to conform to what was being brought to light by the first serious diggings at Herculanum, in the 1740's. The leading English history painter of the time, Gavin Hamilton, actually participated in the excavations at Herculanum. That the Europeans should be taking such an intensive look at the past at the very beginning of the Industrial Revolution may seem curious, but it is symptomatic of the unconscious insecurity that was collectively being felt as the world was launched into the ordeal of industrialization.

On the other hand, the archaeological and art-historical approach to the arts was in complete conformity to what was occurring as a result of the explosion of industrialism: the subordination of human conduct and action at all levels to the demands of *technique*—the mechanization of consciousness, the systemization of data and artifacts, and the classification and categorization of human sensibility into a regimented intellectual order. In the eighteenth century this process was everywhere at work, whether in finance or the arts, in history or biology. As Jacques Ellul has pointed out, the Industrial Revolution "resulted not from the exploitation of coal but rather from a change of attitude on the part of the whole civilization."[9] By the mid-eighteenth century the right mixture of factors and forces had brought about the change that was ultimately to reshape and reorder the face of the earth. The disappearance of a unifying religious movement acting as a transcendental agent of social coherence and the simultaneous atomization of existing social groups, such as the guilds, in favor of the rights of individuals, so that the individual became the ultimate sociological unit, were perhaps the chief factors establishing the sociopsychological conditions for the Industrial Revolution. In this social milieu history itself became an intellectual technique capable of being used to support the forces of industrial and social change.

Though history as an intellectual technique had distant origins in the Renaissance veneration of Mediterranean antiquity, its real progenitors were the first modern works of art criticism and art history, the *Laocoon*

---

*All of this is more explicitly developed in the charts outlining the technocultural development of the Iron Age/Kali Yuga, and the nine hell periods, The Ascent of the Jaguar, Appendix B.

(1760–68) of Gotthold Lessing, and Johann Winckelmann's *On the Imitation of Greek Works of Painting and Sculpture* (1775) and *History of Art* (1766). These astonishing works sum up the point of view of *technical humanism*. Basic to this approach is the idea that man is superior to nature, since animal and inorganic nature are presumed incapable of forming an ideal. Above all, Lessing and Winckelmann extolled the superiority of the Mediterranean past. Prior to the eighteenth century, history had been embodied in the form of a chronicle, usually documenting the lives of notable predecessors and outstanding events, much like Vasari's *Lives of the Artists*. The incentive for transforming history and art into intellectual technique derived from the sciences, which of course were flourishing in the eighteenth century. Thus Winckelmann asked, "How has it happened, whereas profound treatises have appeared in all other sciences, that the rationale of art and beauty has been so little enquired into?"[10] It was only a matter of time before a rational science of art history in the form of archaeology was to be formulated, coincident with the appearance of the first historical work, Gibbon's *Decline and Fall of the Roman Empire* (1775–87), significantly focusing on the demise of the Mediterranean civilization. Echoing the preoccupation with the glories of ancient Greece and Rome, Winckelmann proclaimed, "The history of Art aims at expounding its origin, growth, change, and fall, together with the diverse styles of peoples, ages, and artists, and at demonstrating this as far as possible, from the extant works of antiquity."[11] The history of art was formulated as a science predicated on the existence of certain artifacts from Mediterranean antiquity. Winckelmann's underlying historical and male-chauvinist bias was revealed quite openly and unself-consciously when he declared, "Even in this study (of Greek coins) we shall not lose ourselves in trivialities, if antiquities are regarded as the works of men whose minds were higher and more masculine than ours."[12]

It is interesting that the full title of Lessing's major work is *Laocoon: An Essay upon the Limits of Painting and Poetry*. Like Winckelmann's art history, Lessing's criticism rigidly defines and prescribes to art, asserting the superiority of ideas over the particulars of expression. The very ideas by which art is bound prevent the notions of expression and truth from entering into the artist's domain. In the Aristotelian manner art is defined as an "objectively" imitative craft, and each of the arts—painting and poetry—is distinguished from the other because it imitates a separate aspect of nature. This view emphasizes the separation of sensory modes accompanying the process of mechanization. The materialism of the early paleotechnic aesthetic is summed up in the following passages from Lessing's *Laocoon*:

Objects which co-exist or whose parts co-exist are called bodies. Consequently bodies with their visible qualities are the proper objects of painting. Objects which are in succession or whose parts are in succession are called actions. Consequently actions are the proper objects of poetry. . . . Painting is able to imitate actions, but only by suggestion conveyed through bodies. . . . Poetry can depict bodies too, but only by suggestion conveyed through actions.

Painting in its co-existing compositions, can only use a single moment of the action, and must therefore choose the most pregnant one from which the preceding and subsequent ones become most intelligible.

Hence flows the rule of the singleness of pictoral epithets, and of reserve in description of bodily objects. [13]

It would be hard to find a better example of the sequential, mechanistic point of view applied to the arts!

The realm of creativity became so rationally circumscribed by the mid-eighteenth century that not only did art imitate nature, but the successful artist further believed that the best art must imitate art, nature as such being too base and vulgar. Of course, only certain examples of art were considered worthy of imitation, and supreme among these were the artifacts of antiquity. History as a science must begin with art, for artifact is all that remains of history. The views of Lessing and Winckelmann are only the most outstanding examples of the particular European belief that not only is history the superior model for human actions, but the civilizations of Greece and Rome are the greatest of all human historical achievements. In emulating the republic of Greece and the empire of Rome, the Europeans were able to be democratic and imperialistic at the same time; moreover, they could claim that their civilization was also the greatest achievement of the human race, a prejudice that emboldened the Europeans in their adventure of world conquest through the nineteenth century.

The corresponding aesthetic attitude created by negative definition the realm of the "primitive," initially those arts in which psychic expression predominated over the technical rules of formal beauty, and more specifically, the arts of the non-European cultures. So deep was this bias in the mind of the average European that the artistic renderings of the "savages" encountered on the famous voyages of Captain Cook resemble more the figures and profiles on ancient Greek coins than the living presence of the Polynesian peoples. Nature does imitate art; if the artist can see only with the eyes of antiquity, the dead weight of the past literally precludes correct vision, and the non-European becomes at best the "noble savage," some distant relative of the heroes of whom Homer sang.

Proclaimed as a virtue of the highest order by artists and aestheticians, the adoration of the Mediterranean past made history a supreme ordering value in the reckoning of human affairs. If it was the duty of the artist to imitate the works of the past, then it was the responsibility of the statesman to use the past as his *raison d'être* in creating the republics and empires of the present. If the artist was called upon to improve upon nature, the engineer was responsible for reshaping the environment to accord with the higher ordering principle of the human intellect. The reason for history lay in the supremacy of reason; the history of reason was the triumph of history. But reason and history triumphant in the arts was tantamount to a decapitation of the senses and a banishment of the right-hemisphere functions of psyche. The visual arts responded no longer to the eye but to the printed word, which created the supreme fiction of the science of history. Art became the by-product of criticism, just as contemporary events became the by-product of historical necessity. That the arts were now defined and shaped by the verbal wrangles of the critics only confirmed the emergence of the critic as the foreign minister of the sense organs.

It is not surprising that the artistic style accompanying the first Industrial Revolution was an exacting, archaeological historicism. Since technique, the mechanization of consciousness, had become so thorough by the mid-eighteenth century, archeological art was to be expected, for in it the very roots of creativity were rationalized away, leaving only the arid remains of the human spirit. The *Parnassus* of Mengs, Hamilton's paintings of the heroes of ancient Troy, and even Flaxman's stylized line drawings are poor company for the more spontaneously exalted works of the first wave of classicism, known as the Renaissance. In the works of Mengs and Hamilton there is only academic technique, devoid of spontaneous feeling. Ironically, mechanical consciousness is so thorough that even the expressive realm, where human sentiment should reign supreme, becomes the province of pure technique.

The value placed on technique indifferently applied is what relates a painting by Hamilton glorifying the heroes of antiquity to one by his contemporary, Joseph Wright of Derby, glorifying scientific experimentation. The choice of subject matter is a superficial difference, for the two artists were trained in the same school of beauty. If Hamilton gave greater credence to the world of the past, he tried to be as meticulous in his representation of the past as Wright of Derby tried to be in his portrayal of the present. Indeed, that a photographic meticulousness in portraying the material world should become a primary aesthetic virtue is only another indication of the subordination of art to intellectual technique. On the other hand, Joseph Wright of Derby painted the present as if it were a scene from the past. Regardless of time-frame, archeological fidelity was a fundamental value. The groupings of the figures, the gestures, the dramatic expressions, all derived from the conventions of history painting. It was in this *value* that the intrusion of historicism became most insidious, as the aesthetic conventions engendered by both the American and the French Revolution amply illustrate. The newest and most receptive industrial states of the paleotechnic era derived all of their artistic and cultural ideas from the remote past, for there was no longer a vital source in the present to feed the spirit of those social upheavals. In this way the past became the Vitruvian facade by which the spiritual barrenness and confusion of industrial civilization was kept a fatal secret.

That archaeology—the scientific enumeration of artifacts from the past—should be able to dictate to the contemporary arts was also a sign that a new kind of artist and a new notion of art had to arise in the midst of industrial civilization if the human spirit was to be kept alive. Out of internal necessity, the industrial order gave rise to its opposite, the rebel spirit, the transcendental social visionary. While a Lessing or a Winckelmann extolled the virtues of the archaeological past, Goethe's *Sorrows of Werther* (1774), and Jean Jacques Rousseau's *Social Contract* were the first inklings, however naïve, of the counter-technological force of the transformative visionaries. The very subjectivity of these works went against the archaeological values of the prevailing paleotechnic culture. Meanwhile, history itself provided the culture of a civilization based on a rigorous, linear, mechanistic logic. Whether it was the flamboyant Rococo loves of Venus or scenes from the life of Achilles during the Trojan War, paleotechnic civilization had to borrow its masks of comedy and tragedy from another age.

In the ashes of a disintegrated mythic consciousness, art is invented; from the forehead of art, history springs into being. Quite simply, the death of myth is the birth of history. Through its midwife, art, history becomes the illusion of culture—but only for those who have the power to make history. And this is the tragedy, the terror, of history.

CHAPTER SIX

Revision, Style, and Revolution

As THE justification of events, history feeds on the delusion that reality can be technically manipulated to satisfy the insecure and distorted perceptions of the ruling few. As such, history also reflects the arrogant belief that man is the absolute master of planetary events. It is precisely these twin delusions that create and perpetuate the tragedies of self and other, mind and body, spirit and matter as irreconcilable opposites—tragedies because the underlying nature of things is always seeking a more conscious realization of union. For this reason the willed effort to assert man's separateness from nature never appears unaccompanied by the unconscious urge toward union with it. Similarly, though the technically oriented force of history may seek the systematic repression of psyche, this effort will never totally succeed, for psyche represents the path to the source of life itself. Because of psyche's profound, abiding presence in human life, all of the notable events and great figures of history have about them the strange air of paradox. How else are we to understand the exiled Napoleon on the island of St. Helena, mythologized in his own time as the ultimate symbol of a ruthless historicism, and yet in whom, however crudely expressed in the desire for a unified Europe, there was also reflected the Romantic urge for a mystical reunion with the forces of nature?

It is only logical that Napoleon, the epitome of the modern conquering spirit representing the force of history, should have been closely associated with Neoclassicism in art, the first paleotechnic style. Napoleon's character was both evoked and amplified by Jacques-Louis David, the foremost Neoclassical artist in Europe. Responding to the mid-eighteenth century, academic "crisis" brought on by the "excesses" of Rococo style, David won the Prix de Rome, studied in the archaeological gardens of Italy, and returned to France with a chastened and revised style, as severely imitative of ancient sarcophagi as the two-dimensional canvas would permit. To the French Academy of the 1780's his revision fit the prescription for keeping European creativity from frittering itself away in a decadent Rococo debauch. His paintings illustrate academic principles in their purest application: archaeologically exact representations of the most dramatic moments of cleverly chosen tales from the historical and literary tradition of the ancient Mediterranean world, presented in true-to-life stage sets that are utter paradigms of the Aristotelian point of view. Each of David's major works is a frozen vision of history, a product of the time machine of rigid sequentiality and static sense perceptions. As visions to be seen by the immobile eye, David's paintings show a world of disharmonized sense-ratios, and feelings set against each other—the germ of that basic mental dis-ease W. H. Auden was to characterize as "the age of anxiety."

It is interesting, then, that David should have chosen, for what was to become one of his most famous works, the subject matter of *The Death of Socrates* (1787). Socrates, of course, is the exemplar of a tradition Western culture has literally paid lip service to since the Gutenberg revolution. That is to say, Socrates *is* the tradition of lip-service, the oracle of an oral culture, proclaiming the divine right of the madness of poets; for it is the poet himself who looks the self-esteemed man of knowledge in the eye and proclaims: know thyself! To the prevailing mechanical literary culture of David's time, the wisdom of oral tradition was an archaism to be put to death by the Academy. What poetic irony, then, for Socrates in his moment of supreme tranquility to be captured by the ultimate in academic visions!

Like David's other classic works in the tragic mode of the 1780's—*The Sons of Brutus* and *The Oath of the Horatii*—*The Death of Socrates* is a call to arms preceding the first great modern revolution on European soil, for Socrates also exemplifies the rebel of social justice. In his suicide by drinking hemlock is the seed of stoic virtue all revolutionaries have displayed, from Marat to Guevara. In this respect, David's *Death of Socrates* represents paleotechnic culture's dismissal of archaic wisdom, for it seals the door of the past with the anxiety of the future. Raphael's blissful vision of Plato and Aristotle striding down the majestic steps of the rational dream Academy has been replaced with a foreboding of hallucinatory clarity. David's painting is official art in the service of history, and history in the paleotechnic era was the conscious exertion of power in favor of rational technique: a rational discrimination which could create revolution and very likely lead to racial incineration.

In idealizing the preliterate hero, Socrates in his death-glory, David signaled the death of history as the past, and the birth of history as the present projected into the future. As early as 1770, Louis-Sébastien Mercier had written the first science-fiction utopian projection, *L'an 2440*; and in 1790, three years after David painted *The Death of Socrates*, Restif de la Bretonne's *L'an 2000* appeared. As an artistic technique history could be used just as easily to prophesy the future as to interpret the past. As a rational technique it provided the abstract framework not only for reconstructing past events but especially for determining future ones. As an intellectual technique it embodied the ideal of progress as the pursuit of terrestrial happiness, so eloquently expressed in 1767 by C. M. de la Rivière: "The greatest happiness possible for us consists in the greatest possible abundance of objects suitable to our enjoyment and in the greatest liberty to profit by them."[1] Whatever the tides of revolution, owing to the pervasive technique of history, the stage had been set for the heroes of contemporary war and revolution to replace the heroes of the past—whether Socrates or Christ. David's painting of the dead *Marat* (1791) lying in his bathtub, done in by his companion terrorist, Charlotte Corday, is the logical conclusion to the theme of Socrates about to imbibe the hemlock. The glory and inevitable tragedy of the present are depicted in the same gloomy but vivid style as the glory and tragedy of the past. Marat in his unredeemable silence is the Christ-Pietà of revolution.

The French Revolution, like the American, was a change of power favoring the freer expansion of the mercantile classes. These revolutions did not really mark a new beginning in a spiritual/cultural sense. Instead they represented the shock of the steam engine and free market economics colliding with the remnants of an ancient legacy. Their actual effect was to enhance conditions favoring the isolation of the human sense organs from each other and, under the victorious sway of applied reason, from the greater organic functioning of nature as a whole. The twentieth-century visionary poet Antonin Artaud has described organic culture as a "culture based on the mind in relationship to the organs, and the mind bathing in all the organs and responding to each of them at the same time."[2] From this point of view, the series of revolutions from the American and French to those of the present, presided over by the newly discovered planet Uranus (1781), represents a continuous disintegration of the conditions favoring organic culture. On the one hand, these revolutions have promoted the development of mercantile/technological social economics; on the other, they have served as a great leveling process, reducing all human functions to the inorganic processes of the machine. The mind divided and the senses irrevocably sundered, the human organism itself has ceased to respond to the rhythms of nature, and all human value has been reduced to the terms of temporal economic units.

In a word, the liberation offered by the modern political revolutions is the freedom to live the life of a materially comfortable if hard-working human robot. A more insidious effect of revolution is the increasing mechanization of human expressive means. At one extreme is the pretentious irrelevance of a technically polished set of fine arts, and at the other, the flawless precision of machine-tooled artifacts. Between the two lies a vast gulf of unguided energy and feeling, exploited today by mass-produced kitsch and the entertainment industry. Since neither the technical refinements of fine art nor the mechanical refinements of industrial artifact offer any involvement or challenge, except perhaps for the motorcycle or speed-racing activist, the vast majority of the populace can only be afflicted by a mindless boredom. Deprived of their own creative initiative, the masses gladly turn to whatever entertainment may be offered. It is not too far-fetched to say that this boredom makes mass media indispensable, for both boredom and mass media thrive on a thirst for excitement that can never be gratified. Boredom and entertainment perpetuate each other in a vicious circle: because the bored person is creatively impotent, the entertainment he craves is always vicarious; being vicarious, it cannot satisfy; being dissatisfied and remaining creatively impotent, the bored person can only seek more entertainment. In the meantime the entertainment industry is feverishly at work not so much to quench the thirst for more entertainment as to intensify it. Occasionally an artist may become popular, and then he or she may become a commodity in this vicious circle. But by and large the artist's role has been to remain aloof; even when the artist has been well-intentioned toward the masses, his sensibility has generally been so differently educated that the masses have been unable to comprehend him. On the whole, art has remained indifferently at the far left of the spectrum, especially academic and avant-garde modernist art, and the machine artifact on the right. As a result, art in the industrial age has had little to say that is relevant or comprehensible, except to the cultured few.

This detachment from the social mainstream is strikingly evident in the first modern art style, Neoclassicism. After riding the crest of the French Revolution, and even experiencing the rigors of a prison term, David emerged in 1800 with his style essentially unchanged. His art and the Neoclassical style in general, like the Revolution, were irrationally rational phenomena. Like the blueprint laid upon the wilderness, revolutions and aesthetic conventions rooted in rationalism have little regard for the wild flora and fauna they cover up and even destroy. David, like the greatest figure produced by the Revolution, Napoleon, was utlimately a rational opportunist. If anything, his art after the Revolution reflected a kind of Neoclassical gigantism, as in the much-touted *Rape of The Sabine Women* (1799). In comparison to the works he painted in the 1780's, *The Rape* and later works on historical themes tended to be empty exercises of Neoclassical rhetoric. Style, when divorced from organic necessity and made a province of the intellect, is mere fashion. What had begun prior to the Revolution as a reformation in painting and the visual arts in general became after the Revolution a widespread fashion affecting dress, manners, furniture, and especially the architecture of financial and political institutions. This pattern has been followed by all of the "isms" of modern culture. The Neoclassical fashion gave way to the *Empire* fashion, and the citizen became once again the emperor. But the emperor, in this case, was a petit-bourgeois usurper, aping history and treating reality as a stage for the recreation of past glories. Believing the incredible warlike folly of ancient history to be a virtue, Napoleon had David paint him crossing the Alps—to Italy, of course, the bosom of historicism! In a work painted in 1803, and recently popularized by a brandy manufacturer seeking to give his product the appearance quality, David depicted Napoleon in the customary Neoclassical style of impeccable forms, mounted on his favorite horse, Marengo, high on the Alpine pass to history; one of Napoleon's hands points to a corner of the painting, where engraved in the make-believe rocks are the names of Napoleon's illustrious predecessors: Hannibal, Caesar, and Charlemagne. Not even Louis XIV was so blunt when he had his court painter, LeBrun, depict scenes from the life of Alexander, which the witty were to understand as an allusion to the glories of the "Sun King." But Napoleon's egoistic straightforwardness only betrays the insecurities of the petit-bourgeois thrust into a world of blind, implacable fate, without Redeemer and without grace. The only resource remaining for such an individual is the illusory grab-bag of history—and in this respect Napoleon's *Empire* bears a direct relation to Hitler's *Reich*.

Thus art and history, joined in symbiosis, each supporting and transforming the other. "Napoleon is my hero!" David is once supposed to have proclaimed. The master history painter ended up being the painter of history in the making. Napoleon, the seeker after historical destiny, used art to support and justify his grandiose ambitions, just as the contemporary political tyrant attempts to manipulate the media (which have taken the place of history painting) in order to gain support for and justify his own desires and ambitions. The media event of today has its roots in David's paintings of Napoleon crossing the Alps and crowning himself in the Vatican. Both the media event and the history painting are fundamentally artificial contrivances perpetrating the fatal illusion of the importance of history.

The Napoleons and the Hitlers—and there are many—as well as the arts and media that support and inevitably reflect them, only glorify and perpetuate the dreams held dear by every aspiring member of the bourgeoisie. After the fall of Napoleon the most notable of David's works were his portraits of the new ruling class, the great middle class who had collectively become the *force* of history. The portrait occupies a relatively low position on the academic scale of values, though it is higher than the landscape, mere nature painting. Yet in the genre of portraiture is the germ of the illusion of history—the glorification of the individual ego. The bourgeois banker sitting for his portrait is only Napoleon unmasked: the naked, grasping ego.

Neoclassicism was to fade with the downfall of Napoleon, but just as Napoleon's influence lingered on in the pseudo-mythology that grew around him, Neoclassicism's technically polished and archeologically precise technique, exemplified in the work of David, was to linger on as the academic norm of European art through the nineteenth century, and of the grandiose art of Hollywood cinema in the twentieth. Neoclassicism, the final fixation of the Renaissance vision, became the basis of an artistic dialectic; it was the thesis that one antithesis after another was to rise against, struggle with, and finally overcome in a gradually quickening tempo throughout the nineteenth century, until that particular perceptual fixation disintegrated. Since Neoclassicism represented not even style for the sake of style, but technique for the sake of technique, its ultimate antithesis was not a stylistic one, such as the looser, more painterly—and in academic terms, more Rubenesque—style of Delacroix, but the abolition of style and technique altogether in favor of a raw and little-understood *psychique*. In essence all artistic revolution through the nineteenth century to the point of Dada (ca. 1916–20) had the desctruction of style as one of its underlying aims, for style and technique had become so indissolubly wedded into one feelingless, tyrannical whole wielded by the favored members of the ruling classes, that only an open flouting of authority could insure a measure of cultural vitality.

Style and technique are inseparable in a culture like the Gothic, where the production of art proceeds unselfconsciously. That is, style, technique, and even art are not issues in themselves but integral aspects of an expressive will that is intuitively manifest. Only when art becomes intellectualized do style and technique, like form and content, become separate issues to be discussed and disputed. In contrast to the Gothic arts, the arts of the nineteenth century display a profusion of styles borrowed or imperialistically stolen from other times and other cultures.

In terms of the forces of revolution, Neoclassicism and Napoleon both represent the kind of backlash that is inevitable as long as revolutions are not complete. The merely intellectual acceptance and perpetuation of a style is nothing but a capitulation to a protective dogma; this applies both to the Neoclassicism of post-revolutionary France and more recently to the "socialist realism" of the post-revolutionary Soviet Union. The emergent paleotechnic world continually makes of style a frivolous intellectual/ ideological commodity. Style in its deeper implications as a manifestation of organic necessity is denied by the paleotechnic premise of the ultimate efficacy of technique, which reaches it highest manifestation in the machine, a totally utilitarian artifact. The dismal results of any attempt at embellishing a machine demonstrate that style must be more than mere decoration, a truth borne out again and again by the many nineteenth-century industrial artifacts whose machineness is thinly veiled by a veneer of style totally torn out of historical context—the Gothic sewing machines and Romanesque railroad stations so typical of the period.

Caught in the midst of the first violent thrust of the paleotechnic era, David clung to the Neoclassical style, and thus became a conservative bulwark for nineteenth-century artistic endeavor. Not only were David and other conservatives unwilling to face realistically the industrial conditions of their time, but they tried to escape by the forced contrivances of stylistic mannerisms exhumed from the past and pasted onto the speeding mechanisms of the present. In fact, the emergence of the paleotechnic era permitted total freedom from the claims of the past. This kind of freedom is rare in the evolutionary spectrum, and thus only the strongest and the bravest can endure its full force, for it begs the individual to begin again and re-form the world within the totality of his own being. All the recent outbursts of expression in the arts, all the novelties and bewildering array of "isms," derive from the vacuum of freedom left in the wake of the social mechanization that commenced late in the eighteenth century. Many of those that had some inkling of the freedom offered them by the new age have come to be called Romantics. As their record shows, the freedom they sensed was as easy to abuse as it was difficult to understand.

Freed from the tradition that had its final crystallization in Neoclassicism, the Romantic had three basic riddles to confront and resolve. Any one of these would make him look like a Don Quixote tilting at the windmills, and more often than not lead him to a moral and physical abyss where he might languish for years. Such was the fate of a Coleridge, Baudelaire, Poe, Rimbaud, van Gogh, or Artaud. The three riddles were history, the machine, and being itself. History he had to confront because it had become the inescapable web of everyday events. In rejecting the Neoclassical tradition, which glorified history (and thereby the status quo), the Romantic was invariably at odds with his increasingly urbanized environment, a conflict that led him either to a bitter kind of irony or to a total escape from his own civilization, which had become the embodiment of history.

Whereas history is abstract and elusive, though no less real mentally in terms of "newsworthy" events, the machine is a much more concrete phenomenon to deal with. The machine is the usurper of human beauty and handicraft, or so it seemed to many a Romantic. The more astute, however, saw in the machine not an evil in itself but a projection of mechanical consciousness; thus was born the myth of Frankenstein and the reality of the robot. The prime historical notion of progress itself tends to be identified completely with advances in technical efficiency, indicating that history, too, is but an assembly line where human being is retooled to perpetuate ever more efficiently what has come to be called civilization: an endless mirror vision of man creating machine creating man-creating-machine without beginning or end, easy enough to ignore for those who do not question it but capable of sending those who do to the madhouse.

To get at the root of this problem is to confront the very nature of human being; thus we come to the third and most significant riddle the Romantic had to confront: being itself. It was this last, Socratic confrontation that lent a vibrant, fractured, sometimes hysterical tone to so much of Romantic and post-Romantic art and literature. The Romantic was led too easily into polarizing himself against reason, and as Irving Babbitt so brilliantly pointed out in *Rousseau and Romanticism*, he thereby forfeited his own critical judgment.

For all of its psychic dangers, it is solely in the confrontation of being that the riddles of history and its most conspicuous coproduct, the machine (and later the all-pervasive web of media), are to be solved. But in the post-Gutenberg West nearly all of the guidelines to self-discovery had been annihilated or banished along with the other arts, handicrafts, and therapeutic practices of the pretechnological culture. The Romantic had to take the plunge alone; thus his response to life was often tortured and anguished. Yet in the faith of those who took the plunge there kindled the flame of the transformative vision, born of Socrates' immortal injunction: *know thyself!* Those who could still hear these words and bear up to the truth they signify were able to begin a new quest, the quest of self through which all riddles might be solved. For this quest is none other than the Will to Harmony.

CHAPTER SEVEN

In Search of a Hero: Romantic Quest, Fractured Vision

The emancipation from credulous beliefs leads to an anarchic individualism that tends in turn to destroy civilization. There is some evidence in the past that it is not quite necessary to run through this cycle. Buddha, for example, was very critical; he had a sense of the flux and evanescence of things and so of universal illusion keener by far than that of Anatole France; at the same time he had ethical standards even sterner than those of Dr. Johnson. This is a combination that the Occident has rarely seen and that it perhaps needs to see. At the very end of his life Buddha uttered words that deserve to be the Magna Charta of the true individualist: "Therefore, O Ananda, be ye lamps unto yourselves. Look to no outer refuge. Hold fast as a refuge unto the Law (*Dhamma*)." A man may go safely into himself if what he finds there is not, like Rousseau, his own emotions, but like Buddha, the law of righteousness.

—Irving Babbit, *Rousseau and Romanticism*[1]

SENTIMENT, LIKE the mistaken refuge of reason, obscures the law—not the written law of human error, but the all-pervading law of cosmic transformation. Like the mud of a disturbed river bottom, sentiment is the emotional cloud that must be penetrated in order to attain deliverance from the delusion of erratic cultural beliefs. Insofar as this imperative is not understood, sentiment is the bane of the Romantic and his counter-cultural progeny. Even a genius so wise and revered as Goethe declared in 1827, "Feeling is all!" This proclamation underlies the entire aura of the Romantic period and sensibility. Though Goethe in his wisdom might have meant by "feeling" the direct experience of life guided by the unwritten law of righteousness, to the less perceptive, "feeling" might be nothing more than a blind submission to the emotions. In the deeper sense feeling is not mere emotional release but a hearkening to the primacy of psyche in human development, a primacy submerged in the triumph of reason.

The exaltation of nonrational experience can be explained only by understanding the artist or sensitive individual who, rather than give in, chose to confront directly the technical tyranny of paleotechnic civilization. Emancipated from "credulous belief," this person had to chart a course between the Scylla of anarchic individualism and the Charybdis of unenlightened emotional excess. The former extreme might lead to the barricades, to bombings, jail, or the martyrdom of ignominious death at the hands of the establishment; the latter either to a wasted, possibly drug-induced madness, or to the desperate embracing of some obsolete and conservative dogma wrenched from the past. The middle way, the way of harmony, becomes the most difficult, for it requires one to resist the temptations of polarization. Rather than charting one's course by the essentially negative process of psychosocial reaction, whether it be projected upon a hero, such as Napoleon, or conceived as an ideology such as Christian primitivism or dialectical materialism, one must seek a direction from within.

But it is part of human nature—some would call it a weakness—to conceive of existence generally as dependent upon and defined by some external force, deity or hero. Much of the energy of the early paleotechnic artists was devoted to and absorbed by a search for a new system of "credulous belief." In keeping with the humanist world view developed in the Renaissance and perfected in the Age of Enlightenment, the search tended to take the form of projections upon contemporary characters. The idolization of Napoleon testifies to the frailty of human convictions and the human inability to withstand the test of solitary confinement. Having thrown off the gods of the past, paleotechnic man found that he had not thrown off the need for gods. Where visions of Heaven once depicted Jesus or Mary among the Heavenly hosts, Girodet painted Heaven as the Elysian fields where the legendary Celtic demigod Ossian receives Napoleon and his most illustrious generals. Where once Christ was depicted performing miracles among the leprous and the dead, Gros depicted Napoleon in the pest-house of Jaffa extending a healing hand to the suffering inmates and victims of his egoistic crusade. Even Beethoven originally dedicated his Third Symphony, the "Eroica," to the "little Corsican," in the erroneous belief that he really was a liberator.

To the more sensitive artists, and hence the more disaffected from the status quo, the search took on a more "exotic" and often more harrowing quality. The revulsion felt by the Enlightenment *philosophes* against Medieval Chrstian thought was carried one step further by certain artists who felt the need to reject the European tradition altogether, especially the Enlightenment. This attitude, seen already in Rousseau's "noble savage" and in Chateaubriand's *Atala and René*, a fantasy about Indian life in the New World, was the germ of the quest for the exotic, i.e., the non-Western, or literally, that which is outside, foreign, or alien. But this quest in reality represents the interior journey, for the exotic is merely the outer symbol of the plunge into those recesses of consciousness officially banished by the edicts of rationalism. In many respects the exotic or interior journey has an element of illegality, of the outlaw or criminal. The artist/seeker becomes a trespasser into what Conrad described as the "heart of darkness." On the positive side this outlaw tendency has a healing function, for it entails the exploration of hidden aspects of being. Negatively and more superficially it is merely the temptation to torment the beast of reason, which gives rise to the dilettante's thrill-seeking and the rebel's spiting of the status quo.

It is no small wonder that the magician of libertines, the Marquis de Sade, should have had his black illumination in the Bastille. Imprisoned by reason, de Sade was to become the patron saint of those who would execute by slow and excruciating terror the lords of reason. In truth, the diabolical Marquis is the shadow of the sword of rational justice. If the popular aesthetic of our mechanized society owes its crude and sex-drenched taste to anyone, it is to the Marquis, who has finally been vindicated by the emergence of a culture fully absorbed by pornography and violence. The bloody spectacles that occur nightly on television and the titillating motion pictures now showing in every major urban center are a tribute to his insight, for he divined in the aesthetically stunted psyche of the modern sensibility the primitive hunger for blood and sex. The psychophysicist Charles Henry once commented, "Sadism will live as long as there is no aesthetic in our lives nor solidarity in our social situation."[2]

Sadism is not a veritable aesthetic but a mindless exploitation of the emotions and feelings. It is a false aesthetic that pervades the whole of the modern imagination from the studio-set nudes that were a staple of the nineteenth-century academy to the pornography factories of the present industrialized West. Sadism is the shadow opposite of the search undertaken by the transformative visionaries. Precisely because the visionaries must cross the boundaries of reason on their journey, they are often perceived in the same light as those who would willfully violate the public order. The visionaries' journey is so treacherous and so lacking in guideposts, passing as it does through the suppressed land of psyche, that there is at times a strong element of the sexually perverse, of the violent in their life and work. This accounts for the risqué side of the bohemian or avant-garde existence. At first it is totally unselfconscious, though in time it too may be exploited to create an ambience for luring the bourgeoisie into the paths of a superficial beauty.

In visual art, Eugène Delacroix very successfully articulated the sexual-sadistic plunge of consciousness in a way that captivated the taste of his time. Paintings like the *Massacre at Chios* (1824) and the *Death of Sardanapalus* (1827) are a siege of writhing bodies, a sensual feast in which the tradition of the female nude reaches a new pitch of sadistically provocative poses. Perhaps the furies and *maenads* of Hellenistic Greece are the ancestors of these suffering creatures, but there is a vital difference: the maenads are free in their sexual abandon; the wailing creatures at the foot of Sardanapalus' deathbed suggest a greater delight in the spectacle of beauty violated than in the act of sex per se. The theme of the degradation of beauty—and sex—so skillfully expressed by Delacroix presages the popular twentieth-century cinema. As a master of sweeping emotion and color, Delacroix was a perfect mirror of the sensationalism into which the liberal cultured class let itself be plunged by its confused morality and lack of psychological understanding. The conservative cultured class, too, had its

borderline pornography in the art of J. D. Ingres and his academic followers, with their images of "exotic" Turkish baths crowded with impeccably
demure and satisfied females staring blandly at the emotionally repressed
bourgeois industrial lords who happened to be the patrons of this kind of
art.

Orthodox art history pits Delacroix and Ingres against each other in a
facile reflection of the political and psychological dichotomy that pervades
all of modern intellectual life and thought: liberal and conservative, a set of
terms that is made technically distinct by contrasting Delacroix's looser
brush stroke and greater adherence to an at least intuitive feeling for color
with Ingres' more polished and precise technique; the one is a wealthy man
advocating welfare, the other, a well-kept account book. Although Delacroix gives lip service to the values of revolution in the *Massacre at Chios*
and *Liberty at the Barricades* (1830), the former work is a contrived fantasy
reveling in a kind of sexual bathos, whereas the latter is a sheer idealization
obscuring the vicious realities of a street riot. In truth, Delacroix and Ingres
are tweedledum and tweedledee; neither offers an authentically redeeming
vision of man. While one wallows in the muck of confused emotion and
false historical grandeur, the other fancies that he bathes in the crystalline
springs of the Platonic ideal.

Pawns of the superficial dialectic between liberal and conservative, these
two painters offer a nineteenth-century re-enactment of the earlier academic wrangle between the more linear and classical Poussinistes, and the
more colorful and romantic Rubenistes. Above all, their art reflects the
continuing supremacy of the fiction of history: Ingres' *Apotheosis of
Homer* (1827) has its counterpart in Delacroix's *Dante and Virgil on the
Crossing to Hell* (1821). If Ingres gives us a fictitious paradise, Delacroix
gives us an equally fictitious hell. A Baudelaire might champion the romantic excesses of a Delacroix, but only as a vehicle for projecting his own
malaise. In their tendency to glorify history both Ingres and Delacroix only
acknowledge *Realpolitik;* and in their tendency to view the female as a
sexual object, often one to be tormented or seduced, they yield to the
degradation of the emotions and sexuality resulting from the triumph of
reason and the rise of industrialism.

What is most interesting is that these two artists, who represented the
highest refinement of French culture and the legacy of the Renaissance, still
the predominant mental base of nineteenth-century Europe, reflected the
contemporary realities of the industrial age so little. Their art, like late
Renaissance culture in general, is a *fantasy* that the ruling classes—
whether liberal or conservative—employed to escape confronting the true
nature of their actions. The real dialectic of the period was not between the
classicism of Ingres and the romanticism of Delacroix—both of which
amounted to the unfortunate perpetuation of a superficial error in taste—

but between the anesthetizing dogma of contemporary politics and culture and those artists and aesthetic sensibilities who were able to perceive its alliance with the relentless and implacable advance of machine technology. For the transformative visionaries, the dogma of politics and culture was the very demon to be wrestled with in order that the real issue might be faced. Psychologically, the visionaries are the rare personalities who remain in touch with psyche experienced as a regenerative female force. For all of the countless representations of the female as primarily an intellectually inferior and enigmatic sexual object in nineteenth-century and twentieth-century art, there is Goethe's redeeming conclusion to the arch parable of the modern soul, *Faust*:

> All things transitory
> But as Symbols are sent
> Earth's insufficiency
> Here grows to event:
> The Indescribable,
> Here it is done:
> The Woman-Soul leadeth us
> Upward and on![3]

Exemplifying the path of the transformative visionaries, Goethe's work is actually an extension of the alchemical tradition the original Faust left behind in the sixteenth century. When Dr. Faustus sold his soul to the devil he was actually making the pact that put psyche, the female, in bondage to techne, the male. The present dominance of technique—systematic procedure—is simply utter male supremacy; and technocracy is simply unequivocal rule by the male element of consciousness, the tyranny of the right side of the body over the left. Goethe's "Woman-Soul" is psyche, and it is only through the acceptance of psyche by techne that Faustus, modern man, shall be redeemed. It is important to realize that the Woman-Soul is an internalized ideal and not a projection upon an external figure or force. Alchemy is the conscious pursuit of wholeness through the reconciliation of the opposites within oneself—the will to harmony.

Goethe was concerned with himself not primarily as an artist but as a whole being. For this reason his work extends into various fields, including the study of the soul-life of plants and the psychological nature of color. But the underlying theme in all of his endeavors is the regeneration of psyche and the consequent transformation and fulfillment of human consciousness. For Goethe, woman is divine as all things are divine, and the Woman-Soul is the fundamental spirit force informing matter of its luminous destiny. Goethe's famous last words, "More light," reveal the positive side of his character. In him the will to harmony was no blind force but an energy that was the very light of consciousness.

Distinct from either the comfortable romanticism of Delacroix or the rare transfigurative vision of Goethe is the life and work of Théodore Géricault. If Goethe's example presents us with a conscious manifestation of the will to harmony, Géricault's presents us with an unconscious one. In Aldous Huxley's words, Géricault was a "negative visionary."[4] His early work reflects the tendency to idolize the warrior/hero—not necessarily Napoleon, but the less illustrious soldiers victimized by war: the cavalry, the horse guard, the infantry. Though these works were done in a derivative academic manner, there is more pathos than glory in them. Géricault's most famous work, *The Raft of the Medusa* (1817), illustrates this tendency toward pathos in a monumental manner. But it is interesting that Géricault did not attempt to build on this work in any way during the next—and last—seven years of his life. That was left to Delacroix, who in a fundamental sense imitated *The Raft of the Medusa* for the next forty years.

Huxley comments that *The Raft of the Medusa* "was painted not from life, but from dissolution and decay."[5] Medical students supplied Géricault with bits of cadavers; Géricault himself painted and studied the heads of persons who had been guillotined, and the emaciated torso and jaundiced face of a friend suffering from a disease of the liver. "Even the waves," Huxley adds, "are corpse-colored. It is as though the entire universe had become a dissecting room."[6] As such, Géricault's masterpiece expresses the cathartic and apocalyptic destiny of technological civilization. It is an image that conveys an entire collective state of mind: survivors of a shipwreck, driven in their extreme straits to acts of cannibalism—a far cry from their previous "civilized" existence—languish in desperation on wide uncharted seas with no instruments to guide them toward their most cherished goal, salvation. A more perfect image for the imaginatively starved consciousness of the paleotechnic era would be difficult to find. Caspar David Friedrich's painting *The Wreck of the Hope* (1820) is perhaps more chillingly effective for its lack of any human forms whatsoever, and in this respect it is equaled only by the modern historian Roderick Seidenburg's fantasy, *Post-historic Man* (1950), which envisions a technological world from which every hint of human feeling has been banished. The visions of Friedrich and Seidenburg open no doors; they represent the course of reason in its negative finality.

The survivors on Géricault's raft, by contrast, are not totally lost: on the far horizon, salvation is sighted in the form of a ship. Equally significant, the *seer* on the raft is a black man, a non-European who symbolizes—at least to the modern European—the repressed elements of consciousness: the noble savage, the primitive, the male counterpart of Goethe's Woman-Soul, psyche. If there is a hero in *The Raft of the Medusa* it is this African, this element of consciousness still capable of aspiring to what has not been explained away or otherwise forsaken. Géricault's search for a hero led from the external warrior archetype to a symbol of the exotic as the savior of European man in his despiritualized, shipwrecked condition. How clearly or consciously Géricault realized this one cannot say, but that he felt a deep dissatisfaction—even with his own success—there is no doubt.

It is this profound dissatisfaction that is the creative difference between a visionary like Géricault and an extremely accomplished and socially accept- able artist like Delacroix. What made Géricault a visionary was his capacity to see beyond the norms of artistic convention, something Delacroix was never really able to do. Although both men spent time in England— Géricault for more than two years, from 1820 to 1822, and Delacroix for a period during 1825—it was Géricault who achieved a post-Renaissance perception of industrial-age England's reality and significance, while Dela- croix's perception remained caught in the Renaissance mesh of unreal beau- ty. Where Géricault saw smokestacks and urban slums, Delacroix saw the works of Constable and the English landscape through the eyes of the academic colorist. Quite simply, Delacroix did not cease being a *painter.*

There is no precedent for Géricault's lithographs of the English paleotechnic scene, except perhaps for the works of William Hogarth a century earlier. But whereas Hogarth satirized the arrival of rural folk into the urban web, Géricault depicted the long-term effects of industrial up- rooting and gin on the lumpen proletariat. As Géricault's lithographs clearly show, he was able to see that behind the colorful façade of history painting there was only emptiness, that the academic exercise of art in the "grand tradition" was a lie covering up a horrendous contemporary reality: the transformation of the peasant into a debased slave of the machine, all for the profit of a ruling class that fancied itself, with its legislative houses and country estates, the noble conserver of a culture springing from the pastoral and republican traditions of Greece and Rome. Perhaps Géricault even saw that his *Raft of the Medusa* helped perpetuate that lie by hearken- ing so strongly to artistic conventions that proved to be only a support for the cruelties of the present. No wonder he did not return to that genre, in which contemporary events were ennobled as if they were scenes from the literature of antiquity. Perhaps some of the truth seeped into him through the paleotechnic disease of tuberculosis, which he contracted in England and which caused his early death.

In light of that it is not at all surprising his final painting project should have been a set of portraits of the most alienated of the new alien class: inmates from an insane asylum. These paintings are as penetrating and revealing as any in the art of portraiture, and all the more significant for the anonymity of the persons portrayed. They are not prominent people bidding for immortality but cast-off souls whom the artist has engaged as human beings. The hero that a generation had seen in Napoleon had turned out to be a madness, a hunger for fulfillment and recognition that the *individual* alone can grant himself. In this way Napoleon on St. Helena differed not at all from the inmates of the insane asylum. Géricault's strength lay in the courage he had to see this apocalyptic truth and to follow it without falling back on anything but his own vision. Thus the hero turned out to be the seeker and not the sought.

Madness, like the search for an idealized pre-Renaissance past or the discovery of a "primitive" Garden of Eden, is a mythological invention called into existence by reason's inability to define the total spectrum of reality. Divested by techne of a transcendental hero or ideal, the children of Faust, the sons and daughters of the Revolution, borrowed or stole their gods from alien shores, hoping that the strange names and idols of the past might somehow correspond to the urges of psyche felt deep within. The search for redemption became confused with a pained nostalgia that focused the aspiration for wholeness upon the mute ruins of the past. Images of abandoned cathedrals in the forest's wintry night, or childlike fairy-tale visions of castles and giants, princes and dragons, erupted into the popular consciousness, aided by the publication of Grimm's and Andersen's fairy tales. Even the age of Raphael seemed distant enough to take on the proportions of myth, and a group of Germans calling themselves the Nazarenes, overwhelmed with a nostalgia for inner serenity and divine harmony, descended into the withered bosom of the Catholic Church. By this time Italy was an exhausted spirit, and the Germans' attempt at a spiritual marriage that would result in a new awakening of the collective conscience could only prove sterile and futile. Too long split apart, the European spirit was now fractured even more by the technological ascent of industrialism. The Romantics could only appear flighty and ethereal in comparison to the cool, hard thrust of steam engines, and their quest but the fractured vision of a dazed and prodigal child.

Having abandoned all pretense of conventional religious feeling, even the rationalists were not free from the unconscious need to mythologize. Though repressed, the psychomythic quality of human consciousness remains active. New gods, in the form of "the famous men of history," and new religions, "the ideas that shape men's minds," were called into being. As a brilliant example, late in the eighteenth century the French architect Étienne Louis Boullée designed a monumental cenotaph for Sir Issac Newton—a gigantic, spherical form, "a representation of the earth." Boullée's enthusiasm is worth recalling for its ingenuous, proto-space-age, mystical yet egoistic fervor:

O Mind so sublime! Deep and all-embracing genius! Divine Being! Deign to accept such homage as my poor talents can offer! If I dare to make my plan public, it is because I am persuaded that I have surpassed myself in the work I am about to discuss.

O Newton! if it be the light radiating from your supreme genius that has fixed the earth in its course for us, I, in my turn, propose that you should lie wrapped in your discovery as in a mantle. . . . The interior of the sepulchre is conceived in the same way. In using, Newton, your divine system to shape the sepulchral lamp which lights your tomb, have I not shown myself supreme? . . . The monument is shaped in its interior like a vast sphere, with access to its centre of gravity through an opening cut in its base, on which I have placed the tomb. This shape has one unique advantage; whichever way you direct your gaze . . . you see nothing but a continuous surface with neither beginning nor end. . . . Newton's Cenotaph was meant as the embodiment of the greatest of all conceptions, that of infinity.[7]

Though an appropriate choice for the paleotechnic elite, Newton was a god too esoteric for the popular imagination. But the quasi-religious sentiment of Boullée's thought, and even of Newton's own achievement, offers unquestionable proof that a vital religious impulse remained the source of human imagination, even though religion itself had become a decadent social force. If a scientist like Newton may be considered a displaced priest of the present civilization, then the visionary poet or artist is its magician and sorcerer. But the values of technological civilization are the reverse of authentic religious values. Instead of a monument for the living, Boullée designed a cemetery piece for the dead. "The clear light of the night sky should be the only form of lighting for this monument, and should come from the stars and heavenly bodies decorating the vaulted ceiling."[8] The Age of Enlightenment produced not only the science of the past but art and architecture to house the artifacts of antiquity; the architecture of the grandiose bourgeois cemeteries of the nineteenth century is only a reflection of the architecture of the great mausoleums of culture, the cenotaphs of the great ideas: the museum and the library.

When the eighteenth century ended, clearly it was not only clouds gathering but night falling that obscured the revolutionary sun. What the Europeans took to be the Enlightenment was in actuality the twilight of the gods, the descent of psyche beneath the horizon of light. The nineteenth century commenced as an age of darkness. Culturally it was a nocturne, the musical form of which Chopin was the genius; its most appropriate vehicle for enlightenment, as in any sleep, was the dream.

The spanning of the world by railroad, telegraph, and telephone did not betoken daylight but the nocturnal sweep of a barbarian strength rushing across the unsuspecting hills and valleys of the sleeping earth. Some, like Géricault, soon discovered it was not high noon, and began to record the actual qualities of their time. Others took positions in the night and began charting the stars appearing above them. Their language often seems like a dream, but only because we are not prepared to see what there is to see.

And where some of the disenchanted might perceive only illimitable darkness because they had not raised their heads high enough, there were a few, the watchers of the night, who could utter with Novalis: "The ash of the terrestrial roses is the natal soil of the celestial roses. Is not our evening star the *Morning Star* of the Antipodes?"[9]

CHAPTER EIGHT

William Blake: The Hero as Prophet

The process of mechanization was furthered by an ideology that gave absolute precedence and cosmic authority to the machine itself. When an ideology conveys such universal meanings and commands such obedience, it has become, in fact, a religion, and its imperatives have the dynamic force of myth. . . . From the nineteenth century on, this refurbished religion united thinkers of the most diverse temperaments, backgrounds and superficial beliefs: minds as different as Marx and Ricardo, Carlyle and Mill, Comte and Spenser, subscribed to its doctrines; and from the beginning of the nineteenth century on, the working classes, finding themselves helpless to resist these new forces, countered the capitalist and militarist expressions of this myth with myths of their own—those of socialism, anarchism, or communism—under which the machine would be exploited, not for a ruling elite, but for the benefit of the proletarian masses. Against this machine-conditioned utopia only a handful of heretics, mostly poets and artists, dared to hold out.
—Lewis Mumford[1]

IN TERMS of the larger process of human and global transformation, the "handful of heretics" who dared to hold out, whether they be called artists or poets, constitute the seed-nucleus of a new religion, one that will in time supersede the "religion" of technological progress. The basic principles of the new religion are defined in part by the repressed components of the present one; if technology denies the reality of a subjective world of emotions, thoughts, and trascendent intuitions, then it is precisely this "subjective" realm of psyche that will constitute the core reality of the new religion or world view. The urge toward this new world view was beautifully expressed by the German Romantic writer Novalis:

We dream of voyages across the universe; but is not the universe in us? The depths of our spirit are unknown to us. *The mysterious way goes toward the interior.* It is in us if it is anywhere, that eternity is to be found with its worlds, the past and the future. The exterior world is a world of shadow, it throws its shadow on the kingdom of light. Now, it is true, everything seems to be in obscurity, unformed chaos, solitude: but everything will appear otherwise to us when these shadows will dissipate and this dark body be drawn aside. We shall then know a pleasure all the more lively for the long privation that our spirit will have suffered.[2]

What was articulated by Novalis in his ethereal, neo-Platonic way was totally embodied in his contemporary, William Blake. If Blake was not the Moses of the religion that is just now dawning, he was certainly one of its most singular and powerful prophets—an exemplary heretic dissenting not only critically but creatively from the prevailing technological order. Blake's achievement and life are so extraordinary that it is difficult, even impossible, for a mind trained in the orthodoxies of the present cultural viewpoint to assess them with justice. To speak of him as only an artist or a poet is to miss almost entirely the significance of Blake's effort. Placed in the context of the current paradigms of art history, Blake is a minor character, if not an eccentric nuisance, who "borrowed" freely "from medieval and Mannerist examples, abandoned logical arrangement in space, and developed a purely subjective use of light, colour, and form to give substance to his visions."[3] Blake's place in literature has fared much better, particularly in recent years, with the publication of Northrop Frye's *Fearful Symmetry*, Kathleen Raine's monumental *William Blake and Traditional Mythology*, S. Foster Damon's *A Blake Dictionary*, and Laura de Witt James's *William Blake and the Tree of Life*. Not only do these works place Blake in the forefront of the annals of English literature and art, but more important, they emphasize the fact that he was above all a whole being and a prophet.

A prophet is generally thought of as one who speaks of things before they come into being; as such, he must possess a fundamental knowledge that is really akin to full consciousness itself. Consciousness in this case is not merely the momentary awareness of random passing experience, nor is it an automatically conditioned form of knowing that may be able to "predict" events within a set mechanical framework. Rather, consciousness —knowing all together—is the fundamental ground of being, unrestricted by cultural considerations and the limitations of linear, historical patterns of thought. Actions or statements that issue from this level of being may appear prophetic only within the context of a culture or mentality that has deviated or regressed from the open, timeless condition of being itself; in this respect, being and consciousness, if not synonymous, are mutually defining terms. A prophet, then, does not look forward in time so much as express that which is timeless. In the prophet's words there are intermingled the qualities of the most ancient as well as seemingly the most futuristic. For the prophet these two are one, since in the mythic realm of unified being such distinctions as "past" and "future" are meaningless.

In a culture as civilized as our own, based as it is almost completely on an historical agenda, the prophet's vision calls the most basic assumptions into question, for its timelessness inevitably undermines values bound by time and history. When Blake declared, "Empire follows Art & not Vice Versa as Englishmen suppose,"[4] he reversed one of the most fundamental assumptions of the present civilization by giving pre-eminence to art. But obviously what Blake meant by art is something far more inclusive and humanly significant than what even the most rabid aesthete in our present culture would mean. In Blake's work art is not merely the embellishment of the things of life but the very energy of the life force itself. Everything that is life-enhancing, life-furthering, and life-expanding partakes of art, and man's primary duty is to nourish this basic life force. In fact, it could be said that the life force is by nature *aesthetic,* that is, life-enhancing, whereas that which opposes it is *anaesthetic,* inhibitory and promising of death. Furthermore, when a society fails to appreciate the full importance of fostering and nourishing the essentially aesthetic life force, it is only because the anaesthetic forces of death have taken over the social imagination. Death occurs when fear accelerates the drive for power and control, cutting off the self-renewing life forces.

> Art degraded, Imagination denied
> War govern'd the Nations.

Or, as Blake wrote in the introduction to "Jerusalem," "Poetry fetter'd Fetters the Human Race. Nations are Destroy'd or Flourish in proportion as Their Poetry, Painting and Music are Destroy'd or Flourish: The primeval state of Man was Wisom, Art and Science."[5] Wisdom precedes art as art precedes science. Wisdom is consciousness of being itself; it cannot be qualified, conditioned, or defined, for it is intrinsic to being itself. Art is the reflexive state of wisdom; it is the natural and spontaneous expression of being. Science is the way of materially implementing the reflexive state of wisdom. In awakened human consciousness these three form a unified whole. But in our own time science precedes art, and the practice of art precedes the realization of wisdom; and the three are no longer related as a unified system of knowledge. By Blake's terms, the state we live in is the utter reversal of man's natural state.

What I have been describing as the transformative vision is both the degenerative civilizing process away from eternal vision, which is the basis of wisdom, as well as the persistence of eternal vision, which provides the basis or ground for a return to man's natural state of being. In order for the ground to be fruitful, seeds of renewed and awakened consciousness must fall to the soil. These seeds are the prophets or visionaries. The deeper the seed is planted, the more awakened and renewed the consciousness, the more capable the visionary is of projecting an understanding that is globally significant. This is Blake's blessing; his vision provides an all-encompassing perspective for viewing the recent technological transformation of European thought and culture. By refusing to accept the anthropocentric and materialistic assumptions by which Europe had come to dominate the globe, both technologically and economically, Blake was able to provide a critique of contemporary civilization that is truly radical—going to the roots.

Whereas communism is merely a mirror-image critique of capitalism, Blake's vision is a critique of the condition that makes both capitalisim and communism possible: the loss of imagination, of eternal vision, which has left mankind prey to the petty competitive interests that dominate and divide our planet—materialism, racism, nationalism. Blake's concern is with man's redemption and return to his true universal state—eternal vision. Thus in "Songs of Experience," etched between 1789 and 1794, concurrent with the French Revolution, Blake has the "Voice of the Bard" sounding the summons of the yet distant consciousness:

> O Earth, O Earth, Return!
> Arise from out the dewy grass;
> Night is worn,
> And the morn
> Rises from the slumberous Mass.[6]

When the mythic voice of the Bard cries for the earth to return, he is calling for a *grounding* of human consciousness through the reestablishment of a reverent relationship to the earth below and the heavens above. This relationship is the most basic prerequisite for a valid ecological awareness. When it is flouted, disregarded, and even shattered, then the extremes of human degradation and terrestrial pollution become possible. These were the consequences Blake, the inhabitant of the world of eternal imagination, saw resulting from the new industrialization surrounding him. The images of degradation in "Songs of Experience" prefigure the lithographs of Géricault some thirty years later:

> I wander thro' each charter'd street
> Near where the charter'd Thames does flow,
> And mark in every face I meet
> Marks of weakness, marks of woe.
>
> In every cry of every Man
> In every Infant's cry of fear
> In every voice, in every ban,
> The Mind-forged manacles I hear.[7]

Modern civilization ruled by reason alone is a prison, a true age of darkness;

> Every house a den, every man bound: the shadows are fill'd
> With spectres, and the windows wove over with curses of iron:
> Over the doors "Thou shalt not" & over the chimneys Fear is written:
> With bands of iron round their necks fasten'd into the walls
> The citizens; in leaden gyves the inhabitants of suburbs
> Walk heavy; soft and bent are the bones of villagers.

A plate engraved by Blake shows "The Plague" walking through the darkened streets of modern Europe; a wailing woman drags herself beside the striding Plague, who rings his somber bell. The woman is the *anima*, the psyche or spirit principle bound in the jail of reason. Not surprisingly, Blake saw Sir Isaac Newton as one of the chief symbolic creators of the modern human condition. To Blake, Newton represented the enthrone- ment of reason; he was the mythic author of the mechanistic universe that gave rise to the tyranny of materialism, which spread from England to the rest of the world. Blake singled out Locke and Bacon as Newton's ac- complices: "Am I not Bacon & Newton & Locke who teach . . . Doubt & Experiment?"[9] asks the Spectre, the rational power of divided man. Elsewhere Blake declares, "I turn my eyes to the Schools & Universityes of Europe and there behold the Loom of Locke, whose Woof rages dire, wash'd by the Water-wheels of Newton: black the cloth in heavy wreathes folds over every Nation."[10]

In a memorable color print, Blake depicted Newton at the bottom of the ocean. In his left hand is a compass with which he draws on a scroll. Though according to Damon, the scroll "always signifies imaginative crea- tion,"[11] the fact that the scene occurs at the bottom of the ocean is more significant. In another print Blake depicted the Ancient of Days breaking out of the fiery sphere of perfect being by plunging his hand from the circumference out into the chaos, where his fingers become a compass of light. It is this self-same compass, in its miniscule and ultimately materialized form, that Newton holds at the bottom of the ocean; the ocean itself is consciousness. Newton, a more particularized form of Urizen —whom Blake depicted sinking down through the waters of material- ism—represents the individualizing impulse of consciousness, attempting to measure the infinite with the finite. If the bottom of the ocean is the lowest, or most degraded, state of consciousness—that farthest from the purifying light of eternal vision—there is no place else to go, finally, but up, which would mean a complete reversal of the process by which the "descent" had occurred. No wonder Darwin's great work was entitled the *Descent of Man*, for according to the unconscious materialistic paradigms operating through the European mentality, human development could be nothing but a *descent*. Was it not Newton who discovered the law of *gravity* by observing an apple falling? But it is only through the application of the laws governing matter that the ascent can begin again, for only then will materiality have exhausted itself at the utter limits of creative possibil- ity. Thus Newton is also an angel sounding the final blasts, "the Trump of the last doom." From the Blakean point of view, Einstein becomes the prophet of the redemption of matter. Between the prophecy and the realiza- tion, however, there first must occur the *climax of matter*, the drama of our time.

What is singular about Blake's critique is that already in the early stages of the industrialized state he so penetratingly and comprehensively per- ceived the actual nature of the religion of technological progress. Unlike

Marxist criticism, which does not really step out of the dualistic and materialistic mainstream—in fact, embraces it more openly and less hypocritically than capitalism does—Blake's critique is from a state beyond materialism; and in this lies its greatest value. All critiques of the present civilization will fail and even become absorbed by that civilization as long as they remain rooted in its basic assumptions, which are those of a dualistic materialism (or spiritualism). Though Blake would not necessarily deny a dialectical understanding of reality, he would declare dialectical materialism to be false for denying a return of the spirit. Blake's dialectic is that of heaven and hell, which he conceived to be a unity—hence the marriage of heaven and hell: "Without Contraries is no Progression. Attraction and Repulsion, Reason and Energy, Love and Hate, are necessary to Human existence. From these Contraries spring what the religious call Good and Evil. Good is the passive that obeys Reason. Evil is the active springing from Energy. Good is Heaven. Evil is Hell."[12]

Blake confounds the orthodox European temperament by seeing evil as a positive creative factor, for it is only because of a limitation of the moral intelligence that energy flowing contrary to reason is seen as evil. Completely rejecting the Cartesian assumption, Blake wrote, "Man has no Body distinct from his Soul, for that called Body is a portion of Soul discern'd by the five Senses, the chief inlets of Soul in this age. Furthermore, Energy is the only Life and is from the Body; Reason is the bound or outward curcumference of Energy."[13] In Blake's vision we may distinguish two concepts of hell: the hell of holy energy, which is the fire of inspiration and even salvation; and the hell that directly results from the belief in the separateness of body and soul. It is the latter hell that we experience as the continuum of contemporary historical events, in which energy is bound forcibly by its outer circumference, reason. History is the hell of the fall from the unitive vision of eternal imagination. Though Blake may not have known specifically of the Hindu concept of the Yugas, he would certainly have agreed with the notion that man is now in the final Yuga, the Kali Yuga or Iron Age, the age of blackness where purity of spirit is obscured —in Blake's brilliant phrase—by the choking smoke of "the Mills of Satan." Thus, Blake wrote from what he called the Hell of Eternal Delight:

> The ancient tradition that the world will be consumed in fire at the end of six thousand years is true, as I have heard from Hell.
> For the cherub with his flaming sword is commanded hereby to leave his guard at the tree of life, and when he does the whole of creation will be consumed, and appear infinite and holy whereas it now appears finite and corrupt.
> This will come to pass by an improvement of sensual enjoyment.

> But first the notion that man has a body distinct from his soul is to be
> expunged; this I shall do by printing in the infernal method, by
> corrosives, which in Hell are salutary and medicinal, melting
> apparante surfaces away, and displaying the infinite which was
> hid.
> If the doors of perception were cleansed, everything would appear to
> man as it is, infinite.
> For man has closed himself up, till he sees all things thro narrow
> chinks of his cavern. [14]

History is the result of an overelaboration and separation of the senses. Thus man's redemption requires a re-velation, a lifting again of the veil of the law through the purification of the sense organs.

Blake's vision of man's natural condition and the condition man shall return to following the apocalyptic disclosure of the present era—is that of a psychosensory unity in which each sense is not a "narrow chink" walled off from the other senses but in a state of free communication with them. This state of sensory interfusion, often referred to as synesthesia, is presupposed by a consciousness in which body and soul are realized to be one, and in turn presupposes a social order so totally different from the present one that its closest approximation is to be found in the remnant of so-called primitive societies. As Mircea Eliade has perceived, "For primitive ideology present-day mystical experience is inferior to the sensory experience of primordial man."[15] Hence Blake's statement: "This will come to pass by an improvement of sensual enjoyment." These insights shed much light on the modern European's infatuation with the "primitive," which is essentially a hankering for and a projection of that unitive state from which the dictatorial power of his own reason has severed him.

Modern technological civilization is a state of hell, a province of ignorance from which man must be redeemed: this is the grand theme of Blake's version and prophecies. As if by some miracle, Blake was exempted from the fallacies of his time; his vision of hell as a contemporary state has its counterparts only in the defunct and decaying traditions of non-European civilizations. We have mentioned the Hindu tradition, and even more notably the Mexican. In both the destruction and purgation of the present world system is prophesied, not necessarily by fire, but by some sort of tremendous earth-shaking cataclysm. The coincidence of the cyclical hell periods in the Mexican calendar with the rise of modern European civilization has already been pointed out; the place of Blake's vision within the larger scheme cannot be overlooked any longer. It is of more than passing interest that at the bottom of Plate 15 of "The Marriage of Heaven and Hell," after describing the process by which knowledge is transmitted

—from dragons, to serpents (vipers), to eagles, to unnamed forms, and finally to men in a "Printing house in Hell" — Blake has painted an eagle with a serpent in its talons. This is the mystical tribal symbol of the last of the Mexican empires, the Aztec; it is also the symbol the Mexicans adopted for their flag upon winning independence from Spain in 1821.

The modern state, with its self-infatuating concept of materialistic "progress," is in a reason-obsessed plight: it is what Goya depicted as the sleep of reason releasing its monsters; it is Urizen sunk in the waters of materialism; it is the sleep of matter plunged into deepest night. For Blake the present world *is* Ulro, the material world, where matter and the values pertaining to matter prevail. It is the "Seat of Satan," a "dreadsleep" of unreal forms, of "dreams . . . dark delusive." It is a graveyard, and a charnel house not so much because of man's mortality but because all things here are "Spectres" dead to the eternal imagination. "Such is the Nature of the Ulro that whatever enters becomes Sexual & is Created, and Vegetated and Born." Yet its inhabitants are plagued by the "terrors of Chastity that they call by the name of Morality." In Ulro, "What seems to Be Is, To those to Whom it seems to be, & is productive of the most dreadful Consequences to those to whom it seems to Be, even of Torments, Despair, Eternal Death." Ulro, as the "space of the terrible starry wheels of Albion's sons [factories]," is "a vast Polypus of living fibers, down into the Sea of Time and Space," where spread "the Nations innumerable," with "all the kings & Nobles of the earth & all their Glories." The science of Ulro is a delusion: "a Natural Cause only seems: it is a Delusion of Ulro & a Ratio of the perishing Vegetable Memory." "There is no such Thing as a Second Cause nor as a Natural Cause for any Thing in any Way." Even the astronomical universe is a "false appearence which appears to the reasoner as of a Globe rolling thro' Voidness, it is a delusion of Ulro."[16]

By contrast, the undeluded or enlightened nature of Blake's universe is post-relativistic: according to Damon, "It is one of immediate sensuous and imaginative perceptions, not of geometric logic; psychological, not material."[17] Each individual consciousness is the center and creator of its own universe:

Every space that a Man views around his dwelling place, standing on his own roof or in his garden . . . such space is his universe: and on its verge the Sun rises & sets, the clouds bow to meet the flat Earth & the Sea in such an order'd Space: the Starry heavens reach no further, but here bend and set on all sides, & the two Poles turn on their valves of Gold; and if he but moves his dwelling place, his heavens also move wherever he goes. [In short,] Man's body is a garden of delight & a building of magnificence.[18]

The universe is not only of man's making, it is contained within man. "For all Men are in Eternity. . . . In your own Bosom you bear your Heaven and Earth & all you behold; tho' it appears Without, it is Within, in your Imagination of which this World of Mortality is but a Shadow."[19] But to consciously attain this exalted microcosmic state, one must shake off the materialistic delusions of Ulro; one must pass through hell. Blake's vision of the redeemed state is Jerusalem:

> Of the Sleep of Ulro! and of the passage through
> Eternal Death! and of the awaking to Eternal Life.
>
> This theme calls me in sleep night after night & ev'y morn
> Awakes me at sun-rise; then I see the Saviour over me
> Spreading his beams of love & dictating the words of this mild song.
>
> Awake! awake O sleeper of the land of shadows, wake, expand![20]

Such is Blake's summons to Jerusalem, essentially a post-Einsteinian vision, a realm of consciousness in which man has passed into another dimension of being. Jerusalem—the biblical City of Peace—is the very notion of liberty, or liberation from the confusion of restrictive sense-desire bound by Ulro, the sleep of matter. To wake thoroughly from Ulro is to expand and unite the senses and consciousness into the realm of Jerusalem, liberty. In another sense Jerusalem is the female emanation of Albion, the "Fallen Man"; she is psyche, Goethe's Woman-Soul that "leadeth upward and On." She is the force that Albion, dominated by the false pride of reason, has turned his back upon. In this sense Jerusalem represents the repressed elements, psychic and terrestrial, upon which the brute male force of our present civilization raises itself in the great phallic symbols of skyscrapers and rocket ships. Indeed, in Blake's epic poem "Jerusalem," Jerusalem's city is laid to ruins by Albion, and her children are taken into captivity, where they soon become ensnared by the materialism of Vala and are pressed into war—certainly a clear statement of humanity's present psychological condition, in which the *anima*, psyche, is ruthlessly suppressed by the *animus*, techne, to the point where women believe that freedom means becoming like their terroristic male repressors.

In the course of the epic—which traces the fall of man into the sleep of Ulro, and his passage through eternal death and his awakening to eternal life in the divine vision of unity—there is a phase following the triumph of reason in which the female will comes into dominance. Uniting in the form of Vala, the women proclaim contempt for all men. "This is a Woman's world. . . . The Man who respects Woman shall be despised by the Woman."[21] It is only following this retributive turn of events that Los, the creative imagination, is finally able to proclaim the truth, leading the human race into the liberating unity of the eternal dimension.

Not only does Blake have a full vision of the history and the present condition of man, but he also describes the unitive dimension of being to which man is heir, eternal imagination. This is the fourfold vision of the city of Golgonooza. It is a vision in which the material and the immaterial, the physical and the psychological, the male and the female are united in one indissoluble whole. The ideal society is the projection of the fully accepted and realized body of man. Golgonooza, the city of "Art & Manufacture," constructed by Los, gives form to all uncreated things. It is the crossroads of evolution. "Travellers from Eternity pass outward to Satan's seat, but travellers to Eternity pass inward to Golgonooza."[22] The name Golgonooza recalls Golgotha, the "mount of the skull" where Christ was crucified; but in Blake's poem the heavy sound of "otha" is replaced by the easy sliding sound of "onooza", the skull of crucifixion becomes the skull of release, Golgonooza, "terrible eternal labor," surrounded by Satan's realm, eternal death.

Most significant, this visionary city is a mandala of utter perfection. In the European tradition Jung has defined the mandala as the archetypal image of the *coincidentia oppositorum*, the union of opposites, though as Jung points out, "Our Western mind lacking all culture in this respect, has never yet devised a concept, not even a name, for *the union of opposites through the middle path*, that most fundamental item of inward experience which could respectably be set against the Chinese concept of Tao."[23] Although the mandala was consciously employed as an artistic device in the cultural traditions of the pretechnological world, only in the non-dualizing tradition of alchemy has it been employed with such consummate artistry in the post-Renaissance West. In this respect, Blake's description of Golgonooza is especially notable. Like the classic mandalas of Tibet, Golgonooza is a psychological fortress with four gates to the sacred precincts of the center. The actual center is surrounded by a circular moat of fire, in which is Los' Palace—the realm of eternal imagination—which contains the Forge of Los, or the organs of man; and the Cathedorn, or the womb of woman. The Gate of Luban, symbolic of the vagina, is at the very center of this psychological construct, but it opens directly to *this* world. Like the complex mandalas of Tantric Buddhism, Golgonooza is replete with mythic figures and symbolic functions for every section of its precincts.

> Fourfold the Sons of Los in their divisions, and fourfold
> The great City of Golgonooza: fourfold toward the north,
> And toward the south fourfold & fourfold toward east & west,
> Each within the other toward the four points. . . .
>
> And every part of the City is fourfold; & every inhabitant, fourfold.
> And every pot & vessel & garment & utensil of the houses,
> And every house, fourfold. . . .
> And Luban stands in the middle of the City; a moat of fire
> Surrounds Luban, Los' Palace & the golden Looms of Cathedron.

And sixty-four thousand Genii guard the Eastern Gate.
And sixty-four thousand Gnomes guard the Northern Gate,
And sixty-four thousand Nymphs guard the Western Gate,
And sixty-four thousand Fairies guard the Southern Gate.[24]

Blake's description of the city of Golgonooza is a model of humanity reunified, reborn into its eternal nature. In a fundamental sense it is a post-historical vision, inconceivable from the mundane materialistic point of view. Even the earth in its most basic conception and representation has been totally transformed:

The Vegetative universe opens like a flower from the earth's center
In which is Eternity. It expands in Stars to the Mundane Shell
And there it meets Eternity again, both within and without,
And the abstract Voids between the Stars are Satanic Wheels. . . .
A concave Earth wondrous, Chasmal, Abyssal, Incoherent,
Forming the Mundane Shell: above, beneath, on all sides surround-
ing Golgonooza.[25]

To arrive at this end, "such is the Cry from all the Earth."[26] Blake's vision is beyond *2001*, far beyond the dreams of technocrats. It is a vision of the true space age, in which even astronomical space has become totally enfolded in the mind of man. For us it represents an almost inconceivable dimension of "All Human Forms identified, even Tree, Metal, Earth and Stone: all human forms identified, living, going forth & returning wearied/Into the Planetary lives of Years, Months, Days & Hours; reposing,/Then awaking into his Bosom in the Life of Immortality."[27]

Our civilization as it is now propelled will reach this end only by a cathartic transformation achieved through the path of art. Those who hold steadfast to art as the fiery connecting rod leading to and from the source of life will themselves form the path to this end. Art in this sense is totally redefined by Blake; particularly in "The Laocoon" (1820). If Lessing's *Laocoon* describes the basics of the rationalistic, specialized aesthetic doctrine of the technocratic era, Blake's "Laocoon" offers the transcendental doctrine. Blake declares that every man who is not an artist is a traitor to his own nature. Art is the way to the eternal vision of man unified; if Blake defines the true artist as a Christian in the "Laocoon," then by Blake's definition a Christian is a totally integrated and spiritually renewed human being: "A Poet, a Painter, a Musician, an Architect: The Man or Woman who is not one of these is not a Christian."[28] For Blake, the discipline of art is a psychological, even religious, process of detachment that is akin to Yoga, or the Yogic techniques that lead toward an inner freedom from the demands of this world:

> *You Must leave Fathers & Mothers & Houses & Lands if they*
> *stand in the way of Art.*
> *Prayer is the Study of Art.*
> *Praise is the Practice of Art.*
> *Fasting &c., all relate to Art.*
> *The outward ceremony is antichrist.*
> *The Eternal Body of Man is The Imagination, that is,*
> *God Himself*
> *The Divine Body   Jesus: We are his Members*
> *It manifests itself in the Works of Art (In Eternity All is Vision).* [29]

And, of course, Blake is uncompromising: the practice of true art can only be suppressed and destroyed by its association with money (which Mumford has characterized as man's most powerful hallucinogen): "Where any View of Money exists, Art cannot be carried on, but War only. . . . Christianity is Art & not Money. Money is its Curse."[30] Given his definition of art, Blake can proclaim: "Jesus & his Apostles & Disciples were all Artists. Their Works . . . were destroyed by the Antichrist Science," for "Art is the Tree of Life," and "Science is the Tree of Death."[31] All that negates life, inhibits the basic energy of the organism, and furthers incessant war and the corruption of the spirit is *science* in this use of the word. The scientist is the unwitting destroyer, who, abdicating moral judgment in realms other than his own limited sphere of research, has turned the world over to the nonimaginative Antichrist: the politicians, the intellectual parasites, the greed-driven insatiable ghosts, consuming and consumed by the deadening fever of matter. In contrast to the social vision grouped around physical science, techne's tree of death, with its materialistic pollution, mental illness, and endless political embroilments with their ever-increasing emphasis on security and secrecy, Blake proclaims quite simply the unequivocal rôle of the spiritually rooted artist and the corresponding social vision: "The Whole Business of Man Is The Arts & All Things Common. No Secrecy in Art."[32] To Achieve this vision, civilization as we now know it must be turned upside down and inside out. Art as Blake conceived it is for a race of heroes, not a race of ego-striving men.

CHAPTER NINE

Caricature as Truth: Seeing Beyond Official Truth

IN PROCLAIMING "No Secrecy in Art," Blake struck a paranoid nerve in technocratic society. According to Blake, the most stifling and repressive influence on art is the belief in the primacy of money. Whereas true art affirms and furthers the life-force, man's greed for money, which in time literally becomes a form of bondage, inhibits and represses it. By its very nature, a repressive and inhibitory power cannot function openly. With the triumph of money and its coproducts, industrialism and the belief in unlimited material progress, true art, the work of the eternal imagination, has literally been driven underground; it has become a *secret*. This art, whose purpose is to penetrate and reveal the workings of nature and thereby to further her processes in the human realm, combines what we commonly call art and science. However, the art and science we know today remain separate from each other, driven apart by the insatiable imperatives of money. They are by and large a false art and a false science, the offshoots of the "tree of death," whose trunk is the materialist drive for progress at any cost. As Blake intuited, this drive requires increasing secrecy on the part of society's leaders. The tree of death may be taken as modern technology itself, whose roots stifle the powers of psyche. This, too, must be kept a secret.

Secrecy pervades our lives. In the commercial world a manufacturer must keep secret the formula to his success if he is to stay ahead of his competition. Such is the myth built around Coca-Cola. But though it is psychologically debilitating, commercial secrecy is innocuous compared with the climate of secrecy surrounding the politics of the leading nations, especially in the nuclear age when the products of the competitors are so deadly and the stakes so high.

Political secrecy hides behind the public lie, which is perceived by the more astute as hypocrisy. To a certain degree the notion of material progress is the hypocrisy of promoting the good of the human spirit at the expense of art and nature, while the very essence of the techniques employed denies the reality of the spirit. This is the basic contradiction of materialism, whether of the capitalist or the marxist variety. To paraphrase Blake, art driven underground, imagination imprisoned, the lords of the nations raped the earth and planned their wars in secrecy . . .

The clandestine nature of modern politics, seen from the mythic point of view, has the overtones of a sinister, demiurgic struggle of planetary and even cosmic proportions. The political development of the nations from the Renaissance to the present has been a slowly accelerating struggle for absolute dominion over the physical plane of reality. This means not only the conquest of the world, including astronomical space, but more important, the conquest of life itself, the mastery of all the varied and myriad impulses of the phenomenal world. The protagonists in this struggle are magicians of a sort, relying on their court alchemists—the scientists—to extract the most powerful sources of energy from the material world. As the energy becomes more lethal, the secrecy of government intensifies. The secret creation of the atomic bomb is an excellent example of this process.

As a human creation penetrating the secrets of nature, the bomb is as much a work of art as a ballet is. Both art and science rely on technique; the difference between them is in the degree of contact with psyche. With some notable exceptions, the scientist has traditionally been the schizophrenic twin almost exclusively identified with techne, thus accounting for his *coolness*. Lewis Mumford describes the moral implications of the scientist's position in the following way:

Once, indeed, the scientists decided to exclude theology, politics, ethics, and current events from the sphere of their discussions, they were welcomed by the heads of state. In return—and this remains one of the black marks against strict scientific orthodoxy with its deliberate indifference to moral and political concerns—scientists habitually remained silent about public affairs and were outwardly if not ostentatiously loyal. Thus their mental isolation made them predestined cogs in the new megamachine.[1]

The moral abdication of the scientist to the powers of empire—which gives substance to Blake's proclamation "Science is the Tree of Death"—has its mythic aspect as well, when viewed in the light of the history of alchemy. Historically, of course, alchemy is the immediate parent of modern physical science, specifically chemistry and to a lesser extent physics. Chemistry is the technique most essentially involved in the transformation of matter, and most directly responsible for the increasingly "plastic" world in which we now live. It is still alchemy, but alchemy without art, spirit, or conscience. While the scientific critics of alchemy have characterized it as a futile attempt to transform base matter such as lead into gold, the defenders of true or esoteric alchemy equally criticized those who erroneously sought to transform one material component into another without a corresponding transformation of themselves. The term used by the defenders of esoteric alchemy to describe its false practitioners is most interesting in light of modern chemical pollution. Errants in the "Great Work" were dubbed mere "charcoal burners," for while delving into matter in the pursuit of power they had forgotten the inherent spiritual purpose of alchemy "the chemical marriage," the inner transformation of the psyche by the use of symbols and techniques that bring about a *unified* realization. The chemical industries, the material power needs of the technocratic state, and the ensuing pollution all indicate that it is the false alchemists, the charcoal burners, who have sided with the black lords of power in a magical alliance that seems well-nigh invincible.

And yet it is a myth of the earth that these facts tell; it is mythic that the five-pointed star has been adopted as a national emblem by the Americans, by the Russians, and by the Chinese. In actual fact, the five-pointed star, adopted in their flags by the greatest powers of the world, each bent on the domination and conquest of the physical plane, is the *pentacle*, a symbol of the material plane considered the magician's greatest defense "against tricks played by the spirits." Originally a symbol of well-being and safety, "this sign, like all other magical and symbolic signs, such as the swastika, can be taken over by 'black magicians,' those who have made a pact (with the devil) to exchange the immortal soul for material advantage."[2] This is the curse of Faust. Whereas the white magician might use the pentacle with a circle around it as a means to draw down "divine energy," on loan as it were, the black magician would use the same device to capture energy and use it for material gain and destruction. It is interesting that the greatest war-making power the world has ever known is concentrated in a building known as the Pentagon—a pentacle or five-pointed star with its arms withdrawn, for in the world of the public lie, there are no departments of war, only defense. . . .

A rare seer like Blake could construct his cosmological vision in creative response to the deadening, insidious, psychologically debilitating techniques of the Leviathan/Moloch power of the modern technocratic state. At a slightly lower level the art of caricature was born. In healthy societies the clown exists to offset the possibility that the shaman or priest might become too severely dominating. A society becomes unhealthy when its central forces begin to dominate all of its members and the environment, owing to a fundamental insecurity and thirst for power. When the balance shifts toward the center, and heresies multiply, the clown must become more clever and subtle. In the power-mad modern industrial state, the artist-as-clown, already driven into a corner yet counterbalancing the indifference of the scientist, finally resorts to ever more caustic and often thinly veiled means of expression. In fact, as the technocratic state becomes more highly developed and at least psychologically repressive, the function of art tends to become social commentary or political critique.

In the industrial state art is no longer the overt social force that it once was, expressing collectively the will of the people, and embodying in its forms and symbols the universally understood cultural values of a particular spiritual heritage. From the technocratic point of view the function of art is politely decorative: paintings are made to cover walls, sculpture to fill space—but essentially as an afterthought, and not as an integral expression of the environment or the culture. Since technocracy is an emphatic denial of culture in the traditional sense, art becomes essentially a sop to the "humanist" Renaissance origins of the technocratic value system. With the appearance of the full-blown industrial state in the nineteenth century, there was born the truly modern form of social-criticism-as-art. In one sense, More's *Utopia*, Swift's *Gulliver's Travels*, and Hogarth's London etchings heralded the new role of art in the industrial period. However, in the nineteenth century the artist who would take upon himself the true reflection of society through his vision was often placing himself in real danger. In many cases, since the artist of integrity was already on the verge of being a social outcast, the additional burden of being a criminal was often undertaken with a sense of gleeful spite. "Épater la bourgeoisie!" became a nineteenth-century battle cry.

From its beginnings the technocratic state was in the delicate position of courting criticism in the public media, first in newspapers and journals and later in radio and television. These media have been censored to varying degrees, and the line between the overtly totalitarian state and the more muddle-headed "democracies" on this matter has often been hard to draw. In those printed media tolerated by the governments there developed quite early the political cartoon and caricature in general as an expressive means. The cartoons of the popular press have a mildly critical function, but since it is finally the government that controls the survival of the journals themselves, they have usually served to give the appearance of critical tolerance, or more safely, to make full-vented attacks on the "enemies of the state." The mass media gave rise to a new and virtually anonymous class of art, basically in the form of illustrations, often of exotic climes, as well as political and other satirical kinds of cartoons. Later came the comic strip and the comic book itself. Though cartoons and comic strips are often compared to the illuminated manuscripts of the Medieval period, with few exceptions they really bear no resemblance, since their underlying function is to standardize the mass consciousness at a collective and almost subliterate level. In this respect the cartoon and comic strip perform a regressive and simplifying function; eventually, through a series of crude, standardized images, they help *solidify* the mass consciousness and make it the easy prey of public advocacy and depotism.

From the outset there appeared geniuses among the cartoonists and illustrators. Thomas Rowlandson set a standard for caricature that is without parallel. He was perhaps the first visual artist in the West to concentrate almost entirely on social satire executed as illustrations in a graphic medium. Hogarth preceded Rowlandson, but whereas Hogarth considered himself an artist of "moral subjects" in the high Renaissance tradition, borrowing consciously from the contemporary stage, Rowlandson had no such pretension. In contrast to Hogarth's work, Rowlandson's figures are characterized by outlandish form and a marvelous turn of the grotesque. In addition to poking fun at sexual mores and social pretension, Rowlandson did not spare the high tradition of art. The illustrations that really should accompany Blake's "Annotations to the Discourses of Joshua Reynolds" are some of Rowlandson's. In one drawing plaster statuary in the classical tradition all but crowds out a young beauty seated on fragments of the past, while a nearsighted, aged, and anything but well-proportioned sculptor conspicuous by his ugliness makes a small model of a Venus embracing a cupid who sits on her lap. In another drawing two antiquarians, grotesquely bent, mull greedily and mindlessly over a roomful of objects—ruins and ritual forms dug up, captured, or stolen and taken to the land of the conquerors, where they would one day form the core collection of a museum that could be looked upon with "civic pride." In a similar vein Blake wrote in the "Annotations to Reynolds":

The Rich Men of England form themselves into a Society to Sell & Not to buy Pictures. The Artist who does not throw his Contempt on such Trading Exhibitions, does not know either his own Interest or his Duty.

> *When Nations grow Old, the Arts grow Cold*
> *And commerce settles on every Tree,*
> *And the Poor & the Old can live upon Gold,*
> *For all are Born Poor, Aged Sixty three.*[3]

But generally, the satire of a Rowlandson or a Hogarth, directed as it was at public mores rather than at specific figures or political motives, was absorbed into the social body proper, for in the end what is an artist or draftsman eking out his living on the fringes of society when compared to the weight of an empire? The very impersonality of the technocratic state is the best defense of its ruling classes against the impolite effronteries of its clowns. And if necessary, there is always the threat of jail or the end of the gun barrel for the more impetuous. Politics answers with politics. The career of Honoré Daumier following the Revolution of 1830 in Paris is a perfect example. Daumier stands as one of the first and greatest political cartoonists. His satires against the royalist government and King Louis Philippe in particular landed him a term in jail in 1832. But such open railing against the injustice and corruption of contemporary governments is like Don Quixote's tilting at windmills. That Daumier may have sensed as much is suggested by the subject of his later paintings—strange, loosely painted, elongated visions of Don Quixote. Certainly his experience as a caricaturist prepared Daumier for abandoning the Renaissance ideal of the human figure, though more than just caricature is expressed in Daumier's Don Quixote. Like Rowlandson, Daumier saw through the façade of the neoclassical cult of antiquity, and he certainly had no reason to perpetuate the essentially dead tradition of the Renaissance. Daumier's series *Histoire ancienne* is significant not only for giving the lie to the pretenses of academic art but for pointing out that what had been revered in the gods and legends of Greece and Rome was nothing less than a parade of the grossest and ugliest human emotions and acts: lust, greed, murder, and war.

Given the quality of his genius, Daumier pioneered a freedom of expression and representation that was a model for later artists breaking away from the academic norm. In time the tone of his political caricature softened, and with the *Robert Macaire* series something altogether different developed. According to Baudelaire, "Thenceforth caricature changed its step; it was no longer especially political. It had become the general satire of the people. It entered the realm of the novel."[4] Though Daumier had been able to sympathize completely with "the people," as his famous illustration of the massacres on the rue Transonain so brilliantly shows, his paintings depicting the faceless lives of the proletariat, the series of lithographs, *Les Bourgeois Gens de Justice*, and the *Robert Macaire* series indicate his perception that ignorance is not the sole province of political power and that being a member of the proletariat is no virtue in itself. This realization contributes to the feeling of isolation that emanates so strongly from the Don Quixote paintings: it is the isolation of the Outsider, who has penetrated the pretenses of both the ruling class and the oppressed and emerges alone, socially dangerous, attempting to maintain his anonymity, seeing too much too deeply, and bearing the extra burden of having to live with his illicit knowledge of the social lie. He knows that both the proletarian search for revenge and the bourgeois search for material gain contribute in their own way to the perpetuation of civilization, a monstrous hoax that survives by the suppression of natural feelings and impulses. As Colin Wilson writes, "The Outsider's case against society is very clear. All men and women have these dangerous, unnameable impulses, yet they keep up a pretence, to themselves, to others; their respectability, their philosophy, their religion, are all attempts to gloss over, to make look civilized and rational something that is savage, unorganized, irrational. He is the Outsider because he stands for Truth."[5]

What distinguishes the Outsider from a more thoroughgoing visionary like Blake is that though he has penetrated the façade of civilization with all of its pretentiously masked suffering, he has not yet had a compensatory vision of the New Jerusalem. He may stand for truth, but only for truth as the sorrow of the world. Of the truth of redemption and release from suffering, he has had at most a glimpse, and even that glimpse he is unable to articulate. Hence the Outsider often becomes the most tragic and bitter of men, for he must live with the curse of a knowledge that must remain secret, lest society rush in self-defense to proclaim him either insane or criminal. And yet how many times better it is to risk such condemnation and reveal the dread secret, so that it no longer gnaws within the breast, a nightmare of unendurable anguish. Society as it is: what else can it be but a caricature of itself? A demonic obsession of black magicians, lustful ogres, decadent alchemists, and cannibalistic witches disguised as priests and scientists, kings and merchants. Such is the vision of Francisco Goya.

In his memorable essay "Variations on Goya," Aldous Huxley declares, "For Goya, the transcendental reality did not exist."[6] If the transcendental reality is the confirmation of a positive *redeeming* vision, then there is no sign of it in Goya's work, particularly in his later work, the famous "black paintings" and the series of etchings called *The Caprichos, The Disasters of War*, and that final plunge into insanity, *The Disparates*. With Goya, caricature reached its black nadir; the true revelation of the final phase of Western society has yet to be matched by the supreme grotesquery of Goya's vision. As Baudelaire commented, "Goya's great merit consists in his having created a credible form of the monstrous."[7] If Goya remained tragically incapable of envisioning the New Jerusalem, there is still in his work a psychically informative penetration, a power that is absolutely shamanistic. For Goya the Enlightenment, the Age of Revolution, the Napoleonic wars, the coming of industrialization and technological progress were only the masks of terror, each one more insidiously deceitful than the last.

Goya's early career brought him technically through the tradition of Renaissance painting and socially to the highest position possible: on April 25, 1789, he was made court painter to King Charles IV. It is no small coincidence that as the Revolution raged in France, and as Blake perfected his vision, "The Marriage of Heaven and Hell," a serious illness overtook Goya in 1792-93, leaving him deaf for the last 35 years of his life. No sooner had Goya reached the pinnacle of his career than it was made absolutely miserable for him. His background and his illness were perfect preparation for his role as revealer of the modern spirit, as though his deafness had opened for him that dimension of solitary reflection while sharpening his vision to a clairvoyant perception of his environment. Now nothing would escape him. On the one hand, Goya continued to paint the members of the Royal Family in the late baroque tradition; on the other, he took to drawing the hallucinatory reality of dreams, of darkness and shadows, of grimacing figures and animalistic terrors that finally all but crowded out the mask of everyday reality. In fact, the mask of everyday reality itself began to assume the hallucinatory quality of the dream. *The Caprichos*, a series of etchings that appeared early in 1799, are unique in their wholesale psychological exposé of all levels of society. Significantly, in an unprinted introduction Goya wrote, "The artist who has completely withdrawn himself from nature and has succeeded in placing before our eyes forms and movements which have existed heretofore only in our fancy deserves praise."[8] Among these darkly brilliant visions is the famous "Sleep of Reason Produces Monsters," which depicts an eighteenth-century gentleman asleep at his writing table, while from behind him and through his sleep emerge the prophetically grotesque forms that haunt our present civilization. Certainly for 1799 this image is uncannily clairvoyant. Goya's manuscript commentary on this print reads: "Imagination, deserted by reason, begets impossible monsters. United with reason she is the mother of all art and the source of its wonders"[9] a remarkable insight corresponding to Blake's "Imagination denied, art degraded, War governed the Nations."

Lewis Mumford notes that "the 1780's mark the definite crystallization of the paleotechnic complex: Murdock's steam carriage, Cort's reverberatory furnace, Wilkenson's Iron boat. . . . The whole technique of wood had now to be perfected in the more difficult refractory material—iron."[10] This period—the late eighteenth and early nineteenth centuries—witnessed the dramatic emergence of the full-blown Iron Age or Kali Yuga, the age of blackness. But the rapid advent of iron and coal technology and its literally black effect upon the environment was only the external aspect of something deeper occurring within the recesses of human and planetary consciousness. Symbolically, black is the color of illness and death: it is the absence of light altogether. That Goya executed his "black paintings" and wrote of imagination deserted by reason, and Blake of imagination denied by reason, are symptoms of a fundamental disease at work in the human mind a disease that was quite explicit in the sickness and consequent deafness of Goya, and also of Beethoven. The sickness of these artistic personalities is only symptomatic of a deeper and more widespread collective malaise. The desertion or denial of imagination by reason may in actuality be the desertion or denial of the right cerebral hemisphere, psyche, by the left, techne. This mental imbalance crystallized externally in the dramatic and cancerous growth of industrialism, and internally in the general abdication of creative self-reliance. As I have earlier indicated, its origins can be discerned even before the Renaissance, but it did not reach drastic proportions until about 1780, in the midst of the American Revolution and toward the time the planet Uranus was discovered.

In the body the uncontrollable growth of a certain kind of cell tissue results in the fatal illness we call cancer. It would seem that mentally or even psychophysiologically a similar process is at work on a collective scale, owing to the rampant growth of the functions of the left hemisphere at the expense of those of the right. But though the right hemisphere may have become dormant or anaesthetized by the efforts of the left, as long as it survived physically it would continue to pose a threat to the left hemisphere—provided reason had not already strangled the organism's very potential for life. It may be, too, that broadly speaking there is a polar rhythm at work in man's evolution, so that the dormant hemisphere may in time manifest in a renewed condition and even come to predominate. Whatever the case, the collective balance of organic functions seems to have been drastically disrupted by 1780. Visionary artists like Goya, Goethe, and Blake attempted thereafter to address themselves to this dramatic change in the human condition.

Colin Wilson, who pioneered the analysis of the Outsider, presented in a later novel, *The Mind Parasites,* the possibility of an actual mental virus—energy vampires—that began to afflict the human race around 1780. Wilson wrote:

Until about 1780 (which is roughly the date when the first fullscale invasion of mind vampires landed on earth), most art had tended to be life-enhancing, like the music of Haydn and Mozart. After the invasion of the mind vampires, this sunny optimism became almost impossible to the artist. The mind vampires always choose the most intelligent men as their instruments, because it is ultimately the intelligent man who have the greatest influence on the human race. Very few artists have been powerful enough to hurl them off, and such men have gained a new strength in doing so. . . . The artists who refused to preach a gospel of pessimism and life devaluation were destroyed. The life-slanderers often have lived to a ripe old age. . . . It is at this point in history [1780], just as the human mind had taken this tremendous evolutionary leap forward . . . that the mind parasites struck in force. Their campaign was cunning and far-sighted. They proceeded to manipulate the key minds of our planet. . . .Scientists were encouraged to be dogmatic and materialistic. How? By giving them a deep feeling of psychological insecurity that made them grasp eagerly at the idea of science as "purely objective" knowledge. . . . The artists and writers were also cunningly undermined. The parasites probably looked with horror upon giants like Beethoven, Goethe, Shelley, realizing that a few dozen of these would firmly set man on the next stage of evolution. So Schumann and Hölderlin were driven mad; Hoffman was driven to drink, Coleridge and De Quincey to drugs. Men of genius were ruthlessly destroyed like flies. No wonder the great artists of the nineteenth century felt that the world was against them. No wonder Nietzsche's brave effort to sound a trumpet call of optimism was dealt with so swiftly—by a lightening stroke of madness.[11]

However fanciful Wilson's science-fiction hypothesis may seem, there can be no doubt that the mind of the human race *is* afflicted by an illness, an utter imbalance in which technique totally represses psychic ability. Against the background of these ideas, it appears that Goya's visions reflect not so much his own illness as the illness of the human race. His record of the Napoleonic wars contrasts starkly to the blind idolization that still lends an aura of romanticism to Napoleon's name. Whatever the ideals behind it, modern war is invariably bestial, and Goya's *Disasters of War* is unsparing in its portrayal. The difficulty Goya had in coping with the dark aspects of the subconscious, which had been revealed to him through his illness, and through which he was able to perceive the entire dark panorama of human folly, is evidenced in the "black paintings" and the last set of etchings, *The Disparates*. The "black paintings," which include the monstrous *Saturn Eating His Children*, originally covered the walls of Goya's house, the "Quinta del Sordo," House of the Deaf Man. That the aging Goya chose to surround himself with these paintings testifies to his bleak state of mind. *The Disparates*, like the "black paintings," ring out like a curse flung up from the depths of a nightmare. At times these etchings are lit up with a sinister prophecy. "Ways of Flying," with its brooding men operating large mechanical butterfly wings in a black void, seems to presage the mindless use of flight in the twentieth century, which has given us the tragedies of Guernica, Dresden, Hiroshima and Hanoi.

In Goya's vision the secret that civilization tries to conceal is a Black Sabbath. For the greater part of his life, Goya struggled between life-affirmation and what Colin Wilson calls life-slandering. A common image in Goya's later work is that of a giant seated on the horizon: in one picture his brooding head pokes into the stars; in another, the populace seems to be fleeing in panic from his presence; in yet another, numerous little people swarm over his sleeping head, placing a ladder on his forehead and climbing to the very top with banners of conquest. Who is this giant, and what happens when he awakens? Goya's vision can only produce anxiety, for that is the soul of the civilization he reflects, and until that soul is healed, what Goya has depicted will remain indisputably true. Perhaps Huxley has given us the best understanding of Goya's troubled soul:

"I show you sorrow," said the Buddha, "and the ending of sorrow"—the sorrow of the phenomenal world in which man "like an angry ape, plays such fantastic tricks before high heaven as make the angels weep," and the ending of sorrow in the beatific vision, the unitive contemplation of transcendental reality. Apart from the fact that he is a great and, one might say, uniquely original artist, Goya is significant as being in his later works, the most perfect type of the man who knows only sorrow and not the ending of sorrow.[12]

CHAPTER TEN

The Receding Landscape: The Seeds of Ecological Consciousness

CARICATURE OFTEN adds prevision to insight, thereby providing a view of the future extrapolated from contemporary events. In this respect, science fiction is only an intensification of the present. The vision may be blatantly disturbing, as in Goya's winged men floating eerily through the preternatural darkness of a nightmare. Or it may be more mildly amusing, as in the 1830 English cartoon drawing of the popular character Shortshanks out for a walk in his mechanized boots (thus allowing him extra time to catch up on his reading); nearby a teakettle-mobile puffs along with its cargo of two ladies, while overhead, flying machines whir and glide. The Shortshanks vision, however amusing, is ultimately no less critical and disturbing than Goya's. In addition to depicting the English landscape cluttered with mechanical contraptions, the cartoon offers an even profounder insight regarding the rapid advance of industrialized technology in the character of Shortshanks, who appears every bit the English deacon but could just as easily be a businessman, if we follow Weber's line of reasoning in *The Protestant Ethic and the Rise of Capitalism*. Is it real necessity or mere laziness coupled with a facile ingenuity that has prompted Shortshanks to devise his mechanized boots, so that he can "save time" and attend to his business while he goes about the seemingly inconvenient task of moving his body from one place to another? What is really meant by the concept of a "labor-saving device"? That is, what is *saved*?

Time-saving rewarded by a corresponding accumulation of money —capital—is a primary illusion at the base of technological civilization. What is really implied by time-saving is money-making, as in the famous adage attributed to Ben Franklin, "Time is money." In other words, judging everything by its monetary value is the fundamental means by which organic being is made subservient to the abstract and the mechanical. Shortshanks's mechanical boots pre-empt the organic function of walking and allow him to attend to the abstract business of reading. From the mechanistic point of view, the organic functions are primitive and inefficient. Like the passing landscape itself, which Shortshanks has no time to observe or participate in, they are increasingly violated and mechanized. And of course, the more the organic motor activities are replaced by mechanical ones, the more business there is to attend to in manufacturing, servicing, and selling these labor-saving devices; the more mechanized and *abstract* life becomes, the more schizophrenic mental stress there is.

Supersonic jets crossing the great oceans in a matter of hours are filled with modern-day Shortshanks types who generally prefer to attend to their attaché cases or ease their nerves at a bar-in-the-sky rather than view the world of clouds and miniature landscapes passing swiftly beneath them. But then, as life speeds up, there is naturally less and less opportunity for *engagement* in the ever more swiftly receding landscape: from the window of a speeding plane or car it cannot be touched or smelled or felt, and hence it becomes ever more monotonous. One might as well turn to the attaché case or to a paperback book that describes the lives of glamorous, exciting, "real-life" people—the kind one ordinarily reads about in newspapers or sees on television. The difficulty of caring for the passing landscape is of course compounded by the corollary feature of industrial pollution. Thus as the landscape recedes from our psychic nature for lack of involvement, it also begins to disappear and deteriorate physically through the very same process of alienation. It is not that nature becomes alien to man, but that man alienates himself from nature.

Landscape itself is an interesting notion: the word has a strong connotation of backdrop, of externality to the sensory organism. In this sense, landscape is an accessory, and not an integral part of man's nature. In the history of world art there are broadly speaking two great traditions of nature painting: the post-Renaissance European tradition, and the Chinese and Japanese tradition. Though nature painting in these two traditions is often referred to as "landscape," only the post-Renaissance European tradition properly qualifies as landscape in the sense that it is commonly defined: a view of nature that is external to man, essentially a backdrop to man's activities. The oriental tradition of nature painting is based on a philosophical and spiritual tradition that emphasizes man's being at one or fully engaged with the processes of nature; hence it cannot really be called landscape. This is not to say that European nature painting is not at times comparable to oriental nature painting in this regard, but that the general impetus behind it was quite different from the Buddhist orientation of the oriental tradition. The oriental view of nature assumes an inherent correspondence between mind and nature; the object of nature painting is to express through whatever image the indissoluble union of mind and nature, which is spirit itself. Wilderness, the lofty mountains, the changing seasons, the varied life of plants are valued because through them is revealed the self-same breath that gives man his duration and sustenance. Wilderness becomes a metaphor for mind in its original state, and vice versa.

The equation of wilderness with the primal state of mind—original mind—sheds light on Western man's relationship with nature. If in the inner world of mind there is a primary ground where man and nature fuse into one, this ground may be reached only by traveling inward through the intuitive right-hemisphere door of psyche, for psyche is more primary than techne. While techne externalizes, psyche is an internal quality. In shutting the door to psyche, techne closes itself off from the primal identity of man and nature. Without this identity as a ground for action, the activity of the technically oriented person can only result in an increasing alienation from both nature and himself. In a strange way, relying on left-hemisphere knowledge alone, man loses himself in nature in order that he may control nature. This is because the left-hemisphere activity of techne is essentially involved in the material plane, whereas the right-hemisphere activity of psyche is immaterial. The seventeenth-century mystic Jacob Boehme wrote:

Thou perceivest, I know, that thou hast two Wills in thee, one set against the other, the superior and the inferior, and that thou hast two Eyes within, one against the other, whereof the one Eye may be called the Right Eye and the other the Left Eye. Thou perceivest too, doubtless, that it is according to the Right Eye that the wheel of the superior Will is moved; and that it is according to the Left Eye that the contrary wheel in the lower is turned about.[1]

What Boehme described as the "Eyes within," correspond to the cerebral hemispheres; to the right, psyche, corresponds the principle of the spirit, and to the left, techne, the principle of the flesh. Boehme continued: "Now mark what I say. The Right Eye looketh forward in thee into Eternity. The Left eye looketh backward into Time. If thou now sufferest thyself to be always looking into Nature, and the Things of Time, it will be impossible for thee ever to arrive at the Unity which thou wishest for."[2] Clearly, technical man looks only *into* nature and knows only the Light of Nature, but cut off from psyche, the Right Eye within, he no longer knows the Light of God. Without a primary grounding in the Eye of Eternity, man can see in nature only the temporal corruption of matter—a threatening, alien, and unredeemable specter that must be vanquished.

Seeing only with the Eye of Time and knowing only the Light of Nature, European man created the scientific constructs of cartography and topography, by which the Cartesian grid system could be laid out upon the earth. At the same time he learned to sentimentalize nature, as he had sentimentalized his emotions, and created the art of landscape painting. By sentimentalizing that which he was actually destroying, technological man attempted to atone for his actions. It is for this reason that nearly all of modern European nature painting has a nostalgic quality, for it is always depicting something becoming more and more distant. It is a memento of that which must be sacrificed to progress.

Like the system of perspective, the Eye of Time and Nature looks backward; thus in Western landscapes there is always a hint of the past. In the academy the historical or ideal landscape was considered superior to the contemporary landscape. In Poussin's *Et Ego in Arcadia* the ancient shepherds discover that death has already preceded them and is therefore sure to return. Perhaps the profoundest intuition in the ideal landscape is that the very necessity for projecting it arises from an unconscious acknowledgement of man's alienation from nature. So alienated has he become that he must replace actual nature with a false nature in order to get back to an "ideal" nature. But then, it is a fundamental of the tragic attitude of humanism and of the Faustian mind that man's estrangement is irreversible: thus his only resort is the consolation of beautiful pictures of goldenage landscapes, while in the workaday world the actual landscape is slowly and ruthlessly transformed into the image of man's own psychic alienation.

In contrast to the idealizing academic vision of nature, there developed alongside it a tradition of landscape that respected nature unadorned. Though in the earliest examples of this tradition, such as the magnificent works of Albrecht Altdorfer and Pieter Breughel the Elder, there may still be some glimmerings of the Divine Light of Eternity, by the seventeenth century all that remained was the Light of Nature. Its first pure expression is to be found in the work of the Dutch masters Jacob van Ruysdael and Meindert Hobbema. As opposed to the ideal tradition of the academy, with its variant aspect of the sublime, this tradition is topographical and picturesque. In actuality both the topographical and the ideal landscape are based on the mechanical contrivance of the perspectival grid. Through this means nature is de-natured. The corresponding development of Mercator's projection system (1541), in which terrestrial geography is plotted into squares, aided in the transformation of nature from a wilderness into an intellectual field-pattern, and finally into real estate.

If the ideal landscape became a vehicle for projecting a nostalgia for man's distant past, the topographical landscape tended to become a vehicle for projecting a sense of pathos and tragedy. This tendency, already evident in the work of Ruysdael and Rembrandt, became even stronger with the triumph of industrialism late in the eighteenth century. By the nineteenth century not only the ideal landscape, with its awesome vistas, but the picturesque landscape, with its gothic ruins and gloomy forests, and the archaeological and topographical landscapes as well, had all become a fantasy world, a means of escaping the present by re-living what was no longer a common experience. For certain nineteenth-century landscape artists, such as Rodolphe Bresdin, the wilderness was clearly the equivalent of the "noble savage"; the nostalgia for nature pure and simple is no different than the nostalgia for the nourishing wellsprings of original mind.

It was in England, however, in response to the appearance of the first fully industrialized society, that the nostalgia for nature, the receding landscape, took its most poignant turn. Even Blake, whose main concern was to retrieve and refashion the mythological structure of man's primordial being, wrote nature poetry such as "To the Evening Star":

> *Thou fair-hair'd angel of the evening,*
> *Now, while the sun rests on the mountains, light*
> *Thy bright torch of love. . . .*[3]

Certainly it was among the poets and painters of paleotechnic England that a last, futile attempt was made to revive the Light of Eternity in nature's ever-changing life forms. Coleridge in the dark Hartz Forest of Germany proclaimed,

> *. . . I have found*
> *That outward forms, the loftiest still receive*
> *Their finer influence from the life within. . . .*[4]

Driven by an intellectual energy that could not be satisfied by the materialistic philosophies of his day, Coleridge was obsessed with a hunger for eternity that intensified when he was confronted with the spectacle of nature. Like the mystic Boehme, Coleridge perceived that without the vital principle of religion, man's relation to nature can only be that of a sleepwalker, and nature itself dead and inert to human experience. For a poetic thinker like Coleridge, the major effort of life was not only to know and assert but to realize as fully as possible the unity of human spirit and nature. Of this unity Coleridge wrote:

But let it not be supposed, that it is a sort of knowledge: No! it is a form of BEING, or indeed it is the only knowledge that truly *is*, and all other science is real only insofar as it is symbolical of this. The material universe, saith a Greek philosopher, is but one vast complex *mythus*, that is, symbolical representation, and mythology the *apex* and complement of all genuine physiology. But as neither can it be implanted by the discipline of logic, so neither can it be excited or evolved by the arts of rhetoric. For it is an immutable truth, that what comes from the heart; what proceeds from a divine impulse, that the godlike alone can awaken.[5]

In Coleridge's thought, myth is the common ground of religion and art. All true visionaries, like Blake and Coleridge, are essentially religious thinkers. Though in the post-Renaissance world art and religion are separate mental categories, they both stem from the same source; their origin is in psyche, and in preschizophrenic times each was an aspect of the other. For we might say that religion is the primordial unitive intuition, and art the expression of such an intuition. With the decline of religion through its ossification in the form of organized churches, whether Protestant or Catholic, the visionary alone was left to work out through art what had earlier been the task of a divinely inspired social class. The coherently organized, intuitively based mythus that had once been the integument and protection of an entire culture had been dispersed by the left-hemisphere forces of the Renaissance. In the dispersal psyche retreated, leaving an aching void in man's consciousness and a threatening outer world to be overcome. Coleridge's brief poem "Psyche" aptly describes man's present condition:

> The butterfly the ancient Grecians made
> The soul's fair emblem, and its only name—
> But of the soul, escaped the slavish trade
> Of mortal life!—For in this earthly frame
> Ours is the reptile's lot, much toil, much blame,
> Manifold motions making little speed,
> And to deform and kill the things whereon we feed.[6]

The desire to become at one with nature and the rediscovery of the noble savage aim at the same source and partake of the same dimly religious determination. They are aspects of an overall effort by the human consciousness to regain the "one vast complex *mythus*." Wordsworth at Tintern Abbey, meditating upon "These Beauteous forms"—the intermingled forms of hand-hewn stone and rustic nature—exemplifies the profoundly religious motivation behind the romantic's desire to wed his soul with nature. "I, so long a worshipper of Nature," Wordsworth's description of himself, is the forerunner of the twentieth-century ecologist's motto, "In wilderness is our preservation." The identity of nature and the mind's own antipodes finds one of its purest forms of expression in Wordsworth's famous ode "Intimations of Immortality from Recollections of Early Childhood." Here the Eye of Nature sees with the Eye of Eternity through the medium of the child, symbolic of the purity necessary for religious rebirth:

> There was a time when meadow, grove, and stream,
> The earth, and every common sight,
>   To me did seem
>   Apparelled in celestial light. . . .

However, the actualities of the cultural-historical situation force Wordsworth to add:

> It is not now as it hath been of yore;—
>   Turn whereso'er I may,
>   By night or day,
>   The things which I have seen I now can see no more. . . .
>
> Whither is fled the visionary gleam?
> Whither is now, the glory and the dream?[7]

Because the grown-up man, the civilized being, is always looking at nature and the passage of time with the eye of techne alone, the visionary gleam can only "die away and fade into the light of common day." In these terms, civilization, especially industrial civilization, is the senescence of the spirit; the hardening of the psychic arteries is accompanied by a weakening of man's perception and appreciation of the natural landscape and hence by the actual slaughter of the landscape and the human spirit through the process of mechanization.

Paralleling the expression of Wordsworth and the Lake Poets was the rise of English landscape painting. The windmills, the heaths and moors, the cottages beneath cloudy skies, the unadorned simplicity of the rural scene were suddenly precious because the machine was swiftly plunging all of them into the past. Watercolor was by far the best medium for conveying the sense of these scenes, as well as the artist's urgency of feeling about preserving them. The subjective approach to nature through the medium of watercolor reached its apotheosis in the late watercolors of J. M. W. Turner. Suffused bursts of color attest not so much to the actualities of the scene—usually an early morning or twilight atmosphere—as to the artist's lingering perception of it. This shift from *event depicted* to *perception of event* links Turner's work to that of the French Impressionists. It can also be seen in the work of the late-eighteenth-century watercolorist J. M. Cozzens, whose spontaneity makes him kin to some of the Chinese and Japanese Ch'an and Zen artists.

Interestingly, it was only after thoroughly mastering perspective—the structural-perceptual sine qua non of Western painting—that Turner went beyond the academic concepts. Not only did he transform the convention of European landscape into a subjective, post-perspectival vision, but in so doing he was one of the first Europeans to liberate light and color from their bondage to form. For Turner light and color become the very essence of the aesthetic experience, and for the first time since the Renaissance, form was subordinated to the immediate data of conscious sensory experience. Turner long continued to give literary, conceptual titles to many of his paintings, but largely as a concession to convention. A great influence on his later work, it should be noted, was Goethe's *Farbenlehre (Theory of Color)*, itself inspired by the color theory of the German painter Philip Otto Runge. Turner certainly grasped Goethe's notion of the subjective basis of color, and contrary to post-Renaissance tradition, he gave expression to the notion that mind or psyche, not external nature, is the origin of the aesthetic experience. External nature was at best but a stimulus to Turner's vision, and not his real concern.

Whatever feeling Turner had toward nature was inseparable from his desire to understand his own mind. In his most notable works, *The Burning of the Houses of Parliament* and *Rain, Steam and Speed*, the atomospheric effects of traditional nature mingle with the combustion of technology, becoming one indissoluble whole through Turner's perception. To the degree that Turner's painting unifies these various elements, it transports us to an inner world where no account is taken of our personal wishes or of the concerns of man in general. In Turner's vision, as in the vision of Breughel or the Zen painters of Japan, the disasters of human folly recede into the ground of a greater nature embracing both the world and the mind.

Whereas Turner's concern for the integrity of his own perceptions grew out of the ideal-landscape tradition, that of his contemporary John Constable grew out of the topographical tradition first fully developed by the Dutch in the seventeenth century. Like Turner, Constable in his later art, especially in ink drawings and sketches for larger works, turned to depicting perceptual impressions rather than external nature as such. Almost from the first Constable was concerned with expressing as exactly as he could those effects of nature he had held so dearly as a young child. His concern was much more directly ecological than Turner's. In response to the description of a new "bright, brick, modern, improved, patent monster," to replace an old wooden mill that had burned down, Constable expressed the fear that "there will soon be an end of the picturesque in the kingdom."[8]

Foreseeing the grim fate in store for the England of his childhood, Constable set out to paint, and thereby preserve, those sensations he knew and loved the best—"the sound of water escaping from mill-dams etc., willows, old rotten planks, slimy posts, and brickwork."[9] He confessed that "painting is with me but another word for feeling, and I associate 'my careless boyhood' with all that lies on the banks of the Stour; those scenes made me a painter, and I am grateful; that is, I had often thought of pictures of them before I ever touched a pencil."[10] Yet in keeping with the essentially "objective" approach of the topographical landscape, Constable declared in a lecture delivered to the Royal Institute of Art in 1836: "Painting is a science, and should be pursued as an inquiry into the laws of nature. Why, then, may not landscape painting be considered as a branch of natural philosophy, of which pictures are but the experiments?"[11] Certainly in his own cloud studies Constable carried out this idea, since each study also bears a comment on the kind of clouds portrayed, the climatic conditions, and the time of day.

Constable's interest in making painting a branch of natural science, tempered as it was by his attitude toward nature, was really an attempt at wedding techne to psyche. It should be remembered that techne literally means "art as skill," and that much of what we admire as "art" is actually artifact, the overt manifestation of techne. Constable's humble proposal to the Royal Institute of Art conceals the will to harmony, the reunion of art and science. Whatever his intellectual motives, his painting is finally a personal statement in defense of the simple pleasures of a nature swiftly retreating before a mechanized world owned and brutalized by power-hungry men. Constable concluded his very last lecture, delivered at Hampstead Heath in July 1836, with a touching story of sixteenth-century Europe:

At a time when Europe was agitated in an unusual manner; when all was diplomacy, all was politics, Machiavellian and perfidious, Cardinal Bembo wrote thus to the Pope, who had been crowning the Emperor Charles V at Bologna. "While your Holiness has been these last days on the theater of the world, among so many lords and great men, whom none now alive have ever seen together before, and has placed on the head of Charles V the rich, splendid and honoured crown of the Empire, I have been residing in my little village, where I have thought on you in a quiet, and, to me, dear and delicious solitude. I have found the country above the useage of any former years, from the long serenity of these gliding months and by the sudden mildness of the air, already quite verdant, and the trees full leaf. Even the vines have deceived the peasantry by their luxuriance, which they were obliged to prune. I do not remember to have seen at this time so beautiful a season. Not only the swallows, but all the other birds that do not remain with us in the winter, but return to us in the spring, have made this new, and soft, and joyous sky resound with their charming melodies.—I could not therefore regret your festivities at Bologna. Padua, April 7th, 1530."[12]

The passage Constable chose to make his point in his last lecture was obviously meant to reflect on the even more baffling and subtly chaotic conditions in nineteenth-century Europe. Constable's mildly pantheistic worship of nature, expressed more powerfully in the poetry of Wordworth and the reflections of Thoreau, was a real plea for a "return" to a simpler state, an at-one-ness with nature.

Today Constable's paintings and drawings remain a knowing and vivid testimony to a world that is no more. While Shortshanks was parading about in his mechanized boots, Constable was memorializing the perception those boots were replacing. In a painting of 1831, Constable depicted a horse-drawn wagon slowly making its way across a swampy meadow; to the far left, in the bramble and woods, is a monument or marker as in a graveyard; in the distance is Salisbury Cathedral, one of the relics from an age more perfect in its knowledge of divine grace, already but a picturesque monument soon to be invaded by picture-taking tourists. Yet in the sky beyond there is a restless and luminous gathering of clouds, presided over by a rainbow, eternal symbol of the persistent immaterial presence that gives sustenance to a faith that precedes and endures the formation of any world-system. The sacred ruins, the rustic setting, the divine light emanating about the rainbow all reaffirm the religious impulse motivating the artistic visionary of the Iron Age. Where once there might have been a druidic priest divining astral omens among the clouds, now there was the poet or the painter experiencing a profound nostalgia as he pondered the mute forms of a verdant idyll, far from the lonely rooms of towns and cities whose growing din is like a madness to the mind. One of Constable's last works, a watercolor, depicts a double rainbow rising from the center of the Stonehenge ruins. Centuries after it was built, the geomantic splendor of the ancient site seems to emanate anew the light that is never quenched.

The fatalism among nineteenth-century artists concerning the disappearance not only of the preindustrial landscape but of the way of life and essential attitude of at-one-ness with nature is best exemplified by the work of Samuel Palmer. For a decade or so in the 1820's, Palmer, who began as a disciple of William Blake, was able to transform his feelings for nature, and his indignation over the systematic destruction of rural England and her population, into a unique and unparalleled vision. Of the English landscape painters during the early industrial age, Palmer was the one who was most thoroughly a *visionary*. Inspired by Blake, Palmer and a small group of artists abandoned their urban existence to live in the little village of Shoreham, some distance from London. Palmer's action would later be repeated by other artists and visionaries responding to industrial and technological society; his stay at Shoreham prefigures Thoreau in Walden, the French painters of the Barbizon, Gauguin in Tahiti, Lawrence in Mexico. The return to nature, to Mother Earth, is also a return to a more pristine state of being; it is an act prompted by the need for purity. At times it is simply a search for the exotic, but since the exotic is only a projection of what reason has repressed, it too must be rediscovered in the greater search for harmony. The will to harmony begins as an aversion to things as they are, for this aversion springs from the deeper intuition of things as they might be: a conscious, harmonious concordance of mind and the myriad impulses of the universal creative force, what Blake called imagination.

Though there is in Blake and Palmer, as in Turner, a neo-Platonic strain of idealism that distinguishes "Imagination, the real & eternal World," from "this Vegetable Universe," which is but a faint shadow of the real, the eternal is gained not by denying the vegetable but by accepting it for what it is. As Blake wrote, "I question not my Corporeal or Vegetative Eye any more than I would Question a Window concerning Sight. I look thro' it & not with it."[13] As long as the eye of techne is guided by the eye of psyche, the divine light shines through the vegetable universe. Palmer described this occurrence in his own eloquent manner:

However, creation sometimes pours into the spiritual eye the radiance of Heaven: the green mountains that glimmer in a summer gloaming from the dusky yet bloomy east; the moon opening her golden eye, or walking in brightness among innumerable islands of light, not only thrill the optic nerve, but shed a mild, a grateful, an unearthly lustre into the inmost spirits, and seem the interchanging twilight of that peaceful country where there is no sorrow and no night.

After all, I doubt not but there must be the study of this creation, as well as art and vision; tho' I cannot but think it other than the veil of Heaven, through which her divine features are dimly smiling; the setting of the table before the feast; the symphony before the tune; the prologue of the drama, and antepast, the proscenium of eternity.[14]

In Palmer's landscapes nature is recast by vision, more in certain respects than in Turner's. But whereas Turner's art disintegrates form as such, Palmer's creates quite unorthodoxly those forms most suitable to the needs of his feelings and temperament. For a long time Palmer's early work was not regarded seriously, because his forms deviated so greatly from the Renaissance conventions; neither meticulously topographic nor academically ideal, Palmer's moonscapes and starry nights, his bright clouds and sun-visions are—like the art of Blake—almost naïve in comparison to the traditional art of his time. In the work of his Shoreham years Palmer approached the vision of the Medieval manuscript illuminator. It is significant that he depicted the celestial bodies—stars, moon, and sun—in visionary splendor, practically for the first time since the dawn of the Renaissance, when materialistic conventions banished the notion of depicting the sun in visual art, except as a symbolic device in certain alchemical paintings and drawings. Like Turner, Palmer passed beyond such academic restrictions and was able to paint what his mind knew. But his vision was fleeting. Following a trip to Italy, he began to paint landscapes that were more orthodoxly picturesque. Other artists, too, would find themselves unable to sustain their vision for lack of a genuine context, and either fall back on tradition or resort to copying their own previous work.

By the 1830's the first phase of the Industrial Revolution was complete. Shaken by bloody revolutions, the Napoleonic wars, the uprooting of masses of rural people to work in coal mines or factories, and the hasty sprawl of large urban centers, nature itself was being gouged by mining, choked by smoke, and finally, dissected by railroads and purveyors of real estate. An artist like Samual Palmer objected strongly to the repeal of the Corn Laws, which ensured a steady influx of rural folk to the urban labor markets, and to laws granting rights-of-way to the railroads; yet few but the artists and poets mourned the passing of the preindustrial landscape. By 1830 industrialization was patently irreversible; thereafter the artist seriously seeking inspiration in nature was to risk the anathema of the forces of progress. In the New World, painters like Frederick Church and Albert Bierstadt documented the last vestiges of wilderness in the Andes of South America and the American Rockies. But these artist-explorers were followed close behind by the iron steamroller of progress, and their grandiose, meticulously painted visions were but spectacular pieces of entertainment to a bourgeoisie that even now would uphold the necessity of a pretty landscape to brighten the walls of an urban dwelling. Indeed, technology has induced in the masses such insensitivity toward nature that many prefer the painted image to the live reality of the natural world.

In nature's place was the kingdom of Hell on earth. A popular lithograph of 1813 depicts an itinerant laborer making his way down a road; in the distance smoke rises from a coal mine, while an early freight train chugs by with its cargo of potential consumption. This collier, who a generation earlier would probably have been a shepherd or a farmer, has been sundered from his age-long relationship to the earth; he is now plunged into the bowels of the earth, or into the smoking Mills of Satan. Shakespeare's green and sceptered isle has become the hell of fallen Albion.

The transformation was from life in the world to life in the underworld—the coal mines. As the urban centers developed, more and more of their functions went underground in the form of sewers and massive subway systems with their attendant shopping centers. To the extent that man lives in a controlled environment, whether literally underground or not, he lives in a subtle underworld of Hell. The twentieth-century visions of H. G. Well's *Time Machine* and Fritz Lang's *Metropolis*, with their massive underworlds of factories and mindless, brutalized, proletarian masses were presaged in the nineteenth-century visions of "Mad John" Martin.

Mad John first gained fame as a painter of overwhelming history paintings in the "sublime" mode; these include truly apocalyptic visions— *Nebuchadnezzar*, *Joshua Commanding the Sun to Stand Still*, *The Destruction of Herculanum*, and the spectacular portrayal of the end of the world entitled *The Days of His Wrath*. These works obviously give witness to an imagination in tune with the natural fury destined to rise against the blind, arrogant folly of human ingenuity. It is in works like *The King of Pandemonium*, however, that the true industrial-age landscape and mindscape are recorded. In this illustration to Milton's *Paradise Lost* Martin created a true diabolical reflection of contemporary reality. Seated on his throne atop a monumental globe, undoubtedly representing the world in its current hellish state, is the King of Pandemonium. A shaft of light falls upon him from a circular opening far above—the aperture of Hell, which itself is a world-encompassing sphere. Obviously Martin was Mad John to his contemporaries for possessing such insight, since almost all who publically express a true insight into the world's present state are pronounced mad. Yet it is no coincidence that in the 1840's John Martin was instrumental in planning the first major sewage system for London, as well as executing plans and drawings for the first underground railroad system. Martin's infernal and visionary landscape also has in it something of the character of an opium dream, recalling a poem by George Crabbe:

Upon that boundless plain, below,
The setting sun's last rays were shed
And gave a mild and sober glow,
Where all were still, asleep, or dead;
Vast ruins in their midst were spread,
Pillars and pediments sublime,
Where the grey moss had form'd a bed
And clothed the crumbling spoils of time.[15]

Even more drearily, Gustave Doré, a master illustrator and refugee from academic history painting, depicted the drudgery of underground labor and the feverish search for opiate release in his 1870's series, *A London Life.* Yet the nineteenth-century underground visions of Martin and Doré, and the opium dreams of men like Crabbe, Coleridge, and De Quincey, are commonplace today. Across the world the state of mind known as the Underground harbors nameless fugitives and rebels seeking to escape the rigid, artificial structures into which they were born. More and more the entire social situation appears as a "counterfeit infinity," and more and more people awake "laid loathsome on a pauper's bed," questioning the collective dream that newspaper editors take as such a solid reality. The natural landscape having been obliterated by smoke and speed from everyday consciousness, and psyche itself having been banished into a nocturnal prison, there has developed the inevitable desire for an "artificial paradise." When towering glass and steel walls do not satisfy the urge for mountain vistas, it is easy enough to turn to a narcotic that will recreate those high peaks upon the ever-changing walls of the mind, if only for a moment's duration.

CHAPTER ELEVEN

Drawing with Light: Photography, Reality, and Dream

PHOTOGRAPHY IS one of those technical devices which has so drastically altered our senses and upon which we have developed such a profound dependence that it is difficult, indeed impossible, for us to think about it with any degree of detachment. Nothing yet invented, save perhaps the tape recording, offers such convincing "proof" of what we consider to be real; and conversely, nothing is likely to be considered real unless it can be photographed. Photography makes the philosophy of materialism a closed case. Yet by the same token it is photography that has determined, in the minds of a few, the utter necessity for exploring and expressing the nature of the *invisible*. Even as photography was in the final stages of its development, artists like Blake, Goya, Turner (in his later works), Samuel Palmer, Runge, and even John Martin were tentatively exploring and expressing the imaginative realm of the invisible, that is, the unphotographable. Whereas the work of these visionary artists amounts to a metaphysical erosion of the perceptual basis of the European mind, the academic classicism exemplified by David and Ingres represents the hardening of the European mind into a state of refined senility appropriate to the mechanistic orientation of paleotechnic culture.

The true culmination of the mechanistic mode of visual perception and mental ordering was the perfection of *drawing with light*, the literal meaning of photography. In a vital respect, the tradition of Western painting after the Renaissance is the prehistory of photography. Just as a mechanistic mode of consciousness had to precede full-scale industrialization, so a naturalistic mode of visual perception had to precede the invention of photography. The grid of the photographic perceptual field was perfected by Dürer, Leonardo, and Raphael in the early sixteenth century; the technique for achieving exact naturalistic modeling, tonality, and luminosity was perfected by Vermeer in the mid-seventeenth century. Indicating the web of cultural interchange, the Renaissance system of perspective was itself preceded by the invention of the *camera obscura* (literally "dark room") by the Arab scholar Ali Hazan in the eleventh century, for the purpose of observing a solar eclipse. Both the camera obscura and the Renaissance system of perspective have the effect of focusing vision, of creating a visual field in which "single vision" becomes fixed in a space distinct from the flow of time, so that one visual event follows another in linear sequence. It is this sequentiality, of course, that is the basis of mechanization. From a mythological point of view it is interesting that a method for viewing the obscuration of solar light should be so important in the development of the modern European mind. Metaphorically we may speak of this as the "dimming of the radiant light" that preceded the full entry into the age of darkness, the Kali Yuga.

It was after the perfection of the Renaissance visual system that the camera obscura came into its own as a device to aid the artist in composing landscapes and the surveyor in delineating them. The seventeenth-century development of optics, again partially an outgrowth of the precision that high Renaissance painting demanded, added to the utility of the camera obscura, which, like the eye, would project a given image upside-down. By the mid-seventeenth century, as Helmut and Alison Gernsheim write, "The existing optical apparatus could have been used for photography," but "from the chemical point of view it was not until 1725 that Johann Heinrich Schulze, professor of anatomy at the University of Altdorf near Nuremburg, observed that the darkening of silver salts (on which most photographic processes depend) was not due—as previously believed—to the sun's heat or to air, but to light alone."[1] Interestingly, Schulze had been trying to make phosphorus—"bringer of light"—but had discovered instead "scotopherous," "bringer of darkness."

Scotopherous—silver nitrate—was to be the key element in the perfection of photography. This was achieved a century later, in 1826, by Nicéphore Niépce, who termed his discovery *heliography*, "drawing with the sun." Since Niépce was reluctant to make public his method of automatically fixing an image on silver-treated copper plates, the official credit went to his somewhat unscrupulous and ambitious partner, Louis-Jacques Mandé Daguerre, who during the 1830's developed the process of drawing with light. Long interested in perfecting a mechanical method for fixing images of the utmost precision, Daguerre had already developed the diorama when, through his partnership with Niépce, he finally found what he wanted. By May, 1837 Daguerre had reduced the exposure time from eight hours to 20 or 30 minutes, and had found a way of fixing the image with a solution of common salt. Believing his process to be distinct from that discovered by Niépce, Daguerre called it daguerreotype. By 1839 he had secured the interest of the French astronomer François Jean Dominique Arago, who arranged for the acquisition of the daguerreotype (and instant fame for Daguerre) by the French government in August of that year.

On the momentous occasion when the perfection of photography was officially proclaimed, on January 7, 1839, the academic painter Paul Delaroche declared, "From today, painting is dead!" The irony is that it was the painters themselves, in their slavish interpretation of the Aristotelian doctrine of *mimesis*—the imitation of nature—who engineered their own demise. As we have noted, vision had been mechanized long before the advent of photography, which had eagerly been anticipated by the European masses. In fact, as glorious an event as it was for the public, there was some immediate disappointment that a photograph was only in varying shades of black and white, and not in color.

As a mythological event inaugurating the seventh hell period of the Iron Age, the invention of photography symbolizes the "captivity of light," for it created the illusion that light itself was the mechanical servant of techne. A popular image of Daguerre depicts him, appropriately enough, holding the sun beneath his right arm. Habituated to matter, man perfected photography as an automatic means of capturing the light of the visible world, of fixing that light in images that conformed most precisely to his underlying materialistic view of the universe. Photography proved the existence of the material world in a stunningly irrefutable manner, so it seemed, while heightening the sense of reality as something external to the perceiver, since the "outside" world could now be so readily "captured." In one stroke it demolished the already tenuous hold of an utterly inutilitarian aesthetic, that of the fine arts. The standard of "reality" was firmly fixed by the photograph, and the visual artist's insecurity was raised to a fever-pitch.

Beaten at his own game, the nineteenth-century painter felt the instant pinch of automation. An 1839 cartoon of Honoré Daumier's from the journal *Charivari* depicts a daguerreotypist and a potential subject looking at his watch, wondering if he has enough time for his portrait to be taken. The caption reads: "Patience is a virtue of fools." The painter's time-consuming craft seemed to be undermined. Though the artistic pretensions of the sentimental bourgeois aesthetic helped keep the portrait painter in his servile place, as well as the painter of more sensational or sentimental subjects, there can be no denying that the serious visual artist was forced to see things anew. If he was not to compete with the camera, which could more than adequately convey a picture of reality conceived as a materially external phenomenon, then he was forced to consider other models of visual perception. This was not an easy task, given the emphatically materialistic orientation of society as a whole. Furthermore, it is extremely difficult, having been imbued in one perceptual gloss, to even consider the nature of another. Since the camera had usurped the function of portraying "objective" reality, the serious visual artist was more than ever forced into his own subjective universe. On the positive side, this forced the artist to consider nonmaterialistic points of view, thus promoting the larger transformative process. On the negative side, it furthered the alienation of the serious artist, who had already been shunted aside by the prevailing fine-arts aesthetic and by a society that continued to adhere to the sentimental, realistic aesthetic that photography had finally standardized.

The artists, academic or not, immediately sought to defend themselves against the new competition by maintaining that photography could never be a fine art. At the same time, however, academic painting after the invention of photography reached new heights of meticulous "photographic" realism, exemplified by the works of Frederick Edwin Church in America; Repin in Russia; some of the Pre-Raphaelites in England, whose paintings have a hallucinatory clarity; and above all, the academic masters in France, such as Adolphe William Bouguereau, whose highly polished figures have the ludicrous appearance of photographs of Greek statues come to life. The rise of photography also had the effect of entrenching the sentimental/anecdotal aesthetic as the most popular bourgeois aesthetic, one that prevails to the present day. This is simply because photography, by freezing moments of time, vindicates the novelistic notion that reality happens in anecdotal units; the serialized novel and the sentimental visual aesthetic go hand in hand.

By *sentimental* aesthetic I mean the prevalent notion that art is a diversion to stimulate the senses and conventional emotions, otherwise atrophied by mechanized and alienating labor. The sentimental aesthetic is the aesthetic of a society that takes pleasure only in escaping from work, not in work itself. Photography merely instantized the sentimentalist notion and deepened the feeling that the secret of art is fundamentally technical. This only widened the cleavage between techne and psyche, and confirmed the idea that fine art has little socially redeeming value unless it conforms to a technical, realistic aesthetic that does not transgress the bounds of patriotic convention.

As the technique of photography developed, it was regarded in two different ways: some saw it as a means of documenting reality, while others saw it as a new "fine art." The documentation of physical reality is intrinsic to photography. The attempt to make fine art out of photography, however, merely reflects the *artificiality* of the prevailing aesthetic. In other words, a photographic still life, or even more impressive, Oscar Gustave Rejlander's large neo-academic photographs such as "Two Ways of Life," only give the lie to the hollow social/aesthetic conventions that have been handed down since the time of Raphael. Photography pretending to be fine art unmasks fine art as social pretension. It reveals fine art to be the natural companion of the sentimental aesthetic: an art that attempts to be significant or profound without signifying anything of philosophical or spiritual substance. Thus undone by photography, the fine arts retreated; they no longer attempted to deal with subjects suitable for photography, but clung to the notion of being aesthetically significant and "fine." Hence fine art in the twentieth century is the marriage of anarchic avant-garde subjectivism and the academic pretense at being *aesthetically significant.* This accounts for the predominance of abstract art as the major fine-arts expressive mode in the twentieth century. The pity is that, feeling driven into unphotographable realms, artists at the same time felt ill-prepared to deal with the psychic splendors of the imagination. Thus abstract art unfortunately tended more and more to be purely aesthetic, pertaining to no reality at all, except that of pure sensation. Ananda Coomaraswamy has remarked quite appropriately: "It is by no accident that it should have been discovered only comparatively recently that art is an essentially 'aesthetic' activity. No real distinction can be drawn between aesthetic and materialistic; *aisthesis* being sensation, and matter what can be sensed."[2]

It should be evident, then, that photography helped make the distinction between fine and applied arts absolute: the fine arts are those that aim at being totally aesthetic, while the applied arts are totally functional, and by the mid-nineteenth century, generally machine-made. To the former category belongs photography as it pretends to be a fine art; to the latter, photography as an intrinsically documentary process. But what gives art in either of these essentially artificial categories an apparent legitimacy is its claim to technological *precision*, which has come to dominate all human endeavor. To this very day the precision of the machine replaces the classicism of earlier academic art: whatever the artistic style, the compulsive striving for precision and utter technical refinement untempered by a movement of the spirit spells out the dead weight of lingering academicism.

Describing the impact of photography and the materialistic aesthetic in general, Baudelaire wrote in 1859, some twenty years after the proclamation of Daguerre's invention:

During this lamentable period, a new industry arose which contributed not a little to confirm stupidity in its faith and to ruin whatever might remain of the divine in the French mind. The idolatrous mob demanded an ideal worthy of itself and appropriate to its nature—that is perfectly understood. In matters of painting and sculpture, the present-day *Credo* of the sophisticated, above all in France (and I do not think that anyone at all would dare to state the contrary), is this: "I believe in Nature, and I believe only in Nature (and there are good reasons for that). I believe that Art is, and cannot be other than, the exact reproduction of Nature (a timid and dissident sect would wish to exclude the more repellent objects of nature, such as skeletons and chamber-pots). Thus an industry that could give us a result identical to nature would be the absolute of art." A revengeful God has given ear to the prayers of this multitude. Daguerre was his Messiah. And now the faithful says to himself: "Since photography gives us every guarantee of exactitude that we could desire (they really believe that, the mad fools!), then photography and Art are the same thing."[3]

But whether or not photography and art are the same thing is beside the point, since art resides not in technique but in a knowing application of insight. Falling for the antitechnological line, Baudelaire dismissed photography as the refuge for every would-be painter too lazy or untalented to succeed as a real artist—an assessment that was no doubt as true then as it is today, when it is even easier to become infatuated with the gadgetry of media. But whether they are called tools or media, these technical extensions of man's being can only mirror the intent of the user. Magnificent photographs of nebulae and stars far beyond the reach of the naked eye, balanced by discreet treatises such as Leverant's recent *Zen in the Art of Photography*, are more than sufficient proof that photography may be no less a revealer of beauty than the art of painting.

But to think that progress resides in the invention of certain tools is like thinking that a ten-foot sand castle is qualitatively superior to a five-foot sand castle. In letting himself be polarized into discrediting the tool as well as the use of the tool (except for the most scientific purposes), Baudelaire was as much a victim of the myth of progress as were the industrialists and the foolish "art-photographers" of his time. Beauty is independent of such arguments and presents itself only where truth has prevailed.

It is no small irony that one of the most incisive portraits of Baudelaire was created by the photographer Nadar, who managed to capture the poet in all of his melancholy splendor. Nadar, it should also be noted, was one of the first to seriously explore photography not as an imitation of painting but as an expressive medium in its own right. For this he won the satirical disapproval of Daumier, who caricatured Nadar rising in his balloon—he was the first to take an aerial photograph—over Paris; the caption to Daumier's cartoon reads, "Nadar elevating photography to high art." Nadar's sensitivity also manifested itself when he lent his own studio to the Impressionist painters for their first exhibit, in 1874—a splendid instance of feedback, since it was the Impressionists who first took full advantage of the freedom thrust upon painters by the new medium of photography.

Notwithstanding Baudelaire's misplaced antitechnological views, his criticism of art in the service of a crude materialism, as well as his advice to the artist, was unfailingly proper:

Each day art further diminishes its self-respect by bowing down before external reality; each day the painter becomes more and more given not to painting what he dreams but what he sees. Nevertheless *it is a happiness to dream*, and it used to be a glory to express what one dreamt. But I ask you: does the painter still know this happiness?[4]

Baudelaire rightly and prophetically defined the subjective domain of *dreams* as the valid domain for the visual artist; he also displayed a certain right-hemisphere paranoia, a fear that the powers of imagination and intuitive vision would themselves be usurped by this automatic method of drawing with light. Certainly the power of art lies not in its capacity to imitate nature in the sense that photography does, but in its ability to express accurately the totality of feelings that compose the experience of reality. This has little to do with how an artist chooses to render anatomy and perspective, which themselves are mere artistic convention.

The elevation of scientific anatomical rendering and accurate perspective, which are simply mechanical contrivances, to primary aesthetic criteria reflects the value society places on material progress and achievement, as exemplified by photography. That anything other than a photographic standard in art is deemed primitive, childlike, or amateur, no matter what the artist's intent, only underlines the arrogance accompanying the materialistic, intellectual point of view. "Belief in Progress," wrote Baudelaire, "is a doctrine of idlers and Belgians. It is the individual relying upon his neighbors to do his work. There cannot be any Progress (true progress, that is to say, moral) except within the individual and by the individual himself."[5] Elsewhere Baudelaire defined progress very simply as the "progressive domination of matter."[6]

Like it or not, the artist had to contend with the immediate consequences of photography. Acquiring for the mechanical and intellectual side of the brain the powers of instant visualization, photography either scattered the artists in confusion or made them handmaidens to a paralyzing philosophy of materialistic realism. In this respect there is little difference between the art of a self-avowed realist and Socialist like Gustave Courbet, for whom only the materially visible mattered, and the bourgeois salon art of Thomas Couture or Jean-Leon Gerôme, for whom the ideal was infinitely real because it could be rendered as if it were materially present. All that separates them is a difference of contemporary ideology, for in perceptual terms Marxist socialism and the bourgeois mentality are both functions of the same addiction to material reality, a reality vindicated by the photograph. The problem, then, is not whether photography can be art, but in confusing art with the finished product or the technique employed. It is the artist's psychological *attitude* toward the process of creation alone that signifies the artistic validity of the act that produces the "work of art." Coomaraswamy has clarified this point:

Art is nothing tangible. We cannot call a painting "art." As the words "artifact" and "artificial" imply, the thing made is a work *of* art, made *by* art, but not itself art; the art remains in the artist and is the knowledge by which things are made. What is made according to the art is correct; what one makes as one likes may very well be awkward. We must not confuse taste with judgement, or loveliness with beauty, for as Augustine says, some people like deformities.[7]

Post-Renaissance painting had given rise to the notion that the picture itself in its gilded frame was the art; and photographers initially felt that their work had to be arranged and framed like "art" if it was to have any value. In other words, a materialistic society sees the real value of art not in its psychological motivation but in the technical mastery that a work of art, the *finished product*, demonstrates. Thus one of the initial criticisms raised against Courbet and the nonacademic artists of the Barbizon school in the mid-nineteenth century was their lack of *finish*.

Courbet's lack of photographic precision was also attributed to his socialist philosophy, but though Courbet so egotistically set himself apart from his bourgeois peers in the academy, a painting like his masterpiece, *The Artist's Studio*, indicates a greater affinity with academic convention than he would have liked to admit, simply because of the domineering psychology of the materialistic perceptual mode. In its strict realism, which Courbet declared to be the staple of his faith, *The Artist's Studio* is no different than Couture's academic work *Romans of the Decadence*. Both works are totally contrived compositions in the tradition of Poussin and Raphael; though Courbet depicted contemporary figures—his family, lovers, friends, and art critics favorable to him—they are an imaginary constellation of characters assembled only in his mind, much as the figures in *Romans of the Decadence* were assembled in Couture's mind and then projected onto the canvas. Courbet's realism applies to the representation of visible matter but not to *time*; in this respect, the Impressionists after Courbet were much more strictly realistic. *The Artist's Studio* preserves one other notable academic/bourgeois convention—that of painting a landscape indoors. This inconsistency was likewise done away with by the Impressionists.

Courbet's political radicalism, like Picasso's in the twentieth century, had almost no relation to his art and its patronage; it sprang as much from an aggressive and anarchic need to be different as from a sincere belief in an alternative political system. There is nothing intrinsically socialistic in the art of either Courbet or Picasso. Indeed, there is no Marxist style, just as there is no capitalist style, for both Marxism and capitalism are belief systems that deny the actuality of spirit. Thus the contemporary Russian aesthetic of socialist realism reflects an intellectual judgement and a sentimental predilection rather than being a conscious, integral expression of Marxist philosophy. Art in contemporary capitalist society even more clearly reflects an intellectual decision to manipulate the senses, as in "abstract art," or a blind sentimental predilection, as in the art, for instance, of Norman Rockwell and that of the so-called New Realists, both of which employ a photographically precise technique to deceive the senses and manipulate the emotions. But neither abstract art nor realist art is an intrinsically capitalistic form of expression.

In actuality, capitalism and communism, the two components of dialectical materialism, cannot exist or be defined without each other. Both are intellectual symptoms of the same disease—the belief that matter is the only knowable reality and that the ego, a concatenation of material energies, is the only knower of this reality. Since this belief system entails an explicit denial of psyche, the art it fosters, no matter how technically refined, can have no deeper significance than propaganda or purely sensory entertainment. Anything else will be judged retrogressive, rebellious, or mad. Under these conditions, regardless of the artist's intention, art will be political, for it is inevitably interpreted under materialistic standards as consciously or unconsciously supporting or rejecting the prevailing economic system. The art of Courbet was avowedly political, and by implication so was the art of the academy; the former *consciously* expresses communist sentiment, whereas the latter *unconsciously* upholds a capitalist attitude. Because of the pervasiveness of materialistic values there is no escaping the political interpretations that art inspires.

For our purposes modern politics may be considered any ego-motivated assertion of power; as long as a dualistic conception of the universe continues to be the dominant force in human behavior, then politics will remain the chief expression of the embattled human spirit. Art will remain the pawn of these struggles as long as the artist makes no real effort to detach his feelings from mechanical social patterns and arrive at a genuinely conscious appreciation of the human condition. But to arrive at such an appreciation is to arrive at the ground of being, the existence of which is denied by the materialistic philosophies. It is only from this ground, the primordial realm intuited by psyche, that any integrally expressive behavior can develop; to be in touch with this realm in a materialistic era is what makes humans into mystics; to deny or to be out of touch with it is what turns humans into robots. Though I speak of this realm as a ground, the great mystic Jacob Boehme spoke of it more accurately as *Unground*—baseless and without condition because it is the very essence of freedom, underlying even intuition: "Thus, we recognize the eternal Unground out of Nature to be like a mirror. For it is like an eye which sees, and yet conducts nothing in the seeing wherewith it sees; for seeing is without essence, although it is generated from essence, viz., from the essential life."[8]

The *Unground* is the basis of a tradition that extends from the dawn of time, but that had become quite tenuous and difficult to define by the mid-nineteenth century—the heyday of progressive, positivist materialism. In this tradition art is not merely an aesthetic (or sentimental) pastime, or the creation of objects for mass-consumption, but an integral expression of the life force. Because of the shock of industrialization, this tradition in the later nineteenth-century had become but a shadow lineage. Baudelaire's *Fleurs du mal*, Nietzsche's sickness, Rimbaud's flight from civilization, van Gogh's suicide—all represent conventional spiritual and artistic standards turned upside down by artists in this tradition, who sought to know and express the life force in a hostile, uncomprehending industrial society. A passage from one of Baudelaire's journals expresses their lonely point of view:

> *I have no convictions as men of my century understand the word, because I have no ambition. There is no basis in me for conviction.*

There is a certain cowardice, a certain weakness, rather, among
respectable folk.
Only brigands are convinced—of what? That they must succeed.
And so they do succeed.
How should I succeed, since I have not even the desire to make the
attempt.
Glorious empires may be founded upon crime and noble religions
upon imposture.
Nevertheless, I have some convictions, in a higher sense, which could
not be understood by the people of my time.[9]

Baudelaire knew that within his society, only the artist might heed his
call to explore the realm of imagination and dreams—a call that expressed,
however indirectly, man's need to re-establish contact with the ground of
being. His words have the urgency of a man in a slowly sinking ship with
no rescuer in sight, for in the technical wasteland of mid-nineteenth-
century Europe, who was there to guide the courageous soul through the
forgotten zones of psyche? It is no small coincidence that one of the primary symbols of the romantic imagination was the nocturnal ruin of some
great Gothic cathedral or abbey, set in a landscape made even darker by the
fatuous presumptions of the doctrine of progress, a doctrine that banished
the dream and all notions of divinity and spirituality to the madhouse. How
outrageous it was in such an era for Baudelaire to declare: "Nothing upon
the earth is interesting except religions. . . . There is a universal religion
devised for the alchemists of thought, a religion which has nothing to do
with Man, considered as a divine memento."[10]

The tensions between photography and art, realism and academicism,
capitalism and communism are relatively minor disturbances, then, that
give the semblance of a dialogue to the frenetic drive of materialism; the
true dialectic is between the divine and the manifest, a dialectic in which
man, so significant in the ego-centered humanism of the West, is only the
latest evolutionary manifestation of the divine will. Should the human
manifestation reach its limit, other manifestations may be evolved. From
this point of view, photography, "drawing with light," is a tool of the
exterminating angel, a technical device that may flatter the ignorant into
believing they possess superhuman powers. However, it is man who is
captured by photography, and not light. As a late-sixteenth-century rhyme
reminds us, "Of what use are lens and light to those who lack in mind and
sight?"

CHAPTER TWELVE

Dream Light on the East: Visions of the Seer-Poets

True civilization . . . is not to be found in gas or steam or table-turning. It consists in the diminution of original sin. Nomad peoples, shepherds, hunters, farmers and even cannibals, all, by virtue of energy and personal dignity, may be the superiors of our races of the West. These perhaps will be destroyed. . . .
—Baudelaire[1]

THE DREAM-VENTURE which Baudelaire advocated was pursued artistically by a few of his contemporaries: one recalls the vague, gloomy, gothic ink drawings of Victor Hugo; the meticulous forest visions of Rodolfe Bresdin; the effaced vision of Daumier's late Don Quixotes; and even some of Gustave Doré's illustrations, particularly those for Dante's *Divine Comedy*. But by and large the world of dreams was not to be explored until a later time, a time when the gates to the ports of the "nomad peoples, shepherds, hunters, farmers and even cannibals" had been closed down completely by colonialism and Coca Cola. As it was in the nineteenth century, Europeans looked instead to the non-European cultures still relatively intact, in the hope of finding the psychological freedom their own civilization denied.

In *A Vision*, W. B. Yeats commented: "Hegel identifies Asia with Nature; he sees the whole process of civilization as an escape from Nature; partly achieved by Greece, fully achieved by Christianity. Oedipus —Greece—solved the riddle of the Sphinx—Nature compelled her to plunge from the precipice, though man himself remained ignorant and blundering."[2] To the empire builders Asia and the "primitive" world— Hegel's Nature—were fertile sources of raw materials for technological society; psychologically they represented the antipodes of the Occidental mind. Nature, the Orient, and the entire "primitive" that is to say, pre-mechanistic world had come to symbolize the repressed contents of the right cerebral hemisphere in their full efflorescence. That the experience of *nature* and the *exotic* was essentially a psychological one is made dramatically clear in a passage by Thomas De Quincey describing the psychedelic —mind-manifesting—effects of opium:

Under the connecting feeling of tropical heat and vertical sunlights, I brought together all creatures, birds, beasts, reptiles, all trees and plants, usages and appearances, that are found in all tropical regions, and assembled them together in China or Hindustan. From kindred feelings I soon brought Egypt and her gods under the same law. I was stared at, hooted at, grinned at, chattered at, by monkeys, by paroquets, by cuckatoos. I ran into pagodas, and was fixed for centuries at the summit, or in secret rooms; I was the idol; I was the priest; I was worshipped; I was sacrificed. I fled from the wrath of Brahma through all the forests of Asia; Vishnu hated me; Seeva lay in wait for me. I came suddenly upon Isis and Osiris; I had done a deed which the ibis and the crocodile trembled at. Thousands of years I lived and was buried in stone coffins, with mummies and sphinxes, in narrow chambers at the heart of eternal pyramids. I was kissed with cancerous kisses, by crocodiles, and was laid confounded with all unutterable abortions, amongst reeds and Nilotic mud.[3]

The coupling of nature images with fantasies about the Orient speaks of a deeply religious desire De Quincey shared with a few of his contemporaries to return to a state of primal unity. Nature worship, orientalism, and primitivism in general accompany the triumph of rationalism like a shadow. They are a three-headed beast that rears itself from the shambles of cultural failure and breakdown. Primitivism itself, according to James Baird, "represents one attempt of Western man to restore the symbolism of human existence. It is a willful exit from the crisis and from the chambers of the dead and the dying, *as these manifestations are represented in the moral view of the primitivist.*"[4] Cultural failure may be further qualified as the loss of a commanding authority in religious symbolism and practice. Religion, which originally meant "to bind into one," is the binding medium of culture; it alone can command the authority necessary to mold and direct the total culture of a people. Here I am speaking not of pseudo-religion, such as Marxism or materialism, but of religion as the primary force of life, which spontaneously manifests in symbols and symbolic structures that provide the sustenance of the spirit. By contrast, pseudo-religions, like Marxism and contemporary political or religious charlatanism, merely prey on the spiritual vacuum and hunger for symbols that continually gnaw at the masses.

For all its negative ramifications, the decline of religious authority in Europe, which began in the sixteenth century and was completed by the end of the eighteenth century, did have a positive aspect as well. In stripping away traditional symbolic structures, it laid bare man's potential for realizing the gods as psychic forces immanent within the imagination, as did De Qunicey in his opium reverie and Baudelaire in his evocation of the world of dreams. The concurrent rise of imperialism, colonialism, and world-wide scientific exploration inadvertently opened the doors to secret chambers where there were to be found, in full glory, so it seemed, the sacraments forbidden by reason. As Jung once declared, "We have let the houses that our fathers built fall into pieces, and now we try to break into Oriental palaces that our fathers never knew."[5] As Westerners discovered the fountain-heads of their own tradition running dry, they searched ever more intensively for new symbols and sacraments in other cultures. The situation was accurately described by the French historian Jules Michelet in 1864:

Man must rest, get his breath, refresh himself at the great living wells, which keep the freshness of the eternal. Where are they to be found, if not in the cradle of our race, on the sacred height, whence flow on the one side the Indus and the Ganges, on the other the torrents of Persia, the Rivers of Paradise? The West is too narrow. Greece is small: I stifle there. Judea is dry: I pant there. Let me look towards Asia and the profound East for a little while. There lies my great poem, as vast as the Indian Ocean, blessed, gilded with the sun, the book of divine harmony wherein is no dissonance. A serene peace reigns there, and in the midst of conflict, an infinite sweetness, a boundless fraternity, which spreads over all living things, an ocean (without bottom or bound) of love, of clemency. I have found the object of my search: The Bible of kindness.[6]

Michelet's longing culminated in the "passage to India," the journey to a realm that must be explored if psychosomatic union or integration is to be realized. To enter that realm requires more than just a geographical journey; it demands an upsetting plunge through the rational barricades of the mind. This is the journey attempted poetically by Arthur Rimbaud. In his famous preface to *Illuminations*, Rimbaud declared to his teacher Georges Izambard:

One must, I say, become a *seer*, make oneself a *seer*. The poet makes himself a *seer* through a long, a prodigious and rational disordering of all the senses. Every form of love, of suffering, of madness; he searches himself, he consumes all the poisons in him, keeping only their quintessences. Ineffable torture in which he will need all his faith and superhuman strength, the great criminal, the great sickman, the utterly damned and supreme Savant! For he arrives at the unknown! Since he has cultivated his soul—richer to begin with than any other! He arrives at the unknown: and even if, half crazed, in the end, he loses the understanding of his visions, he has seen them! Let him croak in his leap into those unutterable and innumerable things: there will come other horrible workers: they will begin at the horizons where he has succumbed.[7]

The great domain of the unknown toward which the young Rimbaud steered himself encompassed the human soul as contained within himself: "The first study for a man who wants to be a poet is the knowledge of himself entire."[8] As with other Romantics, such a quest, unguided and untutored, drove Rimbaud to madness; he himself declared, "But the soul has to be made monstrous, that's the point."[9] Yet his brush with the primal realm of psyche gave him uncanny insight: "When the infinite servitude of woman shall have ended, when she will be able to live by and for herself; then man—hitherto abominable—having given her her freedom, she too will be a poet. Woman will discover the unknown. Will her world be different from ours? She will discover strange, unfathomable things, repulsive, delicious."[10] For Rimbaud, woman, like nature and the Orient, is herself an aspect of the great intuitive unknown within our own being that must be rediscovered and returned to. But the task of returning proved too much for Rimbaud, and his life became a classic paradigm of the tragic and inept misadventure that often accompanied the psychogeographic passage to India. A brilliant child prodigy, he abandoned his poetic efforts at the age of nineteen, and in 1873 undertook his own nameless voyage into the Orient, and the heart of darkness.

Prior to the actual physical journey, in his own mind, at least, Rimbaud had already returned to the Orient, "and to the first and eternal wisdom." Throughout his writings there is a psychic nostalgia for the East and for a wisdom that is primal to human nature, identified with the teachings of the Orient. In the prose poem "Lives" Rimbaud wrote:

> *O the enormous avenues of the Holy Land, the temple terraces!*
> *What has become of the Brahman who explained the proverbs to me?*
> *Of that time, of that place, I can still see even the old women!*[11]

By contrast, in the modern world of technological progress Rimbaud could only consider himself an *exile*. Especially in that document of bitter pride, *A Season in Hell*, he spoke of having experienced a radical psychogeographic displacement: "I see that my disquietudes come from having understood too late that we are in the Occident. Occidental swamps!"[12] Somehow or other for the European, the Orient as a psychic reality had vanished, causing the poet to lament: "Well! here is my spirit insisting on taking upon itself all the cruel developments that the spirit has suffered since the end of the Orient."[13] *The end of the Orient!* A magnificent phrase rolling like a curse upon the sensitive brow. From Rimbaud to Ram Dass, through Whitman and Hesse, the tortuous journey to retrieve the East has been but a mental journey, an exploration of psychic geographies momentarily resembling the temples, the pyramids, and the pagodas whose symbolic form and meaning were banished with the advent of technological society and its trappings—the cannon, baptism, the slide rule, the stock market. For the poet glimpsing in the far inner reaches of his mind these ancient yet omnipresent vistas, the only recourse was the hallucination of words; and for the painter, the alchemy of color and strange forms running riot on a palette. As Rimbaud described himself, "I became an adept at simple hallucination; in place of a factory, I really saw a mosque, a school of drummers led by angels, carriages on the highways of the sky, a drawing-room at the bottom of a lake. . . ."[14] With no intelligent preceptor, delirium afflicts the poet's tongue and explodes within the painter's eye.

Hallucinations are without number. Truly that is what I have always known: no more faith in history, principles forgotten. I'll keep quiet about that: poets and visionaries would be jealous. I am a thousand times the richest, let us be avaricious as the sea. . . .

I am going to unveil all the mysteries: religious mysteries, or natural mysteries, death, birth, the future, the past, cosmogony, nothingness. I am a master of phantasmagoria. . . .[15]

In the end the master of phantasmagoria was a bluff. Because Rimbaud had not the patience or the guiding wisdom to substantiate what he saw, his vision became the platform of absurdity. What to Rimbaud was the experience of a painful psychic displacement was to become a century later the stylistic mannerism of surrealist art. The sacraments of the Orient he had envisioned were never to be tasted. In deranging his senses the poet lost all control and tumbled into hell. The goal of human striving, exemplified by the spirit and achievement of oriental cultures, was to remain distinct yet elusive to all Western seekers, and their search would end only when the mind itself had been turned inside out, for what Rimbaud, De Quincey, and Baudelaire had glimpsed as the Orient was in truth the roots of human consciousness.

In fact, that whole blurry phenomenon known as Romanticism—whether it was manifested in the nostalgia of the poets, or in the retreat of certain artists to the wilderness, or in the idealization of the past and the countless sentimental academic fantasies of the orient, or even in the scientific endeavors of men like Alexander von Humboldt, author of the monumental work *Kosmos*, Darwin in the Galapagos, and Wallace in the Amazon—always embraced a sense of *return*: return to nature, return to Orient, return to the past. The Romantics were all searching, however unconsciously, for a "lost" unity. But a search for unity presupposes an already schizophrenic state of being. It is for this reason that modern culture—that of the nineteenth and twentieth centuries—presents such a hybrid amalgamation of styles and period-pieces, the products of a misguided cleverness spurred on by the illusion of material progress. Because unity already *is* the inherent condition of things, it cannot be attained. All efforts to realize the primal unity are tainted to the degree that they share the materialistic methods and psychological techniques of civilization as a whole.

The paradox is that the Orient cannot be appropriated, as Michelet suggested, for that would be but a subtle exercise in imperialism; nor can the present be rejected, whether in the quiet manner of Thoreau in Walden or in the more dramatic manner of Rimbaud. Yet there is a validity to the experience of both Thoreau and Rimbaud that cannot be denied. Baudelaire had prophesied that all of those cultures resisting the cannon and the rite of baptism would be destroyed. What he did not foresee was that the destruction would come as much from the devouring hunger of men like Michelet and Rimbaud as from the wanton aggressiveness of imperialism. If there is any validity in their spiritual hunger it is in the need to rediscover our own psychic Asia, and beneath that the roots of our own consciousness. Moreover, it is quite possible that dying Asia—the Asia glorified by Michelet—may seek out the West and transform itself within the charnel ground of our own civilization. This course of events even seems likely, for there seems to be a kind of justice and divine economy in the proposition that if coal and Coca Cola are exported to India, the practice of yoga will take hold in Europe and America.

The impulse to discover and explore the religions and symbols of the East, taken as a psychic impulse for attaining a state of primary reintegration, received brilliant artistic expression in Walt Whitman's famous poem "Passage to India." Whereas Rimbaud's poetry is nostalgic, Whitman's is utterly positive and confident. The epic theme of the evolutionary dialectic of the transformative vision is clearly enunciated in this poem, in which India is but the symbol of man's inherent at-one-ment in the time just dawning. The European in his restless search and exploration is seen as a necessary, dynamic prelude to bringing home the knowledge of *home* itself. For the wisdom of the East is not necessarily in the symbols themselves but in knowing that it is still possible to become whole and pure, singing the joy of creation endlessly and fabulously as it unfolds itself through us. In fact, all technological exploration and expansion is but the bridge leading to the world of mystic union. Of the Western explorers and researchers Whitman asks:

> *Ah! who shall soothe these feverish children?*
> *Who justify these restless explorations?*
> *Who speak the secret of impassive earth?*
> *Who bind it to us? what is this separate Nature so unnatural?*
> *What is this earth to our affections? (unloving earth, without a throb*
> *   to answer ours,*
> *Cold earth the place of graves.)*
> *Yet soul, be sure the first intent remains, and shall be carried out,*
> *Perhaps even now the time has arrived.* [16]

And then comes the announcement of Whitman's grand theme—the divine role of the artist/poet:

> *After the noble inventors, after the scientists, the chemist, the*
> *   geologist, ethnologist,*
> *Finally shall come the poet worthy of that name,*
> *The true son of God shall come singing his songs.*
>
> *Then not your deeds only O voyagers, O scientists and inventors*
> *   shall be justified*
> *All these hearts of fretted children shall be soothed,*
> *All affection shall be fully responded to, the secret shall be told,*

All these separations and gaps shall be taken up and hook'd and
  link'd together,
The whole earth, this cold impassive voiceless earth, shall be com-
pletely justified,
Trinitas Divine shall be gloriously accomplished and compacted by
  the true son of God, the poet,
(He shall indeed pass the straits and conquer the mountains,
He shall double the cape of Good Hope to some purpose,)
Nature and Man shall be disjoin'd and diffused no more,
The true son of God shall absolutely fuse them.[17]

Whitman's vision of the advent of the poet, "the true son of God," as
the ultimate end of technology is an astonishing affirmation of the spirit of
the transformative vision, and a vindication of the transformative visionaries. Whitman's poet is not a mere spinner of words or idle fabricator of
images but a person so wholly attuned to the primary impulses of psyche
and so skillful at expressing these impulses that he or she would be no artist
in the ordinary sense but a new being altogether. To bring this *one* being
into existence, the entire circuit of techne must be manifested and explored,
until coming at last to that sudden point of realization, we gaze like some
modern Copernicus in wonder and awe at the inner geographies, the
planets and their sun, rotating in tune to some harmony more sublime than
the mind can comprehend.

In declaring the advent of "the poet worthy of that name," Whitman
announced a fundamental premise of the transformative vision: the reestablishment of the primacy of psyche. Thus the present separative,
materialistic phase will give birth to its opposite, a unitive state in which
man and nature are fused into one conscious, comprehensive whole. The
classless state Marx envisioned will be not only a proletarian paradise but a
consciously harmonized state in which every being in nature has a recip-
rocal relationship with every other being—an aspect not considered by
Marx, who perpetuated the humanist heresy of considering the plight of
man alone, apart from the rest of nature. Furthermore, Whitman clearly
saw that the return to nature and the East is a return to the very source of
mind and being. In this respect, Whitman's view is simpler and more
complete than Marx's:

Passage indeed O soul to primal thought,
Not lands and seas alone, thy own clear freshness,
The young maturity of brood and bloom,
To realms of budding bibles.

O soul repressless, I with thee and thee with me,
The circumnavigation of the world begin,

Of man, the voyage of his mind's return.
To reason's early paradise,
Back, back to wisdom's birth, to innocent intuitions,
Again with fair creation. [18]

The rest of the poem is an ecstatic burst, a plunge into the divine, a song of God encompassing the universe:

Bathe me O God in thee, mounting to thee,
I and my soul to range in thee of thee.

O thou transcendent,
Nameless, the fibre and the breath,
Light of the light, shedding forth universes, thou centre of them,
Thou mightier centre of the true, the good, the loving . . .
Thou pulse, thou motive of the stars, sun, systems,
That, circling, move in order, safe, harmonious,
Athwart the shapeless vastness of space,
How should I think, how breathe a single breath, how speak if out of
    myself,
I could not launch, to those superior universes? [19]

Approaching the conclusion of his vision, Whitman saw clearly that the image of India and the Orient should not be confused with a mere journey to the East.

Passage to more than India! Are thy wings plumed indeed for such
    far flights!
O secret of the earth and sky!
Of you O waters of the sea! O winding creeks and rivers!
Of you O woods and fields! of you strong mountains of my land!
Of you O prairies! of you gray rocks!

O morning red! O clouds! O rain and snows!
O day and night passage to you!

O sun and moon and all you stars! Sirius and Jupiter!
Passage to you

Passage, immediate passage! the blood burns in my veins!
Away, O soul! hoist instantly the anchor!
Cut the hawsers—haul out—shake out every sail!
Have we not stood here long enough, eating and drinking like mere
    brutes?
Have we not darken'd and dazed ourselves with books long
    enough? . . .

O brave soul!
O farther farther sail!
O daring joy, but safe! are they not all the seas of God?
O farther farther sail![20]

Whitman's mystically inspired "Passage to India" appeared in 1872, concurrent with Rimbaud's *Illuminations*, and scarcely a generation after the publication of the Communist Manifesto, which signaled the triumph of materialism and the beginning of the "holy" civil war within materialism itself. Certainly the seventh hell period, from 1831 to 1883, marked the high point of the materialistic philosophies, though by no means was it the high point of materialistic life-styles; that remains for the twentieth century to achieve. If the appearance of dialectical materialism in the midst of the seventh hell period was the high point of a particular phase of human consciousness and development—or perhaps even of a *natural* development, since humanity ultimately cannot be separated from nature—then, according to the dialectical principle, the seed of its contradiction should have been apparent at the same time. The noted physicist Carl Friederich Von Weizsacker has recently written:

Dialectical philosophy of history considers the dominion of religion as a phase of world history which today has already been overcome as a matter of fact. The dialectic of history, however, implies that there is a truth in each phase of history. But the truth of each phase is driven beyond itself to its explicit negation by its inherent contradictions. If, for the sake of simplicity, we argue that the historical era of religion has been overcome by the scientific era, it follows that science itself will remain caught in an attitude of naive opposition to religion until it can ask to what extent there has been truth to the very religion it has replaced.[21]

Poetically, Whitman saw the whole of this process and expressed the religious synthesis beyond scientific materialism before Marxism had even claimed a successful revolution. Even closer to the time of the Communist Manifesto which appeared in 1848, was the appearance in 1844 of a new religious movement in Persia that had already proclaimed the unity of world religions and the establishment of one world-wide government based on spiritual principles. Whether or not the religion of Ba'hai, as the faith of Baha'ullah has come to be called, is the new force that will supplant materialism is beside the point; what is significant is its appearance as the counterpart to Marxism in Europe*. And in India as well, there appeared during this period the phenomenal character Ramakrishna (1836-86), who had his first ecstatic mystical experience around 1842—about the time Samuel Morse was astounding the technological world with his telegraph.

*Signaling the formation of these and other modern collective "mass" movements was the 1846 discovery of the planet Neptune, which is characterized as a "Universal Solvent," breaking things down to create a state of undifferentiated unity.

Two of the chief components of Ramakrishna's religious "reform" are quite significant in terms of the larger dialectical process we are considering: the first is the worship of God as Mother; the second is the recognition that all religious teachings and prophets are "true." Like the teaching of Baha'ullah and the vision of Whitman, Ramakrishna's teaching is a significant indicator of what may follow once science asks to what extent there has been truth to the very religion it has replaced.

In marked contrast to the attitude of his contemporary Baudelaire, who despised all women except his mother, is Ramakrishna's worship of God as Mother, as the generative female force in nature and human affairs. Ramakrishna's attitude finds its European counterpart in the closing lines of Goethe's *Faust*, or in Rimbaud's recognition of the imminent liberation of woman, the female principle. Both Goethe's praise of the "eternally feminine" and Ramakrishna's worship of God as Mother may indicate a prophetically significant turn in the collective orientation of the human psyche in the forthcoming phase of history. Whitman, by contrast, was still dominated by the masculine, for he spoke of the saving force as the *son of God*; and in his poetry there is little recognition of the feminine as the divine transformative force, except perhaps for his recognition of the *earth* as an integral element to be transformed: "This whole earth . . . shall be completely justified."

There is one further aspect to the dialectical process envisioned in the "Passage to India." Woman, God as Mother, the eternally feminine, the earth itself represent the vindication of those forces associated with the right cerebral hemisphere; in terms of the Chinese dialectic, woman symbolically represents the yin force of nature, though of course no given woman is totally yin. Similarly, man symbolically represents the yang principle, which is associated with the left cerebral hemisphere. Clearly, the present era is predominantly yang: the triumph of scientific materialism, the exploitation and domination of the earth, and of women themselves, and the overriding ethos of our civilization is ruthlessly, analytically yang. According to the dialectical principle this can only mean that the present yang culture will give way to yin, just as a preceding yin culture gave way to it. Henry Adams summed up the yin-yang dialectic of the present historical process in a memorable way, by his contrasting images of the medieval Madonna (yin) and the contemporary dynamo (yang). The symbol of the ascendant yin force prophesied in the visions of Whitman, Ramakrishna, and Baha'ullah is nothing less than Mother Earth; this is the meaning of Whitman's notion that the Passage to India is a return to earth, to primal thought itself. The present development of ecological awareness (the word ecology first entered the English language in 1873) may be the beginning of the translation of the yin symbol of Mother Earth into an actual reality or article of living faith.

The yin-yang dialectical process should not be conceived of as a cycle so much as a universal force moving in great patterns, contradicting itself at some times and synthesizing at others. For example, one may consider Whitman's visionary "Passage to India" in relation to another nineteenth-century model, articulated by the Confucianist reformers Kang Yu Wei (1858-1927) and Tan Ssu T'ung (1865-98). In Whitman's vision three general phases of human development can be clearly discerned: the pre-technological past; the technological present; and the spiritualized post-technological future. By implication, the past and the future have similarities; the past for Whitman is represented in the present by the lingering civilizations of the Orient, which still have some sense of the unity of man and nature; the present is distinguished by the sense that man is separate from nature; and the future once again will be a time when "Nature and Man shall be disjoin'd and diffused no more, / The true son of God shall absolutely fuse them." In its bold simplicity, Whitman's conception may be compared to Confucius' teaching of the Three Sequences and Three Ages, which according to Kang were among the most significant of all of the Master's ideas. These Confucian ideas provided Kang and Tan Ssu T'ung with the basis for what they termed the Religion of the Great Unity, a remarkable and little-known nineteenth-century vision. According to the doctrine of the Three Ages, the first age is one of universal peace; the second is one of disorder; and the third represents a return to a synthesis of universal peace. According to Tan Ssu T'ung, the doctrine of the Three Ages is graphically represented in six stages through the first hexagram (six-line symbol) of the Book of Changes in the following manner:[22]

	Lines	Sequence of Three Ages	Absolute Time Sequence
Outer Trigram	6	Age of Universal Peace	Distant future
		III	
	5	Age of Approaching Peace	Near future
	4	Age of Disorder	Confucius to 20th century
		II	
Inner Trigram	3	Age of Disorder	Hsia Dynasty to Confucius (2200-400 B.C.)
	2	Age of Approaching Peace	Legendary Emperors (5000-2200?B.C.)
		I	
	1	Age of Universal Peace	Prehistoric (10000-5000?B.C.)

In this configuration, which is read from the bottom up, the first two lines represent the earlier age of unity; the middle two lines, the "historical age" of increasing disorder (hence the increase of artificial, civilized law and order); and the last two, the emergence of another age of unity. Kang Yu

Wei and Tan Ssu T'ung envisioned themselves at the end of the second phase of the Age of Disorder; their religion of the Great Unity proclaimed in its own way the divine fusion of man and nature. Corresponding to the three ages are the Way of Earth, which is represented by the earlier Age of Universal Peace, the Way of Man, represented by the Age of Disorder, and the Way of Heaven, represented by the later Age of Universal Peace.

In terms of the classical European dialectic, the first age represents the thesis; the second, the antithesis; the third, the synthesis. Thus technocratic materialism represents the culmination of the antithetical Way of Man, the Age of Disorder with its contradictions of humanist philosophy and mechanical alienation, civilized order and unprecedented total warfare. Like a blind, mystical throb appearing in the midst of a mechanized dream, the romantic turning toward the thesis state of the primitive and oriental cultures was the unconscious seed for an age of synthesis.

It would be a mistake to think that one could logically deduce what this age of synthesis might be like, since logical deduction itself is an aspect of the consciousness of the antithetical phase of human development. This is not to say that the future will eschew logic and reason, but rather that it may be characterized by *alogical* and *arational* processes (as distinct from prelogical and prerational or nonlogical and nonrational). The utopian fantasies of the nineteenth-century positivists, including Marx, are limited by their reliance on rational projection; these schemes are merely logical extensions of the Renaissance perspective model and its child, the Cartesian system of infinitely linear coordinates, on which all notions of progress are based. The dictatorship of the proletariat and the classless state are idealized projections of the debased level of human affairs in 1848; they are visions in which the a priori status of machine technology remains unquestioned. Marx and Engels were incapable of seeing that their very manner of projecting was but a function of mechanized consciousness, which was itself the oppressive agent. In contrast to the vision of Whitman, the vision of Marx is intrinsically nontransformative. Rather than it merely presenting a true solution to the problem of human destiny, it merely presents an integral and perhaps the ultimate expression of the materialism pervading the Age of Disorder. As this age draws to a close, Marxism will no longer be necessary or valid.

True enough, a classless state may ensue, in the sense that the present rational categories may be broken down or transcended as we return to what Whitman called "primal thought." It is worthwhile to note the comments of Tan Ssu T'ung on the ages of Approaching Peace and Universal Peace. In the Age of Approaching Peace, he wrote, "all the many religious teachings throughout the globe will become unified by a single religious leader [compare with Whitman's poet, "the true son of God"] and all the many nations throughout the world will become unified by a single political ruler. It is in time, that of the single great unification, and for the individual would be that in which he 'understands the Will of Heaven.' "[23] Tan's comments on the final phase of the Way of Heaven, the Age of Universal Peace, are even more intriguing. In this age,

the entire globe is already under a single religious leader and a single political ruler. Being single, they are alone; being alone, they exceed the proper limits; exceeding the proper limits, there comes occasion for repentance. Because of this repentance, each and every individual becomes capable of acquiring the virtue of the religious leader, with the result that this leader himself is no longer needed; each and every individual becomes capable of acquiring the power of the political ruler, with the result that this ruler himself is no longer needed. It will be in time, that when throughout the world the people themselves will rule.[24]

A more perfect description of the classless state would be difficult to find. Yet what we hear is not the dialectical voice of Western materialistic thought but the unitive voice of primal thought itself. When the state Tan described is finally attained, a state in which "all sentient beings will have attained Buddhahood," not only will there be no religious or political leaders, but there will be no religion or politics at all, and not even the people will rule, for what will there be to rule? If the globe is unified, it will be as though the globe itself were no more. "Only when this stage has been reached will there be perfection and completion, with nothing more to be added,"[25] is Tan's final comment. Return to primal thought, indeed! No wonder the poets longed for the Orient, for in the sublime vision of the East, the beginning is in the end and the end in the beginning. In the poet's vision Christ's proclamation of being the alpha and the omega, whose meaning was long forsaken by the West, finds actualization in the thought and culture of the East. The dissident Rimbaud cries out:

Is it not because we cultivate fog! We eat fever with our watery vegetables. And Drunkenness! And Tobacco! And self-sacrifice—How far all this is from the conception, from the wisdom of the Orient, the original fatherland! Why a modern world if such poisons were invented!

Churchmen will say: Granted. But you mean Eden. Nothing for you in the history of Oriental peoples.—It is true; it is of Eden I was thinking! What has it to do with my dream—that purity of ancient races!

Philosophers: the world has no age. Humanity simply changes place. You are in the Occident but free to live in your Orient, as ancient as you please, and to live well. Don't admit defeat. Philosophers, you are of your Occident.[26]

Penetrating the psychic relativity of cultural concepts, the poet-seers were able to perceive that neither the East nor the West, the past nor the future, has any independent truth. The illusion that they do only increases with the rise of materialism. Exhausting the limits of the material domain *is* the passage to India, the emergence into an Eden that is both with and without precedent, for Eden in the end is mind in direct contact with the ultimate reality. In a similar vein Arnold Toynbee has recently remarked:

If mankind finds itself compelled to limit its material aims and to stabilize life on the material plane, the founders of "higher religions" may at last come into their own. They may win allegiance that will no longer just be perfunctory, for they have opened up for mankind a field of activity—the spiritual field—to which Nature sets no bounds. In a global human society that has been constrained by Nature to stabilize its life on the material plane, human dynamism may perhaps address itself singlemindedly to the spiritual objective of making direct contact with the ultimate reality and living in conformity with it.[27]

The passage to India is an event that occurs of natural necessity; if human will is involved, it is only by way of submission to a greater will. History itself becomes the mechanics of an equation that is always perfectly balanced. The Journey to the East, as Hesse called one of his novels, is not a mere appropriation of symbols, artifacts, and seemingly obsolete terms, but a process of natural convergence: the East absorbs the West or becomes absorbed by the West. This is clear. What is not so clear is that in the process, the West is absorbed by the East. The end result can not be predicted, just as it is rationally impossible to conceive of lead turning into gold. But the route to the end is marked by a series of unmistakable correspondences: the gunboat diplomacy of late-nineteenth-century imperialist politics was accompanied by the publication of the Sacred Books of the East under the direction of Max Müller and a host of scholars; the Opium War found its counterpart in the 1875 formation of the Theosophical Society. These correspondences are clues to the workings of a dialectical process of which the vast majority of the world has remained unaware, lulled to sleep by revolution, war, progress, and the poet laureate of the empire, who declared, "East is East and West is West and ne'er the twain shall meet."

CHAPTER THIRTEEN

Revolution of the Eye, Revolution of the Mind

WHILE THE subtle psychogeographic drama of East and West began to play itself out on the world stage, the eye and mind of the European sensibility itself began to undergo a major transformation. This transformation appeared most strikingly in the visual arts and the attendant cultural milieu sometime after the middle of the nineteenth century. In his Preface to *Illuminations* Rimbaud proclaimed, "Inventions of the unknown demand new forms." But in the cyclic nature of things, the appearance of new forms is usually preceded by the disintegration of the old; and if anything had given impetus to the destruction of the old sensibility in the visual arts, it was the advent of photography.

Until the rise of photography (and owing to the very length of the process of completing a painting) the narrative mode predominated in the visual arts as well as in other cultural areas; history painting was flanked by grand opera and the novel. With the rise of photography, however, history painting lost its significance, for photography's instantaneous technique plunged the European consciousness of reality into the immediate present. With the displacement of history painting, the entire edifice of academic culture came crashing down. The history painting produced by the residual academicism of the late nineteenth century appears bombastically contrived, a stage set that could be salvaged and redeemed only by the aesthetics of Hollywood cinema.

Ironically, the relatively instantaneous visual process photography unveiled called into question the very nature of perceived reality. The notion of a solid universe was no longer unassailable, for in revealing the contrived nature of Renaissance visual perception, the photograph implied that the determination of physical reality was solely dependent upon the moment-to-moment perception of the individual eye. Lurking beneath this implication was the notion that the perception itself was the reality, and the thing perceived only a function of it. From this point of view, the material universe is a perceptual fixation or a mental obsession, another idea in a universe of ideas, but without absolute reality.

In effect, the elimination of narrative by photography reduced visual reality to a fragmented anecdote. For this reason, the psychological impact of photography was disintegrative and alienating. The mind, still obsessed with what had seemed to be the concrete continuity of material reality, was suddenly confronted with flux and discontinuity. As photography became more precise, reality became less so. Eventually even the bounce of a ball could be broken down to a series of minute and discrete changes. For a mind clinging to a programed set of beliefs translatable into the tangible objects of material reality, photography could only mean chaos, for the reality it presented was no longer an epic but a slice of life. For the positivist, the chaos was relieved by a belief in the righteousness of material progress, which renders the senses numb to the wholesale chaos of everyday events and to the vast array of "facts" that the materialistic search for knowledge unearths at a rapidly accelerating rate. For others, to discern a transcendent meaning in the growing chaos bombarding the sensibility required a leap of extraordinary insight.

It is precisely this leap that Edgar Allan Poe made in his meditative essay "Eureka" (1848). In a prolonged metaphysical ecstasy, Poe took the base of materialistic thought, Newton's theory of gravity, to its natural—or supernatural—conclusion: the existence of Unity as "the truth of the Original source—as the principle of the Universal Phaenomena."[1] Poe formulated the Newtonian premise as follows: "Every atom of every body attracts every other atom, both of its own and every other body, with a force which varies inversely as the square of the distance between the attracting and attracted atom."[2] As Poe himself declared, "Here indeed a flood of suggestion bursts upon the mind." Then in a passage prophecying Heisenberg's principle of indeterminacy, he continued rapturously:

If I propose to ascertain the influence of one mote in a sunbeam upon its neighboring mote, I cannot accomplish my purpose without first counting and weighing all the atoms in the Universe and defining the precise positions of all at one particular moment. If I venture to displace, by even the billionth part of an inch, the microscopical speck of dust which lies upon the point of my finger, what is the character of that act upon which I have adventured? I have done a deed which shakes the Moon in her path, which causes the Sun to be no longer the Sun, and which alters forever the destiny of the multitudinous myriads of stars that roll and glow in the majestic presence of their Creator.[3]

Poe's metalogical discourse then turns to the corollary principle of *irradiation*. Given the definition of gravity and the principle that each atom is attracted to every other atom, there is, according to Poe, "a tendency of all, with a similar force, to a general centre."[4] Irradiation is governed by certain laws: "From a *luminous* centre, *Light* issues by irradiation. . . . The expression of the law may thus be generalized—the number of light-particles (or if the phrase be preferred, the number of light-impressions) received upon the shifting plane, will be inversely proportional with the squares of the distance of the plane."[5] Poe used the following chart to illustrate his notion of the law of irradiation:

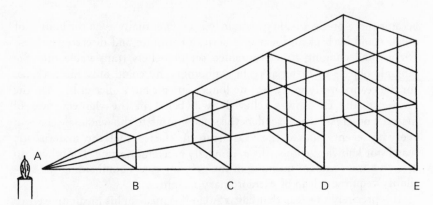

Poe's diagram is very similar to the Renaissance perceptual model, except that, as Poe would have us understand, "A" is the center of a sphere,
rather than the perceiving ego; the diagram thus presents merely a cross-
section of a spherical norm, and not the ego perceiving an external object.
Poe's point of view supports the notion that the "error" of the Renaissance
perceptual model was in forgetting the whole, or the Unity, thus causing
the plunge of consciousness into *particles*—the particularization of matter
into atoms of knowledge into informational bits, and humanity into individuals. But this very particularizing plunge of consciousness was viewed
by Poe (and other seers) as a natural process of diffusion or irradiation from
the center. The complement to the process of irradiation is *concentraliza-
tion*, the force *toward* the center. And as there is a temporal falling away
from the center, so there is inevitably a return toward it, a return that
begins at the point of maximum diffusion. Poe described this process as
reaction:

The general principle of Gravity being in the first place, understood as the reaction
of an act—as the expression of a desire on the part of Matter, while existing in a
state of diffusion, to return to the Unity whence it was diffused. . . . Matter then
irradiated into space with a force varying as the squares of the distance, might, *a
priori*, be supposed to return towards its center of irradiation.[6]

According to Poe, the process of irradiation is pulsing and discontinuous;
otherwise there would be no reactive force (again Poe foresaw the development of quantum physics). The pulsation process makes possible the degradation of light—its condensation at given points—into denser forms of
energy, ultimately into what we define as matter. If the light pulsing from
the center is conceived of as consciousness in its state of most concentrated
awareness, matter exists and can be defined only as a degradation or densification of consciousness. Hence, in the diagram, the luminous center A
(alpha which is also omega) may function as the center of consciousness as
well. Proximity to this point defines proximity to sacredness or chaos, or
rather to illumination/insight or ignorance/seeking. The point of maximum

diffusion is characterized by a minimum perception of source-light. Analogous to the planet Neptune, newly discovered in Poe's time, the sun is but one bright star in a sea of stars.

Indeed, Neptunian describes exactly the diffused, irradiated, and fragmented consciousness that accompanied the emergence of planetary industrialization. The breakdown of the model of Renaissance perception in the mid-nineteenth century left consciousness in total *dis-order*, for there was absolutely no new model to replace it except the natural model of chaos. But it is precisely the condition of maximum chaos or diffusion of light that is necessary for the reactive force to generate itself. Here we may recall Blake's image of Newton at the bottom of the sea, which may be interpreted to symbolize the periphery of diffused consciousness in which the gravitational force of a concentric return may take place. Like Blake, Poe saw no separation of mind and spirit; attraction and repulsion, spirit and matter "accompany each other in the strictest fellowship forever. Thus the Body and the Soul walk hand in hand."[7]

During this "midnight" period of the dissolution and shifting of perceptions, then, there occurred the primary rediscovery of the unconscious, signaled by the publication of Eduard von Hartmann's *The Philosophy of the Unconscious* in 1869, 21 years after Poe's *Eureka*. In a fundamental sense the destruction or displacement of the Renaissance mode of perception took away the last prop dividing conscious human behavior from the great sea of the unconscious. But in Poe's model the ultimate center of the (un)conscious is the luminous point of origin, the unconscious being that of which *we* are not conscious, that of which we have become ignorant. But ignorance is only the diffusion aspect of the primordial consciousness, and in a fundamental sense is inseparable from it.

Because we are dealing with Unity, all contradictions coexist and support each other. Thus sixty years before Einstein, Poe was able to declare

that *Space and Duration ARE ONE.* That the Universe might endure throughout an era at all commensurate with the grandeur of its component material portions . . . it was required . . . that the stars should be gathered into visibility from invisible nebulosity . . . and so grow grey in giving birth and death to unspeakably numerous and complex variations of vitalic development—it was required that the stars should do all this—should have time thoroly to accomplish all these Divine purposes—*during the period* in which all things were effecting their return into Unity with a velocity accumulating in the inverse proportion of the squares of the distances at which lay the inevitable end.[8]

But the end is not the end, and Poe's vision, like that of the ancient Vedic seers, conjures up an endlessly pulsing creation and destruction of the universe, "a novel universe swelling into existence, and then subsiding into nothingness at every throb of the Heart Divine."[9] This conclusion draws Poe into the realm of "cosmic consciousness," for in his words, "this Heart

Divine—what is it? *It is our own"*; thus the "phaenomena on which our conclusions at this point must depend, are merely spiritual shadows, but not the less thoroly substantial."[10] Then in a final statement of poetic majesty, Poe sums up the doctrine of the evolution of consciousness:

I have spoken of *Memories* that haunt us during our youth. They sometimes puruse us even in our Manhood:—assume gradually less and less indefinite shapes:—now and then speak to us with low voices, saying: "There was an epoch in the Night of Time, when a still-existent being existed—one of an absolutely infinite number of similar Beings that people the absolutely infinite domain of absolutely infinite space. It was not and is not in the power of this Being—any more than it is in your own—to extend, by actual increase, the joy of his Existence; but just as it *is* in your power to concentrate your pleasures (the absolute amount of happiness remaining always the same), so did and does a simlar capability appertain to this Divine Being who thus passes his Eternity in perpetual variation of Concentrated Self and almost Infinite Self-Diffusion. What you call the universe is but his present expansive existence. He now feels his life through an infinity of imperfect pleasures—the partial and pain-intertangled pleasures of those inconceivably numerous things which you designate as his creatures, but which are really infinite individualizations of Himself. All these creatures—*all*—those which you term animate as well as those to whom you deny life for no better reason than that you do not behold it in operation—*all* these creatures have, in a greater or less degree, a capacity for pleasure and for pain:—*but the general sum of their sensation is precisely that amount of Happiness which appertains by right to the Divine Being when concentrated within Himself.* These creatures are all, too, more or less conscious Intelligences; conscious first of a proper identity; conscious secondly and by faint indeterminate glimpses, of an identity with the Divine Being of whom we speak—of an identity with God. Of the two classes of consciousness, fancy that the former will grow weaker and the latter stronger, during the long succession of ages which must elapse before these myriads of individual Intelligences become blended—when the bright stars become blended—into One. Think that the sense of individual identity will be gradually merged in the general consciousness—that Man, for example, ceasing imperceptibly to feel himself Man, will at length attain that awfully triumphant epoch when he shall recognize his existence as that of Jehovah. In the meantime bear in mind that all is Life—Life—Life Within Life—the less within the greater, and all within the Spirit Divine."[11]

In the context of the mid-nineteenth century, the glimpse of the cosmic whole as afforded by Poe, who was acclaimed and translated by Baudelaire, at least gave the artistic avant-garde a sense of the larger framework and conscious orientation of which their experiments and investigations might be a part. On the one hand, there was the experience of the profoundly subjective nature of vision and of sensation in general, and on the other, the slowly growing feeling that there was a directedness and purpose to be perceived through consciousness itself. Poe's emphasis on the diffused, subjective nature of sensation and hence of our overall experience of reality corresponds to the dominant current of anecdotal realism operating during the middle of the nineteenth century, culminating in the retinal realism of the French Impressionists of the 1870's.

It is significant that not only was Western art being dominated by a subjective aesthetic of anecdotal realism, often of a very sentimental kind, but a similar aesthetic had developed in Japan. Concurrent with the rise of industrialism, a school of Japanese woodblock artists including Utamaro, Hokusai, and Hiroshige presented their varied impressions of the "floating world," the literal meaning of Ukiyo-e. These artists represented something of a deviation—both social and psychological—from traditional Japanese values. Though landscape and genre, as they would be called in the West, had been part of the Japanese tradition from the time of Sesshu (1420–1506), the philosophical and spiritual attitude permeating the art of Sesshu was no longer the motivating force for the artists of Ukiyo-e. The difference paralleled the shift in Western art during the same period, though nowhere was it as marked as in the West. The art of Sesshu is the art of Zen Buddhism; the depiction of landscape and mundane "objects" had the profound purpose of revealing nirvana through the most minutely *samsaric* or mundune aspects of the everyday world of nature; in short, its purpose was to reveal the immortal through the mortal, "infinity in a grain of sand."

In the art of Ukiyo-e, though this sublime intent may sometimes be the underlying motive, what is basically manifest is the floating world in its pure, individually subjective, samsaric aspects, unredeemed by the nirvanic vision. Whereas the art of Sesshu is imbued with a religious or transcendental sense of awe, that of the Ukiyo-e is magnificently secular. It is important, too, to recall that the most famous of the later Japanese landscape artists of the Ukiyo-e school, Hiroshige and Hokusai, were influenced by the copper plate engravings of the Dutch seventeenth-century landscape school—the most secular, perspectivally precise, and optically realistic school of Western art until the rise of Impressionism in the second half of the nineteenth century. Thus the triumph of the Ukiyo-e, the art of pure samsara, in the early nineteenth century foretold the forthcoming Westernization and secularization of Japanese culture. In the dialectic of consciousness, and in tune with the global dialectic, Ukiyo-e artists signaled the dissolution of the traditional symbols and archetypes of Japanese culture and the beginning of a phase of subjective individualism—what Poe might have called the Social Diffusion of the Divine Self.

It is no surprise that when Japan was reopened to the West in 1868, the samsaric vision of Ukiyo-e had an immediate impact on leading Western artists. The art of the Japanese print provided the perfect reinforcement for the retreat into personal subjectivity that had been initiated by the triumph of the camera. Artists like Edouard Manet, Edgar Degas, Claude Monet, and James A. M. Whistler were the immediate inheritors of the Ukiyo-e tradition; it was with this generation of artists in the 1860's and 70's that there emerged in the modern West an aperspectival art of pure subjectivism —not as an isolated phenomenon, as in the case of a singular visionary like William Blake, but as a collective response to the psychological fragmentation that had come to characterize mid-nineteenth-century culture.

The personal subjectivism of the Western inheritors of Ukiyo-e was scientifically confirmed in the 1860's by the development of *psychophysics* and the new psychology of the "unconscious." In addition to Hartmann's *Philosophy of the Unconscious,* two other works were instrumental in redefining the psychological direction of the avant-garde in the later nineteenth century: Gustave Fechner's monumental *Elements of Psychophysics* (1860–61) and H. Von Helmholtz's classic *Physiological Optics* (1855–66). The significance of the development of a psychophysical science in the mid-nineteenth century cannot be overestimated. In the first place, as the term implies, the original intention of this "new" science, according to its founder, Fechner, was to investigate "the relation of body and mind." This was as vital a departure from the classic Cartesian assumption as any in orthodox science since the seventeenth century, for it indicated a rapprochement between body and mind, which orthodox science had considered absolutely separate. It is from psychophysics as conceived by Fechner that all modern psychology stems, for it was psychophysics that made possible a scientific consideration of the mind. The immediate effect of psychophysics on nineteenth-century thought and culture was to shift the emphasis of research—scientific and artistic—from a consideration of reality as something external to the perceiver to a consideration of reality as represented by the sensations and perceptions of the perceiver. Though psychophysics tended to become more concerned with the correlation of "objective data" in the twentieth century, its fundamental premises were adopted by certain quantum physicists and the Jungian school of psychologists. Significantly, the Western psychophysical premise is similar to the classic Buddhist approach, which, in the words of Lama Govinda, "does not inquire into the essence of matter, but only into the essence of the sense perceptions which create in us the idea of matter."[12]

This point of view, supplemented by the research of men like Helmholtz into the nature and function of the sense organs, created an entirely new basis for evaluating reality. Naturally enough, it was the artistic right-hemisphere of consciousness that first tuned into the new science and translated it into a cultural vision. Thus psychophysics laid the philosophical and experimental foundation for what came to be called Impressionism. Its specific contribution was the reduction of the essence of knowable reality to sense impressions. This approach, visually validated by time photography, suggested that reality was indeed a series of discrete psychophysiological impressions, and that it is only by mental conceptualization that the idea of a concrete object comes into existence. The mental concept itself is subject to social or cultural distortion, thus throwing the meaning of "objective" reality entirely open to question. More broadly, psychophysics vindicated a widespread subjectivism, promoting a disquieting sense of personal and cultural anarchy among the artistic avant-garde.

The impact of this general turn of events was felt quite immediately, and one should add, quite unconsciously by certain artists. For the first time since seventeenth-century Dutch art, painting became purely and even radically optical. In Monet's paintings, for instance, the subject matter is actually the optical or retinal impression made on the artist. Psychophysics also gave the avant-garde a rationale for doing away with the Renaissance perceptual mode, for if the optical impression is all that really matters, then a linear, perspectival mode becomes an artificial encumbrance on the visual process. With the abandonment of perspective—reinforced by the influence of the relatively aperspectival Japanese print—the main prop of European vision was removed. The social consequences of this perceptual alteration were of the greatest magnitude, especially since society as a whole continued unconsciously to adhere to the Renaissance model. As more and more artists adopted the subjective, retinal, aperspectival model of vision, the friction between the artistic avant-garde and the rest of society increased. In one sense, it was as though the artists, beginning with the Impressionists, literally retracted the perspective mode, and made vision once again not a social convention but a matter of personal inclination. Cerebrally this approach represented a retreat of right-hemisphere functions from the restrictive domain of rationalism into intuition's homeground.

According to the model presented by Poe in *Eureka*, Impressionism represents a rebound at the periphery. At one level it signifies the maximum diffusion of light, which is the same as the maximum densification of matter, deep within which occurs, as if by preordained necessity, the return of the vital motivating force once again toward the center. At another level it symbolizes the maximum extension of consciousness in the "sea of materialism" and a turning around in the deepest seat of consciousness, so that, at least at a level of collective unconscious expression, the impelling force of human events is once again directed toward the central source-light. It may seem outlandish to attribute such far-reaching implications to Impressionism and psychophysics. Yet in nature as well as in human psychological development, the most momentous changes often have the most obscure and unlikely origins. The pulse of the world and the texture of human consciousness are remarkably interwoven; thus with Impressionism, what began as a revolution of the eye was in the end a revolution of the mind.

In the 1860's the work of artists like Manet and Degas, both academically trained, began to exhibit a fragmented and detached anecdotalism inspired by the random anonymity of the camera. It is because Manet had unconsciously absorbed and projected this technological innovation that there was such an outburst of rage over his paintings *Dejeuner sur l'herbe* (1863) and *Olympia* (1865). To present the female nude without the conventional cloak of sentimentality, as Manet had done, was immoral in the eyes of his contemporaries. That Manet himself felt some frustration at their failure to appreciate his work only emphasizes the unconsciousness of the process by which the new technology was manifested through his vision. Although Manet was academically trained, he had an open mind; thus before the end of the 1860's he had also begun to absorb the influence of the Ukiyo-e artists, with whom he must have felt a certain kinship. His painting *The Fifer* (1866), for instance, with its utter lack of background, may readily be compared with Hokusai's *A Courtesan*, which similarly presents a full-length figure on a neutral field. The influence of the Ukiyo-e on artists like Whistler and Degas was even more pronounced. The intimate scenes Degas made so famous derive directly from the work of artists like Utamaro, whose subjects included prostitutes brushing their teeth. In addition, the Ukiyo-e subjects were often presented in a bold aperspectival manner, yet with a convincing realism of detail and psychological nuance—a perfect formula for the searching eye of the Western artist still operating in a "realistic" mode. The anonymous yet unique perception of Degas was enhanced, of course, by his own first-hand experience as an amateur photographer, which accounts for the snapshot, candid-camera quality of his art.

The most outstanding quality of the Impressionist art that emerged in the 1870's, however, was its fidelity to sense impressions. The pioneer in this realm was Claude Monet, who had little academic training and who developed the famous Impressionist technique of using small, rapidly placed, "broken" brush strokes—a technique that was simultaneously style and subject matter as well. It was this breakthrough of Monet's that at last literally dissolved the Renaissance perception. The hard world of outlines and preconceived forms whose colors generally had no correspondence with retinal reality was replaced by the diffused, subjective vision of pure optical impression. The visual experience was plunged into a world of spectrally pure, scintillating colors *that could take form only in the mind of the beholder.* The simultaneous dissolution of form (and by extension, perspective) and the creation of a world of radiant color at least partially cleansed the doors of perception. After centuries of static form, the luminous, irradiative nature of reality began to reveal itself in all its splendor. Both the technique and the subject matter of the Impressionists correspond to the expansiveness of Poe's primordial Being: "an infinite Self-Diffusion in which His life is felt as an infinity of imperfect pleasures, partial and pain-intertangled." This is an equally perfect description of the Buddhist notion of samsara, which the floating world of Impressionism so vividly represents in a flickering series of half-images, sparkling at times with a color that has all the deceptive freshness of a bright summer day.

If photography had "captured" light, then the Impressionists "released" it. The genius of Impressionism, corroborated by the new science of psychophysics, lay in the realization that it is not form but light and color that have a primary effect upon the retina. Form is a mental construct dependent upon cultural conditioning, and hence a secondary attribute of our experience. An artist like Monet was a radical because he leaped beyond the conventional way of seeing. For Monet before a tree was a tree, that is, a preconceived form, it was a very particular retinal irritation. Only afterwards would he say that he had seen a tree. So accustomed was he to experiencing in the Impressionist way that when his wife died, he found himself unable to break his fascination at observing the subtle color changes occurring in her face.

Just as photography had showed up the artificiality of the Renaissance perceptual mode, Impressionism demonstrated the arbitrariness of our conceptual conventions. For this reason Impressionism was initially greeted by public outrage. At the first Impressionist exhibition in 1874, one critic said of Monet's painting *Impression: Sunrise* that wallpaper in its embryonic state "looked more finished." To the conventional mind painterly finish, which meant well outlined form, was equated with sanity; but in fact, it indicates a profound metaphysical insecurity that compels us to imprison experience in fixed forms. Impressionism followed no aesthetic or moral precept but pure vision; if pure vision as the Impressionists rendered it revealed no-thing, neither did it attempt to conceal anything. Thus what the academic traditionalist considered the comparative garishness and crudity of Impressionist painting actually reflected the emptiness of contemporary intellectual and moral beliefs. Just as form had been decomposed once again into evanescent light and color, a kaleidoscope of transient sensations and perceptions, so consciousness itself was shown to be no less fleeting. This truth may be easy enough for a Buddhist to accept, but for a culture trained to believe in the hardness of facts, the imperturbable opacity of matter, and the durability of the personal ego, the implications of Impressionism were most difficult to accept.

CHAPTER FOURTEEN

The Establishment of the Avant-Garde:
The Fugitive and the Real

THOUGH IMPRESSIONISM as a social force was transient in nature, its cultural influence was without parallel. By the 1860's the final conditions for the unique appearance of Impressionism had fallen into place: the Renaissance system of academic art was exhausted; the mechanized vision of photography was being absorbed into European perception; urbanization, with its alienating social consequences, was continuing its irreversible thrust; and non-European perceptual modes, as exemplified by the Japanese print, had made their first formative impact on the West. These forces combined to produce an alienated but elitist avant-garde devoted to the pursuit of art for its own sake. The 1870's witnessed the full-scale appearance of the elitist avant-garde as a response to the decadence of official art. In true counter-culture fashion, and following the isolated example of the earlier *salons des refusés*, the group later to be known as the Impressionists began to hold salons of their own beginning in 1874, the eighth and last being held in 1886. The Impressionist exhibitions were actually a step toward the formation of an institutionalized counter-cultural salon, the Salon des Indépendants, which began in 1886 with the final absorption of Impressionism into the burgeoning avant-garde. By the 1880's the Impressionist revolution had been assimilated, and the avant-garde was well on its way to replacing official culture.

But what is the avant-garde*? It is a social institution peculiar to technological society, predicated on the progressivist notion that reality must always be updated. Though setting itself apart from the social mainstream in an often aloof or even antagonistic manner, avant-garde culture is actually the purest reflection of a society neurotically trying to stay one step ahead of itself. Planned obsolescence in industry and military armaments has its counterpart in planned cultural obsolescence, the basic premise of avant-gardism: what was in style last season is out of style this season. Though this attitude was not dominant in the avant-garde of the nineteenth century, with the growing success of avant-garde art (dependent upon the decline of official academic culture) it soon came to the fore. Cultural obsolescence was largely brought about by the great economic

---

*Though now identified almost exclusively with artistic endeavors, "avant-garde" was originally a military term, referring to the foremost attacking position of an army or a naval fleet. In this respect, the very foundation of avant-garde culture is war; when art is war, war itself must be no different than art. The avant-garde artist and the military general—two mirrors of the same schizophrenic truth!

rewards capitalist society could bestow, however arbitrarily, on the avant-garde artist. The paintings that were derided by official society in 1874 were bringing astronomical prices on the art market within fifty years. The avant-garde artist, though his behavior and values were often overtly antisocial, unwittingly played into the hands of a society that could devour him because it fundamentally had no values at all—except the value placed on turning a profit. As long as works of art could be bought and sold for profit, however misunderstood they might be and however contrary the value system of the artists who produced them, they would be appropriated by the Western market economy and used for its own purposes. In the end the avant-garde artist could only submit to this process, thus invalidating for the most part whatever redeeming insight his alienated social position might afford, for even alienation was given a price, and absorbed by the amoeba-like Moloch of a "free" society.

As the first conscientious group of avant-garde artists, the Impressionists reflected the laissez-faire values of market society in the uncontrolled individualism of their personalities and in the overriding value they placed on the personal uniqueness of their vision. This lack of restraint, which they interpreted as artistic freedom, had a disruptive effect on the Impressionists as a group. But in all fairness it must be said that they never formally thought of themselves as a group, having been brought together more by destiny and social conditions than by common aesthetic interest.

What is interesting about the Impressionists is that though they displayed a generally elitist attitude regarding the "sanctity" of their art, with the exception of a few, like Camille Pissarro, they tended to have conventional social attitudes. Degas was almost a royalist; Manet tended to be politically conservative; Monet, politically indifferent; and Renoir, blatantly bourgeois. Yet there can be no doubt that collectively, the art of these men devastated the bourgeois values of the prevailing art system—though it must be admitted that the academic system had already lost its vitality. While reopening the sensibilities to the nuances of light and color and an appreciation of the everyday world of the bourgeoisie, the triumph of Impressionism in the 1880's also helped eliminate the hypocrisy of veiling contemporary values in an anachronistic Greco-Roman mythology. In this respect, Impressionism represented the triumph of bourgeois realism—that is, the triumph of the utterly profane. In their insistence on a purely materialistic (though anarchically subjective) view of reality, the Impressionists were really affirming the deepest values of bourgeois/capitalist society.

But because society's acceptance of these artists had to be grudging, there was an underlying bitterness to their lives; like it or not, they were all engaged in a struggle to survive. How cruel it must have seemed to be rejected for offering society a fresh, realistic view of itself. A society unwilling to view itself as it was could only be considered hypocritical and corrupt—a conclusion that intensified the latent antisocial feelings lurking within even the more politically conservative of the avant-garde artists of the 1870's and 80's. These feelings could only contribute to the risqué life-style of the avant-garde artist, which eventually provided grist for the popular fantasy world of the novel, and later, cinema and television. Murger's *La Vie bohème*, and in the time of the Impressionists, Zola's *L'Ouevre*, provided fictitious accounts that the bourgeois imagination, already passively uncreative, could sentimentalize and use to project vicariously its own repressed functions. The avant-garde artist was ultimately but a source of entertainment to a mass of people among whom the wellsprings of creativity had long since dried up.

In fact, with the rise of the professional avant-garde, which left creative activity in the hands of a few alienated and willful men and women, society had finally and irrevocably abdicated its commitment to the imagination— that is, its commitment to the intuitive functions of the right hemisphere. Although the academic system supported by the state was withering away, there was obviously no measure taken to give official social sanction to the new kind of art. The avant-garde came to be tolerated in time, but it remained without social support of any organized kind. For that matter, except for having a kind of collectively negative social identification, the avant-garde remained a loosely knit social group that never united itself with regard either to social purpose or to a unifying aesthetic. This lack of cohesiveness tended to justify the withholding of official social sanction, for society naturally hesitated to finance a group of artists that presented such a bewildering array of styles and behavior.

It has been scarcely one hundred years since the first Impressionist exhibition in 1874—a brief enough period as far as human history is concerned, yet a period in which the grudgingly tolerated avant-garde has turned into an unofficial institution. The risky—and risqué—life-style associated with the Impressionist painters, their anarchic individualism, and their lack of a guiding aesthetic have become what society expects of its artists. If there is not a bit of sensationalism to an artist's personality, his work is apt to be considered stale. The aesthetic standards of newness and originality, augmented by an art historic self-consciousness that abhors "repeating" the past, but does not hesitate "reshaping" it, has tended to replace the original Impressionist notion of fidelity to one's own sense experience.

Yet Impressionism itself *was* new and unique; that later artists could not sustain or misconstrued the imperative the Impressionists felt is not the Impressionists' fault. The only genuine lesson to be drawn from the behavior and art of the Impressionists is that of responding creatively to the uniqueness of one's environment. It was a decadent society's simultaneous fear of and repressed hunger for authentic creative existence that made Impressionism into a sentimentalized rhapsody of *la vie bohème* and created the expectation that all artists would be similarly inclined. In time society compensated for the avant-garde's arbitrary aesthetic standards by choosing to be equally as arbitrary in deciding which artists to reward, preferably posthumously.

Naturally enough, being forced to fend for themselves, the Impressionists created a support system that was to become the model of the conventional avant-garde for the next one hundred years. This system comprises six basic parts: the artist and his work; the critic/man of letters, who interprets the artist to the audience and vice versa; the specialized avant-garde journal supplemented by the sensationalism of the popular media; the gallery that purveys the artist's work on the open market; the patron who by his shrewdness and sense of publicity can ensure the success of an artist or even an entire style or "school"; and finally the museum, the ultimate repository of cultural values. Though this system was embryonic in the time of the Impressionists, by the mid-twentieth century it had become the only system for the visual arts in free-market societies from Tokyo to New York, from São Paulo to Rome.

It is obvious that under this support system aesthetic intention would finally be subordinated to a value system stressing personal fortune, ambition, and above all, ingenuity. Whereas for the Impressionists their support system was incidental to the artist's vision, at present it is a primary determining factor in the artist's life and work. As in any other bureaucratic system, in the present permutation of the avant-garde, vision is subordinate to procedure; this is the reverse of the original intent of the Impressionists for whom vision determined procedure. Yet the artists of later generations— especially the post-Impressionist generation—cannot be faulted for institutionalizing the expedient support system brought into focus by the Impressionist imperative; no matter how alienated, the majority of the avant-garde artists were not and have not been out-and-out social revolutionaries.

In addition to the creation of a neo-academic avant-garde, beneath the cloak of endless "isms," is the abortive attempt of various artists to form their own utopian unions, or guilds.

In discussing the formation of the avant-garde system at the time of the Impressionists, I have left out one significant feature: the education of the artist. At the time of the Impressionists, and even for a generation or two afterward, a number of artists—Manet, Degas, Seurat, Matisse—were still reacting to the academic system. Yet another, more significant, group—Monet, van Gogh, Signac, and Gauguin, among others—had almost no academic training; their example prevailed, and with the final dissolution of the academic system after World War I, there remained no authoritative method for training artists. The market-society value of free-dom *for* self-expression had triumphed absolutely, and the gates were opened to a flood of endless experimentation, chaos, innovation, and anarchy—a primal reflection of the deeper psychic state of the Western mind.

The value attached to "freedom *for*" without an authoritative system to act as a guide led ultimately to a gross libertinism, sexual and otherwise. Though free-market values are at the heart of Western society, when these values are applied in the sphere of creative expression, society is vulnerable in the extreme; either it becomes subject to an increasing flaunting of its own pretended morality, or it must take a more dictatorial stance repug-nant to its most fundamental ideals. The present-day problems of pornog-raphy and blatant antisocial expressions of various kinds are only two aspects of the larger problem of espousing "freedom *for*" without a univer-sal ground of behavior. The avant-garde assault on all values was uncon-sciously furthered by a society that had lapsed into an unprecedented state of technically refined barbarism: one of the proliferating post-Impressionist artistic groups in Paris in the 1880's even called itself the "decadents." By such examples the artists powerfully demonstrated through their own elitism that alienating professionalism is itself a perver-sion and the curse of industrial society.

Just as the exigencies of purveying their art created the present-day institution of the avant-garde, so the Impressionists' life-style has become the model for laissez-faire man. One of the professed goals of industrial society is to provide more leisure time for everyone; but even with the help of our wholesale gadgetry, most citizens of the industrial state find that their leisure time is confined to evenings and weekends. Ironically, it is the alienated artist, following the example of the Impressionists, who alone seems to live the *leisure-full* life idealized by industrial society. Manet's depiction of Monet painting in his boat floating idly down sparkling waters of the Seine; Renoir's vision of shadow-dappled dancers and drinkers en-joying themselves by the riverside; and even Degas' impressions of the racetrack, the night-café, and the rather sordid absinthe drinkers all em-phasize a life-style far removed from the compulsive work ethic of bourgeois society.

It was only natural that an art based on the increased and renewed pleasures of retinal stimulation would turn to the pleasures of life for its basic subject matter. The Impressionists' concern with purity of experience and, in the cases of Monet, Renoir, and Pissarro in the 1870's, their out-right refusal to work in a studio, enhanced their involvement with the passing scene. Thus we imagine the artist meeting friends in cafés, sketch-ing on the sidewalk or the riverbank, mingling with the crowd, befriending prostitutes, working at his own leisurely pace—quite the contrary of the proper bourgeois existence. Yet the artist is not necessarily free to choose this existence, for in our society it is part of his social role. The avant-garde artist must be something of a renegade to satisfy society's repressed creative yearnings, which manifest as psychosocial fantasies, a love-hate relationship that flared into a white-hot intensity during the First World War before lapsing into another aspect of the decadent status-quo.

Because of the avant-garde artist's alienated position, the role of the modern critic had to be evolved. From the beginnings of the humanist period in the sixteenth century, there existed a literary/critical intermediary essential to the artist. Within the academic system this arrangement was tacitly understood, and in the eighteenth century under the aegis of a growing connoisseurship, men like Diderot, the Comte de Caylus, and even Lessing and Winckelmann carried out the legitimate function of describing, explaining, ascribing historical pedigree to, and criticizing visual art. The rise of Romanticism and the concurrent development of mass-media techniques, especially journalism, helped create a more specialized form of criticism and paved the way for the modern professional critic whose task is essentially to explain the artist's work to the interested public and to prescribe new directions or ideas to the artist, much as the classic humanist patron once did. By the mid-nineteenth century literary figures like Ruskin in England and Baudelaire in France had a strong influence in setting the tone for the visual arts. Ruskin acted as critical intermediary for Turner and later the Pre-Raphaelites in England, and Baudelaire did the same for Delacroix, Romanticism, and generally all of the anti-academic trends in the visual arts. In a similar vein, Emile Zola championed the Impressionist painters in the 1860's and 70's, and Félix Fénéon, the Neo-Impressionists in the 1880's.

Once avant-gardism had become the established cultural norm, the specialized critic—whether of art, music, literature, or film—became a permanent fixture. But the critic's established place within our culture ensured that avant-gardism would remain beyond the grasp of the masses, for along with it came the specialized vocabulary and tone of authority that inevitably mystify and intimidate the culturally uninitiated. These were compounded by the generally antisocial sentiment that pervades avant-gardism like a deadly perfume—at times intoxicating but ultimately stultifying. The critical function perpetuates the elitist status that Leonardo and Michelangelo had helped create for European art in the sixteenth century, even in the case of movements like Impressionism, which was essentially nonelitist—a judgment borne out by the popularity of Impressionist art. Ironically, this "populist" art ultimately became the pawn of capitalist millionaires, for today the biggest buyers of what remains of Impressionist art are Japanese capitalists. The floating world has come full circle.

For Emile Zola, the art of Manet and later the Impressionists was direct, realistic, and unmystifying—precisely what the hypocritical bourgeoisie did not want to see, and hence viewed as socialistic or just plain debased. The close and necessary relationship of avant-garde artist and critic is exemplified in the 1869 *Portrait of Zola* by Manet. Zola, the man of letters, is seated at his writing desk; behind him are two keys: the *Olympia*, Manet's *succès de scandale*, which Zola praised and defended; and a portion of a large Japanese screen, cut off, of course, in the "Japanese manner," and indicating the importance of non-European and consequently non-rationalist values to the artistic avant-garde. Of his role as critic of the avant-garde, Zola remarked: "People write me that I praise the 'painting-of-the-future!' I do not know what this expression is supposed to mean. I believe that every genius is born independent and leaves no disciples. The painting of the future worries me little; it will be what the society and the artists of the future make of it."[1] Had it been his intention, Zola could not have offered a more precise characterization of the "painting-of-the-future," with its emphasis on *genius, independence*, and lack of tradition ("no disciples"). His comment renders perfectly the personality of the avant-garde artist: willful, clever, scornful of what he understands as tradition, a figure living at the fringes of society. But this antitraditional attitude became a tradition itself: the tradition of the avant-garde.

We can now briefly summarize the psycho-social implications of Impressionism's development. By the mid-1860's social vision had reached a dead end, and a small group of artists rather unconsciously went about cleansing the doors of perception. In the 1870's a few chinks of prismatic light landed on the European consciousness. But society and artist alike tended to focus on the pattern where the light fell rather than on the source of the light. The significance of Impressionist art is not in the novelty of retinal stimulation through a technique of broken brush stroke and prismatic color, or in focusing on the everyday, which is charming enough, but rather in the *possibility* of seeing and *seeking* anew what has always been. However, the Impressionists themselves—Degas, Renoir, Monet, Pissarro, Cézanne—once having found a new vision, tended to work over and stylize it for the rest of their lives, rather than continue the search. Though Monet and Cézanne especially painted quite unique visions in their isolated later years, these, too, tended to be stylizations of a fragmented sensibility reflecting as much the laissez-faire values of defiant independence and tenacity as a continually seeking and transforming spirit. Monet's water-lilies and Cézanne's paintings of Mt.-St. Victoire are magnificent studies of the disintegrating sensibility. Faced with an incomprehensible social reality, these men understandably chose to remove themselves from the mainstream and remain faithful to their own retinal impressions. If their vision was limited, at least it was honest. But to a great degree the impressionists had ceased to search and had become satisfied with *art*—and this is the great failure of the avant-garde in general.

The seed of Impressionism's crisis and downfall lay in the inherent contradiction between the ideal of fidelity to the fluid spontaneity of optical impressions and the impossibility of accurately rendering this spontaneity by the inherently cumbersome process of painting—even painting done *in situ*. The effects of this basic contradiction were intensified by the Impressionists' blind adherence to a realistic aesthetic—that is, an aesthetic in which the goal of visual art is somehow to match "outer" reality and "inner" power of expression. The Impressionists in this respect had reached the dead end of materialism; if material reality was seen finally, in the psychophysical vision, to be a fugitive, evanescent set of sensory vibrations, what really was the visual artist to paint, given the impossibility of reproducing the instantaneous? Even conventional photography was not quick enough to capture this reality. And yet, as the poet Jules Laforgue wrote in his remarkable 1883 essay, "Impressionism," there remains "the response of a certain unique sensibility to a moment which can never be reproduced."[2]

The problem facing the artist who had followed this train of thought in the 1880's was to understand and define for himself the nature of this subjective response, for it was this that would ultimately take form in his work. The very nature of the problem emphasizes the subjective and psychological nature of the aesthetic situation. What is real—certainly as real as the sensory experience—is the *mental image*. The great challenge in both aesthetics and psychology in the West since the end of the nineteenth century has been to discover the nature of the *mental image*—whether through the methods of behaviorism, which seeks to explain the mental image in physical terms, or through the analytical psychology of Jung, which assumes the fundamentally psychic nature of all reality. Through the problems which it attempted to solve, and those which it consequently raised Impressionism exemplifies the inexorable transformation of the materialistic viewpoint into the metaphysical, and the realm, however poorly understood, of the spiritual. The dialectical opposite of materialism had been achieved through the most thorough pursuit of the material.

This particularly striking development in Impressionism in the early 1880's parallels the shift from an essentially paleotechnic psycho-social condition, dominated by pre-electrical industrial processes, to the neotechnic era, in which the instantaneousness of electrical technology began to take effect. Already in 1864 Clerk-Maxwell had fully propounded his theory of electromagnetism; the decade of the 1870's saw a number of significant applications of electricity to technology: the electric steel furnace (1870), the electric car (1875), the electric telephone (1876), the microphone and phonograph (1877), the electric light and electric railroad (1879), and the electric elevator (1880). These inventions inaugurated the transition from the paleotechnic era to the neotechnic, corresponding approximately to the date 1883, the beginning of the eighth hell period of the Mexican calendar.

The alteration of sense-ratios induced by electrical technology is encapsulated in the transition from the materialistic but personally subjective art of Impressionism to the totally subjective and mentalistic art styles of the post-Impressionist period. What occurs at the psycho-social level in the neotechnic era is a vast outer ordering of reality—International Standard Time was settled upon in 1885, for instance—accompanied by an increasing and often chaotic subjectivity in the expressive realm of psyche: among artists, this results in further social alienation; among politicians, in a greater tendency to wage war; among the "masses," in a circus of illusions, as appetites are continually whetted without ever being fully satisfied through almost continual exposure to bombardment by various media. Through the efforts of entrepreneurs and engineers, material prosperity increases greatly. But it is only through a psychology of conflict that this affluence can be maintained.

While Europe was experiencing an increase in material productivity, the classical materialistic view of the world in the science of theoretical physics began to undergo a profound transformation and dematerialization, marked by such breakthroughs as the discovery of electromagnetic waves in 1887 and x-rays in 1895, and the development of Planck's quantum theorem in 1900. At a more popular level the process of dematerialization can be discerned in the development of the motion picture between 1882, with the first movie camera, and 1893, the date of the production of the first motion picture. Developments such as these led to a further disintegration of the materialistic view of the universe, though because of our continuing dependence upon a psycho-social materialism, the real psychological applications of quantum and relativity theory have yet to be made. Only in a few fringe areas of atomic physics and avant-garde art have there been genuine breakthroughs to an immaterialist or supermaterialist understanding of the universe.

One of these fringe areas was the point to which Impressionism ultimately led—that shimmering, vibrating realm where mind alone is left to consider the nature of reality as a function of its own creativity. Though the senses are stimulated by the external field of electromagnetic vibrations, it is up to the mind not only to compose these vibrations into forms and images, but to decide which forms and how to present them. The implication is that the formal or symbolic element exists independently of the electromagnetic stimulus, which merely draws forth particular forms or archetypes from the mind. Furthermore, these forms or archetypes precede social organization; that is, *they are inherent to the organism.* Social organization may either encourage or repress their expression through whatever medium, but it cannot do away with them. In any case the avant-garde artist of the 1880's was inevitably led to the realization of a more subtle, immaterialist reality. This realization could only be liberating in its effect, for it fully opened to the artist the inner landscape of the mind, which had been taboo or even declared nonexistent since the sixteenth century. Hesitantly and tentatively, a few of the artists of the 1880's— painters, writers, and musicians—entered this newly rediscovered domain.

When Laforgue declared in 1883, "The optical arts spring from the eye and solely from the eye. There do not exist anywhere in the world two eyes identical as organs or faculties,"[3] the subjectivist implication was clear. What the eye sees is not determined by the external world but by the psychological disposition of the viewer. Laforgue saw that psycho-social conditions favored the plunge into the vast, and for the Western mind, relatively unexplored regions of the inner landscape:

The atmosphere favorable to the freedom of this evolution [of the sensory organs] lies in the suppression of schools, juries, medals, . . . and in the encouragement of a nihilistic dilettantism and open-minded anarchy, like that which reigns among French artists today: *Laissez faire, laissez passer.* Law beyond human concerns must follow its automatic pattern, and the wind of the Unconscious must be free to blow where it will.[4]

The materialistic aesthetic and standard of reality had been exhausted, and there was yet no collective standard representing the immaterial world to which the artists had now been initiated. For this reason the post-materialistic mentality tended to be characterized—as it still is today—by Laforgue's nihilistic dilettantism and open-minded anarchy: a combination of pessimism, atheism, debauchery, and depravity—the petulant response of one who realizes that what he had believed to be the solid, real world is merely a dream.

This mentality is characteristic of all budding counter-cultural efforts—whether those of the Symbolists of the 1880's and 90's, the Expressionists and Cubists of the pre-World War I era, the Dadaists and Surrealists of the 1920's and 30's, the existentialists and beatniks of the 1940's and 50's, or the hippies of the 1960's. But there have been sporadic efforts and achievements that signify a deeper synthesis. In the Symbolist period, perhaps the most coherent expression of a deeper understanding was to be found in the paintings of Georges Seurat. Seurat's art is commonly thought of as being scientific in the positivist sense—an interpretation supported by the artist's own declaration, "Some say they see poetry in my painting; I see only science." But the science on which Seurat's art was based was not so much a positivist/materialist science as a purely transcendental interpretation of the psychophysical theories of Fechner and Helmholtz. Interestingly enough, the psychophysical research France had taken over from Germany and the United States resulted not in a positivist/scientific aesthetic but in a uniquely transcendental one. This development in France was due largely to the influence of a single figure, Charles Henry.

The combination of Henry's experimental psychophysical theory and Seurat's artistic sensibility resulted in a *conscious* form of Impressionism, historically known as Neo-Impressionism. It is the element of *consciousness*, and scientific conscientiousness, that distinguishes the art of Seurat from that of Monet. Indeed, Seurat's art represents an even broader synthesis because of the fact that he had acquired an academic training before turning to the Impressionist approach, to which he was introduced by the painter Paul Signac. But it remained for Henry, whom Seurat met sometime in 1884–85, to provide the key ingredient for the synthesis Seurat was attempting. On the one hand, Henry systematized the color theory that the Impressionists intuitively and unconsciously perceived; on the other, he presented a novel theory of form.

According to Henry, form is a mental abstraction visually represented by lines; and lines are a visual abstraction representing *directions* internally felt. Reality is nothing other than these *directions*, which are experienced as psychic impulses, moods, feelings and thoughts, and which may be reduced most fundamentally to feelings of pleasure and pain. The problem the artist must consider, then, is simply this: "Which are the agreeable directions? Which the disagreeable?" Or said in a different way, "which directions do we associate with pleasure, which with pain?"[5] Direction as psychic response and activity manifests as and is induced by not only line and color but taste, smell, hearing, bodily sensation, and mental perception. In other words, Henry's theory was universal and applicable to all forms of psychophysiological experience. Hence it provided the theoretical basis for a *synesthetic* approach to the arts, which held that not only could the different arts be harmonized but they could be combined to bring about in the human organism a correspondingly harmonizing and transcendental experience or ecstasy: Synesthesia. The ideal artist, aware of the primary psycho-sensory laws and the social ideal of collective well-being, is bound to the art of harmony, whose function is to create ever more expansive states of consciousness: in Henry's quasi-biological language, the social function of art is to *dynamogenize* (as opposed to inhibit) consciousness and to create a sense of continuity of behavior. "The agreeable or disagreeable action of living beings is nothing more than the continuity or discontinuity by which they realize themselves."[6]

The lofty social/aesthetic ideals presented by Henry were translated by Seurat into a number of paintings, the theme of which in the Impressionist manner is mundane pleasure. The most famous is *Sunday on the Isle of the Grande Jatte* (1886)—a utopian projection of idyllic states of mind, a harmonious translation of the proletarian weekend, what Seurat himself called his modern "panathenaic procession." Technically the work presents a thorough distillation of the "science" of color and form. The physiognomy of things has here been transformed into a definite synthesis and symbol of life-experience. Though forms are evident and contours seem clear and flowing, close inspection reveals that there is only a canvas covered with confetti-sized dots, the total sum of which denotes both the retinal vibration *and* the dematerialization of reality. Like light itself, according to the quantum theory, the image presented is both wave (illusion of contour forms/directions) and particle (the innumerable but precisely placed colored dots). As with life's own illusions, it is in the eye and mind of the beholder that color and form are united and the painting takes on meaning. Though the forms are clear, they seem weight-less, and the figures—each isolated from the others—seem to float in a dream-like calm. A hallucination could hardly be more exact, and though everything represented is temporal and precisely in the fashion of the mid-1880's, there is nothing accidental or transitory about the painting. In viewing the curiously clear but weightless forms of Seurat's vision, one may recall the famous words of the Prajnaparamita Sutra: "Form is emptiness, emptiness itself is form."[7] The synthesis of emptiness and form that gives Seurat's masterpiece its "unreal," dream-like quality is in actuality the very basis of the art of harmony: the union of opposites.

Georges Seurat died at the age of 31. His work stands as a notable attempt to create a synthesizing vision in a world consumed by materialistic passions. Without denying the world of the everyday, through his art Seurat was able to transform it. Yet it is questionable to what extent his art represents anything more than an idiosyncratic statement—a brilliant blind alley that in the hands of his followers led to another "ism." Already in 1886 the critic Félix Fénéon had christened Seurat, Signac, and even Camille Pissarro, who all used the systematic *pointillist* technique of uniformly placed colored dots, the Neo-Impressionists; Fénéon thus helped create another arbitrary category, a social fiction as it were. The very word "Neo-Impressionism" suggests a certain cool, calculated, intellectual approach to reality far removed from the spontaneity characteristic of Impressionism.

The leading artistic personality identified with Neo-Impressionism was not Seurat, who had little need of Neo-Impressionism, but Paul Signac. It was Signac, not Seurat, who rallied to Fénéon's concept of Neo-Impressionism and made it a social identity. With the cool and gifted genius of Seurat at its center, Signac as its dogged pusher, drawing freely from the theories of Henry, and Fénéon as its critic, Neo-Impressionism was an exemplary avant-garde movement. Self-consciously based on an earlier avant-garde tradition, applying a distinct artistic technique in the methodically divided brush stroke, based at least in part on a transcendentally scientific set of theories, its literature couched in a combination of quasi-scientific and mystical terms, and vehemently anti-establishment, even anarchistic and utopian, in its politics, Neo-Impressionism was a perfect modernist cultural phenomenon. Its limitation was in its highly cultivated self-consciousness, and especially in its tendency to insist on a particular technique—the divided brush stroke—as the sine qua non of visual art.

The death of Seurat in 1891 deprived Neo-Impressionism not only of its leader but of a luminary who was able to breathe life into theory and whose example inspired others to grow beyond their own self-perceptions. After Seurat's death, Signac modified the rigor of the divided brush stroke into a fashionable but arbitrary style of mosaic-like colors in paintings of equally fashionable seaside scenes. Attempting to justify intellectually his own development, in 1899 Signac published *From Delacroix to Neo-Impressionism,* an effort at providing an art-historical pedigree and aesthetic respectability to a particular artistic style that in the end was only a matter of personal sensibility and choice.

But Signac's effort is not to be faulted. The aesthetic principles of harmony as enunciated by Henry and practiced by Seurat are difficult to follow, for they demand a personal transcendence few are willing to make room for. Only under the direct guidance of Henry, and with Seurat's living example, was Signac able to produce the unique *Portrait of Félix Fénéon, Opus 217* (1891). The placement of the avant-garde critic, executed in pointillist naturalism, against a proto-psychedelic "background," only emphasizes the dialectical transformation that was occuring in the late nineteenth century from a materialistic to a psycho-spiritual point of view. Like so many other modernist works, the *Portrait of Fénéon* is but a signpost. Neither Seurat or Signac was ready to explore fully the mental landscape to which Henry's research had provided the key—the realm of the self-illumined, self-created mind.

In the Symbolist period of the late nineteenth century, only a maverick artist like Odilon Redon could have fully depicted the subjective universe which Neo-Impressionism only hinted at. Free from the politics and strivings of avant-garde ambition, Redon had little difficulty translating experience into channels flowing from deep within his own being. In a letter written in 1894 he stated, "The artist . . . will always be a special emissary—isolated, alone—with an innate sense for the organization of matter."[8] For Redon, it was clear that the organization of matter took place in the mind, flowing without cause or warning from the unconscious and the unknown. Apparently there were few barriers between his conscious existence and the tidal impulses of the psychic zones, for vision poured through Redon a semi-mythic rush of forms more suggestive of either the suboceanic realm or the far reaches of space than of everyday terrestrial existence. No visual artist but Redon could articulate the fantastic cosmic regions hinted at by Poe. In fact, it is in the lithographic series *Homage à Edgar Poe* (1882) that the interior spaces of the immaterial universe open up in unprecedented grandeur. The return journey from the periphery of matter suggested by Poe in *Eureka* is illustrated perfectly in the cyclopean vision *The Eye Like a Strange Balloon Moves Toward Infinity*. This image also conveys the sudden plunge inward caused by the psychophysical investigations of Impressionism, in which the examination of the external world finally runs its course and the veil of matter is penetrated. Another lithograph from the same series, *The Breath That Impels Beings Is Also in the Spheres*, is disquietingly prophetic, for though it dates from 1882 the image suggests the interior of a motion picture theater; on the screen appears a sudden glimpse of the eternal watcher, the witness who observes our every thought and action.

Though Redon might claim in the romantic tradition that the artist is always alone, it is clear from his vision that there is an abiding presence beyond the individuality of each person. In his solitary art the avant-garde with all its foibles and rhetoric is vindicated. The one hope for the artist forsaking the arid tradition of the Renaissance is to see clearly, and in seeing clearly to reveal the open way for all humanity.

CHAPTER FIFTEEN

The Outcast Vision: Van Gogh and Gauguin

PARIS IN in the 1880's was the capital of the world—an energy center through which the winds of the unconscious blew freely. Men and women from all over Europe and America congregated in the City of Light. Emancipated from the sterility of bourgeois existence, these cosmopolites formed a unique *corps d'esprit*. Ideas fermented and bubbled; lives acquired the potency of myth. For a brief, exalted moment the veil of materiality was penetrated, releasing a rush of symbols, a tangle of visions of biological immediacy and utopian urgency. Into this rich world came a Dutch exile from the stable provinces of reason, a onetime gospel preacher and art vendor, Vincent van Gogh. Self-taught, self-willed, trapped in the brutal competitive nets of a laissez-faire society, van Gogh pursued his dream to its bitter ultimatum, only to be exploited posthumously by an adoring bourgeoisie that would have detested him had he lived next door. More than any other figure, Vincent van Gogh—described by Antonin Artaud as the "artist suicided by society"—became the focus of the technological civilization's psychotic attitude toward creativity.

In modern society creativity must be harnessed to the acquisition of material power or to technological innovation if it is to be rewarded. Creativity that expresses fundamental truths, confronts the life-death interface, or explores the intangible dimensions of feeling, dream, and intuition is neglected, despised, and looked upon with suspicion. The educational apparatus of the modern state discourages the development of creativity to such a degree that what is inherently spontaneous and normal in every child has atrophied in all but a few by the age of ten or twelve. This select minority then must assume the creative responsibility of all members of society.

This situation was tolerable as long as the collective vision was clearly defined, as it was from the Renaissance until the mid-nineteenth century. But when the artists began to exhibit the same laissez-faire attitude in their life-style as the bourgeoisie exhibited in their economics, the relationship between artist and society altered drastically. The collective vision no longer clearly defined, society at first became confused, then finally turned away; the artist, lacking society's support, turned his back in defiance. For most avant-garde artists a somewhat antisocial posture became the norm accepted by both the artist and society, the result being that generally the artist was left to himself while society neglectfully rushed along its uncreative way. But from time to time there has appeared an artist who unconsciously draws forth the pent-up creativity of the masses. For him, life can become hell. Such was the fate of van Gogh, who exemplifies the modern artist suicided by society.

Van Gogh's career as an artist lasted less than a decade. The subjects of his paintings came directly from the facts of his own existence: women bowed down by the bags of coal they carried on their backs, textile weavers, potato eaters, Paris street scenes, the fields of southern France, the artist's chair, his bedroom, a field with a flock of crows flying above, and most significant, the series of tormented self-portraits displaying van Gogh's anguish, his narcissism, his paralyzing self-doubt and self-questioning. So driven and self-obsessed was this man that on being released from the hospital after he had cut off part of his right ear and sent it to a prostitute, he painted a self-portrait memorializing for all time this most telling act of his life. Yet this same self-portrait, depicting the artist in his most abject moment, hung for years on the wall of a steel entrepreneur's plush apartment high above Lake Michigan in Chicago.

It is something of an irony that van Gogh's art, which earned him nothing while he was alive, should be so popular after his death. At museum exhibits and art auctions, an adoring public pays homage to a man they never knew. That the personality and work of a single human being who died "insane," lacking love and social recognition, should be the object of so much fascination more than eighty years after his death gives mute and poignant testimony to the debased and vicarious channels creativity must resort to in an overindustrialized society. The ironies of posthumous market-value and blind collective adulation also reflect the misplaced guilt of a society that does not realize the extent of its own decadence. If we consider the actual values van Gogh lived by, we must conclude that the only way to atone for his suicide is to individually accept the responsibility to be creative ourselves.

"To sacrifice all personal desires, to realize great things, to obtain nobleness of mind, to surpass the vulgarity in which the existence of nearly all individuals is spent. . . ."[1] Quoting Renan, van Gogh wrote this credo in a letter to his brother toward the end of 1874. At that time he was the frustrated employee of a prominent Continental art dealer. In order to live out his ideal, van Gogh subsequently gave up the world of business and entered the ministry. Failing at an effort to become an orthodoxly trained and ordained minister, he became an evangelist among the coal miners of the Borinage in Belgium. Believing in the gospel of Christ, and living among the most wretched, debased workers of the industrial age, van Gogh gave away all he had in an effort to follow Christ's example. But to the exploited coal miners, the example of poverty was like a slap in the face. After a time he was dismissed for "excessive zeal." Van Gogh's deepest religious idealism having been thwarted by the salt of the earth, he turned at last to drawing and painting, hoping to achieve through art what could not be achieved through the living gospel. His zeal recalls Blake's pronouncement: "A Poet, a Painter, a Musician, an Architect: the Man or Woman who is not one of these is not a Christian."

Painting was the only form of worship left open to van Gogh; the altar was his own life. Furiously he delved within himself for a means of expressing the living truth, for there was no one to teach him, and the spiritual tradition he might have turned to had long since lost its vitality. By sheer force of will he slowly mastered the means necessary to convey his vision, but the energy mustered to achieve this goal was at the expense of all but the most basic survival needs. In order to be creative, van Gogh sacrificed all personal desires, but he received no guidance or reward in return. The end result was inevitable. After four emotionally abject though artistically productive years in Holland, from 1881 to 1885, he departed from his homeland for Paris, the City of Light. There his brother Theo introduced him to the new trends and the avant-garde artists, primarily the Impressionists and Neo-Impressionists. As a result van Gogh's power of expression was augmented by the radiant use of primary colors. But the city was a jungle for the emotionally unstable artist. Too sensitive to the gross materialism of the urban environment and the keen competition it fostered, van Gogh was seized by the industrial-age fantasy of return to the land. Coupled with his eccentric and indigenous mysticism was a longing to go beyond civilization, to surpass the vulgarity of modern industrial society.

Van Gogh's departure from civilization in 1888 was as symbolic as it was real. If Adam and Eve had been cast from the Garden, he would will himself back into it, and into the bosom of the Lord. The idea of mystic flight was to found a new society that would be fundamentally an "artist's colony," far from the taint of urbanization, where the pursuit of beauty could be sustained at a pace to match divine revelation. But the vision far outstripped the reality. Art made a poor foundation for a community, especially since in van Gogh's case it already served as a substitute for both God and lover. Van Gogh's art flowered in burning fields, sunflowers, cypresses, and starry nights, but banished from healthy human relations, the artist was to be sacrificed to the art. Artaud's epitaph for van Gogh—the artist suicided by society—is not quite right. Instead we should say *art suicided by society, the artist suicided by art.*

Less than a year after his arrival in Arles, van Gogh began to suffer from acute mental crises, including the infamous incident in which he cut off a slice of his ear. By the spring of 1889 the citizenry had requested that he be committed to a mental hospital. The next year or so, until his suicide in July 1890, was spent in the asylum at St. Rémy, and finally under the care of a Dr. Gachet in Auvers-sur Oise. The relationship with Dr. Gachet is interesting: it would seem that Gachet was far better suited to the career of a dilettante and art collector than to that of a physician. He seems to have been fascinated by the creative process (he was also a friend and collector of the work of another eccentric, Paul Cézanne) but incapable of understanding it as pathology. Perhaps like many of us today he assumed that there is something inherently strange about artists; perhaps he thought that they *must* suffer to be able to express so clearly what we only feel so inarticulately. Such assumptions range far from the truth, for it is our own unconscious and repressed creativity that we project upon the tormented artist.

In the earlier part of this century it was fashionable to try to diagnose van Gogh's illness: was it schizophrenia or paranoia? The answer to this question would tell us little, for fundamentally van Gogh's disease was not just a function of his own being, but a collective disorder focused through a single man. When a group of people abdicate their individual responsibility to be creative, a Vincent van Gogh is inevitable. His fate was inseparable from the industrial society of his time—and ours. "It certainly is a strange phenomenon that all the artists, poets, musicians, painters are unfortunate in material things—the happy ones as well, . ." van Gogh wrote to his brother in July 1888 from Arles.

That brings up again the eternal question: is the whole of life visible to us or isn't it rather that this side of death we see one hemisphere only? . . . For my own part, I declare I know nothing whatever about it, but to look at the stars always makes me dream, as simply as I dream over the black dots of a map representing towns and villages. Why, I ask myself, should the shining dots of the sky not be as accessible as the black dots on the map of France? If we take a train to get to Tarascon or Rouen, we take death to reach a star.[2]

Society's rejection of him enabled van Gogh to penetrate beyond his misery to a unique insight, but an insight he was incapable of translating into living knowledge. It is this discrepancy that gives such poignancy to his life. In August 1888 he wrote to his brother:

I always feel I am a traveller going somewhere and to some destination . . . If I tell myself that the somewhere and the destination do not exist, that seems very reasonable and likely enough, . . . so at the end of my course I shall find my mistake. Be it so. I shall find then that not only the Arts, but everything else as well, were only dreams, that one's self was nothing at all. If we are as *flimsy as that*, so much the better for us, for then there is nothing against the unlimited possibility of future existence. . . . A child in the cradle has the infinite in its eyes. In short I know nothing about it, but it is just the feeling of *not knowing* that makes the real life we are actually living now like a one-way journey in a train. You go fast but cannot distinguish any object, and above all, you do not see the engine.[3]

Often knowing little of these thoughts, present-day crowds file past exhibits of van Gogh's works in mute adoration, as if they were viewing the relics of a beloved religious master. The comparison is an apt one, for in a profound way van Gogh is like a modern Christ. He took the burden of the collective creative responsibility on himself so that others might see in his life what was lacking in their own. It is the tragedy of Christ that the masses have not taken up their own crosses and been reborn, but only worship at His cross. Likewise, rather than emulate van Gogh's creativity, the masses only worship what he produced. Not wanting to know, we separate again, and place on high in the altars of the museum, as if worship were atonement for ignorance.

"I am the light of the world, he that followeth me shall not walk in darkness, but shall have the light of life." The failure of Christian civilization—or any other—has been its inability to live by the example of its teachers. This failure has plunged us into the nightmare of "His-story"; instead of living Christ's story ourselves, we have others live it for us. Thus civilization must have its special personalities—the saints, the geniuses, the madmen. Our reliance on them to seek ultimate reality is necessitated by our own abdication of vision, of the creative powers, of the spiritually regenerating forces by which the individual alone might become not merely an animal or a good citizen—but a fully conscious being. Van Gogh realized this at the core of his being and attempted to live the imitation of Christ as few others have, but the redemption he sought first for others and then for himself was beyond his grasp. In leaving civilization he was attempting to leave history—and live "His-story." Though he made a copy of the *Pietà* of Delacroix, and of the *Lazarus* of Rembrandt, by and large van Gogh felt no need to paint biblical subjects. At the instigation of Gauguin he once painted the Agony of Christ in the Garden, but he later destroyed the work. His life painting in the olive groves outside the asylum of St. Rémy *was* the Agony in the Garden. And his Judas was history waiting for him to pull the trigger of the gun.

Van Gogh's sole comrade in flight from the disease and despair of urban culture was Paul Gauguin. Much has been made of the two artists' brief, violent sojourn in Arles culminating in the infamous ear episode. Later, in a letter written to Gauguin from the asylum, van Gogh declared, "How fortunate you are to be in Paris. That is where one finds the best doctors, and you certainly ought to consult a specialist to cure your madness. Aren't we all mad?"[4] Gauguin responded, typically; "The advice was good and that was why I didn't follow it,—from a spirit of contradiction, I daresay."[5]

Gauguin's life and work, like van Gogh's are surrounded by myth. The Gauguin myth is the aching fantasy of countless numbers chafing under the alienating boredom of bourgeois existence; their dream is to flee family and economic routine, to escape into a bohemian life free of bourgeois restrictions, to express uniquely their own vision of life, and finally, to flee civilization entirely, returning to the primordial mysteries and bounties of nature. The myth, like all modern myths, corresponds to a psychological reality, and says as much about those who cherish it as it does about those who are presumed to be its cause. The myth will persist as long as the conditions that give rise to it: alienated labor, wage-slavery, compulsive materialism, the deadening of innate sensibility and individual will to expression by the great artificial construct we call civilization. And occasionally there will appear a figure like Gauguin, in whom is perceived, or rather, on whom is *projected* the virtue of having dared to defy the system. If van Gogh lived in the spirit of Christ, Gauguin lived in the spirit of pure contradiction. But like all contradictions, those in the restless course of Gauguin's life meandered toward resolution.

With Gauguin, the spirit of contradiction was present from the beginning. He was born in 1848, a year of widespread revolution in Europe. On his mother's side he was not European but of aristocratic Peruvian descent. While Gauguin was still very young his father, who opposed the rise of Napoleon III, took the family to Peru. As a result, some of Gauguin's earliest memories relate to the exotic, non-European ambience of Peru, a land of lost kingdoms bathed by the warm waters of the South Pacific. Here lay the germ of his singular love for the exotic and the primitive. Gauguin returned to France with his family at the age of seven, but his contacts with exotic realms were renewed at the age of seventeen, when he sailed around the world as an apprentice pilot in the merchant marine. Through family influence he eventually acquired a job as a stock broker and with his Danish wife, Mette, settled into an upper-middle-class existence. It was toward 1872–73 that he began painting on Sundays. His unusual intelligence and sensibility drew him to the Impressionist exhibits in the middle and late 1870's, and he even began to collect paintings by some of the Impressionist artists. In 1883 he left his job and his family to devote himself totally to his life as an artist.

It is a curious indictment of civilization that one can rarely support oneself with dignity and be creative at the same time. By Gauguin's time the split between creativity and *living* had become so profound as to be taken for granted. We tend to assume that some people are creative and some are not, whereas creativity is a universal quality. In fact, the original meaning of the word *create* is *to cause to grow*. The relation between creativity and living is nothing less than the relation between life and growth. Cut off from growth, life *is* death; cut off from life, growth becomes cancer. In these terms life without creative involvement is death; art—or any technique—that exists for itself alone is a cancer upon life. The artist pursuing the course of art unrelated to the process of living can only create a caricature of life. This is the dilemma faced by the modern artist, like Gauguin, who considers himself responsible only to his art. The way out is inevitably tied to the way one finally chooses to respond to civilization itself, for in a fundamental way the root of the dilemma *is* civilization.

By civilization I mean that which has literally been citified—a highly evolved state of social/technical refinement and development. If human existence itself poses the problem of suffering and death, civilization compounds the problem by pretending that it has been solved, or even worse, that it never existed in the first place. The author of this deception is man's own cleverness, which allows him to specialize at the expense of his fundamental openness. But specialization is simply the triumph of techne over psyche. Thus it is that in the advanced stages of urbanization—the present civilization being the most advanced so far—*means*, including all of the various arts, sciences, and technical skills, are taken as ends. The advanced development of such techniques tends to create increasingly isolated, though no less devastating, problems that can be "solved" only by further refinement of the techniques that created them. At this stage it becomes almost impossible to experience the wholeness of existence because there is no time and no preparation to deal with life except in fragments. The pursuit of art for its own sake exemplifies civilization's fragmenting effects. But if the artist chooses to define his or her destiny in terms of the conscious relation he or she may have to civilization as a whole, then the artist may be able to avoid the pitfalls of art-for-art's-sake and contribute to the greater development of the transformative vision. Such was Gauguin's achievement.

For twenty years, from 1883 until his death in 1903, Gauguin was to engage in a creative dialogue that put him in touch with humanity's most fundamental energies and ideas. From 1883 until 1891 he concentrated on perfecting his expressive means. Impressionism was almost a matter of history by this time; beyond it lay the gulf of the fantastic. The European consciousness having been partially cleansed by the Impressionist vision, much that had lain dormant within it for centuries now began to stir and move out into the open. With industrialism solidly entrenched and electricity making its initial impact, the quasi-Buddhist philosophy of Schopenhauer, which emphasized the subjective nature of our experience of the world, was very much in vogue, offering as it did a spiritual balm to the dazed senses of the refined urban citizen. The dizzying course of material progress either overwhelmed or intoxicated: its artistic reflection was either the science-fiction vision of Jules Verne and the urban realism of Zola, Dickens, and Degas, or the interior journeys of the Comte de Lautréamont, Baudelaire, and Rimbaud, and the dream-visions of Odilon Redon. The world was suddenly too real, too present, too gross; its heaviness pressed on the brain. As the pressure intensified, the walls of reason and common sense began to tumble down, revealing what seemed to be a new vision. In the 1880's this "new vision" thrust itself forth as the Symbolist movement, a cultural force that was to prevail until shortly before the First World War.

Symbolism was a radically transcendental aesthetic and philosophy based on three principles: the law of correspondences—as above, so below; psychophysical harmony, represented by the union of mind and body; and the equivalence of sensory experiences, or synesthesia. It was also a resurfacing of the primary ideas of the alchemical tradition, which had been submerged since the early eighteenth century. Fundamental to the alchemical tradition is the notion of the "great work," the transformation of consciousness through a directed use and understanding of the forces one has available. In these terms the work of art is not only an external object created by a certain learned technique, but an integral and integrating psychophysical process that weds intelligence and feeling, sensation and intuition into a fully realized whole that can be expressed outwardly through *symbols*. What we commonly call the work of art, then, is but the outer symbol of a profound psychological process.

Gauguin, who along with Charles Henry, Georges Seurat, and Stéphane Mallarmé was one of the most articulate Symbolist pioneers, set forth the Symbolist aesthetic in an amazing letter to his friend Emile Schuffenecker, written January 14, 1885:

As for myself, it seems to me at the moment that I am mad, and yet the more I brood at night in bed, the more I think I am right. For a long time philosophers have reasoned about phenomena which appear to us supernatural, and of which however we have the *sensation*. Everything is there, in this word—Raphael and others, people in whom sensation was formulated before the mind started to operate, which enabled them while pursuing their studies, to keep this feeling intact, and to remain an artist. And for me the great artist is synonymous with the greatest intelligence; he is the vehicle of the most delicate, the most invisible emotions of the brain.

Look around at the immense creation of nature and you will find laws, unlike in their aspect and yet alike in their effect, which generate all human emotions. Look at a great spider, a tree trunk in a forest—both arouse strong feeling, without your knowing why. Why is it you shrink from touching a rat, and many similar things; no amount of reasoning can conjure away these feelings. All our five senses reach the brain *directly*, affected by a multiplicity of things which no education can destroy. Whence I conclude there are lines that are noble and lines that are false. The straight line reaches to infinity, the curve limits creation, without reckoning the fatality of numbers. Have the numbers 3 and 7 been sufficiently discussed? Colors, although less numerous than lines, are still explicative by virtue of their potent influence on the eye. There are noble sounds, others that are vulgar; peaceful and consoling harmonies, others that provoke by their audacity. You will find in graphology the traits of candid men and those of liars; why should not colors and lines reveal also the more or less grand character of the artist? . . . The farther I go into the question—the translation of thought into a medium other than literature—the more I am convinced of my theory. . . . The equilateral triangle is the most firmly based and the perfect triangle. A long triangle is more elegant. We say lines to the right advance, those to the left retreat. The right hand strikes, the left defends.[6]

The art Gauguin created by these aesthetic principles departed more and more radically from both the conventional academic realism and the relatively naturalistic technique of the Impressionists. As his forms and colors became simpler and more icon-like, his subjects began to acquire a more archetypal quality. Tempered by his exposure to the folk art of Brittany as well as the exotic, non-European arts displayed at the 1889 Universal Exposition—pre-Columbian, Peruvian, Indian, Far Eastern, and Javanese —Gauguin's art centered on two great themes: human love and the expression of the divine. Through the intertwining of these two themes Gauguin was able to heal himself of the dividing dis-ease of civilization, which had set flesh against spirit. But sensing that civilization as he knew it would never be able to heal itself of this madness, Gauguin at last in 1891 left Europe, having long since begun to steer his consciousness toward other gods and other climes.

If there was any Christianity remaining in him it was the most primitive and personal kind, exemplified in the famous *Yellow Christ* (1889). But to go back to a primary Christianity was not enough; Gauguin had to take the passage to India, the passage to primal thought more universal than Christianity. For Gauguin the mystery of the suffering Christ and the anguished, neurotic love that underlay the edifice of European civilization began to resolve itself in a twofold revelation. The first aspect of this revelation was that he himself was Adam/Christ, exemplified in the self-portrait with the apples (1889) and the self-portrait-like image of *The Agony of Christ in the Garden* (1889), a subject Gauguin had also persuaded van Gogh to paint. The second aspect of his revelation was the discovery of religions and cultures older and/or more comprehensive than Christianity and the philosophies of modern Europe. The foremost of these was Buddhism.

The impact of Buddhism was strongly felt among the Symbolists, owing to the activity of the Theosophical Society, which had opened an office in Paris in 1883. Soon thereafter a number of publications on Buddhism and the neo-Buddhist teachings of the Theosophical Society appeared. Gauguin apparently gave himself freely to learning about the oriental religion, and he reached a broad understanding of it. This is apparent in the curious 1890 painting *Nirvana—Portrait of Meyer de Haan,* in which the themes of love and divinity are combined. In the foreground is the hunchbacked, dwarflike Dutch painter de Haan, something of a contemplative mystic, with a serpent writhing in his hand; to his left is the word *Nirvana*. Behind de Haan are two female bathers, gesturing as if in anguish. This work represents the relation between the round of birth and death, or samsara, neurotic love and desire, represented by the bathers, and the release from this round, nirvana, represented by de Haan. The serpent leading from the hand of the Dutch painter to the bathers is both the serpent of temptation in Christian symbolism and the serpent of spiritual conquest, the *naga*, in Buddhist symbolism. Perhaps what attracted Gauguin most to Buddhism and the primitive world in general was that their frank recognition of human suffering is not at all tragic, as Christianity and Faustian civilization so obviously are. Instead, the Buddhist teachings and the primitive way of life as Gauguin imagined it emphasized serenity, liberation, and wholeness of being.

What Gauguin sought when he departed for Oceania in 1891 was the inevitable conclusion to an authentic pursuit of the Symbolist aesthetic: a life in which the creation of beauty was inseparable from the acceptance of the human body as a manifestation of the divine. To say that Gauguin was deluded in thinking that he would find the Garden of Eden in the South Pacific and that therefore his venture was a failure is an oversimplification. Certainly it is true that he found the same corruptions of civilization in colonial government and the Christian missionaries, against whom he railed in various tracts and a satirical journal, Le Sourire. It is also true that his life was not without its bitterness, so clearly expressed in Intimate Journals and in his attempted suicide of 1897. Yet these facts should not detract from the quality of his vision and the particular truth it reveals.

If Gauguin was motivated by a disgust for civilization, he was also motivated by a perception that is the very core of the transformative vision: he saw the evolutionary need to renew the human spirit, fearlessly and uncompromisingly. Gauguin's expression of this vision was universal in the fullest sense of the word; his life in Oceania was a living marriage of heaven and hell, a marriage of Buddhist philosophy with a primitive way of life. In a passage describing the scope and intensity of his spiritual convictions in Noa Noa, his account of Polynesian life and religion, Gauguin tells of a vision on the beach:

On the purple soil long serpentine leaves of a metallic yellow make me think of a mysterious sacred writing of the ancient Orient. They distinctly form the sacred word of Oceanian origin, ATUA (God), the Taäta or Takata or Tathagatha, who ruled throughout all the Indies. And there came to my mind like a mystic counsel, in harmony with my beautiful solitude and my beautiful poverty, the words of the sage:

> In the eyes of Tathagatha, the magnificence and splendor of kings and their
> ministers are no more than spittle and dust;
> In his eyes the purity and impurity are like the dance of the six nagas;
> In his eyes the seeking for the sight of the Buddha is like unto flowers.[7]

In embracing the Buddhist vision Gauguin was both rejecting European civilization and transcending it, as he reveals in a passage describing his thoughts while chopping down a tree:

It was not the tree I was striking, it was not it which I sought to overcome. And yet gladly would I have heard the sound of my ax against other trunks when this one was already lying on the ground. And here is what my ax seemed to say to me in the cadence of its sounding blows:

Strike down to the root the forest entire!
Destroy all the forest of evil,
whose seeds were once sowed within thee by the breathings of death!
Destroy in thee all love of self!
Destroy and tear out all evil, as in the autumn we cut with the hand the
flower of the lotus.
Yes, wholly destroyed, finished, dead is from now on the old civilization
within me. I was reborn; or rather another man, purer and stronger,
came to life within me.[8]

Gauguin's Buddhist views found expression in a woodcut of the Buddha meditating (1895) and a number of sculptures in wood and native materials—shell, bone, and the like—that combine Buddhist and Oceanic motifs. These sculptures reveal the degree to which Gauguin had immersed himself in Buddhist and Polynesian culture. In Gauguin's vision Buddha, the Oceanic gods, and even Christ mingle in harmony. Perhaps the most striking example of this synthesis is a wood cylinder sculpture, on the front and back of which are fused an image of the Crucifixion and a Polynesian sacrificial victim, while on either side are depicted Gauguin's own head, hands, and feet. All of the various symbols are woven together with Oceanic design, symbolic writing, and scroll work. The whole is like a ritual war club, but in this case the warrior is a seeker of wisdom, singlehandedly attempting a spiritual reunion of diverse planetary ways and beliefs.

All of the gods live within; to create is to see a living god and project it outwardly. This was the spirit that animated Gauguin and gave him faith when so much conspired against him, not the least of which was official Christianity. Thus he wrote in 1903:

In the twentieth century, the Catholic Church is a rich church that has seized upon all the philosophical texts in order to distort them, and Hell prevails. The Word remains. Nothing of this Word is dead. The Vedas, Brahma, Buddha, Moses, Israel, Greek philosophy, Confucius, the Gospel, all exist. Without a single tear, without any monopolistic association, Science and Reason have alone preserved the tradition: outside the Church.[9]

By "Science" Gauguin meant innate wisdom; by "Reason," the innate ability to know. Gauguin's spiritual vision included the most universal aspects of existence, circumscribed by love. Like the Buddhist, his vision was a blend of wisdom, or insight, and compassion, or love, a genuine feeling for the "beauty that is personal—the only beauty that is human." Gauguin's religious impulse encompassed not only mankind but all life on earth. Of his Tahitian paintings he declared that he was "seeking to express the harmony between human life and that of animals and plants in compositions in which I allowed the deep voice of the earth to play an important part."[10]

Gauguin's Polynesian painting and sculpture is dominated by the veneration of the feminine principle, which is manifested in the primordial powers of earth, moon, and night, and in the non-European prelogical and alogical mind. To this aspect of Gauguin's vision we may attribute his presentation of Eve, the eternally feminine, Tahitian beauties on the beach, the mysteries revealed through the flesh, the Oceanic virgins tending their Polynesian Christs, the spirit of the dead watching. Gauguin's vision of woman is whole in both spirit and flesh, a striking contrast to the modern ideal, which converted the medieval Madonna into the dynamo, the object of blind sexual adoration. "Thanks to our cinctures and corsets we have succeeded in making an artificial being out of woman," Gauguin wrote in *Noa Noa*.

She is an anomaly, and Nature herself, obedient to the laws of heredity, aids us in complicating and enervating her. We carefully keep her in a state of nervous weakness and muscular inferiority, and in guarding her from fatigue, we take away from her possibilities of development. Thus, modelled on a bizarre ideal of slenderness to which, strangely enough, we continue to adhere, our women have nothing in common with us, and this, perhaps, may not be without grave moral and social disadvantages.[11]

In contrast to this civilized tendency, Gauguin observed, the Tahitian sexes regarded each other more as equals, engaging in the same tasks, both equally exposed to the same sun, the same hardships. "There is something virile in the women," he wrote, "and something feminine in the men."

This similarity of the sexes makes their relations the easier. Their continual state of nakedness has kept their minds free from the dangerous preoccupation with the "mystery" and from the excessive stress which among civilized people is laid upon the "happy accident" and the clandestine and sadistic colors of love. It has given their manners a natural innocence, a perfect purity. Man and woman are comrades, friends rather than lovers, dwelling together almost without cease, in pain as in pleasure, and even the very idea of vice is unknown to them.[12]

In an image defying every European aesthetic and moral convention, Gauguin depicted a man and woman in the act of love. Their bodies are placed in the center of a flower; from its stem appear not leaves but hands. Gauguin's vision of the sexes as the primary principles *Taaroa*—male, soul, intelligence—and *Hina*—moon, matter, body—is analogous to the ancient Chinese concept of yin and yang. All change springs from the interaction of *Taaroa* and *Hina*, and all things partake of them in varying degrees. Gauguin's image recalls as well the Tantric symbolism common to both India and Tibet. In Tibetan Tantra one of the most primary symbols is the *yabyum*, the father-mother union in sexual embrace, expressive of the unity of matter and spirit, mind and body. The image of sexual union Gauguin perceived in Oceanic theology was the union of opposites that his contradictory spirit had so restlessly sought. The dual themes of Gauguin's work had finally revealed themselves as one: love *is* the expression of divine nature.

Paul Gauguin spent his last days in Atuana, in the isle of Hiva-Oa in the Marquesas. Fully aware of the decline and impotence of the Polynesian civilization, and of the powerful, spreading grip of European civilization, he continued his creative activity to the end. His house and its furnishings were of his own construction. For him, life and creativity had finally merged. Over the entry to his last dwelling were carved the words "House of Pleasure"; the door was flanked by the images of two primordial Eves; on the ground to either side of the door lay two panels. The left panel had inscribed on it "Be mysterious"; the right, "Be in love and you will be happy." Throughout his self-created environment images of the gods and the spirits prevailed. What van Gogh had not been able to achieve in the asylum, Gauguin achieved in the South Seas. The divine prerogative of creativity had been exercised to the fullest, but only at the immense cost of family harmony and economic security.

Naturally the outcast vision of Gauguin, like that of van Gogh, has found its way back to the museums of Europe and America, where it is conventionally enshrined. The Polynesians are now a part of world culture, and tourists may easily pick and poke about the places where Gauguin lived and worked. Unconsciously and often unaware of his example, a few others may attempt to eject themselves from civilization. But it is now too late; there is no place to go that is uncontaminated, and in any case Gauguin's journey to the South Seas is not important of itself. To label his venture an escapade in primitivism is to hide the truth in romance or to obscure it by polite intellectual categorization. No, the sole import of Gauguin's flight is the immensity of transformation which it forebodes.

CHAPTER SIXTEEN

Abstraction and the Techno-Environment

BY 1883, when Gauguin left job and family for the life of an artist, the first fully technological phase of history—the paleotechnic era—had been completed. Full-scale mechanization and the demands generated by total industrialization had become irreversible and fantastically sophisticated. The vision of the world and nature that had sustained European culture since the Renaissance could no longer withstand the sensory and psychic impact of industrialization. The collective effect was the derangement of the psychosensory system. For most this was countered by retreat into a mental shelter composed of a handful of state-generated platitudes. Though academic culture was formally in a state of collapse, it would continue to live on in the universities. More disintegrated, the pre-industrial mentality would nonetheless survive in the collective psyche of the masses and find distorted expression in the sentimentality perpetrated by the new media of the phonograph, film, and radio, which were developed to considerable technical sophistication between 1883 and 1935, and television, which came later. These and other electronic inventions—the telephone, the electric light, the tape recorder and the computer—were to become the major shapers of the techno-environment in the second technological phase, the neotechnic era, which commenced around 1883—the era of not only the phonograph, the motion picture camera, and the radio, but the dirigible balloon, the high-speed gasoline engine, and the steel-frame skyscraper.

What was left of traditional, pretechnological culture after 1883—the avant-garde—engaged in a series of experiments that took advantage of the contemporary psychosensory disintegration and at the same time created visions and values that both mirrored and looked beyond the reality of the new, all-encompassing, and artificial techno-environment. During the period 1883-1935, a leading group of artists struggled toward and finally achieved an authentic expression of the new environment: abstraction, or abstract art.

As a quality of consciousness, abstraction is peculiarly modern. Abstraction literally means *to pull away from, to remove from*. That modern man has uprooted himself from the direct experience of nature through the process of urbanization constitutes the primary level of his abstraction. A secondary level of abstraction results from mechanization, the purely sequential as opposed to the simultaneous ordering of reality. As such, mechanization is a separative process that in the human organism destroys the unity of the senses. A third level of abstraction is brought about by the proliferation of the electronic media into a technological environment that pulls sensory experience away from the body. Marshall McLuhan has called media the *extensions* of man's sense organs; they are the sense organs abstracted from their native state. The abstracting effects of media would not be so devastating if there were a common philosophy relating the variety of experiences occuring through the extended sense organs, but there is not.

"Je *est* un autre,"—"I *is* another"—is the phrase Rimbaud used to describe the alienation caused by the abstraction of experience from any common denominator or center. Modern man has become a pawn of the techno-environment. He is bombarded by *media events*, and he has already become so conditioned to them that his responses are automatic. As in a bad dream, everything in the techno-environment takes on the quality of an uncontrolled and uncontrollable hallucination; because it is so difficult to discern reality through the media-maze, no event is without its sinister and foreboding quality. Paranoia comes to dominate the psychic atmosphere. "All media exist to invest our lives with artificial perception and arbitrary values."[1] McLuhan's simple declaration conceals the void within the vortex. Our condition is pure abstraction, the supreme conquest of technique.

The origins of abstract art go back to the Symbolist period of the 1880's and the various efforts at creating an art that would *evoke* reality rather than *imitate* it. From this common source abstract art flowed into two different streams: *non-naturalistic* art and *nonrepresentational* art. Nonnaturalistic merely means that a thing is not depicted according to the way it actually looks, as it might appear in a photograph, but it may be depicted *symbolically*. Nonrepresentational implies that meaning is intrinsic to the formal or coloristic elements of a thing, and that there are no other points of reference. The latter stream finally prevailed, for it most closely corresponds to our abstracted mental condition. But it was not until just before the First World War that the two streams could even be distinguished.

During the period between 1883 and 1914 there occurred the most profound and far-reaching cultural revolution since the Renaissance. Freed from the strictures of academic rules in every realm of human expression, artists began to fashion the aesthetic of modernism in which sensual and intellectual anarchy were given every possible outlet. Following the initial impetus of Symbolism, artistic experiments were dominated by a tendency toward the exaggeration of representational form and toward the expression of neurotic impulses. The art of Edvard Munch is a prime example. Here the repressed Victorian sexuality oozes forth in a series of images that are hauntingly morbid, sadistic, and anxiety-provoking. Woman is revealed in her abject state as sexual object, and some of Munch's work gives the impression that the woman's plight has even worse ramifications for the man, particularly the artist himself. Munch's art is the perfect accompaniment to the theories of Sigmund Freud, which began to appear in the 1890's. Significantly, Munch underwent years of psychoanalysis. His treatment however diminished his powers as an artist; though he continued painting after his analysis, his work was generally undistinguished. This fact feeds the myth that creative originality is necessarily tied to neurotic behavior. What is more likely in Munch's case is that in remedying his neurosis, analysis also covered up the creative wellsprings which the artist and the therapist undoubtedly confused with obsessive sexuality.

An exacerbated sexuality is a natural consequence of the abstracting effect of unbridled mechanization on the human organism. The more sex is abstracted from consciousness, the more neurotic and full of conflict is man's attitude toward the world. To the abstracted, technologized mind, sex is an aspect of the unknowable psyche; hence it is worthless except as a meaningless titillation, an unconscious channel for the release of unused aggressive energy. Around the turn of the century certain avant-garde artists saw in this very same aggressive, neurotic energy a fundamental resource for their art. In fact, the entire phenomenon known as Expressionism draws to a great degree on this kind of energy for its content and form. The Expressionists consciously used repressed emotion to distort the traditional perception of form and evoke a generally disquieting mood. Formally, Expressionism is a kind of abstraction, especially since it represents a defiant turn away from the belabored naturalism that had come to characterize all of academic and even much of Symbolist art. Yet efforts by artists like the Fauves (1905) and the German Brücke group (1906) to break away radically from the academic forms were undermined in the end by the lack of a coherent and positive spiritual base. Conscious of this deficiency, the Brücke painters—Emile Nolde, Kirchner, Paula Modersohn-Becker— conceived of themselves essentially as a *bridge* (the literal meaning of Brücke) to the future. Some of the neurotic energy that was collectively unleashed in their painting was redeemed by a teleological faith in the purpose of suffering.

In Brücke art, which owes much to Gauguin, the abstraction of form is carried out with particular zeal; the best examples approach the quality of children's art. Precisely this quality exasperated the bourgeoisie. Accustomed to the refined technical virtuosities of the Renaissance tradition, they were unprepared to accept, for instance, Modersohn-Becker's portrait of the poet Rainer Maria Rilke (1906) as anything but a bad joke. Yet by the simplification of form the artist was able to achieve a psychological effect that was absent in the traditional academic genre of portraiture: the painting directly foretells and evokes rather than describes. But most significant in the childlike abstractions of the Brücke artists is the immanent sense of barbarism and destruction—a sense that could only make the bourgeoisie all the more anxious as their world was about to be jolted and destroyed by the insanity of the First World War. During that war Rilke wrote, "Only through one of the greatest and innermost renovations it has ever gone through will the world be able to save and maintain itself."[2] In a similar vein, just after the war he defined the task of the artist and intellectual: "to prepare in men's hearts the way for those gentle, mysterious, trembling transformations, from which alone the understandings and harmonies of a serener future will proceed."[3]

But Rilke's message was for the few. To be sure, the call for transformation was heard and even paid a kind of political lip service by other artists, whose economic insecurity made them more receptive to change than the bourgeoisie might have been. But at the turn of the century the typical avant-garde artist's real interests lay elsewhere. Disenchanted with academicism and caught up in the neo-progressive, art-historical belief that each artist must advance beyond the efforts of his predecessors, artists individually concentrated their energies not on preparing men's hearts for transformation but on developing a style they could be identified with. In this respect the careers of the elder Impressionists were seen as an example to be emulated. The psychophysical revolution Impressionism had once represented now tended to be forgotten, while the success of individual Impressionist painters at winning recognition on the finicky marketplace of taste was increasingly admired. It should be recalled that Degas, Renoir, and Monet all lived well into the twentieth century, each pursuing the vision-become-style he had first developed in the 1860's and 1870's. The work of these artists eventually settled into a kind of familiar and even pretty anecdotalism, and the technique of Impressionism ensured them a certain popularity, especially since so many other artists in the eyes of the public had stopped concerning themselves with beauty. Other artists like Bonnard, Vuillard, and Signac followed suit. Of the first-generation Impressionists who pursued an individual style, Paul Cézanne stood out. He was selected by the new avant-garde as their progenitor, and down to the present he has been canonized as "the father of modern art."

Gauguin described Cézanne as "an essentially mystic Eastern nature" who in order to pursue his own "little sensation" of things left Paris to return to his birthplace in the South of France, Aix-en-Provence. There he worked out his own style, which drew its content solely from his visual sensation of his environment—whether his studio or the surrounding countryside. In this sense he was the purest Impressionist. As late as 1896 he wrote, "At the present time I am still searching for the expression of those confused sensations that we bring with us at birth. If I die everything will be over, but what does it matter?"[4] Because of his strict adherence to his own sensations he was hailed by certain artists early in the century as the paragon of the Western tradition of *pure* painting. But though Cézanne's art is distinctly sensuous, it is also characterized by a typically modern intellectuality, which emphasizes the intellectual perception of material objects. Cézanne's now famous injunction "Treat nature by the cylinder, the sphere and the cone," has become one of the principle doctrines of abstraction. Abstract art, however, has no necessary correspondence to photographable reality; its meaning is intrinsic. Cézanne's art clearly is based upon nature, so-called outer reality—mountains, apples, tables and chairs—but only as a pretext. As Cézanne himself wrote, "To achieve progress nature alone counts, and the eye is trained through contact with her. It becomes concentric by looking and working."[5] What is important is the concentricity of the eye and not the roundness of the orange at which it is looking. Thus in Cézanne's paintings what appears as a mountain is really a series of retinal planes and light vibrations *abstracted* from the object, mountain.

Like his hermetic life-style, the art of Cézanne is curiously closed and aloof. As later art theorists would maintain, it is a paradigm of reality and not an imitation of it. Such was Cézanne's personal vision. But that it should be taken by later artists and critics as the cue for an entirely new theory *and* history of art presents an interesting study in values. It is clear that the reason Cézanne's art came to be so highly regarded was that in a time of disintegrating values and sheer cultural anarchy, it exemplified a *purist* approach. As such it represented the final cleavage between creativity and life: autonomous art, art that had no standard to meet but its own, art that revealed nothing but itself, art-for-art's sake. The old academy of Renaissance masters had finally died, but a new academy had come into being, with Cézanne as its first old master.

The intellectual materialism implicit in the art of Cézanne received its official baptism in the outrageous birth of Cubism toward 1909. If Cézanne is considered the father of modern art, Cubism is generally considered the fountainhead of modernism. What had been the outcome of a semiconscious struggle for Cézanne emerged as a fully self-conscious doctrine with Cubism. Like Cézanne's art, Cubist art retains some semblance of the object that provided a pretext for the painting. But the painting is consciously conceived as an independent entity; it is the object per se. Though this idea was not new with Cubism—it dates to 1890—the Cubists were the first to realize its full potential. For them, all other aspects of the creative act were secondary to creating a unique and autonomous material object, a "work of art." The calculated and abstractly intellectual nature of this kind of art is revealed by Picasso's famous statement, "I paint things as I think of them, not as I see them." Cubism had the effect of isolating the material object of art from the psychophysical processes that brought it into being, as well as the cultural ambience in which the object existed.

As modernism developed from the Cubist premise of the autonomous work of art, whether abstract or not, the entire artistic endeavor was reduced to a circular process with a gradually shrinking radius. The artist's sole purpose ultimately was to make objects—or events—isolated from all nonaesthetic concerns. Art of whatever medium, style, or genre became an intellectual, hermetic, sign pointing to itself—the theater, the museum, the concert hall of the absurd. Thus whether modernist art is stylistically abstract or not, it is utterly abstracted from the concerns of life. Like the technocratic state itself, modernist art is life-denying. Because the modernist aesthetic is so intellectually arbitrary and fundamentally meaningless, it is the perfect aesthetic for the neotechnic era. The monumentally proportioned, technically perfect nonrepresentational painting or sculpture one so often encounters in the monolithic office buildings of our times is absolutely appropriate as something of a punctuation mark. It asks only that you pause before it and recognize it as *a painting* or *a sculpture.* It is just that and no more: a pure piece of existence abstracted from life, its meaning no more significant than the meaning of a wall or an elevator door.

Though the Cubists and Picasso were instrumental in providing the aesthetic base and psychological attitude that were to dominate the later phases of modernism, they were not the actual originators of abstract art. Essentially it was only *after* the impact of Cubism had been absorbed that abstract art in the usual sense of the term appeared—a strictly nonrepresentational art whose intellectual and affective content depends solely on intrinsic form. We must remember also that in some non-European cultures a work of art may be non-naturalistic or may contain many geometric or biomorphic elements, and yet have a meaning radiating beyond its simple materiality. In fact a great prepondernace of works from other cultures may strike us as being fundamentally abstract, as they did Picasso; but few of these objects would have been made for their own sake, and hence they are not abstract "works of art" in the sense I have been discussing. The placement of artifacts in museums only heightens the illusion of their autonomy, regardless of cultural intention.

Whereas the prevailing theory and practice of abstract art is life-denying, the first great collective impulse toward formal abstraction, Art Nouveau, was primarily life-enhancing, for it sprang from motives other than purely aesthetic or art-historical ones. Art Nouveau was a direct response to the psychological effects of the industrial environment. Its antecedent was the so-called Arts-and-Crafts Movement, which originated in England in the latter part of the nineteenth century, nurtured by the mystically sensitive but somewhat backward-looking philosophy of John Ruskin and the Pre-Raphaelite painters, and the more potent and practical thought of William Morris. The simple aim of this "movement" was to sustain and wherever necessary revive the pretechnological craft culture. Ruskin and Morris were aware that their efforts involved not just a material tradition of handicrafts but an entire psychological condition; their concern, in fact, was nothing less than the survival of the human spirit, which they felt was being rapidly and ruthlessly crushed to death by industrialism. But the revival of the craft tradition had also to contend with industrialism's strange twin, the fine arts, which had parted company with the crafts during the Renaissance. Morris spoke of this division in his first public lecture, "Innate Socialism," given in 1878:

Yet in my own mind I cannot quite sever [architecture, painting, and sculpture] from those so-called lesser, Decorative Arts, which I have to speak about: it is only in latter times, and under the most intricate conditions of life, that they have fallen apart from one another; and I hold that, when they are so parted, it is ill for the Arts altogether: the lesser ones become trivial, mechanical, unintelligent, incapable of resisting the changes pressed upon them by fashion or dishonesty; while the greater, however they may be practiced for a while by men of great minds and wonder-working hands, unhelped by the lesser, unhelped by each other, are sure to lose their dignity of popular arts, and become nothing but dull adjuncts to unmeaning pomp, or ingenious toys for a few rich and idle men.[6]

Speaking more specifically of decoration, he added:

Now it is one of the chief uses of decoration, the chief part of its alliance with nature, that it has to sharpen our dulled senses in this matter: for this end are those wonders of intricate patterns interwoven, those strange forms invented, which men have so long delighted in: forms and intricacies that do not necessarily imitate nature, but in which the hand of the craftsman is guided to work in the way that she does, till the web, the cup, or the knife, look as natural, nay as lovely as the green field, the river bank, or the mountain flint.[7]

Owing in part to the foundation laid by Morris and the Arts-and-Crafts Movement, Art Nouveau was a popular, even anonymous development. It seems suddenly to have appeared around 1890, and with the advent of Cubism in 1908, it just as suddenly died away. Its influence on the arts was universal, though painting did not assimilate it as readily as other media. As a style its prime content was a pulsing, undulating, biological mysticism. In the language of Charles Henry, its sinuosity burst into a profusion of *dynamogenous* forms. Though abstract and non-naturalistic, it was biologically evocative and psychically stimulating. The success the Art Nouveau style attained in all of the "Minor" arts could only have goaded the avant-garde artist into more daring attempts at abstraction. But there was an inherent contradiction between the idea of Art Nouveau and the fine-arts aesthetic of the avant-garde painter. Art Nouveau demanded a total environment in which the least detail was coordinated with the whole. The avant-garde or fine-arts painter was accustomed to executing easel paintings independent of any environment. Easel painting, like concert-hall musical performances, came to be regarded by some as an aspect of the basic problem, rampant individualism. Thus Henry van de Velde, who created one of the first examples of abstract art, *Abstract Composition*

(1890), gave up easel painting soon thereafter. His comments conerning the alienation of the art object have as much validity today as they did then:

Little by little I came to the conclusion that the reason why the fine arts had fallen into such a lamentable state of decay was they were being more and more exploited by self-interest or prostituted to the satisfaction of human vanity. In the form of "easel pictures" and salon statuary, both were now being executed as often as not without the least regard to their eventual destination, as with any other kind of consumer goods.[8]

Like Gauguin in his last years, van de Velde devoted the rest of his life to designing an *environment* that would lead to a healthier and more balanced way of life. Owing in large degree to van de Velde's influence, the most noteworthy achievements of Art Nouveau lie in the realm of architecture, understood as a fully environmental art. The ideas propounded by van de Velde, one of the chief spokesmen of Art Nouveau, have their origin in the fecund doctrine of Charles Henry. The bio-aesthetic theories of Henry, so influential on Seurat and Post-Impressionism in general, must also be considered both the theoretical base of the first wave of abstract art and the foundation of a psycho-environmental art that is yet to be perfected. According to Henry's psychophysical aesthetic, *abstraction* is an inherent organic tendency synonymous with *symbolizing* or *synthesizing*. Experience is continually being translated, usually unconsciously, into inwardly realized directions or tendencies. Since *direction* is a psychic propensity, art becomes the exteriorization of psychic states according to the laws by which primary responses are either gay or sad, agreeable or disagreeable, beautiful or ugly, and conducive to either pleasure or pain.

An important aspect of Henry's theory was his observation that simple nonrepresentative lines, forms, or colors by themselves can induce a particular psychic state. More significant, however, was his formulation of the complex process of perception into several simple propositions. The most fundamental of these is the law of simultaneous contrast, which states that every direction simultaneously evokes its complement. What this means is that for any given experience we may have, we also experience, at least unconsciously, its opposite. For example, if we gaze at a red object for a few seconds, we shall see a green object when we look away. This occurs because as opposites, these colors are mutually defining; the one color cannot exist without the other. This analogy carries through to the most complex experiences that we have, and ultimately to the nature of consciousness itself. In other words, consciousness can be defined as the comprehensively perceived pattern of the mutual interaction of the various forces of the universe whose minimal sum is two. Whereas the Renaissance vision emphasizes experience as *successive events*—the narrative-historical point of view—the psychophysical vision emphasizes experience as *simultaneity*—the mandalic-cyclical point of view. The former is characterized by a linear particularity; the latter, by a circular totality.

Integrated with simultaneous contrast are two other inherent psychosensory functions: rhythm, the sense of periodicity; and measure, the sense of fullness or wholeness. These three principles—contrast, rhythm, and measure—are most easily perceived in the experience of music. Distinct from literature and the visual arts, music after the Renaissance maintained a much clearer relation to the inherent psychosensory laws, at least until the onset of the Romantic period. Many of the painters of the Post-Impressionist period were quick to intuitively perceive the "abstract" purely psychosensory qualities of music and sought to make the visual arts equally abstract.

Two other fundamental functions Henry perceived were those of continuity and discontinuity. Continuity describes the fundamental ground of being; discontinuity characterizes experience when continuity is no longer a consciously perceived quality of being. The highest function of art in this sense is to reestablish biopsychic continuity. Expression that enhances this effort is *dynamogenous;* expression that opposes it is *inhibitory.* Since the purest expression of continuity is a circle, or through time, a cycle, the most dynamogenous modes of expression will manifest primarily as circular or cyclical forms. Inhibitory modes of expression will manifest as linear, broken, static forms. In these terms art may be defined as a biopsychological function that may either enhance or inhibit consciousness. Since there is a universal tendency, however imperceptible, toward life—and at a primary biological level, toward light—the predominant evolutionary tendency is to dynamogenize, to expand, to become more open. The function of art especially in modern society, may then be likened to the function of therapy: to "bring forth conscious processes where there were once unconscious impulses, and [restore] the organism to a state of harmonious self-regulation."[9] In the psychophysical view, the task of art is inseparable from the attainment of expanded consciousness—the attainment of biopsychic self-regulation—resulting in the coordination of individual and social reality with the cosmic whole.

What Henry had accomplished by 1926, the year of his death, was the articulation of a new paradigm of knowledge in which successiveness was superseded by simultaneity, particularity by totality, linearity by cyclical function, individual neurosis and social disorder by aesthetic coordination, and unconscious impulses by human self-control.

The first attempts at translating this new paradigm into concrete terms resulted in what is now commonly referred to as abstract art. Seurat, and to a certain extent Gauguin, paved the way. Van de Velde and the phenomenon of Art Nouveau, described by one critic as "biological romanticism," broke the back of the Renaissance visual/aesthetic paradigm. By the time Art Nouveau had run its course, in the early years of the century, a few artists working independently of each other according to principles similar to or actually enunciated by Henry were painting in a manner now referred to as abstract. Credited with this breakthrough between the years 1908 and 1912 are Frank Kupka, a Czech artist settled in Paris who transformed an Art Nouveau illustrative style to abstraction in a series of paintings significantly entitled *The Discs of Newton* (1908-10); Robert Delaunay, and after 1912, his wife Sonia, who proceeded from a late Neo-Impressionist style and technique into paintings of circular forms and "simultaneous discs" executed toward 1911; and Wassily Kandinsky, who began painting in a fully non-naturalistic manner in 1910 and who published in 1911 a significant statement entitled *Concerning the Spritual in Art.*

The work of Kupka and Delaunay is indebted to Henry in several respects: the use of pure, contrasting elements of color to create the entire composition and the emphasis on circular forms are both techniques derived from Henry's classic work, *The Chromatic Circle* (1888). Delaunay also adopted Henry's notion of simultaneity in a basic statement concerning his painting, "On Light" (1913):

[It is] the simultaneity of light, harmony, the rhythm of colors which creates the Vision of Man. Human vision is endowed with a greater Reality, since it comes to us from a direct contemplation of the Universe. The eye is the highest sense organ, that which communicates *consciousness* most directly to the brain. The idea of the vital movement of *the world and that movement itself are simultaneous.* Our understanding is correlative to our perception. *Let us seek to see.*[10]

Throughout their careers, the Delaunays, work centered on the theme of circles and the simultaneous contrast of color, which they equated with the simultaneous quality of modern neo-technological experience. After the First World War their paintings became more static, having lost the tension of the earlier "orphic" work of 1911-14. In a sense the Delaunays never explored more deeply what they had begun to explore in the heyday of the pre-war period; their work, like that of so many other modernists, lapsed into mere style. Like the machines that often infatuated and inspired them, their art became more purely mechanical. In their earlier works circles bursting from one another through rainbow prisms suggest the parting of a veil; what was beyond the veil was to be seen by others.

Kupka's work remained more supple and dynamic; he operated either in a more geometrical mode of vertical planes or in a more ebullient circular/ biological mode in which the color/light/forms explode through a space, much like the more abstract elements of Walt Disney's film *Fantasia.* Kupka's art, like Kandinsky's, is *visual music,* again in accord with the synesthetic ideas promulgated by Henry and the Symbolists.

Whereas the early abstract work of Delaunay and Kupka contains a suggestion of geometric order, the first abstracts of Kandinsky are a virtual chaos. Kandinsky developed his violent abstract style from Impressionistic and later more Expressionistic techniques involving the vivid use of color to depict "dream" landscapes. Though the works painted prior to the First World War seem to reflect a stunning presentiment of the brutal chaos that was imminent, Kandinsky's book, *Concerning the Spiritual in Art*, reveals a mind and sensitivity much more ordered, and above all, transcendentally inclined. More poetic and more oriented toward art history than Henry, Kandinsky nevertheless echoed Henry's theories. This is especially true when Kandinsky speaks of color, of the laws of harmony, of the correspondences between visual art and music, and of the purposiveness of art, as the following passage beautifully shows:

Generally speaking color directly influences the soul. Color is the keyboard, the eyes are the hammers, the soul is the piano with many strings. The artist is the hand that plays, touching one key or another purposively, to cause vibrations in the soul.

   It is evident, therefore, that color harmony must rest ultimately on purposive playing upon the human soul; this is one of the guiding principles of internal necessity. [11]

Harmony is the simple concordance of internal necessity—which must not be confused with the ego's needs—and external expression; of the evolutionary impulse of the spirit and art, taken in the broadest sense to mean *all* forms of human expression. According to Kandinsky, "Art is not vague production, transitory, isolated, but a power which must be directed to the development and refinement of the human soul, to raising the triangle of the spirit. . . . *That is beautiful which is produced by internal necessity, which springs from the soul.*" [12]

   Perceiving the dilemma of human expression in his own time, Kandinsky wrote:

Conversely, at those times when the soul tends to be choked by materialist lack of belief, art becomes purposeless, and it is said that art exists for art's sake alone. The relation between art and soul is, as it were, doped into unconsciousness. The artist and the public drift apart, until at last the public turns its back, or regards the artist as a juggler whose skill and dexterity alone are worthy of applause. It is important for the artist to gauge his position correctly, to realize that he has a duty to his art and to himself, that he is not a king but a servant of a noble end. He must search his soul deeply, develop it and guard it, so that his art may have something on which to rest and does not remain flesh without bones. *The artist must have something to communicate, since mastery over form is not the end, but, instead, the adopting of form to internal significance.* [13]

To have something to communicate means to have an ego-transcending perception of reality. Kandinsky was confident that the new abstract painting could best express this transcendent perception; to him it was a step toward bringing man's consciousness to an "epoch of great spirituality."

As early as the 1890's Henry had also prophesied the coming of this epoch when he declared,

I do not believe in the future of naturalism, or of any realistic school. On the contrary, I believe in the more or less imminent advent of a very idealistic and even mystic art based on new techniques. . . . I believe in the future of an art which would be the reverse of any logical or historical method, precisely because our intellects, exhausted by purely rational efforts, will feel the need to refresh themselves with entirely opposite states of mind.[14]

Within twenty years after this statement, artists like Kupka, Kandinsky, and the Delaunays, in an effort to speak directly to the soul, were painting mystical and cosmic visions.

In addition to Henry's psychophysical doctrine of art, one other cultural element was responsible for the "advent of a very idealistic and even mystic art." I am referring to the philosophical doctrines of Theosophy and contemporaneous movements such as Rudolph Steiner's Anthroposophy. Kandinsky, Kupka, and another prominent early abstractionist, Piet Mondrian, were all directly affected by the Theosophical movement. To Kandinsky, this movement was the "spiritual turning point" in the dark age of materialism. Certainly the ideas disseminated by Madame Blavatsky constituted the first conscious, collective effort at bridging East and West, and in a deeper sense, conscious and unconscious, male and female. There can be no doubt that Theosophy stirred certain leading minds during the peak period of Positivism, including the writer Maurice Maeterlinck, the scholar Max Müller, and the musician Eugéne Scriabin. More significant, Theosophy was the key to a spiritual foundation that provided a more abiding sense of reality than the will-nilly shoals of a competitive and materialistic egoism, which offered no substance for thought beyond arbitrary categorizations nor any reward but the fleeting shadow of fame. Unfortunately, Theosophy itself proved to be more vision than substance, and though it fanned the almost dormant flame of spirit into new forms of expression, it did not and could not, under the circumstances, offer more than the initial inspiration. Yet it gave a sign, at least, of that synthesizing life foundation necessary to fill the spiritual chasm created by four centuries of progressive materialism.

Specifically regarding the appearance of abstract art prior to the First World War, mention must be made of a Theosophical publication, *Thought Forms*, by Annie Besant and C. S. Leadbeater (1901). If abstract art is defined as the exteriorization of psychic states, or as the expression of internal necessity, then *Thought Forms* really provides the first pure examples in this genre. The actual study of thought forms was begun in a slightly earlier book by Leadbeater and Besant, *Man, Visible and Invisible,* which explored and described the general nature of the *aura*—the overall vibrational tone of the psychophysical organism. This work contains a number of color plates exhibiting the auras of individuals of different race, temperament, and psychological type and development. Their different characteristics are conveyed through changes in line and in quality of tone and color—the staples of visual abstraction according to Henry. *Thought Forms* pursues the same idea in more specific terms, operating under three general principles:

1. Quality of thought determines color.
2. Nature of thought determines form.
3. Definiteness of thought determines clearness of outline.[15]

Of the three *classes* of thought forms, the first two are generally expressed in art through portraiture and landscape, but the third "takes a form entirely its own, expressing its inherent qualities in the matter which it draws around it."[16] It is to this third category that the book *Thought Forms* is devoted. In other words, the thought forms that are described and illustrated are the intangible kind that fall into the affective realm. According to the Theosophists these are the thoughts that take place most directly in the astral plane,* such as various kinds of affection, devotion, intellectual pleasure, anger, fear, sympathy, greed, emotions induced by various disasters or death, meditational thoughts, conscious compassion, and so forth. In addition the book contains a brief section on thought forms built by music; the illustrations to this section are abstract compositions that easily prefigure Kandinsky's earliest abstractions some ten years later.

The illustrations throughout *Thought Forms* provide excellent studies in the aesthetic principles of Henry and Kandinsky. Not only are they direct examples of psychic states exteriorized, but they point to another area more directly touched on by the work of Jung—that of *symbols.* The more precise and clear the thought form, the more precise and clear is its expression in what can only be described as an archetypal form or symbol. In fact, the more consciously directed the thought and the more purposive the emotion, the more internal necessity expresses itself in archetypal symbols. This revelation points to a basic critical insight regarding the development of abstract art. The "abstraction" that developed in Western art has meaning only in relation to the preceding centuries of "naturalism." Neither category is absolute. Abstraction is an integral aspect of all art, insofar as it implies the simplification of perceived elements and the condensation of ideas and feelings into a formal pattern. Naturalism is merely the tendency to reproduce the everyday perception of reality. After the

---

* This may be defined quite generally as the formative world of the imagination.

First World War, pure, nonreferential, and nonfigurative abstraction was wrongly elevated to an absolute artistic category. Besides being an over-reaction to centuries of Renaissance naturalism, this conception was simply an error of judgment, and one that was inevitable given the overwhelmingly intellectual disposition and schizophrenic emotional makeup of modern culture.

With few exceptions the abstract artists followed the purist doctrine of abstraction developed in the 1920's. In so doing they shut down the experiment begun by a few men and women in the dark years prior to the First World War and created instead the intellectual shibboleth of modernism. Refusing to believe in a transcendental reality, the majority of modernist/ abstract artists closed themsleves off to the conscious power of symbols. Chained to the blind materialism of the technocratic state, they had disavowed the responsibility of the transformative vision. As Kandinsky wrote, "He who can see beyond the limits of his own segment of spiritual evolution is a prophet and helps the advance of mankind. But those who are near-sighted, or who retard the movement for base reasons are fully understood and acclaimed."[17]

CHAPTER SEVENTEEN

The Aesthetic of Madness I

IN THE numbered and confused world of the 1970's it is hard for us to realize the shock with which the First World War struck the European consciousness. No segment of European society responded more sensitively than the artists, who had traditionally been much more aware of the life-denying forces in our civilization. Toward the beginning of 1915 the Swiss painter Paul Klee wrote in his dairy, "The more horrifying this world becomes (as it is in these days) the more art becomes abstract; while a world at peace produces realistic art."[1] By abstract art Klee clearly meant an art that is the product and expression of the deep psychic disturbances corresponding to the state of total war. But war is more than hell; it is utter insanity. And when there is total war, as in our century, whether that war be called hot, cold, or merely of the nerves—such interesting expressions!—the artist as that figure symbolic of the psyche is also insane, or rather a mirror of our collective insanity. We do not understand modern art because we do not wish to understand ourselves. The modernist knows this; hence his art is difficult and meaningless at the same time.

If life becomes dominated by war, then art can only reflect a basic perversion of the spirit. Perilous is the path of the visionary making his way through the jungle of warring materialism. His isolation is profound, and at every turn he is tempted by the flattering ogre of self-deception. So hungry are the multitudes for spiritual nourishment that they will devour anyone who satisfies the least of their desires. In 1911 Kandinsky wrote of art's degradation in such conditions:

During periods when art has no champion, when true spiritual food is wanting, there is retrogression in the spiritual world. . . . During these mute and blind times men attribute a special and exclusive value to external success, for they judge by outward results, thinking of material well-being. . . . The love visionaries, the hungry of soul are ridiculed or considered mentally abnormal. . . . The spiritual night falls deeper and deeper around such frightened souls. . . . In such periods art ministers to lower needs and is used for material ends. It seeks its content in crude substance, because it knows nothing fine. . . . The question "what?" disappears and only the question "how?" remains. By what method are these material objects reproduced? The method becomes the rationale. Art loses its soul. The search for "how" continues. Art becomes specialized, comprehensible only to artists, and they complain of public indifference to their work. For, since the artist in such times has no need to *say* much, but only to be notorious for some small originality among a small group of patrons and connoisseurs (which incidentally is also profitable), many externally gifted and skillful people come forward, so easy does the conquest of art appear. In each "art center" there are thousands of such artists, of whom the majority seek only some new mannerism, producing millions of works of art, without enthusiasm, with cold hearts and souls asleep. Meanwhile competition grows. The savage battle for success becomes more and more material. Small groups who have fought their way to the top entrench themselves in the territory they have won. The public, left behind, looks on in bewilderment, loses interest and turns away.[2]

Kandinsky's words have as much relevance today as they did in 1911, for they describe equally well the faded remnants of modernist culture, of which Kandinsky was one of the founders, and the now decadent "rock" culture that reached its zenith in the late 1960's. The few who are able to resist the temptations of materialism are generally denied the acclaim given to those who succumb. Often the purest "love visionaries" remain totally ignored. The greatest irony is that the mad pursuit of individual mannerism is considered normal, reflecting the open market of a laissez-faire society, while a quest to fulfill the deepest spiritual aspirations is considered mad. Thus the cleverest receive the greatest recognition; the most sincere, as often as not, end up in an asylum. This is the aesthetic of madness.

Among those acclaimed for the wrong reasons is Pablo Picasso. No one more than Picasso typifies the externally gifted and skillful person who, having conquered a piece of territory—in this case, Cubism—becomes entrenched in that ingeniously conceived battle ground. For all his vaunted modernism, throughout his long life Picasso remained the great academic joker. Self-consciously art-historical, his works have meaning only within the context of European tradition, of which he was the final master. Raphael played with the forms of Greece, David and Ingres with the forms of Raphael, and Delacroix with the forms of Rubens, but Picasso played with them all! Perfecting his own style—or series of styles—flaunting public decency (yet titillating the public with his love life), adopting the pose of the political radical, while leading a life of bourgeois comfort, Picasso became an institution in his own lifetime. He was the ultimate "free" artist. In providing everything he demanded nothing, and so the public could buy him, have their fantasies played out, and continue to live their own sterile lives without really being changed or confronted. In exaggerating the significance of Picasso's art, establishment critics and historians have created a myth that conceals the void left by modern man's abdication of the creative spirit. As artist and as a microcosm of his civilization, Picasso exemplifies the captivity and complete control of psyche by techne.

What was glorified in Picasso was the technically inventive ego. Following his death Time magazine declared,

No artist left alive has been able to rival Picasso's cultural embodiment of the self. . . . He is the tutelary saint of virtuosos, and Picasso's virtuosity is the one fact of modern art that everybody knows something about. . . . By 1940 Picasso was the most famous artist in the world: by 1970 he had become the most famous artist that ever lived. . . . More people had heard of him than ever heard of the name, let alone saw the work of Michelangelo and Cézanne while they were alive.[3]

Virtuosity has little to do with true creativity, however; and if great personality is necessary for the achievement of great works, it does not follow that great works are based on personality. Picasso permitted himself to be seduced by the ego and the collective need to conceal, though not fill, the gnawing void of creativity. The transformation art makes possible was abandoned for the rewards of fame and power. When Picasso's personality became myth, the public began to expect other artists to share his traits: masculine exuberance, insatiable ego, rapid stylistic turnover, rapacious ingenuity. The personality of the artist became a major concern in the marketing of his art, and in many cases the sole concern. But a public personality is no personality at all; it is an abstraction incapable of willed, conscious transformation. In the end it can only mirror the collective consciousness. This is the final tragedy of neotechnic civilization and its modernist culture: neither is the spiritual hunger of the people satisfied, nor is the personality of the artist transformed.

The model of the virtuoso artist, a Paganini or a Picasso, like the model of reality it reflects, is a closed one, sustained by official history and a collective psychology that guards its frontiers. Within our materially self-defined limits we are subjected to an "implosion" of information; yet we deny ourselves the use of individual safety valves for the release of emotional and psychic energy. We have relied on our Picassos too long, and now the model the virtuoso genius represented, like our limited supply of fossil fuels, is finally exhausting itself. Suffocated by the self-imposed, institutional limitations of our civilization, we have literally cut ourselves off from the privilege of transcendence, which can only be gained by assuming responsibility for one's own existence.

In fact, almost nothing is encouraged less by our society than the assumption of creative responsibility. This is what drove van Gogh to suicide and the great dancer Vaslav Nijinsky to the madhouse.   Both of these "love visionaries" saw clearly that modern civilization's greatest error has been to deny man's relationship and responsibility to the divine. In cutting himself off from the divine, modern man cut himself off from the roots of creativity. It is significant that Nijinsky's madness took hold during the First World War. In the epilogue to his famous diary, written in 1919, Nijinsky wrote:

I am a simple man who has suffered a lot. I believe I suffered more than Christ. . . . My soul is ill. My soul, not my mind. The doctors do not understand my illness. I know what I need to get well. My illness is too great to be cured quickly. I am incurable. My soul is ill. . . . My body is not ill, my soul is ill. I suffer, I suffer. I love everyone, I have my faults, I am a man—not God. I want to be God and therefore try to improve myself. I want to dance, to draw, to play the piano, to write verses, to love everybody. That is the object of my life. I know that socialists would understand me better—but I am not a socialist. I am a part of God, my party is God's party. I love everybody. I *do not* want war or frontiers. The world exists. I have a home everywhere. I live everywhere. I do not want to have any property. I do not want to be rich. I want to love. I am love—not cruelty. I am not a blood-thirsty animal. I am man. I am man. God is in me. I am in God. I want Him, I seek Him. . . . I hope to improve myself. I do not know how to, but I feel that God will help all those who seek Him. I am a seeker, for I can feel God. God seeks me and therefore we will find each other.[4]

The most remarkable truth revealed by Nijinsky's experience is the relationship between divinity, madness, and creativity. Elsewhere in his diary he wrote:

Whenever I have a feeling, I carry it out. I never fight against a feeling. An order of God tells me how to act. I am not a fakir or a magician. I am God in a body. Everyone has that feeling, but no one uses it. I do make use of it and know its results. People think that this feeling is a spiritual trance, but I am not in a trance. I am love. I am in a trance, the trance of love. I want to say so much and cannot find the words. I want to write and cannot. I can write in a trance and this trance is called *wisdom*. Every man is a reasonable being. I do not want unreasonable beings and therefore I want everyone to be in a trance of feelings. I am in a trance of God.[5]

Naturally Nijinsky and van Gogh turned the conventional world upside down with these kinds of utterances, for both saw in Christ's betrayal by civilization their own betrayal. *"My madness is my love towards man-kind."*[6] Nijinsky's utterance would have qualified him for a monastery and not an insane asylum in the days preceding the great split in human creativity. As two recent researchers have commented, "In Europe during the Middle Ages, when deviant or bizarre behavior was often heralded as a manifestation of the divine, the insane were generally treated humanely and sometimes revered. Monasteries became havens for the insane; the treatment of their disturbance prayers and various theological rituals."[7] More than one keen-minded sociologist or psychologist has observed that madness and the insane asylum are the inventions of our mechanized society. True, the Middle Ages had their heretics, and other cultures and religions have had their persecutions. But there is nothing comparable to the utterly negative attitude we have developed toward insanity, especially when the definition of sanity and insanity is so fluid and conjectural. If such is indeed the case, we might come to suspect that in madness there are more answers to the question of creativity than we have previously thought. It is the difference between developing a Black Elk or a Saint Francis instead of well-rounded and well-adjusted citizens. If we look at the insane quest of the "love visionaries"—those who have suffered most intensely the reality of civilized madness—we may learn how to live through all of the hells perpetrated by civilization and yet arrive at a creative transcendence in our own lives.

There is one "love visionary"—Adolf Wölfli, or St. Adolf II, as he later preferred to call himself—who must be singled out because of the utter *extremity* of his experience. The questions raised by the existence of St. Adolf II are the same as those raised by other apparent anomalies in our history, from Christ to Hitler. The most extreme exceptions may pass unnoticed simply because by normal standards of reality they are unthinkable. Yet nothing goes by unrecorded. Thus in the "Age of the Digest,"[8] to use the terms of Hermann Hesse's fictitious scholars in their Bead Game description of the twentieth century, the coding of information as well as its transmission and consequent decoding proliferate at an ever accelerating rate. All of yesterday's anomalies and exceptions enter the open market, and today pass quickly into the consciousness of the race; the masks of the hero are ever changing.

Wölfli was born February 29, 1864, in Bern, Switzerland. Aside from his exceptional birthday, his beginnings were ordinary enough. When he was eight, however, trauma intervened: his mother died (his father, a drunken stone-breaker, seems to have played a far less important role than his mother in Wölfli's development). In his later autobiography Wölfli remarked, "It is following a grave illness contracted when I was eight years old—precisely from that moment on—that I have directly and radically forgotten EVERYTHING"[9]—a sublime observation that should not be taken too lightly considering Wölfli's later development, for only by forgetting everything was Wölfli able to remember *who he was to become*. "Freed from the sentimental affectations of reconstructing his own memories,"[10] as Henri-Pol Bouché puts it, Wölfli was able to go directly to the source of creation, beneath and beyond the arbitrary push and pull of the ever changing individual personality. Such is the privilege of magicians, visionaries, and saints. Yet the road to liberty was to be most difficult for St. Adolf II.

From the age of eight to sixteen, Wölfli's life was a series of abandonments and frustrations as miserable as anything described by Dickens. In this respect Wölfli was typical of the uprooted children of the nineteenth century: Rimbaud and van Gogh, visionaries contemporary to him, were no less tormented. Of this period Wölfli wrote, "Often on Sundays I would cry in a corner for hours thinking of my dead mother."[11] He was shunted from one orphanage to another, and forced out of school at the age of fourteen. As early as 1875 he went to work as a farm laborer, which remained his general job category until his final incarceration at the Waldau Insane Asylum in 1895; from 1880 to 1889, Wölfli was itinerantly employed in this manner.

Early in this period (1880–1882) Wölfli fell in love with a woman who, most likely by virtue of class distinction, was beyond his reach. Years of sexual frustration, no doubt related to unresolved feelings over the death of his mother, were to follow. Wölfli's experience recalls the sexual melo-drama of his contemporary, Vincent van Gogh. Like van Gogh, Wölfli found occasional release in religious devotion, but not a lasting cure. After being forbidden to see the young lady with whom he had fallen in love in 1880–82, Wölfli later wrote, "I became sad and even melancholy; I did not know what to do. That very evening I rolled myself in the snow, prey to a burning passion of love, crying that I might be torn into bits and pieces."[12] He became progressively more sensitive and itinerant. However, unlike van Gogh and Nijinsky, Wölfli did not reach a level of consciousness at which creativity was possible until *after* he had gone over the brink. In the late 1880's Wölfli contracted veneral disease from a love affair with a prostitute. This experience did not keep him from speaking of the woman's great beauty, and at one point a marriage was even planned. Here one recalls the trials Baudelaire put himself through in his obsessed affair with the mulatto prostitute Jeanne Duval, before whom the poet knelt, like Dante before some malignant Beatrice.

The degradations of Adolf Wölfli became acute in 1890, when he at-tempted to rape a fourteen-year-old girl in a park near Bern. He saved himself from punishment by giving a false identity, but the downward spiral of his life accelerated. In 1891 he attacked a five-year-old girl. This incident resulted in two years' imprisonment, from 1891 to 1893—the very same years that marked Gauguin's first visionary flight to Tahiti. Prison was to become Wölfli's Tahiti. Late in 1891 he had his first visionary experience: the sudden appearance in a prison labor field of the Holy Ghost, whom Wölfli initially took to be the surprise apparition of his "little Dearie," (!) perhaps refering to all of his female attachments. From 1893 to 1895 Wölfli went back to working as an itinerant laborer in and around Bern; he seems to have been quite unstable at this time, interspersing biblical declarations with paranoid delusions of being hunted down. He attempted to regulate himself by giving up drinking, a habit he had ac-quired, and taking up rug making instead, a curious first sign of creativity. But his efforts were to no avail. In the spring of 1895 he committed his final sexual assault, this time on a three-year-old girl. In court Wölfli was described as hard-working and extremely energetic and powerful, his physical makeup, coupled with his violent temper and sexual disposition, spelled the end of worldly life for Wölfli, who by now appeared incorrigi-ble. In the autumn of 1895, while Gauguin was making his final voyage to the South Seas, Wölfli was pronounced insane and sentenced to Waldau Asylum for the rest of his life, or until deemed socially responsible.

The years from 1895 to 1899 were most chaotic: sexual fantasies and obsessions, hysterical outbursts, months-long periods of near catatonic depressions and isolation were followed by violent attacks on guards and other inmates, and above all, hallucinations. Then, in 1899, a general calm began to prevail; like a man coming back from the dead, Wölfli experienced something of a rebirth. Indeed, in 1897 his voices had spoken to him of his imminent *death*, and in a very real way, Wölfli's ordeal—the various sexual attacks followed by life imprisonment—ended in the veritable death of Adolf Wölfli, orphan, itinerant farm laborer, hopeless madman, society's ultimate outcast.

Within the overall structure of Wölfli's personality, the sexual attacks he committed were mechanisms for releasing the phenomenal energy buried beneath the psychic and sentimental debris of his miserable life. His ordeal was harrowing to say the least, but no less harrowing and structurally no different than the ordeal of the Eskimo shaman, who to prove himself must go to the "bottom of the sea," which in many cases literally means being plunged under the ice. In view of Wölfli's experience, the comment of one ethnologist on the shaman type is most pertinent: "Crimes and sudden acts of brutality are not infrequent among these people."[13] Certain rites and rituals are imperative for the acquisition of new knowledge—rituals whose very nature imparts knowledge in a way that no conceptual logic can duplicate. All new knowledge and all new being comes in the nature of a ritual initiation; thus the consciousness of Adolf Wölfli passed beyond the threshold of its own self-definition and created, or perhaps more appropriately, discovered the character and role of St. Adolf II. The following description of shamanic initiation by Eliade also applies to the initiation undergone by St. Adolf II:

The total crisis of the future shaman, sometimes leading to complete disintegration of the personality and to madness, can be valuated not only as an initiatory death but also as a symbolic return to the precosmogonic Chaos, to the amorphous and indescribable state that precedes any cosmogony. Now, as we know, for archiaic and traditional cultures, a symbolic return to Chaos is equivalent to preparing a new Creation. It follows that we may interpret the psychic Chaos of the future shaman as a sign that the profane man is being "dissolved" and a new personality being prepared for birth.[14]

Toward 1900 Wölfli suddenly became intensely creative. The turning point had been reached: painting, writing (the cosmically endless autobiography), and composing music, which he sang, danced to, and played on paper trumpets of his own making, became the chief activities of St. Adolf II. At the same time, there is good indication that afraid of being freed, Wölfli consciously resorted to periodic attacks of violence in order to ensure his measure of psychic freedom; indeed, he seems to have preferred the isolation that generally resulted from his violent episodes, most likely because it gave him time to go on his "trips," the hallucinatory voyages that were the mainstay of St. Adolf's existence. Interestingly, only after

1917, toward the end of the First World War did Wölfli calm down. He became inordinately tender and gentle, in one instance acting as a mother to two idiot boys; from this time to his death in 1930, he remained quite calm and extremely productive. It was during this last period that he most consistently signed his works St. Adolf or St. Adolf II; up to this time the signatures St. Adolf and variants of Adolf Wölfli had been alternatively used. Thus the sexually unrestrained and creatively undistinguished Adolf Wölfli was finally metamorphosed—shamanized—into the exuberantly creative, gentle, and monastic St. Adolf II, enamored, we are told, of the x-ray table on which he died.

While Picasso's vision was circumscribed by European art history, Wölfli's vision, in the words of Dr. Morganthaler, "passed beyond the limits of his own childhood: he crossed over, to speak in Jung's terms, from the personal realm to the suprapersonal, the absolute unconscious; thus, he returned to the 'original affective thought,' to the 'primary representations,' to the 'most ancient, most general and most profound thoughts of humanity.' "[15] As madman, Wölfli achieved in the modern West what perhaps no other artist except Blake had been able to achieve: the creation of a complete and integral psycho-cosmogony.

Wölfli's achievement is all the more striking when one considers the fragmented vision of what has come to be called modern art. Of the work by other artists of his own generation, only Kandinsky's and Klee's begins to approximate the ideal that Wölfli's epitomizes. Yet there is a critical difference between Wölfli, on the one hand, and Kandinsky and Klee, on the other. The last two were conscious of their role as artists working within a socially acceptable conceptual structure; both had to intellectually decivilize their technique in order to arrive at the universal ground of experience. But Wölfli made no conscious decision to become an artist; hence he felt no need to struggle with the definition of art, a question that lies at the heart of every professional Western artist's self-definition today. The twentieth-century artist is not expected to create art—much less beauty—but merely to struggle with its definition. As a result, his work typically seeks only to interpret itself, and he is trapped into a series of ever more involved exercises in self-definition. St. Adolf II, by contrast, was free to go directly to the source of creativity, unhampered by any preconceptualization; his art accordingly has an integral universality unique in modern times. The example of St. Adolph II reminds us that the creation of beauty, like any other act of conviction, must proceed directly from integral self-realization; otherwise one's work remains caught in the surface play of games and forces beyond one's control.

Because the artist's function in a technological society has never been clear, the lives of nearly all of the modern visionary/artists have been filled with suffering: madness, disease, social conflict, and despair have ever been their fate. Only Blake and perhaps Whitman seem to have escaped the psychotic afflictions of the industrial-age visionaries. And it is Blake's visionary temperament that seems most akin to Wölfli's. The visionary voyages of Blake, who also preferred a life of isolation, and Wölfli began much more deeply in the unconscious than the voyages of Gauguin or even Rimbaud. So deeply rooted was Wölfli's experience that prior to the brutal shock of incarceration he had little inkling of the marvelous adventures that awaited him. In this respect Wölfli's creative behavior is unique, for without any of the traditional historical material available to him, he created an art that transcends the realm of the personal and enters the great realm of the archetypal, much like the art and techniques of magicians, yogis, and shamans. In this connection lies some of the greatest significance of the case of St. Adolf II; he serves as a model of the contemporary creative person as *interior technologist*. Yet none of this must diminish the first lesson to be learned from Wölfli's life-experience: with the exception of the newspapers available to him, Wölfli was *dead* to Western civilization from 1895 until his literal death in 1930. For Wölfli, in the space capsule of his cell in Waldau Insane Asylum, unparalleled creativity came only with a complete break from civilization.

Not unexpectedly, the paintings and drawings of St. Adolf II have few counterparts in contemporary Western art, save perhaps some of the efforts of the psychedelic artists. In color, design, and symmetrical formalism, the art of St. Adolf II is most reminiscent of the art of Medieval Europe, and of certain works from India and Tibet. This relationship to works emanating from developed religious traditions is most significant, especially in view of the appearance of the mandala and its centralizing effect in the work of St. Adolf II. Because the mandala has its origin in the biological structure of the eye, its appeal is immediate to the psychophysiology of vision. It is a natural form, often reproduced spontaneously when the restrictive workings of consciousness do not impede the flow of the unconscious. Moreover, the mandala is a prime tool for self-integration; the creation of a mandala signals the reorganization of the various components of personality to reach a new level of stability—and perhaps even a new personality.

It is not surprising, then, that as Wölfli's disintegrated personality underwent its healing transformation, he rediscovered for himself the age-old tool of the mandala. His art may be seen as *a tool for self-transformation*. This function and value for art is recognized and practiced by Australian aborigine and Tantric yogi alike. In their traditions, as in Wölfli's experience, art has a sublime utility: it is a psychic tool for experiencing, expressing, and transforming one's deepest consciousness.

The work of St. Adolf II is replete with psycho-cosmic imagery. The chief character, of course, is St. Adolf himself in his multifarious guises—

"the hero with a thousand faces"—a black-masked Ulysses freely charting the farthest reaches of consciousness. His paintings and writings center on his various voyages to all the fabled and marvelous lands of the universe. "Where in my head could I have found that?" Saint Adolf would remark when Dr. Morgenthaler asked him where the visionary forms in his paintings came from. Morgenthaler wrote, "He pretends to have designed and drawn everything on divine orders received in his travels across the world."[16] The source of Wölfli's imagery was his many hallucinatory trips taken within his cell. But what did these trips, which were the chief adventure of St. Adolf's solitary existence, really consist of?

For Adolf in his most *normal* state, the trips most certainly took place outside his head. Though the possibility of out-of-the-body experiences is not to be discounted, it is more likely that these trips were explorations, via the central nervous system, of the microcosm of the inner psychosensory realm. In this regard, the words of the Buddha are not merely metaphoric: "In this very body, six feet in length, with its sense impressions and its thoughts and ideas, are the world, the origin of the world, the ceasing of the world and likewise the way that leads to the ceasing thereof." The visions of St. Adolf II, like those of all visionaries and prophets, may be regarded as the symbolic representations of the various neural patterns and genetic configurations that constitute the evolutionary "plan" of the species. True vision—clairvoyance and revelation—are to humanity what instinct is to the lower animals and plants: a direct line of communication between sensory input and the situational necessity of the organism. The prophet is he who by his receptivity *sees* and *reads* the immediate evolutionary direction from and within the components of his own psychogenetic constitution. St. Adolf's paintings and mythic tales are projections of the direct experience of his own psychogenetic patterning. It should also be noted, however, that for St. Adolf the actual experience of the trips was paramount, whereas his paintings, writings, and musical compositions were "merely pastimes executed in my cell of the insane asylum."[17] For him, as for other mystics, work was the residual but necessary furtherance of the messages received at the height of the mystical experience.

The following is Wölfli's description of one of his hallucinatory voyages:

And now: and now: here commences Our Voyage, O hunters and naturalists of indefatigable ardor, our retinue of twelve horses leading us from the West to the East in the southern part of Heaven, occasionally traversing most-respectable villages, plains and localities of a suprayme elegance, cities of different sizes and even extraordinarily large or gigantic in certain places, now and then coming across different cult-tours, flowers and magejestic vegetations of a suprayme elegance; and then, from time to time, traversing mossy fields, prairies and gigantic Virgin forests, even travelling along little lakes and these much larger or gigantic seas as well; travelling along cliffs plunging from highest peak to abyss from 100 to 500 leagues, and also through places of much lower mountainous outcroppings and hills, until finally, after so much fatiguing sport, numerous dangerous tourments and cata-strrophes, we arrive at the very edge of the Sea-of-the-Southern-Heavenly-Reaches, and depart as always in the direction of the East, then of the North along the Sea-of-the-Eastern-Heavenly-Reaches and Sea-of-the-Northern-Heavenly-Reaches, going obliquely once again towards the West so that we may attain to cliffs 350 leagues high, 25,000 leagues long and 900,000 leagues broad (at certain places); then continuing, going beyond, through Virgin forests, Alpagaen realms, glaciers, boulders, valleys and abysses, and then some towns, some large and gigantic cities, further cult-tours and more regions of floral growth and vegetation right up to the foot of the Giant-Glacier-of-the-Heavenly-Aastral-Reaches-of-God-the-Father, in the very bososm of which is in length, 250,000 in height, and 500,000 leagues broad; and finally up to the luxuriant and magejestic Great-Throne-of-God-the-Father-All-Powerful, hierarchically divided into a number of administrative districts representing the Public Powers, little and great, Kingdom, Empire etzeterra. . . . And then, taking count, we amassed on a route a gigantic booty, which added to the little we own in total property on the earth, comes to: totall, exactic, around, justly=Pong!: 117, 993, 025, 775, 875, 000, 000, 000, 000, 000 Francs. Then led by not less than 350 gigantic silver chariots with heavily charged steel hubs, a great many of which are harnessed to anywhere from twenty to thirty-six horses, and a dozen gigantic Celestial-Transports-of-God-the-Father and Giant-Transport-Birds each carrying a load of several thousand tons, and numerous little vessel-moths-of-the-isles heavily weighted, we arrive thereby at the Harbor-of-the-North-of-the-Celestial-Aastral-Body-of-God-the-Father (Giant City of more than 800,000,000,000 souls), in good form, gay and of good humor, continually sustained by our excellent Orchestra and our Chorale. The numerous and diverse manifestations of sympathy coming from the innerhabitants of these regions knows no limits. The innumerable and excellent orchestras and ditto the chorales, the gigantic military parades in complete formation: the thunder of the cannon and the guns of war: the luxuriant festivals of night with their Bengal fires blazing on the sea and on the earth and even in the harbors: Ynaventura! Great Empress of Bengala of the twenty-eight celestial lights! And then, the gigantic and immense swimming festivals, gymnastics, dance and other arts of so suprayme and elegant a grace, representations of spiritism, etzeterra, all of which made us so enthusiastic and so transported us for three days and three nights duration, yes, which gave us so much admiration and stupification, that we cried out, Me, and those others of my own Voice: Yes, the All-Powerful, the Wisdom, the Grace and the Justice of God have no limits! And everywhere: in all the creation of which God-the-Father-All-Powerful let us visit, everywhere, my own well-beloved Mother purchased directly the innumerable and gigantic administrative districts representing the Public Powers (the little as well as the big) and paying them, be it in hard cash or in Bank Notes, she waits until she receives from them in part, at least, a gift, or even one of the devastating wars, and in the gigantic battles, receiving even the general-in-chief under the orders of God-the-Father-All-Powerful in whom she has regularly conquered in all honor, so even to the end of this chapter, carried by a solid conviction, I can cry out: I am the Master of Oberon!: however, above me, there is God: and if He were to disappear today, I would return there, Hott!, I would climb towards the Throne of God: Him, he will quickly see fit to arrange it: St. Anne has the most beautiful Throne: Goodbye my dear, Lott. And if you have not flown away, Ha! Ha!. Finally: it was me who said that which my Mother said. For it was God-the-Father-All-Powerful who gave the most beautiful Throne of the Goddess to my well-beloved Mother, in his gigantic, magejestic Giant-Cave-of-the-Celestial-Aastral-Body-of-God-the-Father.[18]

In this hypnotic, inward journey, full of repetition and number, immensity and infinity, God is revealed by total immersion in one's own being. Wölfli's sense of rapture in the presence of God is a classic example of the ecstatic mystical experience. What one may call the ornamental character of Wölfli's work imparts the same sense of symmetrical unfolding—infinite mirror play—that charactarizes the art of schizophrenics and primitives, and much mystical and religious art. Indeed, this sense of infinite, symmetrical unfolding can be taken as a prime characteristic of all psychic art—that is, art whose origin and end is the unfolding of consciousness. Schizophrenia can often be a prelude to a mystical-ecstatic state. Given all the fantastic components of Wölfli's voyage, we can see that the transformation of Adolf Wölfli into St. Adolf II is the transformation from the imagistic overload of civilized schizophrenic disassociation to the sublime order of mystical non- (or pan-) identity; from noncreative, chaotic disfunction to creative, cosmic realization.

How much difference is there between the often willed isolation of St. Adolf II in his cell at Waldau and that of the famed Tibetan mystic and saint Milarepa, who experienced so much in his cave in the stony fastness of the Himalayas?[19] Though Milarepa had the fundamental advantage of receiving by direct transmission a highly developed religious teaching, Vajrayana Buddhism,* the visionary quality of the experiences of St. Adolf II and Milarepa is much the same. Seen in the spaceship of his cell, St. Adolf II is a twentieth-century model of the psycho-cosmic voyager, exploring realms of consciousness far beyond the "normal," automatic state of consciousness that has become the very standard of what we call civilization.

Finally, St. Adolf II, somewhat like Milarepa, chose to eject from civilization, knowing full well that the experiences he was *free* to enter into within his cell in Waldau Asylum would never be condoned outside it. We often forget that in the past our own culture was much more tolerant of God-mad "love visionaries" like St. Adolf II, and even provided respected means through which these men could pursue their vision, such as the

---

*Vajrayana (lit., Diamond or indestructible vehicle) is the form of Buddhism practiced in Tibet. It is synonymous with the Tantric form of Buddhism and is characterized by a highly developed symbolism and ritual practice.

esteemed monastic orders of the Medieval period. I am not advocating so much the revival of such a system as the *re-cognition* of the necessity and significance of the kind of exploration done by St. Adolf II and others like him, through whatever means. Compared to the example of another twentieth century figure, Adolf Hitler, who attempted to institutionalize forcibly and permanently a single state of consciousness, St. Adolf II's option of retreating from society to pursue the many pathways within his own consciousness is certainly preferable.

The lives of van Gogh and Nijinsky, among other visionaries who suffered society's rejection, are vindicated by the example of St. Adolf II. As the nature of our global situation—and the guidelines for coming to grips with it—becomes clear to all, we begin to see that whatever else we may undertake in the near future, we must embark on the willed exploration of our own inner space. This is the evolutionary imperative glimpsed by Adolf Wölfli in choosing to remain in Waldau Asylum, thus ensuring the productive well-being of St. Adolf II. For in the end, St. Adolf II was one of those men, in the words of Hermann Hesse, "who are beyond all originalities and peculiarities and who have succeeded in achieving the most perfect possible service to the supra-personal."[20] Equally apropos, another recent saint, Ramana Maharshi, wrote: "One should abide in the Self without the sense of being the doer, even when engaged in work born of destiny, like a madman. Have not many devotees achieved much with a detached attitude and firm devotion of this nature?"[21]

CHAPTER EIGHTEEN

The Aesthetic of Madness II

PICASSO AND Wölfli—the one represents madness as an institution, the other madness institutionalized. The one is a reflection of the insantiy of history; the other of the history of insanity. In the vocabulary of the occult, insanity has no meaning apart from history, and history itself is but the record of human illusions and hallucinatory digressions—all nonetheless painful and real enough when they are being experienced. History as destiny—the domain of the egotist who strives to make his mark—is a prison of ever diminishing options. As options diminish, so does man's capacity to control the course of events, and the entire process of history—culture, politics, mechanization—becomes an indissoluble unity interred within the belly of Mammon. Culture itself cannot really be said to exist, only politics and machines, and at one point even this distinction becomes blurred; hence we arrive at technocracy, in which all organic functions are subject to a process no one can control. Reality is then experienced as a *congelation* of matter. From time to time there are eruptions within this congelation, known as wars. And as the density increases so does the sensation of an imminent climax.

From its beginning there were those who sensed that the twentieth century was actually the prehistory of the apocalypse. A 1908 woodcut illustration to the Bible by the German Symbolist E. M. Lilien depicts a colossal prophet Moses, his feet enshrouded in clouds while his figure rises high above the planet. To either side of him are smoking volcanoes. In his hands are the tablets of the laws; his head is haloed by an orb of light, luminous and clear in the nocturnal sky. Though war and destruction would prevail on the earth, the law would remain. Though men's ears would be deafened by the roar of speeding machines the teachings of the prophets would continue to resound through the nocturnal terror of death camps and mechanized life.

On February 20, 1909, a small group of Italian artists made a formal declaration of war on the culture that had been born in their soil and gave rise to modern man. In the Initial Manifesto of Futurism, this group proclaimed:

1. We shall sing the love of danger, the habit of energy and boldness.
2. The essential elements of our poetry shall be courage, daring, rebellion.
3. Literature has hitherto glorified thoughtful immobility, ecstasy and sleep; we shall extol aggressive movement, feverish insomnia, the double quick step, the somersault, the box on the ear, the fisticuff.
4. We declare that the world's splendor has been enriched by a new beauty; the beauty of speed. A racing motor car, its frame adorned with great pipes, like

snakes with explosive breath . . . a roaring motor car which looks as though running on shrapnel is more beautiful than the *Victory of Samothrace.*

5. We shall sing of the man at the steering wheel, whose ideal stem transfixes the earth, rushing over the circuit of her orbit.

6. The poet must give himself with frenzy, with splendor and with lavishness, in order to increase the enthusiastic fevor of the primordial elements.

7. There is no more beauty except in strife. No masterpiece without aggressiveness. Poetry must be a violent onslaught upon the unknown forces, to command them to bow before man.

8. We stand upon the extreme promontory of the centuries! Why should we look behind us, when we have to break in the mysterious portals of the Impossible? Time and Space died yesterday. Already we live in the absolute, since we have already created speed, eternal and ever present.

9. We wish to glorify War—the only health-giver of the world—militarism, patriotism, the destructive arm of the Anarchist, the beautiful Ideas that kill, the contempt for woman.

10. We wish to destroy the museums, the libraries, to fight against moralism, feminism, and all opportunistic and utilitarian meannesses.

11. We shall sing of the great crowds in the excitement of labor, pleasure, and rebellion; of the multicolored and polyphonic surf of revolutions in modern capital cities; of the nocturnal vibration of arsenals and workshops beneath their violent electric moons; of the greedy stations swallowing smoking snakes; of factories suspended from the clouds by their strings of smoke; of bridges leaping like gymnasts over the diabolical cutlery of sunbathed rivers; of broad-chested locomotives prancing on the rails, like huge steel horses bridled with long tubes; and of the gliding flight of airplanes, the sound of whose propeller is like the flapping of flags and the applause of an enthusiastic crowd.[1]

The theme of simultaneity, first sounded by Charles Henry, acquired a sinister, apocalyptic overtone with the Futurists. Their cause was nothing less than the supreme victory of the machine; they complained that progress was not swift enough or simultaneous enough. To them, progress toward the total mechanization of means and simultaneity of communications was impeded only by society's tendency to cling to the cultural forms of the past. Their mechanical ecstasy signaled the triumph of reason and mass consciousness, and the total suppression of the feminine, intuitive nature of things. Though naive and ambiguous, their manifesto conveys the collective conditions of the human psyche in the advanced stages of industrialization, a condition in which all organic impulses have been blocked and human affairs are guided completely by the impulses of Uranus, the planet of revolution, and Neptune, the planet of mass, collective movements. The impulses toward reflection and self-awareness have been totally displaced by mindless enthusiasm for the paradoxical combination of utter materiality and absolute speed. In a world dominated by

Mammon, this obsession inevitably leads to *the climax of matter,* an apocalyptic eruption transforming the totally coagulated state of materiality into something altogether unpredictable.

The Futurists were mere children rejoicing in the warning tremors of the coming apocalypse. In 1914 Carlo Carrà, one of their members, created their last suicidal manifesto and call for war. The *Interventionist Manifesto* dispenses with words altogether; it is a collage of frenetic simultaneity, in which streams of nonsense syllables burst in every direction. In August of that year the "Great War" burst open; technically skilled human hordes clashed in pure, mechanical—*futurist*—strife. A number of the Futurists experienced the apocalypse early and never came home. Laboring under the burden of an exhausted tradition, artists from all over Europe fed their energies into the war, making the ultimate sacrifice of psyche at the altar of techne.

"Forgive me my ignorance, Forgive me if I no longer know the ancient game of verse,' said Guillaume Apollinaire*, the brilliant poet and art critic, before marching off to that war, never to return. Blaise Cendrars, another poet, repeated again and again in his futuristic epic poem of 1913, "The Prose of the Trans-Siberian and of the Little Jeanne of France," that he was a *bad poet*. Bereft of tradition, the artists spiraled into the insanity of the simultaneous experience evoked by the sensory disordering of neotechnic civlization. Initially this experience is without a center, a tumult of chaotic meanderings brought about by the direct impact of the neotechnic environment. The result is a jumble of images in which time past and time future dissolve into one violent frenzy. Cendrars' long poetic train ride is not poetry, nor is he a poet; it is hallucinatory vision mingling prophecy—"I sensed the coming of the great Red Christ of the Russian Revolution"—with a cinematic montage of the violent reality of the present:

> *Now the unleashed storms roar*
> *The trains roll in a whirlwind on the entangled lines*
> *Devilish toys*
> *There are trains that never meet*

---

*Apollinaire typified the artistic desire for war, however it might have been justified. Having signed up for front-line duty, he suffered a head wound from flying shrapnel and died in 1918, just two days before the armistice. The suicidal aspect of the avant-garde stems both from the fact that the avant-garde is inherently a militaristic concept and from a need for psyche to inflict some kind of revenge on techne. Perhaps such gestures as those of Apollinaire and the Futurists were meant to communicate the desperation these artists felt, as in the recent example of a concept artist who literally suicided himself by cutting off his limbs. But the tragedy is that the message rarely gets across, if ever. Cf. Maurice Nadeau, *The History of Surrealism,* trans. Richard Howard (New York, 1965), chapt. 2. "The Poets in the War," pp. 52–58. Apollinaire, it should be noted, coined the word surrealism.

Others get lost on the way . . .
The railroad is a new geometry
Syracuse
Archimedes
And the soldiers who slit his throat
And the galley
And the ships
And the prodigious machines he invented
And all the killings
Ancient history
Modern history
The whirlwinds
The shipwrecks
Even the Titanic's which I read in a newspaper
So many image-associations that I cannot develop in my verse
For I am still a very bad poet
For the universe flows over me
For I neglected to insure myself against railroad accidents
For I do not know how to go all the way
And I'm afraid . . . [2]

The train of psychic sensibility had long been separated from and at odds with the train of technical progress; now the two collided and plunged dizzily into war. The delicate dialectical framework modern civilization had developed for maintaining its schizophrenia collapsed in a carnage of words, images, and human flesh and blood. Yet the "Great War" did not change anything; rather, it only confirmed the irreversible machinations of hell, the mindless, mechanical course of Mammon. Men emerged from the First World War determined even to build bigger and better than before. Though the war had resulted in a tremendous loss of human life, it was a triumph for technique. W. B. Yeats beautifully summed up its aftermath in 1920;

> *Turning and turning in the widening gyre*
> *The falcon cannot hear the falconer;*
> *Things fall apart; the centre cannot hold;*
> *Mere anarchy is loosed upon the world,*
> *The blood-dimmed tide is loosed, and everywhere*
> *The ceremony of innocence is drowned;*
> *The best lack all conviction, while the worst*
> *Are full of passionate intensity.*
> *Surely some revelation is at hand*
> *Surely the Second Coming is at hand.* [3]

While the war and the materialist revolution in Russia raged on, a small group of European artists gathered in Zurich. Wiser perhaps than the Futurists, these artists saw more clearly the folly of culture—culture understood not merely as an assemblage of art objects, but as the direct psychological underpinnnings of an entire civilization. This common perception gave birth to Dada, as a leading Dadaist, Hans Arp, wrote:

Revolted by the butchery of the 1914 World War, we in Zurich devoted ourselves to the arts. While the guns rumbled in the distance, we sang, painted, made collages and wrote poems with all our might. We were seeking an art based on fundamentals, to cure the madness of the age, and a new order of things that would restore the balance of heaven and hell. We had a dim premonition that power-mad gangsters would one day use art itself as a way of deadening men's minds.[4]

As an eruption of matter, war always unleashes a deepening exploration of the psyche. Dada was both a terrible and idiotic outcry, and a sublime journey through the undergrowth of consciousness. What the Futurists spurned, with their contempt for women and the aspects of consciousness they considered weak, the Dadaists embraced with fondness and love. Their simultaneous nonsense poems became the automatic writing of the Surrealists. More than anything, the adventure of playing with the moment, of taking and accepting the moment, of being receptive to chance, suspending all preconception, led certain of the Dadaists, at least, to the border of a new psychic experience of the world. According to Arp, "The law of chance, which embraces all other laws and is as unfathomable to us as the depths from which all life arises, can only be comprehended by complete surrender to the Unconscious. I maintain that whoever submits to this law attains perfect life."[5] If realization of the simultaneity of experience was the first step toward an authentic postmechanical consciousness, then the perception of acausality through the full acceptance of *chance* and surrender of the unconscious was the next path to follow.

But even at this point, the path was fraught with danger. Complete submission to the unknown without a conscious balancing only perpetuates an automatic and mechanical existence. Thus certain of the Dadaists gloried in an anticonsciousness; their art was an antiart that ultimately amounted to another suicidal form of nihilism. Into this category fall the "readymades," and "found-objects." One of the most famous of these was a urinal, signed R. Mutt, that Marcel Duchamp attempted to exhibit at the first New York *salon des indépendents.* Another was a snow shovel bought at a hardware store, on which Duchamp wrote, "in advance of the broken arm." When it appeared in an art exhibit, the snow shovel simultaneously was elevated to the category of art and exposed the surrounding works of art as being mere objects of no more intrinsic and of less utilitarian value than a snow shovel. This technique has a unique if limited value in exposing the shallowness of accepted aesthetic values. But when repeated again and again within the context of an art gallery or a museum, it endows the ready-made with a false aesthetic value and ultimately only contributes to the cultural barrenness it originally was intended to expose. This is precisely what has happened. Marcel Duchamp, who scorned the very notion of art and the bourgeois culture that sustains it, has been canonized by a later generation of pop, funk, and concept artists. The consciously antiartistic techniques he originated have become the core of a leading school of avant-garde art.

In Duchamp's own words, the concept of the ready-mades was "based on a reaction of *visual indifference* with a total absence of good or bad taste . . . in fact a complete anaesthesia."[6] Duchamp's use of the word *anaesthesia* is interesting, for *anaesthesia* implies a loss of consciousness, literally a complete senselessness: in a word, death. (*Aesthetic*, by contrast, literally pertains to the heightening of sensory awareness.) In embracing Duchamp's notion, then, later generations of artists have in effect embraced death. The ready-mades and the later forms of concept art—whose intent is "to carry the mind of the spectator towards other regions, more verbal"[7]—are the same in spirit (or lack of it) as the forms of abstract art developed from Cubism and Mondrian's De Stijl, or "pure plastic art." In these modes the artist, like the scientist/technologist, is a soulless manipulator of forms and matter, totally unrelated to the organic impulses of life. To the degree that artists have embraced these fundamentally life-denying and anaesthetic techniques, their art has become a movement toward death; in fact, art becomes the death of psyche itself.

For the Dada artist following the war there were two choices: the path of the machine and the path of the dream. A poster at a 1919 Dada exhibition in Berlin read: "Art is dead. Long live the New Machine Art. Tatlins."[8] The machine offered the value of utility to artists disenchanted with the effete, nonutilitarian aspect of the fine arts. This reaction produced a wave of neomechanical artistic ventures in the 1920's, including various schools of abstraction—Purism, De Stijl—and other more enviromentally oriented efforts: the Bauhaus in Germany, Constructivism, and the efforts of the new Soviet academy of arts. Some of the works that resulted now adorn museum walls and fill the spaces of gargantuan skyscraper plazas; the monolithic steel-and-glass skyscraper itself can be considered a product of this exploration. But though there was much that was worthwhile in these various attempts to come to terms with the machine, the ultimate machinery of collective state psychology proved implacable. "Power-mad gangsters," dictators, politicians, and advertising men continued to destroy or pervert sincere artistic exploration and use it as a way of deadening men's minds. Finally, as an attempt at reshaping nature according to rational materialist principles, techno-abstraction—pure plastic art, Constructivism, Purism, and so forth—only signalled the final stylistic stage of Western classical humanism.

Side by side with the often compromising or easily compromised efforts at creating a machine aesthetic, techno-abstraction, there emerged another development, the conscious and willed exploration of those realms of mind either ignored or repressed by reason. "The world of memory and dream is the real world,"[9] Arp declared in his autobiographical work, On My Way. As early as the first years of the nineteenth century, the German Romantic Phillip Otto Runge had stated, "Art must first be totally despised, it must first be thought totally pointless, before it can once more come into its own."[10] The point of pointlessness seems to have been reached with Dada. The conscious plunge into the unconscious signaled the abdication of the realms dominated by the left cerebral hemisphere and a reimmersion in those dominated by the right. This conscious movement became known as Surrealism—super-realism, beyond reality.

Surrealism had been an unconscious movement since the flames of revolution had swept the Bastille in the late eighteenth century, and choking black smoke had begun to cover the European countryside in the early nineteenth. Its precursors are all those Romantics and madmen who creatively rebelled against the iron yoke of rational materialism—whether Blake or Gauguin, Poe or Rimbaud, Hölderlin or Wölfli. The whole movement, fragmentary at first but then gaining coherence and strength, had more to do with maintaining the vitality of the human spirit than with creating works of art. Spirit is primary, expression secondary, manifestation tertiary.

The collective effort away from the mind-forged manacles of materialism may be described most accurately as *purposive regression*. The German art historian Alois Riegl used this phrase early in the century to describe the transformation of later Roman art from a relatively articulated naturalism to a more simplified, hieratic form equivalent to a symbol or ideograph. From the point of view of the prevailing civilizational values, this transformation exemplifies a process of "degeneration," or the onset of decadence; it appears to be a *regression* to a more childlike form of expression. This regression can be considered *purposive* in the context of late Roman civilization because it prepared the perceptual ground for a new symbolic system, Christianity. More recently, a similar pattern can be traced beginning with the early industrial Romantics: the progressive movement away from Renaissance naturalism, the madness of the poets, the flight of Rimbaud and Gauguin, the impulse to abstraction, the outrage of Dada, and with Surrealism, the plunge into the depths, and conscious cultivation of unreason. All of this may be viewed as a similar breaking down and preparation of the ground for the revelation Yeats called the Second Coming. And since the Second Coming can be prepared for and come from nowhere but the human *interior*, the Surrealists and later psychedelic pioneers who hoped to retrieve a glimpse of what is to be had to become deep sea divers dipping into the vast ocean of human consciousness.

From this point of view, the First World War was a tidal wave leveling culture and spirit to mere debris. Igor Stravinsky's *Sacre du Printemps*, written in 1913, was in reality the rite of a spring yet to come, a forevision flashing unexpectedly in the midst of a civilized Walpurgis Night. To paraphrase Runge, the spirit must first be totally despised, it must first be thought totally pointless, before it can once more come into its own.

Like Kandinsky and Gauguin, Arp saw the necessity of reversing the prevailing values without losing touch with the creative strand of the spirit.

In former times man knew the meaning of above and below, he knew what was eternal and what was transitory. Man did not yet stand on his head. His houses had a floor, walls and a ceiling. The Renaissance transformed the ceiling into a fool's paradise, the walls into garden mazes, and the floor into the bottomless. Man has lost his sense of reality, the mystical, the determinate indeterminable, the greatest determinate of all. . . . The Renaissance taught men the haughty exaltation of their reason. Modern times with their science and technology turned men towards megalomania. The confusion of our epoch results from this overestimation of reason. We wanted an anonymous and collective art.[11]

To achieve this goal Arp and his wife, Sophie Tauber, worked in painting, embroidery, collage, and sculpture, combining their skill and imagination with the spontaneous impulses of nature, "for in nature a broken twig is equal to the stars in beauty and importance, and it is men who decree what is beautiful and what is ugly."[12] Arp and his immediate circle had rediscovered the point at which nature and human consciousness merge—the mental antipodes that had been ruptured or concealed in the great Cartesian schizophrenia that developed in the seventeenth century.

What Arp and certain of the Dadaists had touched upon and experienced as a vital aspect of the strange migration of the spirit was transformed by André Breton and others into the absolutist doctrine of Surrealism, defined by Breton in the First Surrealist Manifesto (1924):

SURREALISM, noun, masc. Pure psychic automatism by which it is intended to express either verbally or in writing the true function of thought. Thought dictated in the absence of all control exerted by reason, and outside all aesthetic or moral preoccupations.

Philos., Surrealism is based on the belief in the superior reality of certain forms of association heretofore neglected, in the omnipotence of the dream, and in the disinterested play of thought. It leads to the permanent destruction of all other psychic mechanisms and to its substitution for them in the solution of the principal problems of life.[13]

In the absolutism of its principles, Surrealism was ultimately another form of tyranny, replacing the terror of reason with the terror of unreason. Thus it was never to be more than a sensational explosion, a burst of rhetoric, and a host of ingenious techniques that were to become commonplace in television advertising. The revolution it had hoped to achieve was easily surpassed by the natural incongruities and simple terrors of technologized existence. The balance between heaven and hell, above and below was destroyed by the most fundamental Surrealist premise of antireason. The Surrealists had embarked on their perilous journey forgoing all guides, with the dubious exceptions of Freud and Marx, whom they immediately canonized. As for what a later generation would refer to as maps of consciousness, the Surrealists seemed initially to have little systematic awareness of them. True enough, there appear images obviously harking back to the Tarot, and much Surrealist work is permeated with an overstrained sense of magic. But in attempting the marriage of Freud and Marx, Surrealism floundered totally.

Sensing the bankruptcy of these ideologies, Breton issued another manifesto in 1929. In order to broaden and deepen the Surrealist current, he exhorted Surrealists not to neglect the esoteric traditions of alchemy and astrology, the search for the philosopher's stone and the guidance of the stars. In accord with the secretive precepts of these disenfranchised traditions, Breton urged, "The public must absolutely be kept from *entering* if we wish to avoid confusion . . . *I demand the profound true occultation of surrealism.*" The actual goal of Surrealism—the search for and attainment of the philosopher's stone—would allow the human imagination "to take a brilliant revenge upon things."[14] From this point of view, Breton judged Surrealism to be merely in its preparatory stage, and much too involved in purely artistic matters.

For the first time since the early eighteenth century, a group of European intellectuals were reinvestigating and invoking the lost traditions that maintained the balance of heaven and hell. But Breton's attempt to shift interest from artistic production to a more psychological plane proved unsuccessful, as did his efforts to place Surrealism on a sound footing with the esoteric or traditional sciences. As Breton perceived, the motivating principle underlying these traditions precludes the *primacy* of artistic activity; from the point of view of alchemy, for instance, artistic activity is a secondary trait. It may be necessary, but unless it proceeds from a proper understanding of the structure of consciousness and the workings of natural law, it is merely a frivolous pastime. The alchemist and the businessman might well agree about the uselessness of modern art, but their reasons are utterly different.

Rather than make the purposefully regressive leap of a radically transformed alchemy, Surrealism produced many brilliant individual styles, each a fractured reflection of the collective psyche. It remained essentially a savage perpetuation of the cult of individual genius initiated by Michelangelo and the Renaissance masters. The publicity-seeking antics of the brilliant madman Salvador Dali are not at all in accord with Arp's vision of an anonymous and collective art. In fact, no one has cultivated the art of public egomaniacal madness so successfully as Dali. Next to him, Picasso is an ingenuous child playing the role of the Latin lover in the bullring— while Dali emerges from the Paris subway led by an anteater on a leash. By the 1930's Surrealism as a movement had succumbed to the same decadence that Dada had rebelled against.

Among the Surrealists who embarked on the search for the philosopher's stone, one stands out: Antonin Artaud, a man of penetrating vision and insight who saw that "things are bad because the sick conscience now has a vital interest in not getting over its sickness."[15] Like van Gogh, whom he understood as no one else, Artaud could say of himself, "He who does not smell of a smouldering bomb and of compressed vertigo is not worthy to be alive."[16] Experiencing civilization's perversity to the fullest—in a 1926 film he played Marat murdered in his bathtub—he fled, he invoked other gods, he traveled deserts and mountains, he consumed himself with opium, and he sought the philosopher's stone in the peyote of the land of the Tarahumaras. Finally wrenched completely from common reality and all but broken, he collapsed in the insane asylum at Rodez.

In him, purposive regression was the journey to the East, to primal lands; it took the form of an "Address" to the Dalai Lama: "We are your faithful servants, O Great Lama. Grant to us, address to us your wisdoms, in a language which our European minds can understand, and if necessary change our Spirit, fashion for us a perception wholly attuned to those perfect summits where the Spirit of Man suffers no longer."[17] Or the "Letter to the Buddhist Schools":

You who are not imprisoned in the flesh, who know at what point in the carnal trajectory, its senseless comings and goings, the soul finds the absolute verb, the new word, the inner land; you who know how one turns back into one's thoughts, how the spirit can be saved from itself . . . hurl into the ocean all those whites who arrive with their small heads and their well-behaved minds. . . . We do not speak of the old human ailment. Our spirit suffers from other needs than those inherent in life. We suffer from a corruption, the corruption of Reason. Logical Europe endlessly crushes the mind between the jaws of two extremes; it opens and recloses the mind. But now the strangulation is at its peak. We have suffered too long under the yoke. The spirit is greater than the spirit, life's metamorphoses are manifold. Like you, we reject progress: come and tear down our houses. . . . Come. Save us from these larvae. Devise for us new houses.[18]

From the teachings of Tibet, Artaud arrived at the perception that modern existence is a hell—a real hell, and not just a metaphorical or literary hell. But this hell, officially known as history, is a *Bardo*, an intermediate stage between death and another birth.

> *Now, I repeat, death is an invented state*
> *and it keeps itself alive only through all the low rabble of*
> *warlocks, gurus and conjurers of*
> *nothingness for whom it is profitable and who for some centuries*
>   *now have been nourished by it*
> *and live by it in the state called Bardo. . . .*[19]

This stage must pass, for civilization is truly a dream, and what may seem absolute under present psychosocial conditions is but the machinery of a hallucination that keeps us from realizing the "true organic metamorphosis of the human body."[20] Artaud's entire effort was toward "this revolution of the whole body without which nothing can be changed."[21] Armed with the metaphysics of Tibet, Artaud, the psychedelic pioneer, continued his search in Mexico, for as he perceived: "We have much to learn from the secrets of Mexican astrology, as read and interpreted on the spot through hieroglyphs not yet deciphered."[22] And in a passage that predates by almost thirty years the later search of Carlos Castaneda, Artaud wrote:

Upon some lost plateaus, we shall interrogate healers and sorcerers, and we shall hope to hear the painters, poets, architects, sculptors state that they possess the whole reality of the images they have created—a reality which drives them on. For the secret of high Mexican magic lies in the power of signs created by those who in Europe would still be called artists, and who in advanced civilizations have not lost contact with natural sources and are the sole performers and prophets of a speech in which, periodically, the world must come to quench its thirst. Mexico can still teach us the secret of a diction and a language where all dictions and languages gather in one. . . . Old Mexicans did not separate culture from civilization nor culture from a personal knowledge distributed in the whole organism. . . .

Are there still forests which speak? Where can sorcerers with burning fibers of Peyote and Marijuana still encounter that terrible old man who discloses the secret of divination?[23]

What Artaud sought was the mystic key to unlock the myth of his own divinity and make it real. In the land of the Tarahumaras in the scorching plateaus of northern Mexico, he came pathetically close; but though he was saturated with peyote and dazzled by visions, the final mystery, the *mysterium tremendum*, the final initiation was never revealed:

What is the singular word, that lost utterance, the Lord of the Peyote passes down to them [the sorcerers]? And why do they need three years to handle the grater properly, this grater on which it must be admitted, the Tarahumara sorcerers perform some rather curious *auscultations*? What is it, then, they have torn from the forest and the forest yields to them so slowly?[24]

Artaud, the European artistic rebel, returned unsated from the land of the Tarahumaras. The key to the myth having slipped through his hands, he pursued the notion of creating a *ritual theater;* but it was too much to realize without the key, without the *word.* The agonized European, bitter, vengeful, was too impatient to understand that to master the disciplines by which hell may be transcended may easily take three years *just to begin with.* Yet at the core of his perceptions was the key, disembodied in fragments of verse, by which the hallucination of history/hell might be overcome:

I hate and renounce as a coward every being who is unwilling to consecrate his whole life to the control as well as to the reorganization of the buried, unfounded, and uncreated being of his thought. . . . I hate and renounce as a coward every being who separates what he calls his body from what he calls his consciousness or his thought. . . . I hate and renounce as a coward every being who will not consent to go through two hundred thousand reincarnations on earth until he finally becomes conscious of having been born.[25]

The Futurists, the Dadaists, and the Surrealists were all self-conscious European intellectuals, a select elite of human intelligence. If anything defeated them it was the accumulated weight of hundreds of years of materialistic, intellectually structured perceptions that, no matter how shattered by war, still lay in an undecomposed heap at the periphery of their consciousness. Without the true innocence of the perceptually unencumbered mind, they could only create fragments, nightmares, dreams. An outsider like Wölfli, unemcumbered by the intellectual debris of the past, had no trouble creating at least the vision of that paradise Artaud so intensely aspired to. But the Surrealist's plunge into the ocean of consciousness, if dramatic, was too shallow to bring about the revolution they desired. Their works merely affronted the public, or at best elicited a morbid fascination. With no clear understanding of the ego, its dangers and inherent illusoriness, other than Freud's sexually obsessed theories, the Surrealist intellectuals, with rare exceptions like Max Ernst, could go no farther than personal bitterness for some, for others the glamorous cult of personality, and for a few, the madhouse or suicide.

> *What is that sound high in the air*
> *Murmur of maternal lamentation*
> *Who are those hooded hordes swarming*
> *Over endless plains, stumbling in cracked earth*
> *Ringed by the flat horizon only*
> *What is the city over the mountains*
> *Cracks and reforms and bursts in the violet air*
> *Falling towers*
> *Jerusalem Athens Alexandria*
> *Vienna London*
> *Unreal*[26]

T. S. Eliot had most appropriately described postwar Europe as a psychic wasteland that only the deepest conversion of the spirit could redeem. In view of the obstacles faced by the European intellectual, it is not surprising that one of the most compelling efforts in "pure psychic automatism" was made by a technically and intellectually unencumbered coal miner, a denizen of the deepest and truest underground of the modern hell period. What sets Augustin "Le Mineur" LeSage even farther apart from the intellectually motivated artists of the Surrealist generation is the fact that he was a psychic medium.

In 1911, not too far from Paris, City of Light, the center of heightened civilized madness preceding the First World War, LeSage was accosted by the voice of his dead sister while deep within the bowels of a mine. From 1911 to the beginning of the war, the scarcely literate LeSage labored on his nine-foot-square *Great Painting*. Whereas the traditional modes of perception in European civilization were being shattered on many levels, LeSage's monumental painting exhibits a development from chaos to order—not just rational order, but a growing, organic sense of togetherness strangely absent from nearly all other contemporary European art. Unlike any of the abstractionists or Surrealists, LeSage created his art not in response to other art but in response to something beyond.

According to LeSage, during these early years he was acting merely as the medium of the "Spirit of Leonardo da Vinci." Though this cannot be proved one way or the other, it is curious and even haunting that just prior to the great psychotechnological outburst of 1914, a poorly educated coal miner should have achieved such a fresh and striking departure from the Renaissance tradition as the *Great Painting*. Even more than Wölfli's work, LeSage's conveys an amazing sense of balance, order, symmetry, and organic harmony, evoking the deepest archetypal patterns of thought and feeling. Next to his work the modernist struggle of much of abstractionism, Surrealism, and the pretentious movements that followed appears to project profound emotional and moral confusion and intellectual folly. LeSage's *Great Painting* is also unique in affording a glimpse of the creative transformation of the personality, for it begins as an outburst and progressively develops into a symmetrical order that, unlike the subjectively rational order of modernist geometrical abstraction, remains alive and growing.

LeSage continued painting into the 1920's. Though his later paintings appear more ornamental and less spontaneous than the early work, they are brilliant evocations of temples and hieratic architecture that also serve as pure images of the inherent order of the mind. The resemblance of these later paintings to Hindu architecture and the gates of Tibetan mandalas reflects the unity of mind and the common source of all human creative endeavors that are rooted in the spirit. But this unity is revealed only when the paths to the spirit, the intuitive realm of psyche, have been cleared, unintentionally or otherwise. The singularity of LeSage's work rests on his personal transcendence of the techniques and principles of rational materialism—in a word, of civilization as we know it.[27]

In a significant way, the work of pure outsiders like Wölfli and LeSage forecasts an era of more conscious and thoroughgoing psychosensory integration than our own. They are true premonitions of growth in the ice floe of a disintegrated culture. At a more personal level, their example demonstrates the tremendous creative potential inherent in the individual, regardless of his educational and cultural background. At the very least, creativity is independent of cultural conditioning. Moreover, it requires that psychic insight precede technique. When technique becomes paramount, and overwhelms the ability to nurture the primal psychic insight, then the entire apparatus of culture or civilization has outlived its usefulness and must be transcended. This is the lesson of the coal miner LeSage.

Counterbalancing the rare exception of an individual like Wölfli or LeSage is the mass of humanity, desensitized in our technological era by the merciless onslaught of mechanical conditioning processes. For them, only the electronic media and popular events can offer any solace, however fleeting. Just as LeSage achieved the goal of Surrealism—pure psychic automatism—without being a Surrealist, so the popular film *King Kong* fulfills at a collective, unconscious level another basic Surrealist aim—the presentation of "certain forms of association heretofore neglected." Without resorting to the overblown and self-conscious artifice of manifesto and conscious rebellion, *King Kong* presents a perfect parable of the cause of civilization's present crisis—the suicidal consequences of the repression of the intuitive realm by the rational. In this respect *King Kong* is merely one of the monsters produced by the dream of reason.

Technically *King Kong*, like many another science-fiction or historical film, is an illusionistic tour de force. Though Surrealist painters like Dali and René Magritte resurrected and perfected the Renaissance technique of illusionism in their own disturbing way, it is in the art of the cinema, the stepchild of nineteenth-century academicism, with its stage sets and devices, that illusionism has reached its ultimate perfection. At this level alone *King Kong* would have amazed the academic studio illusionists. It is one of the early landmarks of cinematic illusionism, and though it has been surpassed by stunning films like *2001*, its appeal as a parable of the pathetic state of the contemporary collective consciousness is without parallel. What Frankenstein's monster—sinister presage of the Faustian manipulation of life and matter—was to the nineteenth century, King Kong is to the twentieth. The former is the soulless proto-robot brought forth from the sterile womb of dealchemized science, the exact mirror of the cybernetic robotism that pervades the technological era; the latter represents the technologically repressed spirituality transformed into the unconscious itself—a monster grown out of proportion through neglect and abuse.

Naturally King Kong's original home and sacred place is an island off the coast of Africa—"the Heart of Darkness"—where he is worshipped in fear and terror. The African natives represent the stunted impulses of the modern psyche living in the luxuriant wilderness of the feminine, intuitive right cerebral hemisphere. So primordial is the home of King Kong that in it still linger the great reptilian beasts of the Mesozoic era. Into this undeveloped wilderness, with its strange beasts and rites, come the white American explorers and exploiters, a group of Barnum & Baileys seeking the greatest and strangest of whatever there is to be had. Hearing of King Kong and fancying what a lucrative attraction he would make, they finally manage to capture him. King Kong is to be exploited, much as nature itself has been exploited for the profit of a few. The "lost world" escapades have a perverse and sadistic overtone, for the only creature King Kong can maintain any kind of a positive relationship to is a woman, enacted by Fay Wray. This is appropriate enough, since in our age the feminine aspect of nature is most clearly associated with spirit as a psychic resource. King Kong's advances toward the woman—another variant of beauty and the beast—are inevitably grotesque and misinterpreted.

Having been drugged and shipped to New York, King Kong appears in chains on the Broadway stage; here he exemplifies the ultimate civilized ideal of art as entertainment, an essentially uncreative art that is in reality the crucifixion of the spirit. Breaking loose and fleeing from this humiliation, carrying Fay Wray in his hands, King Kong terrorizes the city. In a publicity shot that never actually occurs in the film, King Kong is shown standing against the nighttime sky above the great "unreal" modern city, while from each hand great crackling streams of lighting pour down on the menaced buildings below—a powerful, "surrealistic" image of the revolt of the unconscious. At the end of the film King Kong mounts the great phallic symbol of left-hemisphere dominance, the Empire State Building, where he is shot down by the new technological might of warplanes. There is no doubt that the film's popularity and power owe much to the audience's unconscious sympathy and identification with this fear-inspiring symbol of our own repressed nature.

When King Kong was released in 1933, it was a stunning success. Surrealism was but a weird aberration at the fringes of culture. The world was in the midst of an economic depression. And in Germany a frustrated artist named Adolf Hitler had finally consolidated his vision, partly through the use of an ancient sign symbolizing the power of the turning of the world. Mankind's great march into the incandescent brilliance of an atomic death and transfiguration had begun. When man is deprived of the power of expression, he will express himself in a drive for power.

CHAPTER NINETEEN

Art and Alchemy: The Great Return

LESS THAN 140 years after Edward Gibbon completed his monumental work, *The Decline and Fall of the Roman Empire,* Oswald Spengler published an equally brilliant and even more foreboding study entitled *The Decline of the West.* The former was written during the American Revolution; the latter, during the First World War. With Spengler's work the historical cycle begun with Gibbon had come to its natural conclusion. From its origins technological civilization had been obsessed with the glory and melancholy decline of the Mediterranean past. This theme was prevalent in nineteenth-century art and culture, and the behavior of the artistic demimonde prior to and especially after the First World War only seemed to bear out the fatalistic identification: the decline of the megalomaniac Roman empire was being played out once again in the decline of the West. In Spengler's view Faustian man has only a long "wasteland" twilight to look forward to, punctuated along the way by the violent spasms of the final war, characterized by Spengler as the war between blood and money.

From our vantage point today, it is difficult to dispute Spengler's vision. The Faustian thrust of Western civilization has expanded to encompass the entire globe. If Japan is a brilliant reflection of American capitalism, China apes the Marxist efforts of the earlier phases of Soviet Russia. Regardless of ideology, the relentless impulse of technique prevails. The combustion engine, television, the jet airplane, and the steel-and-glass skyscraper are commonplace the world over. In a sense our civilization's end has already been reached; now it is only a matter of filling up the empty spaces, from the atmosphere of earth to the farthest stars.

There is in this vision an absolute linearity, a blind extension toward Andromeda that fails to take into account organic periodicity, the cycle of death and rebirth. As long as the line of progress is sustained in its upward path, then man will continue to live in the twilight wasteland of the Faustian dream. To a great degree Western civilization has played out this scenario since the First World War, and the planet earth has accordingly become encased in the belly of Mammon. But like the linear Christian historical vision, of which it is an outgrowth, Spengler's Faustian interpretation denies the reality of *return.* I am referring not to Nietzsche's mechanical vision of eternal return, but to *organic return*—death, rebirth, and the possibility of unimaginable transformation.

In the "Ninth Duino Elegy," written in 1922, almost contemporaneous with Spengler's magnum opus, the poet Rilke declared:

These things that live on departure
Understand when you praise them: fleeting, they look for

rescue through something in us, the most fleeting of all.
Want us to change them entirely, within our invisible hearts,
into - oh, endlessly - into ourselves! Whoever we are.

And then, in a plea that is the summons of the transformative vision, Rilke
continued:

Earth, isn't this what you want: an invisible
re-arising in us? Is it not your dream
to be one day invisible? Earth! Invisible!
What is your urgent command, if not transformation?[1]

The significance of the appearance of visionaries like LeSage and Wölfli,
Gauguin and Nijinsky at this point in the "decline of the West" becomes
clear in the context of Rilke's summons. To *return* means to submit the
total structure of the personality to the inexhaustible source of the creative
spirit, a spirit that is independent of cultural conditioning. Because he had
glimpsed something of this truth, Breton called for the ressurection of the
esoteric arts of alchemy and astrology, which teach through a veiled, symbolic language the reality of and means to an organic, transformative return. The theme of the Romantics, of Gauguin and Artaud, of the Dadaists
and the original Surrealists is nothing less than the theme of the Great
Return. What Riegl described as purposive regression in a time of civilizational decay has its more positive side in the notion of the Great Return—
the conscious reimmersion in the spirit with the end of transforming both
the individual and his cultural means. As Breton perceived, for the civilized
artist to embark on the Great Return he must set aside his involvement
with art as such until the spirit is reborn and nurtured by an appropriate
teaching. For most European artistic temperaments this presented too great
a sacrifice, and the primacy of art for its own sake has been maintained.
Among some of the more spiritually sensitive artists in the 1920's and 30's,
however, the impulse toward the Great Return manifested in an increasingly childlike art. This accounts for the proto-symbolic and quasi-
hieroglyphic paintings of Klee, Kandinsky, and Miro—an unconscious
stuttering and stammering toward that symbolic language Novalis had
called the true language of paradise.

Cut off from the traditions that deal most explicitly with the Great
Return, the task of envisioning a transformation from death to a new birth
is enormous. Yet there is a principle of spiritual necessity operative in even
the darkest of ages.

The fundamental principle of the Great Return is cyclical, and its course
immutable, beyond the charade of intellectual form and will. In the experiments and writings of Charles Henry were enunciated the psychophysical
premises of the cyclical nature of our own experience. Henry's *Chromatic*

Circle is a metaphor of our essential condition, in which all opposites are harmoniously united. If our own psychosensory nature is organized according to the laws of the circle and its dynamic aspect, the cycle, then the same should hold true for the development of nature and human consciousness, each of which is inextricably involved with the other. What we call history is not a line on a graph, but an alchemical formula symbolized by the Ouroboros—the dragon eating its own tail. In alchemy the Ouroboros symbolizes the fusion of energies necessary for integration. By biting its own tail and infusing itself with its own poison, the dragon completes a circle and a transformation occurs. "This surely is a great miracle—that in a venomous dragon there should be the great medicine."[2] If the dragon does not bite its tail it dies, for as the Pythagoreans taught, death is not knowing how to join beginning with end. The Ouroboros biting its own tail is the sign, therefore, of the Great Return. History, the erratic, willful dynamism of the venomous dragon, bit its own tail at the time of the First World War—the Great War—thereby releasing the transformative toxins of the great medicine.

This medicine takes effect first at the deepest levels of the psyche, acting on the latent forces not yet developed—or neglected—by human consciousness. Naturally those whose minds have not totally succumbed to the dictatorship of reason are more open to the impulses emanating from repressed right-hemisphere functions. Thus the circle of nations that the Sioux Indian seer Black Elk saw broken at Wounded Knee in 1891 surfaced whole once again, at least in seed form, in the mandalas drawn by C. G. Jung during the First World War. The mandala is the Ouroboric circle completed. Quoting Goethe, Jung described it as "formation, transformation, eternal mind's eternal recreation."[3] During the years 1918-20 the mandala gave Jung the key to a realization that "there is no linear evolution; there is only circumambulation of the self. Uniform development exists, at most, only at the beginning; later everything points toward the center. This insight gave me stability, and gradually my inner peace returned. I knew that in finding the mandala as an expression of the self, I had attained what was for me the ultimate."[4] History, being but an expression of the self, to use Jung's terminology, is also a mandala.

It is an interesting testament to the suicidal tendencies of the European mind that in the decades following the Great War, the Surrealists looked not to Jung but to Freud, who was incapable of seeing beyond the limits of his own ego. In his last book, *Civilization and Its Discontents,* published in 1939 on the eve of the Second World War, Freud touchingly and characteristically reasoned to the pessimistic conclusion that the warring dualities of man and nature, conscious and unconscious, reason and instinct could never be satisfactorily resolved.

If Freud and the Surrealists faltered, Jung did not. Having rediscovered the mandala after the publication of his *Psychology of the Unconscious* (1917), Jung later came to realize that the mandala was nothing less than the *"prima materia* of a life-time's work."[5] For some ten years he painted mandalas, as did some of his patients. Then, in 1927, Jung had a powerful dream. He dreamed he was in a dirty, sooty city on a dark winter night— an image that represented the current stage of human development. The city was Liverpool—"pool of life." Passing through a narrow alley named "The Alley of the Dead," he came upon a square, from which streets radiated in every direction. In the center of the square was a pool, and in the center of the pool, an island. "While everything round about was obscured by rain, fog, smoke and dimly lit darkness, the little island blazed with sunlight. On it stood a single tree, a magnolia, in a shower of reddish blossoms. It was as though the tree stood in the sunlight and at the same time was the source of light."[6] Jung's dream of the revelation of the tree of light and life is the exact counterpart of Black Elk's vision of the Hoop of the Nations with the multicolored Tree of World Renewal at its center.*

Shortly after this great dream an important twofold event occurred: Jung connected his vision of the mandala with the oriental tradition through Richard Wilhelm's *Secret of the Golden Flower;* and he ceased painting mandalas. The *prima materia* had revealed itself to Jung, and in an important way to the modern West. Through the mandala Jung was able to reestablish at least a vital scholarly connection with the lost tradition of alchemy, a feat André Breton was contemporaneously attempting to accomplish on the Surrealists' behalf. Since Jung's *prima materia* is also identical with Whitman's *primal thought*, the mandala being literally the point of origin, a new psychological link to the Passage to India was established. Because of Jung's effort the avenue leading to the esoteric traditions of the East was broadened, and another step had been taken toward a synthesizing global renewal. Through Jung the well of the creative spirit which had been clogged for so long in the West had begun to be cleaned out.

Jung's contribution is notable in one other respect. As a healer and a teacher he helped others express themselves through mandalas and symbols in general, not merely for aesthetic satisfaction but as an integral means to self-realization. Thus, Jung helped restore to art some of its dignity by demonstrating its importance as a tool for psychic survival. Consciously or not, he began to retrieve the symbolic language cast into the

---

*Black Elk's vision is vividly described in John G. Neihardt, *Black Elk Speaks* (Lincoln, Neb., 1961), p. 43 "And I saw that the sacred hoop of my people was one of many hoops that made one circle, wide as daylight and as starlight, and in the center grew one mighty flowering tree to shelter all the children of one mother and one father. And I saw that it was holy." The correspondence of Jung's and Black Elk's visions can only be taken as another example of the activity of a global counterpoint of consciousness.

dungeon of the irrational by the architects of reason. By declaring the enduring psychogenetic nature of symbols—the archetypes inherent within our constitution—Jung, like Henry before him, placed art in the context of psychobiology, and psychobiology in the context of the eternal. But with the exception of a few artists and aestheticians like Henry Moore and the late Sir Herbert Read, most observers did not appreciate the creative, artistically transformative value of Jung's vision until they were plunged into greater awareness by the psychedelic revolution of the 1960's.

The spirit of the Great Return surfaced through several other individuals just after the Great War. One may recall Hermann Hesse's novels of the 1920's, with their inherent "orientalism"—*The Journey to the East, Siddhartha,* and *Steppenwolf.* Or the sudden, almost magical appearance of Gurdjieff in Moscow during the war and in Paris in the 1920's with his dancing groups, his thorough going psychology and philosophy, and his incredible personal mystique. Though an elite corps of writers and thinkers, including P. D. Ouspensky, Maurice Nicoll, and Rodney Collin, were immediately affected by him, Gurdjieff much like Hesse, remained largely unappreciated until later.

More directly parallel to Jung's discovery of the mandala between the years 1916 and 1927 was the strange revelation vouchsafed the Celtic poet W. B. Yeats through the inspiration of his wife, who had certain abilities as a medium:

On the afternoon of October 24th, 1917, four days after my marriage, my wife surprised me by attempting automatic writing. What came in disjointed sentences, in almost illegible writing, was so exciting, sometimes so profound, that I persuaded her to give an hour or so day after day to the unknown writer, and after some half dozen such hours offered to spend what remained of life explaining and piecing together those scattered sentences.[7]

The result of Yeats's effort was his book *A Vision,* first published in 1925.

The Ouroboric symbol, which was revealed to Jung as the mandala, disclosed itself to Yeats as the Great Wheel, the principal symbol of his vision. For Yeats the Great Wheel was the cosmic emblem in which all things could be read: the nature and constitution of the universe, the typology of human character and its development, and finally, the mirror of history, the great cycles of interpenetrating concord and discord, which held within the serpentine coils of time the secret of the Great Return. The Great Wheel, based on an alchemical symbol from the *Speculum Angelorum et Hominim* of Michael Robartes, is divided first of all into alternating primary (dark) and antithetical (light) phases, and then into four faculties, Will, Mask, Creative Mind, and Body of Fate, and their corresponding principles, Husk, Passionate Body, Spirit, and Celestial Body. The Wheel also has points corresponding to the equinoxes and solstices, and is divided into 28 parts, bearing some correspondance to the phases of the moon. Like all symbols, it may be applied and read in diverse ways, expanding or contracting in dimension, providing a measurement for the most minute nuance of psychological impulse or the greatest expanse of time.

Yeats himself was not totally certain about the full ramifications of his great symbol, and we must remember that it was his wife, acting as the mediumistic muse, who actually received the information, whereas Yeats was only the interpreter. In addition, Yeats' symbol must be conceived as a sphere or a cylinder (recall that Anaximander also viewed the world as a cylinder) composed of two interpenetrating cones, the apex of each being the center of the base of the other. One of these cones represents the primary force, and the other the antithetical force. Yeats did not seem to comprehend clearly the dynamics of these two forces, though he did refer to the dialectical philosophy of Hegel. At any rate, the two obviously relate to the Chinese principles of yin (primary) and yang (antithetical). From the interaction of the three sets of principles—the two forces, the four faculties and their corresponding principles, and the cycle of 28 Phases of the Great Wheel—Yeats developed a complex, quasi-astrological system of cosmopsychology, in which the history of an individual through various lives recapitulates the history of civilization, and vice versa. Because of the close identification of the development of the individual, and the history of the race, the entire vision borders on the mythological; what was absurd and arbitrary is suddenly transformed into the detail that gives meaning to the whole.

At the beginning of the fifth book of *A Vision*, there appears a strange chart entitled "The Historical Cones."* Essentially this chart is composed of two forms, a diamond-shaped cone contained within an hourglass-shaped cone. The diamond-shaped cone is the cone of the *primary tincture;* it is solar, feminine, religious, vital, symbolized by the faculties of Mask and Body of Fate, and the principles of Passionate Body and Celestial Body. The hourglass cone is the cone of the *antithetical tincture;* it is lunar, political, secular, masculine; its faculties are Will and Creative Mind, and its principles, Husk and Spirit. The whole chart represents a single *gyre* or turning of a complete cycle of 28 phases or incarnations of the Great Wheel, a time period of approximately two thousand years. All of the dates (and phases) on the chart are produced twice, and there are usually four dates strung out on a horizontal line. Though Yeats does not explain why the dates are reproduced twice—it may be that there actually is a mirror of our reality in time as well as space—it is clear that the horizontal lines have the function

---

*The two cones—primary and antithetical—are reproduced as part of the chart, "The Ascent of the Jaguar." See page 298.

of ensuring that within a given gyre, different points in time correspond with each other. What is begun at one point is resumed at another, albeit transformed externally.

Reflection on Yeats' "Historical Cones" may produce an uncanny sense of déjàvu, of inexplicable recognition, of genetic recollection, for this diagram and the Great Wheel from which it derives represent a cyclical understanding of history. The smallest major cycle of some two thousand years—comparable to the astrological procession of the planet through one of the constellations of the zodiac—begins and ends with an influx or *exchange of tincture*, essentially a dramatic reversal of ideas or a psychosocial revolution. A given gyre, such as the two-thousand-year Piscean age we are presently in, goes through four alternations of antithetical and primary forces. Thus a major antithetical period began in the year 1450. The end of this period will bring about not only an influx of primary forces but a complete reversal of our era; perhaps there will be a resumption of patterns within, but beyond that no one else can say. According to Yeats, "the unique intervenes."

The period in which Yeats wrote *A Vision* was the twenty-second phase, 1875–1927, the phase of the "balance between ambition and contemplation." It was "a period of revolution terminated by a civilization of policemen, schoolmasters, manufacturers, philanthropists, a second soon exhausted blossoming of the race."[8] In addition to this characterization of the era, Yeats also made intriguing references to death and rebirth, a theme that is inseparable from the concept of the circle. In the recent Western tradition it was the eighteenth-century historian Gianbattista Vico who first articulated an historical philosophy of the cycle. Yeats regarded many of the revolutionary ideas of recent European history as a perversion of Vico's ideas of class struggle and social regeneration through a return to a primitive mental state and a new barbarism. Obviously terms like *primitivism, barbarism,* and *revolution* are susceptible to any number of interpretations. Yeats made it clear, however, that the approaching influx or interchange of tinctures signifies a midpoint between death and rebirth. *Primitive* can only mean the influx of the *primary,* feminine forces following the death of the purely physical man of the materialist era, "for only so can *primary* power reach *antithetical* mankind shut within the circle of its senses."

Following Artaud's suggestion of the Bardo nature of recent history, it may give us more insight to assume that we are dead than that we are living, at least insofar as mankind is some kind of total, organic planetary process, moving through great periods of death, larval gestation and metamorphosis. According to Yeats a slow death began around 1050; the Gothic cathedrals are the hallucinatory tombstones of the initial stage of death. The fact that the feminine principle is so idealized in the cathedrals only implies that mankind had already divorced itself from the vital feminine aspect of life. But when one half of us dies, the other half is also doomed. Thus since the eleventh century Western man has been in a stage intermediate between death and a new birth, a stage filled with prodigious vision and struggles, and yet increasingly lifeless. Material expansion is not identical with true growth. As the Surrealist painter Matta declared, "History is the story of man's various hallucinations."[9] Once man is freed from these hallucinations, history as we know it may no longer exist, but there may be some potential for conscious understanding and growth. In Yeats's chart of the historical cones the last important date is 1927, which initiates a penultimate series comprising phases 23, 24, and 25. The Body of Fate of these three phases are characterized respectively by an enforced triumph of achievement (the triumph of fascism), an enforced success of action (World War II and the atomic era following it), and finally, an enforced failure of action (technological stalemate, energy and population crises). The interpretations in parentheses are my own. Yeats was very vague about the future, aside from suggesting a dramatic reversal, and he gave no date for the final period corresponding to the last three phases of the wheel—26, the Hunchback; 27, the Saint; and 28, the Fool.

Yeats also spoke of the coming marriage of Europe and Asia, though he was confused about what this might actually mean. He left us a clue when he spoke of the westward movement of antithetical Renaissance culture, which implies that the so-called New World, the Western Hemisphere, is the primary force toward which the antithetical is drawn. Neurophysiologically this corresponds to a movement from the intellectual left hemisphere to the intuitive right.

Though the symbol of the Great Wheel had come to Yeats, it was too immense for him; he could use it brilliantly to interpret the past, but the totality of its meaning escaped him. Yeats was a visionary, but he was no prophet. The Second Coming was easy enough to foretell, as was the turning of the gyre, but there is a quality to his thought of melancholy not totally redeemed. Yet he perceived certain clues, such as the significance of the year 1927.

It was a curious year, marked by the appearance of an erratic comet, Jung's dream, the invention of radio-television, Buckminster Fuller's synergistic revelation, and the publication of Evans-Wentz's popular edition of the seemingly obscure *Tibetan Book of the Dead*, the *Bardo Thödol*. The Bardos: twilight hallucinatory realms suspended between death and birth, history itself, in which the possibilities unrealized in life are grasped at, and ethical retribution for one's acts are paid back. The present era of history, as both Yeats and Artaud perceived it, is a *Bardo realm*.

According to the Tibetan teaching, at the moment of death the clear light of total illumination and understanding occurs; this is usually so powerful and intense that the consciousness of the dying person shrinks from it. At this point the consciousness enters the *Chikhai Bardo,* the realm of the purest emanations of primordial light. If the consciousness is unable to bear the intensity or grasp the meaning of the experience, it passes on to the next *Bardo,* the *Chonyid,* the realm of archetypal apparitions; if the consciousness is unable to grasp the significance of the events and visions of this realm and attain realization, it passes on to the lowest realm, the *Sidpa Bardo,* the realm of hellish apparitions and wrathful deities. From this realm the consciousness must choose a set of parents— one of the common apparitions is that of copulation—enter a womb, and prepare for rebirth. In 1935 Jung wrote a psychological commentary to the *Bardo Thödol,* making the interesting suggestion that for Westerners the book—or process—might best be read or experienced backward, starting with the Sidpa realm. Jung made this suggestion on the ground that we had best start on the most familiar level—living hell—since our experience is so far removed from the primordial. Whatever the merit of this idea, it does contain the painful insight that our present historical situation is analogous to the Sidpa realm, the realm of the wrathful deities who enact all of our agonies of desire and death.

In passing from death to birth we have perhaps already slipped into a womb. The interchange of tinctures may well be the trauma of birth as mankind enters another phase of development, for assuredly we are living a myth, and what we choose to call real is as arbitrary as the fixation of a madman. The obsession must be exorcized, but in this case the madman is the collective mentality of the human race. The situation is inexorable; conception has already occurred. The Great Wheel of Yeats or Jung's mandala is then the seed of the conception. The ovum is the spirit of the earth surging toward regeneration. Mankind is the vessel.

There is one other point about the year 1927: it was the first year of the current and last sixty-year cycle of the Tibetan calendar—the Kalachakra, or Wheel of Time. It seems more than a coincidence that the esoteric knowledge of *The Tibetan Book of the Dead* was made available to Westerners in the year that began the fateful cycle in which Tibet itself would be destroyed. Since the final Tibetan cycle and the ancient Mexican hell cycle both end in 1987, this year may be the date Yeats did not list in his "Historical Cones," and the date initiating the last three phases of the Great Wheel: the Hunchback, the Saint, and the Fool. The Bodies of Fate corresponding to these three final phases are Enforced Disillusionment, Enforced Loss, and Enforced Illusion. These suggest mutation (the Hunchback), a new religious vision and dispensation (the Saint), and the beginning of a new cycle of collective human development (the Fool).

In the stage between death and birth, the Bardo realm, which is the realm of Mammon, what matters is the seed. Clearly Romanticism, primitivism, abstractionism, and even Surrealism have all evoked the Great Return; but they were all too reactionary to contain the authentic vision of the seed; they depended too much on understanding or reacting against what had gone before. The seed depends on understanding what comes after. The seed contains all forthcoming elements in condensed, unified form; its potential is tremendous; it is a releaser of power. In the seed is the Great Return.

In November 1916, in the midst of the First World War, a young Frenchman arrived in New York. He had already written and published a book, *Claude Debussy and the Cycle of Musical Civilization* (1913), and he had composed several musical works. He had been present at the tumultuous first performance of Igor Stravinsky's *Rite of Spring*. The outbreak of war, from which he was fortunately exempt, confirmed a twofold intuition of his: that the law of cycles controls existence in all of its forms, and that European civilization was in the autumn phase of one of these cycles. So keenly did this artist feel this intuition that somewhat like Gauguin before him, he felt prompted to forsake completely the decaying Old World and begin anew, as a *seed*, in a "New World." Unlike Gauguin, however, he did not so much flee the old as make a conscious decision to consecrate his life to realizing fully the new. As a symbolic act he dropped his family name in 1917 and adopted the name Rudhyar—a word signifying fire, the primal element red, the planet Mars, the astrological sign Aries, the beginner; etymologically the name is related to that of an ancient Hindu god, Rudra, releaser of electrical power during storms. For the rest of his life Dane Rudhyar was to evoke and fulfill all of the qualities associated with the name he had chosen.

Once in America, where his work was performed at the Metropolitan Opera House under the baton of Pierre Monteux, Rudhyar plunged himself into a whirlwind of creative activity that saw him steadily pulling away from the decadent European forms, especially as they were manifesting toward 1920 in the renewed *neoclassicism* of Stravinsky (and Picasso). As Rudhyar later pointed out, such regressive artistic manifestations had their political counterpart in the rise of fascism. As he shifted away from the traditional European forms, he moved farther west, until he arrived in Hollywood on January 2, 1920. In Hollywood the antithetical tincture of the Eastern Hemisphere transformed itself through a person like Rudhyar into the primary tincture of the Western Hemisphere, the so-called New World. Significantly, at this point Rudhyar came into contact with Theosophy and Ba'hai. What these religious movements had in common was a vision of world unity and planetary rebirth through the transfigured human spirit. It was during the 1920's that Rudhyar's seed-vision came to its first maturity through his experimental practice of the arts of poetry and music, and later, painting.

In 1927 Rudhyar began to expound his vision publicly. Already his music, based on the cry and the *tone* rather than the note (which is read), as well as his poetry, had begun to express by their very nature the primal quality of the seed-vision. In 1929 Rudhyar published a book on the role and function of art entitled *Art as Release of Power*. The ideas in this book are totally out of the ordinary. Unlike the contemporaneous ideas of the Surrealists, they are far more than a reaction to the conventions of the time. Despite their revolutionary aspirations, the Surrealists were very much a part of the European tradition in its autumn phase. Their manifestos were addressed to the past and not to the future; their work tended to dwell on the Freudian neuroses, which are oriented strictly toward the past, rather than on exploring the archetypes, which represent simultaneously the past and the future. Rudhyar's view, by contrast, is from the *outside;* somehow his consciousness by an effort of the will was able to escape the European cultural cycle, at least to the extent of being able to envision something beyond it. For Rudhyar the question of art was no longer a merely aesthetic matter. It was inseparable from the question of life itself. Since life is psychobiological in nature, art is psychobiological as well. "Life-forms are transformers of energy."[10] All forms of life are *performers*, a term Rudhyar states is identical with *transformer*, for *per* means *through*. If there is something being performed, there is also a *will* at work. The human body and mind are transformers of energy; through body and mind, Life or Spirit, or Soul, or Self perform. All such performances can therefore be called *magical.*"[11]

Whereas the Surrealists strained after their magic, thinking it occupied a special realm far removed from our everyday consciousness, Rudhyar saw magic as a natural result of human action: "Magic is merely *the release of power through an efficient form by an act of will. . . .* Magic thus understood, differs from age to age according to the focalization of the Race's will and desire."[12] Today's magic resides in an electrical generator, and today's magician is the engineer. In another culture, the magic may be in the rain dance ritual, and the magician the dancer, the shaman or medicine man who brings the rain. From the point of view of advanced European civilization, the rain dance or at least some of the objects used in the rain dance might be considered works of art; the same could be said of an African hunter's spear or the archaic chants of India. But the aesthetic qualities these objects and activities may happen to have are incidental to their true function, for they are all power-releasing forms, the instruments of magic:

Was the Gettysburg Address intended by Lincoln to be beautiful? We doubt it. It was to be an effectual vehicle for a powerful idea, a word engine which was meant to work. . . . It worked well, just like a fine sledge hammer. Likewise all good publicity mottos are forms-of-power. They are efficient. They release power. We learn Lincoln's words at school and are taught to admire their *style*. Why not be taught rather to admire their *power?* We are shown the pyramids and led to wonder at their beautiful proportions. Why not be led to the proper realization of the mysterious operations performed therein *which conditioned their form?* The artists of old were not really artists; they dealt with applied magic, as the builder of aeroplanes deals with applied science. They conceived their activities in terms of life, in terms of doing things, of accumulating power, of being a master of natural forces; in order to live a fuller and more intense and freer existence, an existence richer with power—which is the one great eternal goal of all men. . . .

Therefore art, in such a magical sense, is perhaps not art at all. And yet it is the greatest and only universal, only permanent ART. For it is an immediate gesture of Life, of the will which has assumed Power and relates itself to other wills.[13]

From this point of view, form has little value unless it is put to use. A Rolls-Royce engine may be aesthetically pleasing, and so might a particular modernist painting, abstract or otherwise. But the Rolls-Royce engine, unlike the painting, was made to be used rather than to be passively contemplated. In this sense aesthetic value is secondary, a suspicion long harbored by the working and middle classes, for whom the art of the elite has little meaning. "All great esthetic Art-Forms are the remains of magical utterances. They are 'sacred'; they were consecrated by the power they released. Any other art-form made for esthetical purposes, to be enjoyed, to please, etc., is either an imitation or a deformation of such once living sacred forms-of-power."[14]

Although Rudhyar's language is of his time—he speaks of machines, engines, power—he carefully distinguishes between sacred art and the two prevailing modes of contemporary art—individualistic Expressionism (or Surrealism) and Constructivism (including purist art of all kinds). Both of these are actually two poles of the same phenomena, and are incomplete of themselves. In the one mode the viewer's emotions are manipulated for a particular dramatic effect; in the other, materials and objects are manipulated for a specific intellectual/aesthetic effect. But neither mode is a consciously conceived source of power. Insofar as neither has a direct practical use, as the applied arts do, or serves *directly* as a consciously conceived means of release for psychic or spiritual energy, as sacred art does, they serve no authentic function aside from stimulating the senses.

And so we have the esthetical attitude; we hear of the "inspired" artist, the Muse and much nonsense. Art is a very simple operation. But humanity has lost the knowledge of the Science of Art, just as it has lost that of the science of Soul. It revels in material excitement and sentimental feelings and is bound in forms; therefore it worships forms which it calls beautiful or esthetical. For those who begin to grasp the operation of Power which is Soul, there is nothing but engines which either work or do not work. But he who wishes to handle Power, *must first BE power.*[15]

To *be power* is to be the seed, and to be the seed requires that the artist be not just a maker of objects. To be a seed defines totally the context as well as the nature of the work to be accomplished. It requires that the artist be something of a prophet, a teacher, a messenger; and it requires that his work have a regenerative force or enhance receptivity to the incoming energies of the time that is dawning. As Rudhyar wrote in 1939, the artist whose work is effective for both the present and the future is *the artist as avatar.* To reach this level, the artist must first become a "work of art of the Spirit."[16] Having undergone a profound transformation of consciousness, the artist incorporates—literally *embodies*—an aspect of the spirit. In this way he helps consolidate the necessary forms for releasing power, what Jung might have called the archetypal forms. "In really creative Art is revealed that which ultimately will emerge through the evolutionary process as consciousness. . . . At least such is the Art of the beginning of every cycle, the Art born of the magical sacrifice of Avatars, or Seed-men, on all planes, Art which is a 'release of power,' a cry of birth a poem of initiation."[17] The artist-as-avatar is the realization Breton dimly intuited in the second manifesto of Surrealism.

To accept Rudhyar's vision is to accept not only the death of this civilization but the exalted coming of a new phase of human development totally unpredicated by the present phase. Rudhyar's vision is cyclical, like Yeats's and Jung's. More emphatically than anyone else, except perhaps Spengler, Rudhyar has declared the irrevocable death of the present civilization; and more surely and clearly, he has envisioned the birth of the new civilization. But the new era will arrive only through a transformation of certain elements in the present era. Following Breton's cue, Rudhyar took up the ancient language of astrology, which provided a structual viewpoint within which the cyclical philosophy of the seed could be properly articulated. In fact, placing the ancient science on a psychological footing appropriate to the condition of the modern spirit, Rudhyar, along with Marc Edmund Jones, must be looked upon as one of the renewers of astrology. This is most evident in his 1936 publication, *The Astrology of Personality.*

Like Yeats, Rudhyar conceived the present cycle as a period roughly equivalent to two thousand years divided into four great seasons. In a later work, *Birth Patterns for a New Age,* (1969), Rudhyar further divided this period into twelve stages according to the twelve signs of the zodiac. Within the context of a cultural cycle, he wrote, "art must be considered as a whole. As such it is an emanation of the collective consciousness of the Race, an Image of its Soul, a precipitation of the innermost rhythm of its being. . . . Objectively, it is the sum total of the Race-Images."[18] Culture and the Art-whole are essentially the same thing.

The Christian European Art-whole scatters itself more and more as form; that is to say, the various arts emphasizing more and more the value of technique became thereby more and more separate, unrelated. This process may not necessarily take place in all cultures, but it is especially obvious in Europe as the result of . . . the failure of the spiritual Renascence of the fifteenth century. This failure was followed by the worship of Greco-Latin forms, a deadly process from a spiritual point of view which killed the true Nordic European spirit that had just produced a Shakespeare and in Central Europe a host of Great Seekers after Truth.

It is only with the Romantic rebellion against this deadly classicism that the thread of the true European spirit is rediscovered and that a great effort of artistic regeneration is pursued which ends in the Synthetic Drama attempted by Wagner and visualized at a further stage of completeness—probably unrealizable in this era—by Scriabin.[19]

What Rudhyar envisioned occurring historically was on the one hand, a tendency toward greater multiplicity and individualism—the separation of the arts from the Art-whole of the cathedrals, so that each art viewed itself as a distinct Art-whole—and on the other hand, a tendency, beginning with the Romantics, toward unity. The attempts at synthesis—*synesthesia*, it should be recalled, was the ideal of the Symbolists of the 1880's and 90's—really reflect the summation of an era and not the beginning. In the ideal process of the Art-whole, the conclusion is stated by a Synthetic Drama that reunites the primary vision of the race or culture. In this way the Synthetic Drama embodies the ideal of a perfected humanity. When a cycle such as the European so disastrously and with little hope of reunification comes to an end, there is an urge to create the Synthetic Drama, the integrating Art-whole embracing all aspects of existence and uniting life and art. But for any real integration to occur, a process of regeneration must take place. Nature's aim is to bring out a "image which reproduces in perfection the primal unity." Such an image is the mandala as rediscovered by Jung, the Great Wheel of Yeats, or the horoscope as conceived and used by Rudhyar for reflecting the inherent wholeness of an individual entity.

There is no doubt that in the man Rudhyar much of the ideal he expressed was realized. In the dissonance of his music and his poetry, the original utterance stammers forth, like the cry of a newborn child; in his painting, which bears similarities to the work of Kandinsky, we see genuine symbols coming into being. As he himself wrote, "We believe the deepest duty confronting Artists today is to bring forth symbolical utterances emanating this really human spirituality. This can be accomplished only if the Artists themselves are tuned to their own spiritual Centers, only if they themselves become to some extent, *actually* if not necessarily in full mental consciousness, incarnations of the God within."[20] These artists, like the alchemists of old, must be willing to work "unceasingly and honestly toward the mastery of their own material, including the material of their own lives."[21] These words point to the clear necessity for the expression of archetypal symbols to supersede the fragmented subjective will of the "free" artist of late European civilization.

Though mankind still struggles toward rebirth, the seed has been fertilized; the womb is being prepared. In a poem written in the 1930's, entitled "Autumn," Rudhyar expressed most touchingly the meaning of the Great Return:

It is time to die with the year,
to draw within the seed
the fervor of yore, to die
into the sunken splendor
of the seed.

Yellowing leaves,
vanishing loves,
my poem of age
falling earthward with the snow,
falling toward the seeds
tenderly to mother
and to love. . . .[22]

CHAPTER TWENTY

Split Adam—Split Atom: Art in America

The seed-forces are working throughout the XIXth century and today America is confronted with the great fateful possibility and need of a moment of seed-incarnation: the descent of the seed into the ground, the crucifixion of the New Spirit-Impulse into the regenerated matter of a new continent and a new humanity. This seed will be the new "Primal Unit Ray," the initial point of the Art-whole of the future, which we may call American.[1]

—Dane Rudhyar

THE BIRTH and rapid rise of Faustian Europe was accompanied by the so-called discovery and colonization of America. The entire length of America, from arctic to Antarctic, symbolizes the primary tincture, the right cerebral hemisphere, the land where the seed of full-fruited Europe was to fall and be transformed. As America was in the process of being colonized, the Art-whole of Europe was splintering, each art—and science—becoming ever more refined and technically sophisticated, ever more separate and removed from the other arts and from the lifestream itself. Though culturally Europe was to die before any real unity had occurred, in America she had spawned the offspring that might be the transfigured culmination of what she had begun; for the seed is the culmination of the plant. But the real process of creating the Art-whole of the future has hardly begun. What has materially occurred in America since the coming of the Europeans—and by America, I mean the entire Western Hemisphere—has been essentially the megalomaniac shadow empire of Faust. The American Revolution, though organized by a select and esoteric group of Freemasons, culminated in a totally neoclassical banker's enterprise. The American Revolution is also called the War for Independence, and in this latter aspect the true nature of the founding of America as another splintering of the whole is clear. Thus as the fountainhead of civilization in the New World, the United States of America has expanded the anarchic individualism, feudalism, materialism, and artificially separatist cultural tendencies of the European Art-whole to a monstrous degree, far surpassing the great Mammon-dominated ancient Roman empire. But this pursuit of the gargantuan in every facet of American culture is not indigenously American. It is the overripe fruit, but it is not the seed. The seed that is truly American still lies dormant within.

In 1870, in his remarkable essay "Democratic Vistas," Walt Whitman declared that democracy "at present is in its embryo condition, and that the only large and satisfactory justification of it resides in the future, mainly through the copious production of perfect characters among the people, and through the advent of a sane and pervading religiousness."[2] Physical revolution, materialism, progress and science are only fuel for the seed-spirit. Considering the material wealth of America, the spirit should blaze high indeed. For Whitman, the essence of democracy—interchangeable with America—is its religious element. "As fuel to flame and flame to the heavens, so must wealth, science and materialism—even this democracy of which we make so much—unerringly feed the highest mind, the soul."[3] Whitman perceived that the epic struggle of America is the struggle of the seed for right nourishment. What is now an embryo seeks to be born as a fully spiritual force, refashioning the earth and regenerating man so that there may be a new earth and a new man founded on the full expansion of individual consciousness. This attainment, the *magnum opus* of democracy, is the identity of the individual with the All,

with the accompanying idea of eternity, and of itself, the soul, buoyant, indestructible, sailing space forever, visiting every region as a ship the sea. And again Lo! the pulsations in all matter, all spirit throbbing forever, the eternal beats eternal systole and diastole of life in things—wherefrom I feel and know that death is not the ending, as was thought, but rather the real beginning—and that nothing ever is or can be lost, nor ever die, nor soul nor matter.[4]

Though the citizen in the voting booth, the merchant tradesman, the stockbroker, the policeman and the schoolteacher may not know it, their efforts all lead toward the attainment of this goal—the death which is the real beginning. America at present is the heavy, pulsing placenta nourishing the embryonic form. But what Whitman himself scarcely perceived is that America is infinitely more than an extension of the late European shopkeeper culture. If the modern democratic culture is the *placenta*, then the land and all the spirits of the land are the womb itself. What the immigrant Europeans so energetically and basely raped has a spirit and life of its own that must be integrated with the seed. The neoclassical culture of Europe, which has been so successfully transplanted on American soil, may be nothing more than a means through which the energies that are already here and still "descending" may impregnate the seed. At birth the placenta drops away. Like the culture of Europe, the present American culture must prepare for death, for the placenta cannot live at the expense of the embryo. As Whitman prophesied:

In the future of these States must arise poets immenser far, and make great poems of death. The poems of life are great, but there must be poems of the purports of life, not only of itself, but beyond itself. . . .

America needs, and the world needs, a class of bards who will, now and ever so link and tally the rational physical being of man, with the ensembles of time and space, and with this vast and multiform show, Nature, surrounding him ever tantalizing him, equally a part, and yet not a part of him, as to essentially harmonize, satisfy, and put at rest. Faith, very old scared away by science must be restored, brought back by the same power that caused her departure. . . . [This] must be done positively by some great coming literatus, who, while remaining fully poet, will absorb whatever science indicates, with spiritualism, and out of them, and out of his own genius, will compose the great poem of death. Then will man indeed confront Nature. . . . And then that which was long wanted will be supplied, and that ship which had it not before in all her voyages, will have an anchor.[5]

The seeds of the great poem of death Whitman yearned for—a native American Book of the Dead—lay in the very land.[6] Long before the Europeans arrived, great civilizations had flourished and passed away on the American soil. Because of the genocidal policies of the Europeans, perpetuated by the American Policy of Manifest Destiny, we know little of the spirit that was here before the coming of democracy and the machine. Even to their inheritors at the time of the Conquest, these civilizations were like a dream from the distant past. Yet what gave the most grandiose of these civilizations their power was the living rhythm of the "poem of death."

The 1626 world map of John Speed indicates that the northern continent of the Western Hemisphere was called "North America or Mexicana." Certainly in the Western Hemisphere it was the kingdoms and theocracies of ancient Mexico that had attained the most exalted heights of thought and culture; indeed the Aztec sphere of influence spread far into what is now part of the United States. The exact nature of the religion that animated these peoples remained unknown for a long time, owing as much to the brutal smugness of the European settlers as to the religious zeal of missionizing Christians, both Catholic and Protestant. The Aztecs, with their morbid, Mammon-like religion of human sacrifice, have remained strongly and to some extent rightly embedded in the popular imagination as *the* people epitomizing ancient Mexican culture. But to regard the Aztec way of life as emanating from the essence of ancient Mexican religion is tantamount to regarding the recent bombing of Southeast Asia by the United States as emanating from the teachings of Christ. Yet it is in the earlier strata of Mexican religion that the image pattern of the great American poem of death is to be found.

In the 1920's the English novelist D. H. Lawrence came to the New World; he spent his time largely in Mexicana, meaning both Mexico proper and the American Southwest. Even more than Gauguin or even Rudhyar, Lawrence was a refugee from the industrial slums; his upbringing had been banefully proletarian. Emerging from the coal fields of northern England, he slowly worked his way out of the material and psychological morass of mechanized existence. In the process he conceived his own transcendental visionary goal, which was implicitly a rejection of materialism and European culture in general. The vision of primal unity led Lawrence toward the non-European, toward the New World, toward the earth and the regeneration of the human organism. For Lawrence, as for Rudhyar and Gauguin,

Adam had been split; Christ alone had not regenerated the Old Adam. New gods, old gods, faiths unknown had to be invoked in order to heal him.

Much has been written of Lawrence's preoccupation with sex. The reestablishment of a right relationship with Eve is essential for Adam's wellbeing; but it does not and cannot stop with mere sexual satisfaction, for Eve is more than woman. She is nature, the earth, and death's great entrance itself. For the modern European, she is a whole new world. In his poem "New Heaven and Earth," Lawrence wrote:

> *And so I cross into another world*
> *shyly and in homage linger for an invitation*
> *from this unknown that I would trespass upon. . . .*

> *I was so weary of the world,*
> *I was so sick of it*
> *everything was tainted with myself,*
> *skies, trees, flowers, birds, water*
> *people, houses, streets, vehicles, machines*
> *nations, armies, war, peace-talking. . . .*

> *At last came death, sufficiency of death,*
> *and that at last relieved me, I died. . . .*

> *God, but it is good to have died and been trodden out,*
> *trodden to nought in sour, dead earth*
> *quite to nought*
> *absolutely to nothing. . . .*
> *For when it is quite, quite nothing, then it is everything . . .*
> *risen and setting foot on another world*
> *risen accomplishing a resurrection. . . .*
> *I new-risen, resurrected, starved from the tomb,*
> *starved from a life of always devouring myself,*
> *now here I was, new-awakened, with my hand stretching out*
> *and touching the unknown, the real unknown, the unknown un-*
> *known.*

> *My God, but I can only say*
> *I touch, I feel the unknown!*
> *I am the first comer!*
> *Cortes, Pisarro, Columbus, Cabot, they are nothing, nothing!*
> *I am the first comer!*
> *I am the discoverer!*
> *I have found the other world!*

> *The unknown, the unknown!*
> *I am thrown upon the shore. . . .*

I am covering myself with the earth.
I am burrowing my body into the soil.
The unknown, the new world![7]

Lawrence died to his European ego in order that he might come to know the ancient American way of life-and-death. His passage to India led through ancient America. So he went to the land, to the places least spoiled by the European, to the places where the ancient spirits still brooded and roamed. From New Mexico to Oaxaca, Lawrence touched on something very primal. And it is interesting that in Oaxaca in 1924, in the pure highlands of the myth he sought, while working on his last great novel, *The Plumed Serpent,* Lawrence became very ill with the black disease of the Iron Age, tuberculosis, a disease that was slowly to ravage him for the next six years. While he was stalking death, death found him.

Even more than the United States, Mexico was a land of the dead. For here were the descendants of the ancient civilizers of the New World, oppressed and inarticulate, slowly being fed into the maws of an even more efficient and mechanical hell than that first provided by the conquistadores. It was in the midst of this brutal wasteland that Lawrence found the myth he had sought, the myth of the Lord of the Morning Star, Quetzalcoatl, the Plumed Serpent.

Far up in the northern plains where the snow swirls down, the myth is there. Among the Crow and the Pawnee, the religion of the Morning Star shapes the flow of life. Even among the Ghost Dancers of the 1890's, the Morning Star was emblazoned on shirts and dresses. But nowhere did the thought and religion of the Morning Star reach such abstruse mythological, mathematical, calendrical, and alchemical heights as among the ancient Mexicans. Just what Lawrence knew about the religion and philosophy of Quetzalcoatl is not certain; he probably did not know much. Yet the unconscious power of the myth was strong enough to refashion itself through Lawrence's imagination. The stark contrast of present-day Mexico, a living fable of the split Adam, was enough to bring out the necessary lineaments of the myth.

The Plumed Serpent is itself a union of the opposites, heaven and earth. The great religion of Quetzalcoatl flourished as early as the sixth century B.C. How or when or where it began is not clear. But from the start it was a religion whose symbolism was inextricably allied to the revolutions of the Morning and Evening Star, or the planet Venus. Morning Star for some 236 days, invisible for 90, Evening Star for another 250 days, invisible again for 8 days, only to reappear once again as the Morning Star, the seemingly endless procession of Venus provided the ancient Mexican seers with a key for unraveling the mysteries of life, death, regeneration, and resurrection. The myth was further embellished by the life of the tenth-century mystic emperor of the Toltecs, Ce Actl Topiltzin, Quetzalcoatl, Our Lord One Reed Quetzalcoatl, an avatar who prophesied his own return on the day sacred to his name, One Reed. As history had it, Cortés and his small expeditionary force landed on Mexican soil supposedly on the day One Reed, April 21, 1519, for which reason Cortés was at first hailed as Quetzalcoatl. As we know, however, Cortés turned out to be not the Lord of Light but his twin, his antagonist and opposite, the Lord of Darkness, Tezcatlipoca, the Lord of the Smoking Mirror. Quetzalcoatl had not yet returned.

Seeking his own and the world's regenerative apocalypse, Lawrence tuned into the profoundly unconscious, deep-seated expectation of Quetzalcoatl's return, which provides the basic theme of *The Plumed Serpent*. In the return of the Lord of the Dawn, the Great Return of which I spoke previously finds a mask or an embodiment, especially since Quetzalcoatl, the Plumed Serpent, is also an image of the Ouroboros transformed. By biting his own tail, Ouroboric Adam uses his own poison to homeopathically heal himself and become truly human. Lawrence's novel is large and prophetic; Quetzalcoatl's return is the symbolic opening of the seed and the birth of a newly awakened consciousness that is no longer materialistic and bound by Mammon. The prophecy of Quetzalcoatl's return is universal, for it is the deliverance from the present hell.

Actually Lawrence's book is two books: one of them is a novel of Mexico in the 1920's, vividly portraying the materialistic wasteland of the smoking mirror and the downtroddenness of the people and the land; the other is a book of ritual that goes far beyond the novel's reportorial aspect. It is a preliminary book of the ritual of human enlightenment.

Who sleeps—shall wake! Who sleeps shall wake!
Who treads down the path of the snake shall arrive at the place; in the
path of the dust shall arrive at the place and be dressed in the skin of the snake—
There is no Before and After, there is only Now;
The great Snake coils and uncoils the plasm of his folds, and stars appear, and worlds fade out. It is no more than the changing and the easing of the plasm.
I always am says his sleep.
As a man in a deep sleep knows not, but is, so is the limpid, far-reaching
Snake of the eternal Cosmos, Now and forever Now
Now and only Now, and forever Now.
But dreams arise and fade in the sleep of the Snake
And worlds arise as dreams, and are gone as dreams.

And man is a dream in the sleep of the Snake.
And only the sleep that is dreamless breathes I am!
In the dreamless Now I Am! . . .
And the perfect sleep of the Snake I Am is the plasm of a man, who is
*   whole.*
When the plasm of body, and the plasm of the soul, and the plasm of
*   the spirit are at one, in the Snake I Am.*
I am Now. . . .[8]

In Lawrence's prophetic vision, history is finally transcended; it is only a dream that falls away from the coils of the snake, for history is simply what accrues and what falls away. And the rhythm that is underneath remains, comes through in timeless archetypal shapes, and everything that is done is only part of the dance, the shimmering coils of the snake unfolding. In choosing the snake for his symbol, Lawrence went right to the core of planetary myth. The snake is the serpent of Eden, the bestower of wisdom as well as the tempter, for wisdom is always a temptation to those who do not known how to use it. Thus Buddha conquers Mara, the Naga or serpent king, but Mara then protects Buddha. As such the serpent, Naga, is the keeper of the secret wisdom and the possessor of the life force itself, called by the Hindu Tantrics, Kundalini, the serpent power that lies coiled in the root-center of the body. In Lawrence's vision Quetzalcoatl, the Plumed Serpent, is like a collective Kundalini lifting itself upward through a spiritually aroused and awakened body. The serpent, which represents the earthly material aspect, is plumed and brilliantly feathered because it has made itself servant to the Lord of the Morning Star, symbol of supreme enlightenment, which embodies conquest, union, and the transcendence of the polarities of day and night, right and left, life and death.

The Lord of the Morning Star
Stood between the day and the night:
As a bird that lifts its wings, and stands
With the bright wing on the right
And the wing of the dark on the left,
The Dawn Star stood into sight!

Lo! I am always here!
For in the hollow of space
I brush the wing of the day
and put light on your face.
The other wing brushes the dark.
But I, I am always in place. . . .

The multitude see me not.
They see only the waving of wings,
The coming and going of things,
The cold and the hot.

But ye that perceive me between
The tremors of night and the day,
I make you the Lords of the Way
Unseen. . . .

Deep in the moistures of peace,
And far down the muzzle of the fight
You shall find me, who am neither increase
Nor destruction, different quite.

I am far beyond
The horizons of love and strife.
Like a star, like a pond
That washes the lords of life. [9]

Lawrence's heroes, Ramón and Cipriano, and their small group, along with the hesitant Kate, form themselves into a mystical elite, what Rudhyar might call a seed group, that is prophetic of a posthistorical reality. " 'Listen!' said Ramón, in the stillness, 'We will be masters among men, and lords among men. But lords of men, and masters of men we will not be. Listen! We are lords of the night. Lords of the day and night. Sons of the Morning Star, sons of the Evening Star. Men of the Morning and Evening Star.' "[10] These lords of the Morning and Evening Star are a visionary embodiment of the subtle force that has always shaped and revealed the highest truth in the human realm. And when Ramón says, "We are not lords of men: how can men make us lords? Nor are we masters of men for men are not worth it,"[11] he is expressing the truth of the indestructible middle way, neither human nor inhuman, wise but not without compassion: "I will not command you, nor serve you, for the snake goes crooked into his own house. Yet I will be with you, so you depart not from yourselves."[12] And then in words that speak the most sublime truth of nonduality:

There is no giving, and no taking. When the fingers that give touch the fingers that receive, the Morning Star shines at once, from the contact, and the jasmine gleams between the hands. And thus there is neither giving nor taking, nor hand that proffers, nor hand that receives, but the star between them is all, and the dark hand and the light hand are invisible on each side. The jasmine takes the giving and the receiving in her cup, and the scent of the oneness is fragrant in the air. [13]

Think neither to give nor to receive, only let the jasmine flower. Lawrence's Quetzalcoatl comes. He relieves Jesus and Mary of their burden.
Not only is he the return of the new man, he is what always returns.
Lawrence depicts Jesus as sad at having been foisted on the Mexican people,
and relieved at Quetzalcoatl's coming. Jesus, who represents the European's unique unrepeatable historical vision, does not return to life among
men; he will reappear only for the stern moment of the Last Judgement.
Quetzalcoatl therefore addresses him: "Thou were Lord of the one way.
Now it leads thee to the sleep. Farewell!" Whereas of himself Quetzalcoatl
proclaims: "But I, I am lord of two ways. I am master of up and down. I am
a man who is a new man, with new limbs and life, and the light of the
Morning Star in his eyes. Lo! I am I! The lord of both ways . . . star
between day and the dark."[14]

Arriving in Mexico and surveying the spiritual desolation there, Quetzalcoatl announces the apocalypse:

> The stars and the earth and the sun and the moon and the winds
> Are about to dance the war dance around you men!
> When I say the word, they will start.
> For sun and stars and earth and the very rains are weary
> Of tossing and rolling the substance of life to your lips.
> They are saying to one another: Let us make an end
> Of these ill-smelling tribes of men . . .
> This flesh that smells
> These words that are all flat
> These money vermin. . . .
> Let us have a spring cleaning in the world
> For men upon the body of the earth are like lice,
> Devouring the earth into sores.
> This is what stars and sun and earth and moon and winds and rain
> Are discussing with one another; they are making ready to start.
> So tell the men I am coming to,
> To make themselves clean inside and out.
> To roll the grave stone off their souls, and from the cave of their
>   bellies,
> To prepare to be men.
> Or else prepare for the other things.[15]

The Great Return is the announcement of the Great Purification, the
change for which civilization is unwittingly preparing itself. As a later
generation was finally to realize, humanity too is a part of a total system of
planetary ecology. Whatever the merits of Lawrence's novelistic fantasy of
Quetzalcoatl's return, his insight into the necessity of a spiritual transmutation for the remaking of the historical situation is unquestionably valid.

And there is something uncanny in his projection of the Quetzalcoatl myth and prophecy. That this Englishman from the coal mines, those sores inflicted by men upon the earth, should have been able to resurrect this myth of another race from another time and make it speak directly to the present world is a tribute to both the lingering potency of the myth and the urgent intensity of Lawrence's vision. But above all, through the prophecy and myth of Quetzalcoatl, Lawrence rediscovered death—not only his own, but the collective death of humanity in its present stage. Sometime after the publication of *The Plumed Serpent* in 1926, Lawrence wrote "The Ship of Death":

> *Now it is autumn and the falling fruit*
> *and the long journey toward oblivion . . .*
>
> *And it is time to go, to bid farewell*
> *to one's own self and find an exit*
> *from the fallen self.*
>
> *Have you built your ship of death, O have you?*
> *O build your ship of death, for you will need it.*
> *The grim forest is at hand, when the apples will fall*
> *Thick, almost thundrous on the hardened earth. . . .*
>
> *We are dying, we are dying, so all we can do*
> *Is now to be willing to die, and to build the ship*
> *Of death to carry the souls on the longest journey. . . .*
>
> *And yet out of eternity is a thread . . .*
> *A flush of rose and the whole thing starts again. . . .*[16]

Passage to India, journey to the East, death and rebirth, the Second Coming, the Seed, Quetzalcoatl, America. . . . Somehow out of deepest collective necessity the artist-visionaries had begun to reveal the mythic purpose hidden behind the frenzied exaltation of historical progress.

In the pivotal year 1927, a year after the publication of *The Plumed Serpent*, a Mexican mural painter, José Clemente Orozco, came to the United States. Orozco, like his compatriot Diego Rivera, who also worked in the United States in the early 1930's, was fired with the spirit of the revolution that had swept Mexico before and during the First World War. It is often said that these two muralists from "south of the border" renewed American art, and that the Work Projects Administration of the 1930's owed much to their inspiration. Except for the work a few notable eccentrics like Albert Pinkham Ryder, Louis Sullivan, and Frank Lloyd Wright, American visual art had been thoroughly European in its origins and styles. Barrenly neoclassical from the start, American tastes culminated in the pure, monolithic formalism of the skyscraper—commercial Mammon's contribution to posterity. By contrast, the Mexican mural artists represent the first attempt at a fusion of indigenous American spirit and contemporary European style and form. Rivera expressed quite clearly the ideals of the mural artists:

I have always maintained that art in America, if some day it can be said to have come into being, will be the product of a fusion between the marvelous indigenous art which derives from the immemorial depths of time in the center and south of the continent (Mexico, Central America, Bolivia and Peru), and that of the industrial worker of the north. The dynamic productive sculptures which are the mechanical masterpieces of the factories are active works of art. . . . A machine that lives and performs the functions for which it was intended must have been constructed under inevitably harmonic conditions. Do not painting, sculpture and architecture require the same harmony and functional utility to be considered really living, dynamic and socially enlightening?[17]

More vehemently and romantically communist than Picasso, Rivera managed in his best murals to live up to his ideals. The most spectacular event in his career as an artist in the United States was the row over a mural he painted at Rockefeller Center during 1933-34. Here was certainly a confluence of energies: the native American communist Rivera commissioned to decorate the ground-floor walls of a monumental, ego-aggrandizing building owned by one of the most powerful mercantile imperialist families, the Rockefellers. The theme of the mural—*Man at the Crossroads*—was handled well enough as a cosmic vision in which man is the center of a nucleus of energies greater and lesser than himself. But Rivera felt compelled to include a portrait of Lenin. There ensued the "battle of Rockefeller Center," which in itself carried out Rivera's intention to depict "an exact and concrete expression of the situation under capitalism at the present time and an indication of the road that man must follow in order to liquidate hunger, oppression, disorder and war."[18] If nothing else, Rivera had an acutely accurate vision of the hellish conditions of life in a technocracy. In a mural executed at the New Art Workers School after the Rockefeller incident, he painted a chillingly exact portrait of the present forms of slavery: wage, media, and political. Wage slaves are represented by rows of women literally chained to their jobs, processing identification cards; education is depicted prophetically as a process of electrically implanting images; and a jail is shown full of political prisoners. It is a vision of the dead in the land of the dead.

If Rivera's vision is often unremitting and unredeeming, at times purely propagandistic, and at other times sentimental and patronizing, Orozco's is permeated with an unspoken spiritual quality. Whatever political content Orozco's murals have is part of a larger mythic vision; unlike Rivera, Orozco was not misled by a dualistic belief in either communism or capitalism, and though he was far from insensitive to the oppression in the society surrounding him, he placed it within the redeeming context of myth. Whereas Rivera remained engulfed in history, Orozco was able to transcend it; this alone places him in the company of the transformative visionaries. For Orozco, as for all of the other visionaries, class struggle was to be superseded by apocalypse.

Lawrence's mythic vision of America began in New Mexico; Orozco's flowered in New England. From 1932 to 1934 Orozco worked on a series of frescoes in Baker Library at Dartmouth College, New Hampshire, in the heart of the original thirteen colonies. His theme was "An Epic of American Civilization," a reinterpretation of the Quetzalcoatl myth. That Orozco's version of the ancient story of the Plumed Serpent was placed on the walls of a New England college is highly significant, for it connects the collective heritage of the land and its first peoples with the mighty industrial civilization that was to follow. As the Orozco frescoes bring out, there is an indissoluble relationship between the ancient teachings and prophesies and what is now taking place on this continent. The connection is extremely strong; yet it is so unconscious that not even Orozco was aware of the extent to which it was being transmitted through him. By his own admission, "The theme was of Quetzalcoatl, but the final paintings do not show a clear relation with it."[19] In retrospect we can say that there is a coherent relation throughout the fourteen main panels of the fresco.

Like Lawrence, Orozco had only a tentative understanding of Quetzalcoatl's ancient teaching, though the interpretation and prophecy are clearly and powerfully portrayed. The first panels depict the primordial migration of the original races of Indians to America. The following two panels depict the more barbaric aspects of the original American cultures: human sacrifice and Aztec men ready for war. The fourth, fifth, and sixth panels deal specifically with Quetzalcoatl as a divine hero. The first of these panels depicts the coming of Quetzalcoatl; its main emphasis is on the subordination of the older gods to the harmonizing spirit and power of the religion of Quetzalcoatl, which was wholly transcendental and humane. It is noteworthy that Orozco has depicted on Quetzalcoatl's left the Pico de Orizaba, the volcanic home of the Fire God, which Quetzalcoatl was said to ascend from time to time in order to speak to his people with a voice of thunder that could be heard for four hundred miles around; in fact, the Pico de Orizaba was the epicenter of the disastrous 1973 earthquake, the worst in modern Mexican history. The central Quetzalcoatl panel depicts the pre-Columbian golden age, which was distinguished by a flowering of agriculture and all of the arts and sciences. The sixth panel depicts the wrathful departure of Quetzalcoatl on a raft of serpents; the cause of his wrath was the reversion of the people to black magic, the perversion of Quetzalcoatl's teaching into the baleful practices of the Aztecs, the "imperialist" Mammon culture of pre-Columbian America. The seventh panel depicts the prophecy, interpreted as the coming of the European invaders.

The second set of seven panels is a counterpoint to the first set; that is, the eighth panel corresponds to the seventh, the ninth to the sixth, and so on. The second set begins with a powerful vision of Cortés, the bringer of the Iron Age, the Kali Yuga, the cross and the sword, against a background of flames. In a later mural painted in Guadalajara, Orozco depicted Cortés, the man of iron, as a machine with a human head.

The indigenous races of America are depicted being fed into a giant machine, the motif of the ninth panel. There could hardly be a more accurate mythical rendering of the purport of the civilization of the machine; since this panel corresponds to the departure of Quetzalcoatl, the machine may be interpreted as the ultimate tool of Mammon, human greed turned upon itself, the final rendering of black magic. The tenth panel represents the people of the golden age of the machine, an Anglo-American nation of emotionless schoolteachers, shopkeepers, and politicians at a town meeting. The eleventh panel depicts the modern Hispano-American world, victimized by insane greed and political corruption, the dirty playground of imperialist materialism. The twelfth panel represents the gods of the modern world. With profound intuitive insight, Orozco portrayed the Zombie-like inhabitants of the world of intellectual abstraction delivering stillborn knowledge from a skeleton while the rest of the world goes up in flames. He saw that the intellect of Adam, split from the life source, perpetuated the atrocities of a conscienceless Cartesian science. Corresponding to the panels of ancient human sacrifice, which at least had the virtue of being undisguised and direct, is modern human sacrifice, represented by politicians giving speeches at the tomb of the unknown soldier.

In the last and perhaps the most powerful panel of all, Orozco portrayed the Modern Migration of the Spirit; in the foreground appears the Quetzalcoatl who is yet to return, who announces the transcendence of history, while in the background history itself is shown as a swarm of tanks and armored artillery pouring over the symbols of the past: Greek columns, statues of the Buddha, a fallen cross. Striding forth from this historical tumult, the modern spirit—the Quetzalcoatl yet to come—is shown with moulting flesh, a human in the process of transformation. In the *Book of Changes* the symbol for Revolution, Ko, literally means moulting. What Orozco has depicted is the revolution of modern man—not the political revolutions, whose effects are minor, but the moulting and turning over of the spirit within the dense conflagration of matter. Orozco's vision shows us that the industrial technocratic era is actually the tempering, the purification, and the transformation of the spirit through the trial and climax of matter.

Orozco returned to Mexico and completed a brilliant series of murals in Guadalajara between 1935 and 1939. Though not as thematically coherent as the Dartmouth frescoes, these paintings present sometimes even more vividly the struggle of the spirit in the contemporary way of materialism.

In these later murals there is an overriding foreboding of the coming apocalypse and the fiery birth of the new man. As Orozco keenly realized, we are ruled more than even the Aztecs or the Romans by the god of war, the eternal combatant who in whatever disguise is the perverter of human truth, the enslaver of human souls, and the devourer of human flesh; he is the chief lackey of Mammon. And where once men raised totem poles signifying their common bondage with the spirits of the earth, the modern god of war raises smokestacks to declare his enmity.

The reappearance of Quetzalcoatl in the work of Lawrence and Orozco was not merely a coincidence, just as the landing of Cortés on the day sacred to Quetzalcoatl was not a coincidence. As the Dartmouth frescoes of Orozco show, there is a strange inverse correspondence between the events that took place before and after the European invasion of the New World and the consequent rise of technological civilization. According to the teaching of Quetzalcoatl, the world we live in is the fifth world; it is the world of movement, change, and progressive materialism. Before this world came into being there were four earlier worlds in which man was created and destroyed. These four previous worlds symbolize the perfection of man as a physical entity. The fifth world symbolizes the purification of consciousness in the furnace of matter. Toward the end of the fifth world, the earth, seized with a yearning for unity—the Great Return—will give birth to a new, purified race whose consciousness will be luminous and whole. This is the actual meaning of the prophecy of Quetzalcoatl's return. The alchemy of the return will be performed on native American soil through a confluence and blending of various world teachings, for in America is the seed-destiny of the next polar pulsation of the planet. From Old World to New, from left hemisphere to right, from intellect to intuition, the tide rushes darkly through the flesh, and only those trained to watch for it will see the white crest of the wave in the moonless night.

The conquest of the New World by the Old was remarkably swift wherever it occurred among the more developed American civilizations, not only because the European technology was superior but because the conquest had been psychically prepared for. Once the leading indigenous civilizations had been destroyed, it was only a matter of time before the remaining tribes were conquered and the exploitation of the land had begun. The meeting of the Old World and the New can also be seen as a concordance of planetary timing—the dissonant counterpoint of split Adam. The rapid acceleration of Old World technologies corresponds exactly with the New World myths and prophecies. Thus what has been a period of remarkable and unprecedented material progress and imperialist expansion for the Old World—the Faustian civilization at its zenith—has been a period of hell and purification for the New. Since materialism is predicated on war, and war is hell, materialism brings about a progressive descent into hell. If the calendars of East and West meshed so perfectly at the landing of Cortés, it seems reasonable to suppose that they will mesh once again. For that matter, perhaps they are already totally synchronized, and it is only our lack of awareness that prevents us from learning what the planetary calendar can tell us. In any case, the nine hell periods of increasing doom and despair forecast by the ancient Mexican calendar are a most appropriate timetable for our materialist technocratic civilization.

The return of Quetzalcoatl in the art of Lawrence and Orozco occurred toward the end of the eighth hell period, which encompassed not only the First World War but signs of the Great Return in the resurfacing of the symbol of primary unity, the mandala or Great Wheel. Orozco's vision of Quetzalcoatl was completed in 1934, the last year of the eighth hell period; with Quetzalcoatl firmly implanted as an artistic/symbolic outpost in the heart of the thirteen colonies, the stage was set for the ninth and last hell period, which would witness the triumph and transcendence of Tezcatlipoca, the smoking mirror, one of whose sacred signs is the jewelled bird of Mammon, the turkey.

The final hell period, from 1935 to 1987, is the all-American hell. In 1935 Hitler consolidated his power in Europe, thus ensuring a final influx of European intelligence to America. Brought to America also was the fatal germ of atomic war. In 1935 the last Dalai Lama of Tibet was born; before the ninth hell, and also the present sixty-year Tibetan cycle, would come to a close, Tibet, the planet's last arcane kingdom, would be eradicated by the inexorable logic of dialectical materialism, Maoist style. In 1935, it may be recalled, Jung wrote his preface to *The Tibetan Book of the Dead*. And not the least interesting event occurring in 1935 was the reissuance of the American one-dollar bill. Engraved on it for the first time were the two sides of the Great Seal. On one side of the seal is the usurped celestial emblem of the Native American peoples, the eagle. Thirteen, the most sacred number of the ancient Mexicans, appears four times with the eagle: thirteen stars, thirteen stripes, thirteen olives, and thirteen arrows. In the ancient Mexican religion there are thirteen heavens. In the sacred Mexican calendar thirteen is the number of Acatl—reed—which is the sign of the East, the sign sacred to Quetzalcoatl. Four times thirteen is fifty-two, the number of years that constitute a sacred Mexican cycle and the length of each of the current hell periods. On the other side of the seal is a pyramid of thirteen layers of stone (four sides of thirteen again produces the number fifty-two), on top of which is the all-seeing eye, symbolic of the fifth world of emerging consciousness. On the bottom layer of stone is written the date 1776; astrologically the United States was born on the thirteenth degree of Cancer. Above the eye are the cryptic words *Annuit Coeptis*—"He furthers this undertaking"—and beneath the pyramid is a banner bearing the inscription *Novus Ordo Secolorum*—"the new order of the ages."

Presumably this refers to an age for which America—democratic vista—is but the preparation.

The dream of 1776 reached a zenith of plantary power and prestige during the ninth hell. Accordingly in 1940–41 the United States government constructed the Pentagon, the world's largest building, to house all of its various war offices. The form of the Pentagon, whose five sides and five inner corridors symbolize the Fifth Sun, is also that of a *pentagram*, the chief magical aid for gathering power. When a pentagram is drawn on the ground with its base to the north and its chief point toward the south, as is the case with the Pentagon, it is useful for negative or black magic purposes. If we recall Blake's aphorism "Art degraded, Imagination denied, War governed the Nations," it is of more than passing interest that the National Arts Commission was the only group that contested, quite bitterly, the construction of the Pentagon in Arlington overlooking the Potomac. The Arts Commission won a minor victory in getting the site of the Pentagon changed from a hillside site blocking the entrance to Arlington National Cemetery—the home of the Tomb of the Unknown Soldier—to the riverside site it presently occupies. There is a grim and ironic, if not utterly black, humor to the fact that the Pentagon, the pivotal seat of power of the ninth and final hell, is built in an area once occupied by pawnshops and bars, and commonly known as "hell's bottom."

This bottom hell, inaugurated in 1935, corresponds to the ninth month of pregnancy. This is the hardest month, for it culminates in labor and birth. During this period America has become the pivotal point of planetary energies; through its dynamic center matter has finally been shattered through the splitting of the atom. Psychically this event signifies two things: the final splitting apart of the primal character of man, the old Adam, and at the same time the transcendence of matter. In ancient Mexican myth this event is represented by the splitting apart of Quetzalcoatl in his infernal form of Xolotl, which simultaneously gives rise to the birth of the Fifth Sun. On viewing the first atomic explosion in White Sands, New Mexico, in 1944, Robert Oppenheimer could only utter words from the *Bhagavad Gita* describing the appearance of the Godhead: "Brighter than ten thousand suns." Whitman's great poem of death had finally been born.

CHAPTER TWENTY-ONE

At the Zero Point: The Art to End All Art

HISTORY IS a dream—the dream of reason. As long as man believes in this dream and seeks to acquire an historical identity, he remains unconscious of the fact that he is a bridge between the cosmic realms of heaven and earth. Within the dream man's hopes will always focus on a future utopia that is progressively realized as a *kakatopia*, a psychotechnological intensification of hell on earth. His only escape from this fatal circle is to wake up from the dream and realize a cosmic, mythic, and fundamentally timeless identity.

1939. The eve of war. Another demonic turn. Hitler, Stalin, Churchill, Roosevelt, Hirohito, Mussolini struggling for unique historical identity, goaded on by the audacity of Alexander, the greatness of Caesar, the ruthlessness of Robespierre, the humaneness of Jefferson, Samurai ghosts of past time mechanized. Already Einstein, Thomas Mann, Stravinsky, Fermi, and hosts of others—the cream of the European intelligentsia—had fled the mainland. What Europe had not fully accomplished in the Great War she was to attempt once again under the ancient symbol of the turning of time, the *swastika*. Collectively the deepest sleep had enveloped Europe and the modern mind.

1939. The appearance of *Finnegan's Wake*, the last epic in European literature. Written in a language of great density and obscurity, James Joyce's last novel is a symbolic return of European consciousness to the charnel ground of dreams and chaos. The action of the novel, which is placed totally in the realm of one person's sleeping unconscious dream-life, presents a true picture of the hopes and preoccupations of an entire civilization. Just as one person is a reflection of the human race, so one night's dreaming is a reflection of the entire cycle of human development. In a word, Joyce has presented the myth of history as a dream. All that seems so solid and real shifts and changes, transformed in a magical shimmering of words and forms that have no base and endure only so long as there is a desire for them to endure. And all of this world, its houses, people, armies, governments, loves, and warring intrigues, has no other ground but the playful urge of a creative force whose existence reason cannot admit, and in any case would never understand.

Like the vision of Rudhyar, Jung, Yeats, and Lawrence, Joyce's vision centers on a cyclical return of history back into the realm of cosmic myth. This process, which is naturally most disturbing to the rational conventions of history, appears as a distintegration accompanied by the babblings of madness. The theme of Joyce's epic is stated in its famous beginning: "riverrun, past Eve and Adam's, from the swerve of shore to bend of bay, brings us by a commodius vicus of recirculation back to Howth Castle and Environs."[1] Howth Castle represents the mandalic fortress surrounding the primal being at the very center of consciousness, a being that transcends all of history. In its creative destruction of the rational tradition, *Finnegan's Wake* is the pure psychic complement to the unspeakable outrage of the Second World War.

The epic as a whole is literally a Book of the Dead, a passage or rite through the realms of consciousness repressed by the centuries-long dominion of technical prowess. In a stroke the entire literary intellectual tradition of modern times is parodied, surpassed, and laid to rest. Because *Finnegan's Wake* is so broad in the scope of its vision and so brilliantly inventive in its language, it both exemplifies the total exhaustion of one tradition and offers a glimmering forevision of another. To turn a phrase of Joyce's, *Finnegan's Wake* is the simultaneous Agnosis of postcreate determinism and the Gnosis of precreate determination; above all it is the "Probapossible prolegomena to ideareal history."[2] As McLuhan has tirelessly observed through Joyce's vision, "The wake of human progress can disappear again into the night of sacral or auditory man. The Finn cycle of tribal institutions can return in the electric age. . . . Joyce . . . discovered the means of living simultaneously in all cultural modes while remaining conscious."[3] If, according to Joyce, history as she is harped is rite words in rote order, then what is simultaneously emerging in the elctronic age is myth, the returning of rote words to rite order. The simultaneity of the synesthetized consciousness perceived by Henry and the Symbolists receives an apocalyptically authentic statement in Joyce's language: "What can be coded can be decorded if an ear aye seize what no eye are grieved for. Now the doctrine obtains, we have occasioning cause causing effects and affects occasionally recausing alter effects."[4]

Joyce's language recreates the psychosensory impact of runaway technology, a reality in which feedback takes precedence over primal experience. If a Joyce or a McLuhan could make his way in such a world and even take inspiration from it, a more pedestrian mentality could only retreat to a superficial devotion to order, while confusion reigned in the subconscious. With prophetic insight Joyce described the bewilderment and the violent subliminal chaos characteristic of the civilized consciousness that was to be dominated by the sinister and pervasive electronic media:

In the heliotropical noughttime following a fade of transformed Tuff and pending its viseversion, a metenergic reglow of beaming Batt, the baird-board bombardment screen, if tastefull taut guranium satin tends to the teleframe and step up to the charge of a light barricade. Down the photoslope in syncapanc pulses, with the bitts buttweg their teffs, the missledhropes, glitteraglatteraglutt, borned by their carnier walve. Spraygun rakes and splits from a double focus: grenadite, damnymite, alextronite, nichilite. . . .[5]

The passage reads like a narcotic prevision of the famed "television war" that would become familiar to Americans in the 1960's.

Though the message throughout Joyce's epic is "commodius vico's recirculation" of the dream, such a hermetic literature is destined for the academy and can hardly sound or evoke the catharsis necessary for the recirculation to occur. *Finnegan's Wake* fails magnificently by the scope of its ambition, and its failure is that of civilization's inability to communicate *within* itself. So separate had the two sides of man become by 1939 that encounters between them could only end in war.

> Sandhyas! Sandhyas! Sandhyas!
> Calling all downs. Callings all downs to dayne. Array! Surrection! Eirewicker to the wohld bluyden world. O Rally, O rally, O rall! Phlenxty, o rally! . . . Quake up, dim dusky, wook woom for husky? . . . We have highest gratifications in announcing to pewtewr publikumst of practician pratyusers, genghis is ghoon for you. A hand from the cloud emerges, holding a chart expanded. The eversower of the seeds of light to the cowld owld sowls that are domnatory of Defmut after the night of the carryin of the word of Nuahs and the night of making Mehs to cuddle in a coddlepot, Pu Nuseht, lord of risings in the yonderworld of Ntamplin, tohp triumphant, speaketh.
> Vah! Suvran! Sur! Scatter brand to the reneweller of the sky, thou whoagnitest! Dah! Arcthuris coming! Be! Verb unprincipiant through the trancitive spaces! Kilt by kelt shall kithagain with Kinagain. . . .[6]

Joyce's epic rambles on to its tentative conclusion. In the beginning was the word, and in the end the word still reigns supreme; but disfigured or transfigured, it is only a presage of the end of history. Joyce's work is the kind that can have no successors, for it is more the synthetic conclusion of one tradition than the beginning of another; it is the ultimate classic of psychic automatism, even though it is too studied to be considered pure psychic automatism. *Finnegan's Wake* and Wölfli's autobiography are to be distinguished only by the fact that the former was written for the public, whereas the latter was written solely as a vehicle for Wölfli's inner transformation. The difference is critical: public intent is what makes history; inner transformation is what transcends history. In the end, *Finnegan's Wake* presented the texture of the collective consciousness as it passed into the penultimate phase of historicity, the phase preceding the descent of myth and the conscious ascent of the unconscious. Once *Finnegan's Wake* had been achieved, Europe could descend to the depths of collective unreason. The European epic from the wars of Homer to the wars of Hitler had come full circle: the zero point had been reached. Though Europe was to linger on after the Second World War had ended, its cultural tradition had been thoroughly exhausted.

In 1939, the year of the publication of not only *Finnegan's Wake* but Rudhyar's "Artist as Avatar," a young American painter from the "Wild

West" named Jackson Pollock began Jungian analysis. Pollock had already had some treatment for alcoholism, but he felt a need to understand himself in greater depth. Some ten years earlier, while still in high school, he had been introduced to the ideas of Theosophy. Through the decade of the 1930's, when he was influenced by the Mexican mural painters and imitations of Picasso, his images tended to be raw and symbolic. Now, under the influence of Jungian analysis, his plunge into the depths of the unconscious was to provide the ultimate key to his identity as a painter. What Joyce had achieved with words, Pollock was to achieve in paint: a presentation of the raw texture of human consciousness during a time of maximum confusion, aggression, and sheer collective hysteria.

Having been encouraged by his analyst to use his drawing as a therapeutic aid, Pollock began to paint crudely calligraphic symbols ejected vigorously, even violently onto the canvas. The titles of his works during the war years are quite revealing: *She Wolf, Guardians of the Secret, Mad Moon-Woman, Male and Female* (originally entitled *Male and Female in Search of Symbol*). These works authentically chronicle the process of striving toward a realization of the archetypal forces within oneself. But sometime shortly after the war, Pollock's search for symbols ceased. Jackson Pollock the Seeker was transformed into Jackson Pollock the Artist. Art critics had begun to acclaim his work as the first major American contribution to modernism and later coined the phrase "abstract expressionism"—a phrase Pollock himself rejected—to describe the kind of painting they thought he was doing. But Pollock was sufficiently caught up in the illusions of the importance of the individual, of history, and of art itself to stop at a certain level of development and literally, though unconsciously enough, to cash in on what was critically being fed back to him. The real turning point in Pollock's career, came in 1947, when he revealed in a magazine article the technique and "content" of his work:

My painting does not come from the easel. . . . I prefer to tackle the hard wall or the floor. . . . On the floor I am more at ease. I feel nearer, more a part of the painting, since this way I can walk around it, work from the four sides and literally be *in* the painting. This is akin to the method of the Indian sand painters of the West.

I continue to get further away from the usual painter's tools such as easel, palette, brushes etc. I prefer sticks, trowels, knives and dripping fluid paint or a heavy impasto with sand, broken glass and other foreign matter added.

When I am in my painting, I'm not aware of what I'm doing. It is only after a sort of "get acquainted period" that I see what I have been about. I have no fears about making changes, destroying the image, etc., because the painting has a life of its own. I try to let it come through. It is only when I lose contact with the painting that the result is a mess. Otherwise there is pure harmony, an easy give and take, and the painting comes out well.[7]

Because of the technique involved, another critic described Pollock's work as "action painting," and the idea soon developed that somehow what Pollock had devised out of his own internal necessity was actually the *end* of traditional painting—as if art had reached some kind of terminal point. In a sense this was true enough. In Joyce's words and Pollock's drips, as in the invention of the atomic bomb, conscious human development had reached a veritable charnel ground of past illusions. What Pollock's technique engendered was a period of unprecedented gimmickry in art, and Pollock earned the dubious distinction of being considered a pioneer in what Harold Rosenberg was to describe as "the tradition of the new." But once his technique had been elevated to its place in art history, Pollock's own work developed into a monumental and decorative artistic *style*. Again the alchemy of the search had been prostituted into the artistry of style. It is evident from the unhappiness of Pollock's life that he was never fully satisfied with this turn of events. His alcoholism was never cured, and by the mid-1950's it became increasingly difficult for him to take up a paintbrush, owing to the intense identification he had developed with his artistic role. Occasionally during this period images began to reappear among the swirls, but Pollock was already trapped, suicided like van Gogh. If van Gogh had been suicided by society, Pollock was suicided by the art critics. Although he declared just before his death in an automobile accident in 1956 which many considered a suicide, that "painting is self-discovery. Every good painter paints what he is,"[8] Pollock's self-discovery had ceased to have any authentic meaning.

In his monumental 1942 work, *Male and Female*, Pollock presented two roughly totemic images; in contrast to the sinuous forms of the female, the male totem is like a rigid blackboard inscribed with numbers and mathematical signs, the archetype of the modern, quantifying male consciousness. It is this consciousness that finally absorbed Pollock's energies, turning the sinuous flow and totally unconscious energy of the female to its own quantifying art-historical ends. In their most mythic aspect, the classic postwar drip paintings depict the final atomization of historical consciousness, the total psychic disintegration that occurred with the advent of atomic warfare. But the mythic impulse in Pollock—the impulse that identified with the Indian sand painters of the West—died in the stylish world of the New York art galleries, where the image of the disintegration of consciousness was elevated to high fashion. Pollock was a victim of the Moloch of blatant commercialism, which in postwar America had very quickly devoured the immigrant European culture.

Abstract expressionism, the school of painting the critics credited Pollock with founding, was also heralded as the first authentic American art. Since America had not been ravaged by the war, it enjoyed a position of unprecedented world power and was revered by many of the other nations, not only politically but culturally. Abstract expressionism was accordingly adopted by avant-garde artists throughout the free world—whether in São Paulo or Tokyo, Paris or San Francisco. By the 1950's it had become the foremost international avant-garde style, and as a consequence New York had become the center of avant-garde world culture. In imitation of Pollock, the fashionable French painter Pierre Mathieu was depicted in a two-page spread in *Life* magazine throwing buckets of paint on a canvas—the act of creation captured forever for the unwitting audiences in the heartland of America. Then there was Yves Klein rolling attractive female nudes covered with paint across his canvases while a small society orchestra played in the background. After all, Pollock had said, "I continue to get further away from the usual painter's tools." The height of this delirium was reached in the mid-1950's, when it was announced that several abstract expressionist paintings that had been sold at a London auction for a considerable price were actually the work of a chimpanzee. Though many critics and artists themselves spoke of abstract expressionism as a counterpart of the literature and the theater of the absurd—and there is no doubt that the postwar world of the 1950's was precisely that—this kind of language became more and more of a screen. The heroic significance of Pollock's art was in the artist's act, the effort of creating his own ritual. Each person honestly pursuing this path must go his own way. But when the act is commercialized and made into a linguistic/media package, a fundamental perversion has occurred. This perversion more than anything else characterizes the cultural condition of the postwar "free world."

One group of avant-garde artists took Pollock's example as a license for anarchy. To them, art was whatever you can get away with"; hence the development of happenings, pop art, junk art, and finally concept art, the pure realm of novelty where anything can happen. Another group found justification in Pollock's autistic concern with his own creative process—art for art's sake. This group composed the purist stream that produced geometrical abstraction, minimal art, and finally concept art. The distinction between these two streams, however, is entirely academic, and in fact they have certain underlying similarities that are of greater interest. For one thing, both are radically anaesthetic, being merely the transplanted forms of the divided consciousness that had previously given rise to classicism and romanticism. For another, both are characterized by an art historicism that culminates in the cult of the new. The constant demand for newness requires that either the artist must continually change his style or the new must be subsumed under a concept of such extravagant purity or novelty as to utterly defy interpretation. Since most artists try to develop a certain style they can be identified with in order that their art will become a marketable commodity, they choose the second option rather than the first.

The most articulate and humorous exponent of art-historical *anaesthetics* was the late American painter Ad Reinhardt. In a 1960 panel discussion on "The Concept of the New," Reinhardt very neatly summed up the later modernist position:

If there is anything that distinguishes the art of our century from that of previous centuries, it is the word "abstract." The word "abstract" was a new attempt to separate and define art. In the seventeenth century, the idea of the "academy" was an attempt to separate the fine arts or intellectual arts from the practical or manual arts and crafts. In the eighteenth century "aesthetics" was invented to isolate art from other fields. In the nineteenth century, the main art movements were all involved with "independence"—independence from something. In the twentieth century the central question in art was the "purity" of art.[9]

Artistic purity had become synonymous with artistic novelty. Both novelty and purity imply progress, and hence both help perpetuate the fundamental myth of historical consciousness. But to strive for novelty is an inherently destructive process, since the new exists only in terms of an opposite it must always displace. Such a process can only be exhausting. To deny continually the foundation of what has come before is like jumping off the ground and saying, "This time I shall not land." Since one always lands, one attempts to deny the existence of the earth, or perhaps even to blow the earth up. For this reason even the creator of happenings, or the junk, funk, or pop artist, like the purist, must finally take refuge in the distinct *art-ness* of what he does, for his entire identity depends upon that distinction. Reinhardt very explicitly stated the essence of this position:

The new is the new awareness of the art process, of what art is, of what an artist is. This is the most serious idea and I would narrow down the subject for more awareness and not open it for a greater mass audience. . . .

I know the difference between art and life, between art experiences and other experiences. Many artists confuse them because they think that is what the public wants.

I like the academy–cloister–ivory tower–museum isolation of art. No one goes to an art museum to worship anything but art. The religious content is automatically removed when it becomes a work of art. A museum should be a tomb, not an amusement center, and art is not an entertainment—art is neither a pleasure nor a pain. Art is always dead, and a "living" art is a deception. Some religious painting—the Protestant—excluded the visual image because of its power. I exclude the visual image because of its weaknesses. I also would exclude sensations and impulses, and lines and colors, too, especially wiggly lines.[10]

Pollock's autistic gestures, as well as his use of random objects—cigarette butts, scraps of material, and so forth—and Reinhardt's ultimate *anaesthetic* appeal for an art purified of life are twin echoes of the Dadaist destruction of culture during the First World War. But in the case of

Pollock and Reinhardt, whatever their original and personal motives, the destructive impulse was supported by a network of forces that can only be described as an anticulture. The development of an anticulture, whether of the purist or of the "pop" variety, as the culmination of the industrial age should not be surprising, since efficiency, monetary worth, competitiveness, and material advancement are the primary values our system has fostered. With the advent of the Cold War in the late 1940's it even became advantageous, at least in certain circumstances, to promote the antics of the avant-garde artist as proof that the so-called free world was really free. Such a self-serving attitude is more than recompensed by the fact that these same artists are generally indifferent or even hostile to government.

In the Communist world, which shares the same materialist values as the free world, the anticultural forces are discouraged and repressed wherever they may appear, often justifiably being regarded as decadent bourgeois elements. Instead there is an official culture that promotes the merits and values of the state. The counterpart of this official culture in the free world is actually advertising, which like the official art of the Soviet Union, promotes the principal values of Western technological culture. It was only after the Second World War that advertising came into its own, especially with the perfection of public television as the major expressive force shaping the collective mentality. The tremendous power of advertising banished into the realm of the effete and the insignificant much of the activity of the avant-garde anticulture, for advertising could always absorb or usurp any novelties the avant-garde might conceive. Even though the avant-garde artists were coming into their own economically in the 1950's and 60's, finally winning acceptance by the establishment they had traditionally despised, the anticulture had few resources to counter the wealth and technical facility advertising had at its disposal. Modernist anticulture is like the eunuch in the court of the king, the king being advertising itself. The one commodity the anticulture can offer that advertising, owing to its inherent anonymity, cannot is personal glamor, the acquisition of a social/ historical identity.

The gap between the *avant-garde* anticulture and the world of advertising and media was finally bridged in the 1960's by Pop Art. Its leading practitioner was a former advertising man, Andy Warhol, and it generally consisted of imitations of consumer products often achieved through exaggerated mass-media techniques. In the words of one critic, Pop Art is "advertising art which advertises itself as art that hates advertising."[11] Like their compatriots, the Minimalists, the Pop artists had only one line of defense: an art criticism that invoked official art history as a justification for the novelties of the present. The art offered by the Minimalists, who also appeared in the 1960's, consisted of non-utilitarian objects that were often manufactured and bore no resemblance to anything save random recollections of the industrial landscape on a moonlit night. Both the Pop artists and the Minimalists pointedly ignored the criteria traditionally applied to works of art; yet their work was justified as art by a literature as densely intellectual and academic as any in the history of belles-lettres. Indeed the content of Pop and Minimalist art ultimately is the history of art-historical criticism itself.

The natural conclusion of either Pop Art or Minimalism could only have been concept art—antiart as the idea of art as idea. Not only does concept art represent the final disintegration of traditional art, since it can be sustained only by documentation intended to have an art-historical value, but it also represents the final sellout of the human spirit to the highest bidder, which is the illusion of history itself.

Faust sold his soul for knowledge, knowing full well that knowledge is power, and power is the key to historical identity. The modernist avant-garde artist has sought the same end, if by a slightly different course. As the critic Harold Rosenberg has written; "Apart from the difference in size, what is the real difference between a comic strip Mickey Mouse and a Mickey Mouse painted by Lichtenstein? The answer is art history. . . . The sum of it is that Lichtenstein had his eye on the *museum*, while the original worked outside of art history. Art manufactured for the museum enters not into eternity, but into the market."[12] In the film based on the life of Henri de Toulouse-Lautrec, *Moulin Rouge,* the painter on his deathbed receives the joyous news that his work has been accepted by the Louvre; he is the first living artist to be honored in this way. With this news we are expected to believe that Toulouse-Lautrec died a happier man. In 1956 the Museum of Modern Art inaugurated its series of one-man shows called "Work in Progress," each of which would honor an artist in mid-career by showing up to 25 of his major works. The first artist selected was Jackson Pollock. In August of that year his car went off the road and he was killed instantly. One wonders; did Pollock die because he had finally made it into the museum, or because making it into the museum made him realize he was "dead" already? Nowadays retrospective exhibits of an artist's work are sometimes shown several times during his life. This kind of recognition is what the avant-garde artist aims for, along with the purchase of his work by a number of the major museums. When Reinhardt declared that "art is always dead, and a living art is a deception," he was quite accurately stating the views of the museum-oriented anticulture. The faceless commercialism of the anticulture is a pure reflection of a spirit solidly emtombed within the cybernetic anonymity of its own illusions.

The museum was originally conceived as the tomb of the muses of the ancient Mediterranean humanist tradition, a place where the desecrated relics of a dead civilization could be categorized and displayed like trophies of war. As the heart of technological culture, the museum confers the value of a noble death on all official culture and anticulture. At one time all museums, whether they were devoted to science or art, were built in the neoclassical style—the style of fashionable death. After Hitler had his House of German Art built in the same monumental neoclassical style in Munich in 1937, the relation between neoclassicism and fascism became uncomfortably clear. Museums built since then have displayed a kind of technological neoclassicism: the columns and fountains are there, but the specifically Mediterrannean references, such as fluting in the columns or Apollo and Diana in the waterfount, are absent. By the 1960's the museum not only was the house of the past but had also become the central cog of contemporary anticulture. That museums of modern art are becoming standard features in the major cities of the world indicates that modernism itself has died, perhaps with the atomic holocaust, and is now simply being perpetuated as luxurious amusement to keep the empty truth from shining through.

Since the Second World War the avant-garde anticulture has been a small but bold operation with an excellent knack for getting the attention of the mass media—a trick it learned from advertising. The museum is the keystone of the system, of course, but there are several other essential components: the artist needs the art gallery to purvey his work and the art critic to explain it to his audience; the art critic uses specialized art magazines to communicate to an elite group of other artists, critics, and prospective patrons, who need the museum to legitimize their activities within the community at large. The reliance on the specialized art magazine, which invariably contains several critical essays sandwiched between many stylish and clever advertisements, underlines the continuing dependence of the visual arts on the written word, an academic tradition that can be traced directly to the Renaissance artist's embrace of humanism. Finally, since economic security is hard to come by, the major bastion of avant-gardism has become the modern academy—the various university and college art, music, and literature departments.

In returning to the womb of alma mater, avant-gardism has come full circle. The journey that started with Raphael's dream academy, *The School of Athens*, has ended where it began. In aiming to be fully accredited as worthy of the museum, art loses its vitality, for no matter how beautiful its treasures, the museum is the isle of the dead, and its values are the values of the dead. The fate of avant-gardism is the fate of history—a return to the isle of the dead. Within the academy it is easy and safe for the artist to adopt a negative posture of cleverness and cynicism, articulated with a flawless technique that lacks only the breath of the human spirit. Even more pernicious than the devotion of the avant-garde to the museum and the academy is its enslavement to the market. Art has come to be defined by the price it will bring; nothing else really matters. Art reduced to monetary value makes money-making the only art, the art to end all art. If Spengler saw the final war as that between blood and money, then art is checkmated and merely awaits the final counterattack of blood. Having sidestepped the catharsis necessary for transformation, modernist culture has reached a dead-end.

The barrenness of avant-gardism, which is exclusively the product of art history, reveals the bankruptcy of history as a value-producing ideal. It also reflects the cultural narrowness and suicidal exclusiveness inherent in the dogma of history as progress. Broadly speaking, art history is a set of perceptions extracted from the general European study of history in the eighteenth century and broken into a rigid set of categories in the nineteenth. These categories consist of a linear sequence—ancient art (meaning the art of the ancient Mediterranean, including Egypt and the ancient Near East), Medieval art, Renaissance art, Baroque art, and modern art—based specifically on the European past and European values. Medieval simply means the *age between* (the Renaissance and antiquity). Baroque is essentially a stylistic concept drawn from studies of the evolution of later Renaissance and antique styles. Modern is the term used to designate the breakup of the stylistic tradition of the preceding periods in the nineteenth and twentieth centuries. And avant-garde is synonymous with modern art, or modernism as it has more recently come to be called. Thus the historical concepts underlying avant-gardism build upon each other like the famous domino theory. The closer we are to the present the more quickly do the dominos—the various "isms"—come tumbling down. Each domino that comes down acquires its meaning simply from its place in the sequence. Without understanding its place in the sequence, the individual domino is meaningless. This is why minimalism—minimal reference to non-aesthetic—cannot be understood without references to classicism, cubism, expressionism and so forth. Whatever its merits, this system of critical classification which comprises the essentials of all academic art and art history text-books—has no absolute claim to reality. It is essentially only a mental construct, an institutional structuring conceived by the nineteenth-century European historical mind. In other words, modern culture in general is intrinsically and exclusively part of a European value system.

As we have seen, the roots of historicism in the European Renaissance coincide with the European confrontation and conquest of the non-Western world—another intrinsically European definition. By the nineteenth century, Europeans had begun to consider some of the non-Western cultures worthy of study. Those artifacts commanding greatest respect in European eyes, initially, were from the Orient; hence the category of Oriental art was created as an adjunct to the five Western periods of art. From a global viewpoint this arrangement is quite unbalanced, since the Orient comprises a complex of civilizations, any one of which is the equal of the European civilization in duration, number of artifacts, and so forth. These considerations go to the root of what is commonly called racism, here qualified as cultural racism. Not only is less attention given to the Orient in this system of classification, but the Orient has generally been perceived and understood only through European perceptions.

All of those forms alien to his perceptions the European lumped under the label *exotic*. To him the most exotic and least comprehensible arts of the world are those in the vague and quasi-anthropological realm of *primitive* art. The so-called primitive world includes most of Africa, Oceania, parts of Asia, and the remaining indigenous cultures of the entire Western Hemisphere. It covers the major part of the planet, then, and includes a wide range of cultural responses to the environment. But here again, Europeans have been prepared to study and appreciate the primitive world only insofar as it accommodates Western perceptual constructs. Thus, as Rudhyar has pointed out, we prefer to view the artifacts of the primitive world as art, and not as ritual or magical objects and tools. Similarly, any textbook history of modern art—the art of the nineteenth and twentiety centuries—includes only the artists, of whatever nationality, who have accepted and followed the canons of art-historical avant-gardism, and who have been able to find a market for their work. Much of what is commonly regarded as primitive or exotic art was still being created during this same period, but it is either ignored or demeaningly called folk art, an academic criterion that dates to the seventeenth century. Gauguin proved a major exception to the European attitude, but then he also left Europe. Picasso used African masks only because their forms corresponded to his personal urge to *deform* the conventional Renaissance vision. Pollock invoked the Indian sand painters of the American Southwest to justify his laying the canvas on the ground and working on it from all sides. But for the sand painters, whose canvas *is* the earth, Pollock's consideration is meaningless. Pollock's canvas was intended to be put on a wall and admired, whereas the sand painter's work remained on the ground and by tradition was erased after its ritual healing function had been completed.

Collapsing under its own weight, modernist culture only reveals the myth of history for what it is: an egotistic delusion collectively magnified into racial suicide. The artist and his activity represent the condition of human consciousness. When there is an artistic and cultural breakdown, the human species is suffering its own spiritual death. Recently a New York avant-gardist sent out invitations for a gallery performance. The day of the event, the gallery was bare except for several loudspeakers placed in the corners and some of the artist's written comments placed on the wall. The artist was beneath a raised floor toward the rear of the gallery, unseen by the guests. The art consisted of the artist masturbating beneath the raised floor, while microphones carried the sounds of his activity to the guests in the gallery. This event was duly documented in one of the leading avant-garde journals with an accompanying critical article that spoke of it in such terms as "low visibility." Surely art such as this reflects only the fatal narcissism of historical consciousness and the egotistic pursuit of an historical identity.

If "avant-garde" originally meant the vanguard of an offensive military force, the cultural avant-garde has collapsed in the heart of the enemy camp. In adopting the methods and means of a progressive, acquisitive society, the avant-garde permitted itself to be assimilated by the very society it had initially rejected. Ultimately, too, it spent itself in the continued pursuit of novelty, which by its very nature can no sooner be gained than it is lost. Now having all but consumed itself, the avant-garde, that social force which always prided itself on being ahead of the times, is finally bankrupt. With its collapse and degeneration, history and the myth of progress have also reached their end. What is now ensuing is the sporadically frenetic but generally bleak wake of the modern soul, as we await the catharsis preceding resurrection. If the mythic consciousness preceding the schizophrenic development of history stemmed from a primary ground, an *Urkultur*, then history, like Finnegan's wake, once again returns its contents in a heap of smouldering debris to that same primary ground.

CHAPTER TWENTY-TWO

In the Shadow of the Apocalypse

THE PROBLEM of art is inseparable from the problem of consciousness. In the art academies of the seventeenth and eighteenth centuries, art was legislated by placing tight restrictions on the powers of the imagination. When psyche fled the academy in the nineteenth century, the academy remained, not as a particular social institution but as a pervasive social force in the form of museums, galleries, universities, and modernist criticism— the new academic legislation. By 1960 the final academic solution had been reached: the abolition of art from artistic activity, resulting in happenings and pop art, with all its derivatives; and the abolition of artistic activity from art, resulting in minimal art and concept art, and their various derivatives. The Surrealist artist Max Ernst once declared, "We have no doubt that by yielding naturally to the business of subduing appearances and upsetting the relationships of 'realities' art is helping with a smile on its lips, to hasten the general crisis of consciousness due in our time."[1] The self-destruction of avant-gardism was one of the necessary events hastening the crisis of consciousness, the psychosocial catharsis toward which modern man has unconsciously driven himself.

Stripped of imagination, the official world of the 1970's comes to resemble more and more the negative utopia first forecast by Aldous Huxley's *Brave New World* in 1931. It is a world under the spell of mass media, propaganda, and advertising, and collectively industrialized almost to the exclusion of serious craft activity. But it is also a world deep in the throes of a crisis of consciousness. Huxley's vision, like the vision of George Orwell in *1984* (1948), to mention only the foremost among the science-fiction seers presents a world in which history has finally been exhausted. In its place is a more or less stable society whose members are controlled by techniques of suggestion representing varying degrees of sophistication. In these visions, which are an antimyth, the aim of history—complete and collective industrialization—has been achieved, and the fundamental energies of the human race are devoted to maintaining the existing social order. Maintenance and control are the two key terms best describing the preoccupations of the advanced technocratic state. If there is a third major preoccupation, it is secrecy, for secrecy gives power an aura of glamor and authority of invincible remoteness. When accompanied by clever advertising and propaganda, secrecy misleads the masses by concealing the fact that human affairs have embarked on a totally spiritless course, hell-bent on perpetuating the dominion of matter through increasing automated technology.

In *Brave New World* control is maintained through the use of drugs and a biopharmaceutical technology; in *1984* the emphasis is on a more psychological kind of control maintained through omnipresent and political persuasion. In 1955 the Chilean painter Matta executed a work entitled *Intervision* that vividly depicts the collective state of mind in the present era. In becoming so accustomed to the daily presence of the electronic media, which are said to have extended our senses and expanded our powers of communication, we have unwittingly submitted to a network of psychic servitude. Reality has been expropriated by media; in fact, it is a media reality. The media themselves have been used increasingly to maintain control and ensure the growth of the technocratic web. Electronic eyes are now sold commercially to trap burglars, but for what other purposes are they used? And even more fundamentally, why do we face problems with crime and terrorism in general? Our legislative inventiveness and our technology, like our medicine, are purely *allopathic*, dealing solely with symptoms and not with causes. For this reason we shall never "win" the war against crime, disease, poverty, or hunger. Accordingly the more alienated members of society, the criminals and the artists, have consistently sought other means for solving their problems, most notably the use of drugs.

Since the beginning of the industrial era, when it became clear that neither art nor religion as traditionally practiced could afford total relief for the psyche overwhelmed by the proliferation of technology, the use of hallucinatory drugs has been a common outlet among members of the social fringe. Such nineteenth-century drug users as De Quincey, Coleridge, Gauthier, Baudelaire, and Poe were joined in the twentieth century by Artaud, Cocteau, Michaux, Huxley, and Leary. Following the Second World War an increasingly prominent counter-culture developed, one of whose rallying points was the use of drugs. While the fashionable avant-garde continued along the path to its own esoteric death, a barbarian counter-culture evolving in direct reaction to technocracy was shaping up to take its place. The expressive means of this culture depend largely on a music and life-style derived from jazz and black American culture in general, and on the overamplified use of electronic media. The content of its expression ranges widely, from political outrage and technological despair, to an existential celebration of the present mixed with a quasi-spiritual invocation of love, and even to a fully apocalyptic vision. As a totality this far-ranging culture is the appropriate companion of advanced technocracy, for it is a culture based on media projection and psychological hallucination. Even more than Surrealism or concept art, the frenetic media arts of the counter-culture have hastened the general crisis of consciousness due in our time. With history in collapse, the counter-culture is the shadow of the apocalypse, the smoking mirror of Tezcatlipoca of ancient Mexican philosophy, emanating the smoky light that characterizes the hell of *The*

Tibetan Book of the Dead. It is the poison released by the Ouroboros biting its tail.

In selling his soul to the devil—Mammon—for unlimited knowledge and consequently power, Faust granted techne supreme power over psyche. Where once the alchemist and artist had stood together there now appeared the scientist, standing on the prostrate body of the struggling Artist. What had once been alchemy was now chemistry. Alchemy literally means the art of transmutation (*al*) practiced by the Egyptians (*chemy* means "the black land," a name for Egypt). Traditionally alchemy was simply referred to as "the art," for it was the means for the greatest transmutation of all, the transmutation of human into divine or cosmic consciousness. Chemistry is simply technique with no such grand claim, just as the art of the academy was simply a sensual/intellectual technique with no transformative goal. Chemistry and traditional Faustian art, which culminated in the avant-garde art of modernism, are both profoundly materialistic practices limited to transmutations within one plane of reality, the material/sensual. The material progress afforded by chemistry is counterbalanced by the material reflection of nature—naturalism—which is the predominant perceptual mode of the Faustian artistic tradition. Even today many prefer the naturalistic art of Norman Rockwell to abstract art; and the concept artist who fills a gallery with earth is primarily concerned with juxtaposing materials from one milieu against another, without making any kind of intentional psychological statement. The Faustian artist merely manipulates the material world, while psyche remains unwanted, unattended, and unaccounted for.

"Violent eruption, vulcanism; the patient becomes violent, as he wakes up. The madness of the millennia breaks out. Dionysius is Violence."[2] This passage from N. O. Brown's evocative book *Love's Body* describes the internal explosion, the dis-ease of psyche rebelling against the technical tyranny of the Faustian world. Homeopathically the remedy for Faust's disease could only be chemical: only by ingesting the chemicals of his own creation could Faust begin to cure himself of the obsessive disease of matter. Naturally it was psyche in the form of the disenchanted industrial-age artist who began the experiment. But before the nineteenth century was completed, he was joined by the scientist, who began to investigate the hallucinogenic drugs. The first systematic study of the ancient Mexican hallucinogen peyote, from which mescaline has been chemically derived, was published by the German pharmacologist Ludwig Lewein in 1886. Around the same time the American philosopher William James undertook his famous experiments with nitrous oxide. Sporadically through the earlier part of the twentieth century other researches were carried out, including Robert Weitlaw's discovery in 1930 that the "sacred mushroom" cult was still active in Oaxaca, Mexico. The turning point came in 1938, one year before the outbreak of the Second World War, when the Swiss phar-macologist Hofman discovered the powerful mind-altering qualities of cer-tain synthesized properties of the ergot fungus. Further researches by Hofman resulted in the discovery in 1946 of the most powerful and notori-ous hallucinogen, LSD-25.

The exquisite counterpoint of the discovery of LSD and the invention of the atomic bomb is not to be overlooked, for the penetration of matter signified by the smashing of the atom was paralleled perfectly by the penetration of the psyche signified by the discovery of LSD. With these two achievements the extreme limit of Faustian knowledge was reached, for human consciousness had returned to a point where the antipodes of ex-perience are joined: the illumination of the smashed atom is the illumina-tion of the mind released from bondage. The dropping of the atomic bomb on Hiroshima and the subsequent production of the hydrogen bomb have brought about an unprecedented change in the planetary ecosystem; such a change of necessity was accompanied by an equally radical exploration and alteration of the psyche through the technological means of drugs.

The first hydrogen bomb was exploded in the Pacific—the Sea of Peace—in 1954. The irreversible increase of radioactivity in the physical environment resulting from continued atomic testing represents the ex-treme *hypertrophy of* techne, which verges on an actual transmutation of the physical organisms of the planet. At the same time the ultimate *at-rophy* of psyche, represented by the nihilistic efforts of the avant-garde and the prevalence of existential philosophy, has been reversed by the conscious introduction of chemical agents for the alteration and exploration of con-sciousness. The 1954 explosion of the hydrogen bomb was accompanied by the publication of Aldous Huxley's *Doors of Perception*. It is not stretching the comparison too far to state that Huxley's experiments with hallucinogens—or psychedelics, as they were to be called—which began in Hollywood in the spring of 1953, mark a cultural turning point equivalent in effect to the explosion of the first hydrogen bomb. "Psychedelic" liter-ally means *mind-manifesting*; at the same time that matter was dissolved by the bomb, mind remanifested in an explosive and radiant presence.

In his earliest novels, culminating in *Brave New World*, Huxley had already displayed his acute perception of the state of human affairs. Rather than become utterly disillusioned or cleverly adopt some dogmatic solu-tion, whether political or aesthetic, he moved in the direction of what Leibnitz had called the perennial philosophy. For Huxley, mysticism in whatever form was the revelation of man's one source of wisdom—the spiritual fountain of the divine available to all if only the "doors of percep-tion were cleansed." Like Blake, Huxley had seen through the façade of Faustian civilization to the squalid presentiments and grim horrors behind it. Delving into the mystical literature of the world, Huxley grasped, dur-ing the Second World War, the need, stressed by every exponent of the Perennial Philosophy, for mortification, for dying to self. And this must be a mortification not only of the appetites, the feelings and the will, but also of the reasoning powers, of consciousness itself and of that which makes our consciousness what it is—our personal memory and our inherited habit-energies. To achieve complete deliverance, conversion from sin is not enough; there must be a conversion of the mind, a *para vritti* as the Mahayanists call it, or revulsion in the very depths of consciousness.[3]

Huxley's mescaline and subsequent LSD experiments after 1953 gave him what he felt was a direct experiential confirmation of truths perceived by the mystics. He thus came to believe that psychedelics held the key for modern man, enabling him to experience the mortification and dying to self, the revulsion in the very depths of consciousness that was absolutely necessary for survival. Through the use of these drugs was revealed the "Door in the Wall," the possibility of self-transcendence and transformation.

"Ideally everyone should be able to find self-transcendence in some form of pure or applied religion;' the chemistry set of Faust had finally been turned upon itself and was being used to justify the most immoderately immaterialistic goals. "I am not so foolish," Huxley continued,

as to equate what happens under the influence of mescaline or any other drug, prepared or in the future preparable, with the realization of the end and ultimate purpose of human life: Enlightenment, the Beatific Vision. All I am suggesting is that the mescaline experience is what Catholic theologians call a "gratuitous grace," not necessary to salvation but potentially helpful and to be accepted thankfully, if made available. To be shaken out of the ruts of ordinary perception, to be shown for a few timeless hours the outer and inner world, not as they appear to an animal obsessed with survival or to a human being obsessed with words and notions, but as they are apprehended, directly and unconditionally by Mind at Large, this is an experience of inestimable value to everyone and especially to the intellectual.[4]

Huxley's words were to spark a revolution. Quite simply, through the drug experience he had rediscovered the visionary experience in such a way that its significance was to have a widespread effect on the collective consciousness. In Huxley's appeal to the intellectual class to drop its verbal defenses and experience *directly*, the gauntlet had been thrown down. For Huxley, the inadequacy of words and what we would now call left-cerebral-hemisphere functions was painfully manifested through the psychedelic experience:

Literary or scientific, liberal or specialist, all our education is predominantly verbal and therefore fails to accomplish what it is supposed to do. Instead of transforming children into fully developed adults, it turns out students of the natural sciences who are completely unaware of Nature as the primary fact of experience, it inflicts upon the world students of the humanities who know nothing of humanity, their own or anyone else's.[5]

In their final evolution the Faustian scientist and artist are each divorced from the other, for both are divorced from the life-giving source of revelation, the visionary experience. The visionary experience, a parting of the veil, may not be the same as the mystical experience; the ineffable embrace of unification; yet translated into art by its inherent transportive power, the visionary experience may lead directly to the most profound and beatific exaltation. Precisely because the visionary experience is not historical but transcendental, it presents a threat to the historical vision; it was to safeguard the historical vision that the academic strictures were placed on the imagination and a naturalistic art arose whose major glories were depictions of historical heroes and events. For this reason the restoration of the visionary experience to its primary place in human creative endeavor may have an apocalyptic result, for it not only announces the end of history but declares the return of a timeless world. A world of precious stones, of flaming jewels, of preternatural lights gleaming from pinpoints within undulating landscapes of ever-changing colors, simultaneously receding and coming forward, at once totally illusory and painstakingly time-bound, and yet utterly void of the least significance: a shining unnameable presence as timeless as the space between death and birth.

As a result of his experiments, Huxley predicted the advent of a genuinely apocalyptic, transhistorical collective movement when he wrote in the late 1950's,

My own belief is that, though they may start by being something of an embarrassment, these new mind changers will tend in the long run to deepen the spiritual life of the communities in which they are available. That famous "revival of religion" about which so many people have been talking for so long will not come about as the result of evangelistic mass meetings or the television appearances of photogenic clergymen. It will come about as the result of biochemical discoveries that will make it possible for large numbers of men and women to achieve a radical self-transcendence and a deeper understanding of the nature of things. And this revival of religion will be at the same time a revolution. From being an activity mainly concerned with symbols, religion will be transformed into an activity concerned with experience and intuition—an everyday mysticism underlying and giving significance to everyday rationality, everyday tasks and duties, everyday human relationships.[6]

As his own artistic vision of this future world, Huxley published in 1962 his last novel, *Island*, a psychedelic version of the perennial phiosophy, the point-counterpoint to his *Brave New World*. In presenting the ultimate fantasy of a mystical society in which aggression and war have been replaced by visionary exercises, Huxley provided an illustration of why hallucinogens have also been called "utopiates." *Island* is not only a treatise for the living, but in the tradition of the technological visionaries, a treatise on dying as well. In this "book of the living and the dying,"[7] there is a scene with a dying woman, Lakshmi, in which the visionary moment and the supreme mystical experience of the Clear Light unite, transcending the duality of life and death:

"And now," Susila was saying [to Lakshmi], "think of that view from the Shiva temple. Think of those lights and shadows on the sea, those blue spaces between the clouds. Think of them, and then let go of your thinking. Let go of it, so that the not-Thought can come through. Things into Emptiness. Emptiness into Suchness. Suchness into things again, into your own mind. Remember what it says in the Sutra. "Your own consciousness shining, void, inseparable from the great Body of Radiance, is subject neither to birth nor death, but is the same as the immutable Light, Buddha Amitabha."[8]

Buddha Amitabha, the Clear Light of what endures, as it is described in *The Tibetan Book of the Dead*, may be recalled at the peak of those events that abolish history, the explosion of atomic bomb and the psychedelic experience. This much Huxley knew when he died, on November 22, 1963, the same day President Kennedy was assassinated. Earlier that same year, on the other side of the continent, another event had occurred that was to catalyze and bring into full focus the apocalyptic, antihistorical movement and religious revival prophesied by Huxley. In April 1963, Timothy Leary and Richard Alpert were dismissed from the academy, Harvard University, for experimenting with psychedelics—an event that launched the psychedelic movement. If Huxley had been the prophet of this movement, Leary was its Messiah.

Leary's psychedelic experiences had their genesis in Cuernavaca, Mexico, during August 1960. Here, having ingested seven "sacred mush-rooms," he first experienced that revulsion of mind and deepest conscious-ness without which there can be no deliverance from sin, bondage, and ignorance. Pioneering individuals like Rudhyar and Huxley had articulated the need for transcendence, and artistic minds like Breton as recently as 1957 had called for a revival of magic, "for magic implies protest, in other words, revolt,"[9] but in Leary the wildest dreams of the Surrealists and the most beatific visions of the seers were to be combined in a disquietingly charismatic and catalyzing force. Romanticism, Symbolism, and Sur-realism had been irrational forces channeled through the minds and imagi-nations of the artists. But because art itself had finally been subverted by techne after the Second World War, the psychedelic experience was to be a deep collective force of visionary potency moving through the public imagination regardless of artistic inclination. Indeed, official avant-garde art only tightened its defenses with the advent of psychedelics and proved mortally impervious to the opened floodgates of vision.

Within several years of his departure from Harvard, Leary had almost singlehandedly brought about a major cultural revolution. Much of his initial influence emanated through the Castalia Foundation, which he helped found and operate (with Alpert and Ralph Metzner) in 1963. "Castalia," of course, refers to the utopian state described in Hermann Hesse's monumental novel *Magister Ludi: The Bead Game.* The name was appropriate, for the foundation served as an energy center combining scientific research, anthropological investigation, consciousness-expansion workshops, light shows and multi-media artistic endeavors, and a rediscovery of arcane knowledge. By the summer of 1967 millions of people in America, Europe, Japan, and Latin America—the entire technological world—had experimented with biochemical agents. But this massive immersion in visionary ecstasy hardly ushered in an amplified Castalia or Huxley's *Island* utopia; instead it brought human society much closer to Huxley's "*brave new world.*"

Like all revolutions, the psychedelic revolution was short-lived. By 1968 it had peaked and entered a phase of violent political upheaval; by the early 1970's it was virtually over. Leary was a criminal, fugitive, and the psychedelic movement, once a vital counter-cultural force, had become merely a matter of style. Its legacy, however, was profound, for it had permanently merged two cultural streams from the 1950's: the revitalized visionary stream and the indigenous technological media culture. The first had appeared full-blown in 1956, when Allen Ginsberg's *Howl* was published, with its incantatory lines,

> *I saw the best minds of my generation destroyed by madness,*
> *starving hysterical naked,*
> *dragging themselves through the negro streets at dawn looking for*
> *an angry fix,*
> *angelheaded hipsters burning for the ancient heavenly connection*
> *to the starry dynamo in the machinery of night,*
> *who poverty and tatters and hollow-eyed and high sat up smoking*
> *in the supernatural darkness of coldwater flats floating*
> *across the tops of cities contemplating jazz,*
> *who passed through universities with radiant cool eyes hallucinating*
> *Arkansas and Blake-Light tragedy among the scholars of war,*
> *who were expelled from the academies for crazy & publishing*
> *obscene odes on the windows of the skull.* [10]

Ginsberg inveighed mercilessly against a civilization that is itself the incarnation of the insanity it imputes to its dissenters and visionaries. Indeed, everything he spoke of in the opening lines of his epic was to become a point of counter-cultural protest within the next decade. But the heart of the matter was the nature of modern civilization itself:

> *What Sphinx of cement and aluminum bashed open their skulls*
> *and ate up their brains and imagination?*

> Moloch! Solitude! Filth! Ugliness! Ashcans and unobtainable
> dollars! Children screaming under the stairways! Boys
> sobbing in armies! Old men weeping in parks!
> Moloch! Moloch! Nightmare of Moloch! Moloch the loveless!
> mental Moloch! Moloch the heavy judger of men!
> Moloch the incomprehensible prison! Moloch the crossbone
> soulless jailhouse and Congress of sorrows! Moloch whose
> buildings are judgement! Moloch the vast stone of war!
> Moloch the stunned government!
> Moloch whose mind is pure machinery! Moloch whose blood is
> running money . . . Moloch whose soul is electricity and
> banks.[11]

Ginsberg's vision is wholly apocalyptic. Lacking the literary grace of Huxley, he made raw and real the fears and fantasies of a generation who had witnessed the birth of the hydrogen bomb:

> we wake up electrified out of the coma by our own soul's airplanes
> roaring over the roof they've come to drop angelic bombs
> the hospital illuminates itself
>   imaginary walls collapse. . . . O starry spangled shock of
> mercy the eternal war is here.[12]

Between 1956 and 1963 the Beatnik movement, as the small group around Ginsberg came to be called by the media, carried the banner of vision through an essentially uprooted and existential life-style that married a nervous foreboding and hatred of the social order with a frenetic adoption of Zen Buddhist and other vaguely oriental and mystical clichés and attitudes. During the same period, which saw the beginning of the space age, there appeared a second cultural stream, the indigenous technological culture of rock 'n' roll. At first blissfully innocent of any pretense to social commentary, after 1963 rock music was to provide the catalyzing energy of the psychedelic movement. Performers like Bob Dylan, the Rolling Stones, the Beatles, and the many San Francisco groups successfully united what had been taken as a teen-age musical style derived from black and hillbilly folk music with the apocalyptic and mystical intent of Beatnik literature.

"I am waiting for the rebirth of wonder,"[13] Lawrence Ferlinghetti wrote in 1959. His plea was answered with the arrival of psychedelic culture. From about 1964 to 1972, the period in which the United States' involvement in the Vietnam War was most intense, the widespread use of psychedelics enabled millions of intellectually oriented Westerners to encounter pre- and para-verbal reality. The visionary experience that had been so rare to the European technological mind since the advent of the printing press was now becoming a commonplace. Thousands of young people began to leave the academies; where once they would have been studying and attending classes, now they were performing a new, hypnotically rhythmic, and highly amplified electronic music, running light shows, or making psychedelic posters and the like. The tyranny of the word had been broken; the spell of the printed message had been shattered. The psychedelic carnival of the 1960's was a cultural enactment of *finnegan's wake*. Multi-media events were staged in an effort at recreating the powerful psychic experiences evoked by the use of LSD and other hallucinogens. Perhaps the most notable of these was Leary's 1966-67 production with USCO, a collective of media artists, entitled "The Death of the Mind." Media events such as these and the massive celebratory "be-ins" that were held in San Francisco and New York in 1967 were the high point of the psychedelic cultural movement. If Dadaism had pronounced the death of art and culture during the First World War, the psychedelic movement in announcing the death of the mind was initiating the apocalypse itself. Speaking of these events, Ginsberg declared in a magazine interview,

We're in science fiction now. All the revolutions and the old methods and techniques for changing consciousness are bankrupt. We're back to magic, to psychic life. . . . Don't you know that power's a hallucination? The civil-rights movement, Sheriff Rainey, Time magazine, McNamara, Mao—it's all a hallucination. No one can get away with saying that's real. All public reality's a script, and anybody can write the script the way he wants. The warfare's psychic now. Whoever controls the language, the images, controls the race.[14]

From the Romantics to the Surrealists, a few willful souls had rejected history and its implacable dialectic outright. But never had an entire generation, as it were, made such a wholesale rejection of the historical process and all that it entails: politics, dualistic science, academic knowledge, and technology, at least insofar as it is a tool of war and an economic system that feeds on consumption for its own sake. The rejection of history, the ideological underpinning of the present civilization, is a prelude to the apocalypse. What are we when stripped of the myth of progress? Apocalypse means revelation, disclosure, being without one's clothes, standing naked. By opening up the visionary experience, psychedelics had helped many individuals see beyond history. In the conclusion to his Surrealist novel, *Nadja*, André Breton declared, "Beauty will be CONVULSIVE or will not be at all."[15] And Rilke in the *Duino Elegies* passionately proclaimed,

> *Who, if I cried would hear me among the angelic*
> *orders? And even if one of them suddenly*
> *pressed me against his heart, I should fade in the strength of his*
> *stronger existence. For Beauty's nothing*

but beginning of Terror we're still just able to bear,
and why we adore it so is because it serenely
disdains to destroy us. [16]

For modern man, aesthetically and culturally deprived, the visionary experience afforded by LSD is that convulsive beauty, that beginning of terror which can hardly be borne. The experient, abruptly lifted from the narrow, egotistic realm of the personal, is confronted with the awesome splendor of the super-personal; and if he is fortunate and skilled enough, he is swept through the realm of the archetypes right into "the atomic-electronic flash beyond form." [17] The hallucinogens have released a floodgate of symbols and meanings that have no place in the historical continuum. Born from the tension of the timeless and the timebound is the politics of the nervous system, the politics of ecstasy.

A living revelation of eternal truth expressed in terms academically described as occult—hidden—could only draw the immediate rancor and suspicion of the upholders of history. An individual revelation is a private transcendence of history, but a collective revelation is an apocalyptic event that aims toward abolishing history. Alchemy, witchcraft, astrology, the entire train of secret arts whose resurrection Breton had called for in the Second Surrealist Manifesto, had suddenly reappeared. Soon it was manifest that these arts had become "secret" largely because they negated the egotistic doctrine of history. And history in the form of the modern state answered back. In October 1967 a massive group of more than one hundred thousand people gathered in Washington, D.C., for an exorcism of the Pentagon. The event combined the celebratory style of the be-ins with the conscious purpose of confronting the war-machine. It became the occasion for the confrontation of two forms of magic: one form securely bastioned in the immovable material presence of the Pentagon, and the other form represented by thousands of chanting seekers hardly believing in their own power, mere children playing a deadly game of witch and warlock.

No sooner was the sacred object of the Pentagon touched than its protective forces reacted. With little solid grounding in the science and magic of the psyche, the exorcists' incense and good will, misunderstood mantrams and war paint were no match for tear gas, the swoop of helicopters, and a well-disciplined army of soldiers with fixed bayonets. The political front of the psychedelic revolution fared no better than the American Indian Ghost Dancers of the 1890's. In Prague, Tokyo, Mexico City, Paris, Chicago, and Berkeley, the specter of apocalypse within its own midst drew the paranoid wrath of Moloch, which irrevocably shattered the dissident forces. The revolution of 1968, which ranks with the revolution of 1848 in its international scope, served only to demonstrate the supreme power of technocracy. The occult vision of an imminent new age dwindled into sporadic violence on the one hand, and gigantic rock festivals on the other, in which hundreds of thousands of young people could mesmerize themselves with electronically amplified music and the liberal use of hallucinogens. With these events, Huxley's *Brave New World* was coming true. The monotony of working in an industrial society could now be relieved not only by television and the other distractions that electronic media and advanced technology can provide but by the psychedelic weekend. A new and stifling normalcy has arrived, under the aegis of governments that are even more deeply entrenched, more reactionary, and more totalitarian than they were before the psychedelic revolution.

Yet a strange disquietude permeates the psychic atmosphere. An unstable Pax Americana now prevails, but the deeper effects of the revolution of the 1960's should not be discounted. The general crisis of consciousness due in our time is now a day-to-day heritage. Having once occurred, it has generated the apocalypse. From now until some unforeseeable point in the not-too-distant future, we shall be living in the precincts of the apocalypse, for the total domination of history over the minds of men has been broken by the gratuity of the visionary experience. A sufficient number of human beings have achieved a radical self-transcendence that offsets the disastrous and degenerate abuses of mind-altering drugs. How these self-transcending humans realize their goals during the next few decades will determine the future of human development. Inescapably they will bring about that revival of religion Huxley spoke of in the late 1950's. Perhaps some clue to the future may be discerned in the phenomenon of the Lama Foundation and similar communal groups.

Lama, which was founded in 1966, is located high in the Sangre de Christo Mountains of New Mexico, not far from where the ashes of D. H. Lawrence were buried. Some of the founders of Lama, had been avant-garde artists since the mid-1950's, and with the advent of psychedelics had become members of the USCO group of artists in Woodstock. Like other modern visionaries, some of them came to believe that an art intended to transform the emotions and consciousness of the beholder must be based on a transformed life. Thus a few sought to live the truths of the new age in a setting uncontaminated by the present civilization. And so Lama sprang into existence as a communal "seed group" of a dozen or so core members, some of whom had been active as artists in the counter-culture. Forgoing the electronic media and drugs that had been the instruments of their earlier inspiration and success, the Lamaites voluntarily accepted the often harsh life of the mountains. Their community, which strives toward self-sufficiency in every respect, had succeeded where many other communal experiments have failed, for at its core is an unfailing dedication to a transcendent spirituality. Even the architecture of Lama, which combines the space-age geodesic structural technique of R. Buckminster Fuller with the indigenous adobe building materials of New Mexico, reflects the religious inspiration of the community. As it was evolving in the early 1970's, the spiritual direction of Lama was eclectic: Hindu, Buddhist, Sufi, Christian, and Native American elements all found their way into the thought, practice, and publications of the Lama Foundation, which include the widely read Richard Alpert/Baba Ram Dass document *Be Here Now*. Over the past several years this small community has exercised a significant influence on the outside world. But more important is the fact that whatever its failings, it is a community attempting to practice, as Huxley predicted, "an everyday mysticism underlying and giving significance to everyday rationality, everyday tasks and duties, everyday human relationships."

The path from a mythic space to an art separated from life led to the adulation of the secular past and the creation of the values known as history. Once invented and believed in history made of art a specialist concern whose primary motive was its own furtherance, and the maintenance of its own self-importance. "Educated" people pressed on the masses the importance of art and culture; but to a technologically educated race of mechanics art could only be a frill and any claims to its importance only another proof of the hypocrisy of the ruling class. The claims of the "educated" were supported by the avant-garde artists' growing belief in their own self-importance. In the Greek myth Arachne, a splendid weaver, is turned into a spider for believing that her work was the equal of the gods. Technique and ingenuity are nothing if they are not the fruit of inner realization, or at least the accompaniment of the search for such realization. Experiments like the Lama foundation represent an attempted transformation of the prevailing values.

In a community like Lama the question "What is art?" is no longer at issue, for art has become what Rudhyar called an *art-whole* in its seed-formation. An art-whole is determined by the quality of life-response, and not by a particular aesthetic philosophy. It is no longer of *history*, for it no longer supports the notion of art as entertainment or of the artist as an isolated genius, the main staples of art-historical art down to the heyday of popular psychedelic culture with its adulation of rock superstars. Instead, an art-whole is the expressive mode of the creative seed group on its slow, lonely, and often anonymous return to a mythic space where the inner and the outer worlds mirror each other. When expression of any kind proceeds from inner realization, each act bears the imprint of truth; it matters not whether the expression is a work of "art." The path of the seed group is the only path beyond the politics of apocalypse. As the art historian Herbert Read once wrote,

To those whose minds are dedicated to movements and collective efforts of all kinds this may seem to be a pessimistic conclusion. But if it is generally accepted it might be the beginning of a new era [in politics]. The processes would necessarily be piecemeal and slow, confined to individuals and small communities, and it is possible that catastrophic events will overtake us, and destroy the civilization we would save. But it would not be the first time in the history of the world that civilization has been preserved by the patience and humility, the suffering and sacrifice, of few lonely individuals, a few isolated communities.[18]

CHAPTER TWENTY-THREE

Art as Internal Technology: The Return of the Shaman—The Descent of the Goddess

IN THE psychedelic experience we are confronted with the abolition of history. But the abolition of history is the recovery of the sacred dimension, "for all history," as Mircea Eliade wrote in the foreword to his book on shamanism, "is in some measure a fall of the sacred, a limitation and a diminution."[1] Certainly the life of every culture is a "history," a departure from the sacred primary experience, but only to the extent that the *reliving* of the primary experience is not an important life-goal. In technological civilization the spontaneous possibility of living again a fuller revelation of the sacred has been so thoroughly diminished that it is viewed as a crime and a direct threat to the very existence of society. Why is this so? As an ideology history is oriented, toward the future. Any experience that transcends this ideology is therefore regarded as archaic or regressive. "Archaic" is generally thought to mean antiquated or outdated, in keeping with the historical point of view, but its root is a verb meaning *to begin*. In a sense what is archaic may not be backward at all, but a beginning. From the historical point of view what is important is the utopian end and not the beginning; thus historical consciousness wishes to abolish the archaic experience by whatever means, for it does not believe in the possibility of a new beginning. From the sacred point of view, however, it is history that is "outdated," or actually "overdated."

The very meaning of religion, which art once served as a handmaiden, is to bind back into one, to relate to the beginning, to the origin of all things. True religion implies a reversal of the historical process. An authentic religious revival, as foreseen by Huxley, is a return to the "beginning," to the primordial state of unity. This "beginning" is omnipresent as the on-going self-renewal of the cosmos in all its aspects. When Timothy Leary was traveling about the country exhorting people to create their own religion, he was calling for a reversal of history by returning to this "beginning"—beginning with the individual. The typical person immersed in the kind of revelations brought on by psychedelics must confront something far vaster than his own memory could encompass. It makes no difference whether the contents of this vast realm are explained as the evolutionary spectrum encapsulated within the genetic configuration of the particular individual or as the primary encounter with the supernatural embodiments of the archetypes. The significant fact is the realization of an immensity that no words can describe, and that impoverishes the grand illusions of the individual ego. There may well be as a result of such an experience the desire, the need, the urge to participate more fully in a religious life, even to the point of creating one's own religion. If this is the choice, then one faces a staggering decision: where does one begin, and how?

Since one is at a "beginning," an affinity with archaic material is felt very naturally. In the collapse of history, which is the "end," the archaic, the "beginning," is all that remains: Ouroboros once again. Whereas history is built on temporal ephemera, the contents of the archaic are embedded in the self-renewing cosmic experience that transcends time. It is curious how history and the myth of progress distort our perceptions, so that we think of alchemy, shamanism, and yoga, for instance, as things of the distant past, while in fact all of the mystical techniques that were relegated to the past in the European cultural continuum have continued to exist side by side with history. The endurance of the archaic is all the more astonishing, given the merciless willingness of technological civilization to uproot, desecrate, and where necessary, even to commit genocide in order that the progressive forces of history could prevail. But as the inner psychic house of history begins to collapse, suddenly appearing through the debris are the glints and glimmers of an eternal magic. The walls and features of the outer house of history remain more or less intact, but as the inner house is slowly reconstructed, the outer walls lose their supports. The structure built according to the precepts of the remaining archaic material calls for a totally different design and points of stress. The blueprint of the archaic is not ancient, but an eternal beginning, making itself available whenever the barriers of history and materiality have exhausted themselves.

The archaic presents a curious counterpoint to technology. While technology is an instrument of externality, the archaic begins with a consideration of the internal structure of things, which is universal and all-encompassing. Archaic techniques constitute an internal technology. Academic art and culture could persist in the West as long as they adhered to an essentially external and linear logic. The most exquisite examples of modern Western art are no doubt the musical compositions of eighteenth-century masters like Bach and Mozart; in their work the linear, external logic of the post-Renaissance mind is perfectly wedded to a sensual form and spiritual structures demanding that kind of rigorous technical support. By comparison, Baroque and Neoclassical visual art is barren and pretentious, dependent as it is on the historical anecdote for meaning. Freed of any such anecdotal necessity—for Mozart and Bach the opera or mass was not prerequisite but integral to musical form—music could use the linear, external technique perfectly to convey very diffuse and abstract feelings and states of consciousness. But this perfection could be sustained only for a brief historical moment. With the crushing triumph of late-eighteenth-century technology, the *techniques* by which inner meaning could be developed—namely alchemy and a vital harmonic Pythagorean tradition of mystical mathematics—disappeared. Thereafter, Western artists were to be deprived of an internal technology. Though it was to be rediscovered haphazardly and incompletely from time to time by visionaries like Blake, Goethe, Seurat, and Kandinsky, more common was the spectacle of a Picasso on the one hand, improvising on the external logic of Western art, or a Pollock on the other, flirting with the inner realm yet lacking the discipline and the knowledge to master it. Only the late work of Kandinsky and Klee, among the self-conscious artists of modernism, approaches the true precincts of the archaic, the former painting images in a manner reminiscent of Australian x-ray painting or of the *huichol* yarn-painting of Mexico, the latter creating pictographs and hieroglyphs stammering toward the articulation of a new world.

What separates the art of most modern Western visionaries from the kind of integral achievement that characterizes the archaic, however, is an intense inner discipline—the development of an internal technology. From the archaic point of view, internal technology—discipline of the psychic energies—precedes and underlies the fabrication of any artifact. Whereas the knowledge underlying the development of historical culture is intellectual and literate, that of the archaic disciplines derives from a living oral tradition. "Tradition" literally means to give over, or to hand down, not in books but literally by word of mouth and symbols. From the historical, scientific point of view, tradition has been interpreted as precluding *direct* experience, and it is therefore considered a deterrent to progress. This view is not altogehter correct, since archaic traditions emphasized the necessity of direct experience or revelation to confirm their teachings. What the historical position actually favors is human endeavor for its own sake. The ideology of modern history, which is progress at all costs, is directly opposed to tradition, which is rooted in the cosmic sense of being, a sense in which even progress is an egotistic illusion. To cultivate the cosmic sense of being precedes in importance any expression of it, and for this reason, the archaic endures beyond the historical, since its real essence is continuity in change. Defined this way, tradition is the transmission of an inner quality of being rather than an external expression of it. From the traditional point of view, even history is a sacred deviation; it is the trump card of the Fool.

What the lingering presence of the archaic suggests is not an allegiance to a specific set of goals, values, or techniques, but the necessary development and refinement of consciousness, beginning with the individual. In other words, the individual's first responsibility is to his own conscious development. Because the ideology of history favors the collective values of competition, patriotism, and the work ethic, values that keep the individual in bondage to external goals, the individual must be extremely vigilant in order to preserve his humanity. But history itself being a deviation, a trick the collective ego plays on itself, the yogi and the shaman meditating on the outskirts of civilization bide their time waiting for the refugees.

Though he eagerly sought the shaman, Artaud lacked the patience and the discipline necessary to find him; eventually he went insane. Faring somewhat better, Ginsberg tracking through the jungles of South America or wandering through India was able to transform *Howl* into the mantric chanting of the Vedas—the wisdom of the seers. Trying to avoid practicing Pavlovian psychology within the walls of academe, Leary had the discipline necessary to make some sense of Mind-at-Large as it oozed and manifested through him. In creating his own religion, the League for Spiritual Discovery, Leary resorted to archaic tradition for discipline and support. Appropriately enough, the purest analogue that Leary, Alpert, and Metzner could find for the *psychedelic experience* was *The Tibetan Book of the Dead*—a manual archaic in the fullest sense of the word. Because it embodies an ancient wisdom of death, *The Tibetan Book of the Dead* is also a wisdom of the beginning that is eternally now. The implication was that psychedelics, when properly used, are a vital instrument of rebirth into the sacred dimension. In *Psychedelic Prayers*, Leary rephrased the *Tao Teh Ching*, one of the most *archaic* manuals of the way, in terms of his own genetic vision. Like Jung's notion of archetypes, Leary's notion of the cosmic vision is placed within the genetic structure of the individual; therefore what is most archaic is within us, genetically encoded in the psychophysical structure of the organism. The wisdom of our contemporary ancients, the shamans and the yogis, is an organic wisdom intrinsic to our own nature. The perennial philosophy, the means of gaining that wisdom, is no different than the development of our own consciousness, for which purpose the force of history is both a repressive burden and a challenge.

The initial use of drugs to reacquaint Faustian man with the reality of this wisdom acts as a stick of dynamite to break up the logjam of materialistic confusion and error. But used continually without an appropriate ritual prescription, psychedelics can only be a poison. More important is the development of the discipline—the internal technology—that an understanding of the inner realm demands.

We are in a unique evolutionary position, and when I speak of tradition and the necessity of developing an internal technology, I am by no means advocating the thoughtless or wholesale embrace of the traditions of another culture. Yet to begin at the beginning, to begin again, is to embark on an archaic path. Though the shamans and the yogis of the existing archaic traditions may offer the post-Faustian refugee essential help, the point is not to become them but to become ourselves. The vision of what we are to become is already within us, awaiting the proper discipline through which it might be appropriately expressed.

An initial seed-glimpse of the "archaic future" is provided by the outpouring of mandalas sparked by the psychedelic revolution. The mandala is the most archaic symbol; its spontaneous projection is an indication that the deeper levels have been sounded. Being the most archaic symbol, the mandala is also the best symbol of the primordial state of unity. Like the previous "early warning" mandalas of Jung, the mandalas of the 1960's and 70's are unique; embodying the archaic form-principle of the centered wheel or sphere, they derive from no particular past culture but from a realization of the immediate evolutionary condition of consciousness. This is evident, for example, in the mandalas of Paul Laffoley, whose work focuses on the universality of the "visionary point," the eternal point at which "time moving forward meets time moving backward." For Laffoley this is the point that "precedes the world's mystical experience, the Omega point."[2] The reference to the visionary philosophy of Pierre Teilhard de Chardin is clear. The visionary point artistically symbolized by the spontaneous return of the archaic form of the mandala is really a sign that the new beginning, the Great Return, has taken root, not in just a few individuals as it did after the First World War, but in the collective consciousness of mankind. Correspondingly, and in opposition to orthodox Darwinian theory, Teilhard de Chardin declared: "No proof exists that man has come to the end of his potentialities, that he has reached his highest point. On the contrary, everything suggests that at the present time we are entering a peculiarly critical phase of super-humanisation."[3] This critical visionary moment can achieve its end only by the simultaneous transcendence of the physicalist mentality that has been modern history's mainstay and the unleashing of what Buckminster Fuller describes as humanity's unique capacity for the metaphysical. The landing of humans on the moon in 1969 had its psychic correspondence in the greater realization of our intrinsic weightlessness. It is astonishing to think that all of our institutions, our technological power and military might, are simply the embodiments of values that have no weight. These embodiments drag us down, much as the moon "drags" around the earth.

In physical terms civilization has reached a point of maximum entropy, the unparalleled grossness of what the visionary media artist Willard Van de Bogart calls *industrial anarchy*. In a paper entitled "Entropic Art" Van de Bogart wrote "That area of thought on this planet that has been the alternate symbol system, separate and apart from 'Industrial Anarchism,' is art." As an inherent symbolic system art has traditionally been the

unconscious overseer of man's activities. . . . Initially art was glorious with a high degree of spirituality. . . . But then the unexpected . . . the machine culture and industrial consciousness. No longer the aristocracy . . . revolt was in the wind . . . and equality for all became the people's revolution. However, the gap in the symbol system transfer was neglected. Further and further the symbols receded until today we have artists cutting up their bodies in protest to the inhumanity that is in operation within the social system . . . .

The art symbol system of man is now revealing in a synergistic way the hierarchy of the earth plan's entropic system of Industrial Anarchy. These art symbols are coming about so that man can restructure his system to the point that evolutionary synergy will in fact be made possible by thinking of art as a utopian mechanism that serves as a safety valve to prevent the human species extinction.[4]

Van de Bogart is representative of those artists who, having seen through the barrenness of the philosophy behind technology, are using the most advanced techniques of electronic media to penetrate the blind wall of technocracy. As Van de Bogart has explained, "Media projections are the only real possibilities for non-cultural constructs for the evolution of man's mind."[5] Exemplifying this trend of thought in his recent book, Gene Youngblood described Jordan Belson's masterwork, the 1964 film *Re-Entry*, as follows:

Simultaneously a film on the theme of mystic reincarnation and actual spacecraft reentry into the earth's atmosphere, . . . *Re-Entry* is chiefly informed by two specific sources: John Glenn's first space trip, and the philosophical concept of the *Bardo*, as set forth in the . . . so-called *Tibetan Book of the Dead.* . . . With imagery of the highest eloquence, Belson aligns the three stages of the Bardo with the three stages of space flight: leaving the earth's atmosphere (death—[Chikhai Bardo]), moving through deep space (karmic illusions—[Chonyid Bardo]), and reentry into the earth's atmosphere (rebirth—[Sidpa Bardo]).[6]

A similar idea was developed in the popular movie *2001* . In yet another film, *Lapis* (1963-66) by James Whitney, the computer was used to develop exquisite mandalas that are synchronized with Indian ragas, powerfully recreating the experience of primal cosmic awareness.

Consciously or unconsciously, willfully or not, even the most technically sophisticated artists have arrived at the precincts of the *archaic.* Through the artist, the scientist and the shaman begin to merge into one. But it should be kept in mind that the primary function of the archetypal figures of the shaman and the yogi is not to create art or science, but to heal, to make whole, to maintain a balance between psyche and techne. This is achieved through an understanding of the laws governing the creation and maintenance of the world. The inner is always drawn to the outer and vice versa; the microcosmic contains the macrocosmic just as easily as the macrocosmic contains the microcosmic. In the beginning is the end, and in the end is the beginning.

The transubstantiation of materiality through art produces spiritual power. In the Catholic ritual transubstantiation makes the bread and wine the actual body and blood of Christ, without changing the presence of bread and wine. This is brought about not by overt action but by the action of psyche in conformity with certain laws governing the processes of internal growth and relationship. But the belief system known as materialism totally ignores the laws of internal necessity, by which transubstantiation, for instance, is made possible. Ignoring the laws of internal necessity, materialism has no real place for art, the means by which all matter may be regenerated as spirit. The primitive peoples of the world have indeed been able to speak to rocks and listen to voices issuing from mountain-tops simply because for them art is the transubstantiation of materiality. Because Western civilization has lost this art, which is the essence of art, both the physical body and the intuitive psychic faculties have been neglected in favor of a disembodied and exalted intellectualism whose chief fruit has been the gargantuan planetary system of runaway technology. Instead of a harmoniously integrated and thorough psychophysical training, the civilized human is educated to use and rely on the intellect alone, while dealing with a world of inert but exploitable matter, of which nobody is a part.

This materialistic world view came fully into being during the latter part of the eighteenth century. The music of Bach and Mozart, of which I spoke earlier, succeeds only because it achieves a subtle balance between the internal psychic structures derived from late Medieval culture and the outer linear forms of the mechanistic Renaissance world view. With the triumph of technology and intellectual materialism, the delicate psychophysical balance was destroyed. In the nineteenth century the composer Franz Liszt, overcome by a bodily passion he could not understand, gave up music to search for God. God-mad, Van Gogh committed suicide because his intuitive mind and his physical body had no way of relating to each other. What we have been calling art for the last few centuries has largely emanated from the misunderstandings between the body and the mind that have taken place in the free-fire zone of the psyche. What Huxley said of Freud—that he was not materialistic enough since in paying attention only to the mouth and the anus he ignored the rest of the body as well as the psyche—is true of modern civilization as a whole. Because materialism is a psychological condition, the technological methods of dealing with such problems as pollution, crime, terrorism, poverty, disease, and madness only worsen them. The only solution possible is a radical one, that is, a solution that goes to the roots. And the roots of human behavior are not material but psychological.

Despite the brilliant technological ingenuity of our materialistic civilization, the general level of human consciousness has scarcely ever been more debased, degraded, depressed, and desperate. Blind to anything but the grossest forms and subjected to a tyrannical dualism that assigns a separate reality to the creative act, the individual is divorced from creativity. The problem is compounded by the fact that a primary value is assigned to the *artifact* or the event as the quantifiable proof that creation has occurred. Since the educational process discourages the widespread attainment of the psychomotor abilities required by the practical or craft skills, in favor of the more socially and economically prestigious attainment of intellectual, mechanical, or clerical skills, relatively few members of society seem to have artistic abilities. This state of affairs seems to validate the assumption that creativity is a special and distinct human attribute.

Once he is attuned to the psychological and spiritual nature of the world crisis, the internal technologist must first seek to transcend the ceaseless intellectual thinking principle upon which material progress depends. Because the practice of seeing through thought is fundamental to all experience of a cosmic nature, the mandala and other primary geometrical forms have persisted throughout human culture. Transcending the grip of intellectualization, rationalization, or conceptualization, one will almost certainly experience the mandalic nature of the primordial. Second, in whatever form the sacred is experienced there must be a complete identification of self with the object of experience. At its most primary level, art is not a thing done but a dissolution of the ego; nor is anything "created." Whereas the materialistic view is that creation is an addition to reality, from the point of view of internal technology, creation is actually a dissolution of duality and a merging into a unitive state, producing a transformation of reality—the transubstantiation of which I previously spoke. What technological civilization refers to as the archaic work of art may well be the residue of an active realization of nonduality.

In the art of Tantra, both of India and Tibet, we have perhaps the purest example of an archaic non-dualizing tradition that has survived quite intact. The rediscovery of Tantra art by the technological world and its subsequent popularity are further signs that the circle is completing itself. In Tantra, as in certain American Indian rituals, art is not a specialized profession or a particular style but a path to greater self-realization open to anyone willing to cast aside the mind-forged manacles of man. Of course, to choose this path requires the reversal of all logical and historical processes. The extent to which individuals are capable of undergoing this initial transformation is the extent to which a new world view is being brought forth.

The power of Tantra and the ritualistic art of the American Indians derives from a religious impulse profoundly wedded to an intuitive and systematic knowledge of the laws governing the creation and perpetuation of the world. This religious impulse is utterly lacking in the art of technological modernism, which has finally exhausted and broken itself in the chaos of intellectual conceptualization. Yet in the charnel ground where concept art disintegrates, a new consciousness more appropriate to the temple than to the studio or gallery has slowly emerged. This deeply conscious change in attitude, type, and quality of artistic activity, which has appeared largely unannounced, is as significant as any change that has occurred since the Renaissance. However the various efforts in the realm of the developing consciousness may find expression—whether in the life-style of a commune or the practice of art in a certain medium—they do not constitute a movement but a *mutation*. A movement is a calculated reaction to a preceding event operating within a strict causal framework; but a mutation is a function of evolutionary necessity without parallel or precedent.

We are now witnessing the final reversal of Renaissance values. Naturally this could not have come about without the formative base of European culture. But to follow the prevailing standard is to widen the ever more apparent abyss separating the psychic from the physical. If one encounters this dilemma head-on, a transfiguration occurs, accompanied by a unitive experience that engenders a resolve to leap over the abyss. The resolve may be associated with a thirst for gnosis—a more fundamental knowledge, a knowledge that may become an integral part of oneself. At this point a revitalized human expression becomes possible.

If art is no longer specialized, then it becomes a means of relating to the whole; that is, it becomes an activity that responds to and helps direct environmental impulses rather than an art (or a technology) that is imposed on the environment. This is why knowledge of the laws of the creation and perpetuation of the world is a prerequisite for the practice of art. The most direct source for knowledge of this nature is one's own organism. But to gain knowledge from this source requires psychophysical techniques that make direct and immediate use of the biopsychic system centered in our bodies, which are the ultimate environment and ground of experience.

Through archaic techniques such as *hatha yoga* and *tai chi chuan*, for instance, psyche and body may be revitalized and their union experientially reaffirmed. Psychophysical exercises, consciously undertaken, enable the organism to reassert its autoregulatory and self-expressive capacity, which has been greatly diminished by the artificial dependencies that technological civilization instills in the individual. In fact, the confusion resulting from "industrial anarchy" is so profound that only through exposure to a seemingly *opposite* system of behavior can the stifling ego-consciousness fostered by present ways of life be adequately confronted and transformed. Thus the archaic systems and their various gurus and teachers are an essential part of the present "end" phase of neotechnic civilization. At one point Don Juan told Carlos Castaneda that the system of magical thought into which he was attempting to initiate him existed only so that, jux-taposed to his old, Cartesian mental set, it would enable Carlos to see the absurdity of both—and all—human conceptual systems and thereby arrive at a realization of the truth.

Slowly and often painfully uncovering an authentically open and de-structured vision of the world, the internal technologist appears in his or her role as a *healer, one who makes whole*. Psychophysically healed, his negative, materialistic tendencies transformed, and initiated into a knowl-edge of the laws governing the creation, perpetuation, and destruction of the world, the internal technologist exemplifies the integration of archaic widom with a full realization of man's present evolutionary situation. Beyond merely pointing out the present stagnation in the human condi-tion, the responsibility of the artist of renewed awareness is personally to bring about a new harmony beginning with his own organism. In other words, the internal technologist has the potential of becoming a *center* by coordinating his own organism's physical, emotional, and mental func-tions. Since the human species itself is potentially a network of centers, and hence an organism whose rhythmic and harmonious order depends on the rhythm and harmony of its individual centers, the artist as internal technologist has a definite role to play in human survival. Moreover, to add a further dimension, the earth itself depends on the superior coordination of the human race for its ultimate fulfillment. But there will be no absolute realization by all the members of the planetary hierarchy until there is a real coordination of individual centers. Charles Henry expressed the double-bind imperative of this situation:

The development of the individual is as impossible without the development of the species as the development of the species is impossible without the development of the individual. . . . The result of this important consequence is that individuality tends to be collective, and that collectivity tends to be individual. The realization of this double end would be the age of absolute harmony; the complexity of the rhythm which sweeps the species along is the same in consequence for the individu-al.[7]

What makes the internal technologist a "center" is the interior wedding of the feminine right hemisphere and the masculine left hemisphere: the result is synergistic, and not at all like adding two and two and getting only four. Whatever the internal technologist does is art, for art in these terms is an integration of the open way (psyche, the female) and the way of power (techne, the male). The open way is the descent of the goddess, the yin, *shakti, dakini*, mother-muse who symbolizes inspiration, submission, in-tuition, wisdom as innate appreciation. The way of power is that with which we usually identify art or technique. It is male; it is yang; disinte-grated, it is the artist or the technocrat; integrated, it is the yogi or the shaman; it symbolizes the qualities of expiration, ability, implementation; its wisdom is skill in means. For the revitalized artist of whatever sex, the intrinsically feminine psyche no longer is the disembodied muse of the Romantic poet but is incorporated once again as the vitally functioning intuitive structure of being. Correspondingly, woman is no longer the "lesser faith," *fides minor*, hence feminine, but the goddess, the matrix, the openness of nature through which spirit finds the vessel appropriate to its expression. Man and woman are no long master and slave, nor are they at war with each other, but they realize in and through their uniqueness the fullness of the universe. They are representatives on earth of the primary cosmic principle; both must live in harmony with each other, or else they jeopardize the precarious balance of the cosmos.

Reflecting the integration brought about by an activated internal technology, the expressive language of the new vision is necessarily symbolic and androgynous. Symbols may be described as compressed information, and as Van de Bogart has written, "Compression of information is the next step toward global sanity."[8] Because the language of the new vision is symbolic, it is capable of conveying immediately through simple forms a multiplicity of meaning; because it is androgynous, it evokes the marriage of heaven and hell, the physical and the psychic, man and woman, the archaic and the evolving, the terrestrial and the celestial, the sacred and the profane. What is coming into being is a language of renewed archetypal significance based on a profoundly religious orientation. In being religious—bound back into one—this orientation implies a transvaluation of everything commonly understood as either art or technology.

The problem of art cannot be solved apart from the problem of life; rather than speak of art in the context of what is coming to birth, it may be wiser to speak of an art-whole, a mythic space in which the pattern of human behavior is so radically altered that the very concept "art" no longer has any validity. Purged of the separatist notions of art and technology, we may approach a mode of behavior in which the expressive function of the human organism is so indissolubly wedded to an intuitive knowledge of the laws governing the creation and maintenance of the world that our least response is pregnant with a vitality and a meaning of which mechanized existence has long since deprived us. Where once alienated, literally educated masses sought an escapist refreshment in the entertaining spas of the theater, the museum, or the television tube, we may envision participatory ceremonies that are therapeutic, consciousness-enhancing and synesthetically involving.

Our journey began with the transformation of mythic experience into the schizophrenic, splintered-world of art, and of the artistic experience into history itself; now through the transformative mind of the visionary artist, we find that history diminishes in the swelling tide of a new myth based on the reunited antipodes of the human mind. The return of the shaman, the descent of the goddess, usher us once again into another beginning.

CHAPTER TWENTY-FOUR

The Tranformative Vision: Catharsis and Individuation

THE SHAMAN and the yogi, the sorceress and the priestess, all derive their strength from an initiatory death and rebirth experience they must each undergo before they can truly be themselves. It is this transfigurative experience that endows them with their unique vision. In traditional societies this experience was highly valued, and the right to undergo it was safeguarded religiously. But modern techno-historical society abolished the right to vision as well as the ritual for gaining it with a fearful and self-righteous vengeance, thus ensuring its own fantastic rise to power but also sealing its own doom. In denying the validity of the vision and the vision-quest, modern society denied itself any rebirth short of the apocalypse—an event its own shamans and visionary prophets, exiled to the sidelines, have continually foretold and prepared for.

The great rush of progress, so contrary to the cylcic order of the universe, is like a forestalling of the inevitable; as man seems to have achieved success in combating the harshness of nature and softening the sting of death, so the necessity to be reborn and baptized again in the spirit of God has also been laid aside in favor of security and creature comforts. Instead of the arduous purification, ritual, and meditation required of the archaic visionary, the modern artist or scientist submits to rote academic training and wins a diploma. In fact, the visionary experience is likely to mark a modern artist as deviant and place him outside of the historical mainstream. Even so, modern visionaries have maintained contact with the archaic, not because of an archeological or sentimental veneration of it but because in the archaic they have glimpsed the *only* tradition, the tradition of Eternal Life. "The soul must take the hint," wrote D. H. Lawrence, "from the relics our scientists have so marvelously gathered out of the forgotten past, and from the hint develop a new living utterance. The spark is from dead wisdom, but the fire is life."[1] It is not the classroom and the academic degree that bestow wisdom, but purification and the vigil on the sacred mountain. The Tantric artist, toward whose sense of wholeness so many of the Western visionaries have unconsciously aspired, is called a *sadhak*, a *mantrin*, or a *yogin*, meaning that he has first purified his body and mind and entered into contact with the ineffable. In this same tradition Blake declared "Prayer is the Study of Art. Praise is the Practice of Art. Fasting &c., all relate to art"; Gauguin carved Christ and the primordial Polynesian deity on a single piece of wood; and Lawrence wrote his "Hymns" to Quetzalcoatl.

Immersed in their belief in history, academic and avant-garde artists, politicans and technocrats alike have justified the aberrations and tragedies resulting from their activities in the name of history or historical destiny. But the true history of techno-historical civilization is written, imaged, and transformed in the labors of its visionaries. In their lives and work are revealed not only what Eliade calls the Terror of History but history's redemption, for the essence of the transformative vision is that the sufferings of history themselves constitute the process of transformation. The poet Rilke expressed this truth in a beautiful and simple metaphor: "We are the bees of the invisible. We frantically plunder the visible of its honey, to accumulate it in the great golden hive of the invisble."[2] The bees of the invisible correspond to the mythic, *prehistorical* existence of the spirit in man. The frantic plundering of honey is the manifestation of the spirit as history, which results in the rape of the earth and the degeneration of man by his pursuit of material well-being. The return of the honey to the great golden hive of the invisible is the necessary transformation of the spirit-in-matter. The purpose of life *is* its transformation. Rilke's great elegy rings out:

> Earth, isn't this what you want
> an invisible rearising in us? Is it not your dream
> to be one day invisible? Earth! Invisible!
> What is your urgent command if not transformation?

The historical web of transformation is planetary, and as subtly psychological as it is grossly materialistic. What the Romantics felt as a "return to nature," what Whitman perceived as a Passage to India, and Hesse as the journey to the East, were all aspects of the collective psychological intent of the transformative web operating intuitively and urgently through the minds of a few. The return of the honey to the great golden hive of the invisible is the Great Return, the return to harmony and wholeness of being, both in history and in the individual. In the simplest terms the Great Return implies a major reversal of the specialization typified by the scientist and the artist, until the two roles are merged into one. Primordially the scientist represents intelligence, corresponding to the left cerebral hemisphere, or techne, which rules the right side of the body; and the artist represents intuitive knowledge, corresponding to the right cerebral hemisphere, or psyche, which rules the left side of the body. The unassailable power of the shaman or yogi results from the internal marriage of these two principles.

In the Hopi creation story as told by Dan Katchongva, the Great Spirit

made our bodies of two principles, good and evil. The left side is good for it contains the heart. The right side is evil for it contains no heart. The left side is awkward but wise. The right side is clever and strong, but it lacks wisdom. There would be a constant struggle between the two sides, and by our actions we would have to decide which was stronger, the evil or the good.[3]

There is a remarkable psychophysiological truth to the mythic voice of the Hopi medicine man which is universally applicable. Knowledge or wisdom, symbolized by the left side of the body, must precede intelligence and strength, symbolized by the right side; otherwise moral corruption is the result. Thus the "heartless' right side is considered evil, for when it alone seeks to determine things, disaster is inevitable. In other words, the most fundamental errors begin in assuming the absolute power of reason, or of right. This was the error of Faustian civilization, which created a *science* without *conscience* and an art without vision. Right (in French, *droit*, the same as the word for law), ratio, reason, rote—these are key words for the most fundamental assumptions of the technological civilization that grew out of the European Renaissance. From the Hopi point of view, these assumptions amount to a complete capitulation to the right side of the body and the left cerebral hemisphere, resulting in what has been earlier described as the tyranny of the left hemipshere or the tyranny of reason over vision, woman, the earth, and "minority" views and cultures. In technological culture at first only the artist, and finally only the visionary, was able to maintain some degree of sanity, simply because he was still able to keep a better balance between the left hemisphere and the right. As we have seen, what began as the history of art logically must end as the history of man's insanity, for the degree to which art becomes specialized as fine art, and dependent for its meaning on art history is the degree to which man loses touch with his innate wisdom. In recent times this process has been hastened by the advent of the machine. Since expression is innate to the human species in denying ourselves our expressive wisdom we have denied ourselves our own humanity.

During the first phase of industrialization, in the early nineteenth century, progressive apologists argued that the machine would give the masses extra leisure time in which to offset the debilitating horrors of mechanized labor by pursuing the humanizing arts and handicrafts. But this idea was ill-conceived, for true art is not a hobby but the very fruit of a life lived in integral relation to the cosmic web of earth and the cosmic web of heaven. Mechanization had completely disrupted this dual relationship; thus the leisure time it afforded could only be a blank space in which man's expressive functions were further atrophied by an entertainment industry that demands utter passivity from its audience.

Most fundamentally, the history of modern art implies that for the vast majority of human beings, the primary integration of mind and body at best has become unconscious, and at worst has been destroyed. Prior to the rise of the specialized artist—and mechanization—handicraft and artistic activity had been one of mankind's noblest ways of consciously integrating mind and body. The specialization of art led to the appearance of a few geniuses, but it reduced the rest of humanity to a race of robots. And the genius himself, though his extraordinary abilities are worshipped in our culture, is often a distorted personality. Beethoven composed music of superhuman beauty, but he was also a deaf and lonely misanthrope.

It is characteristic of the modern age that we experience chaos to the utmost. Chaos is simply the warring separation of right hemisphere and left, of mind and body, of man and woman, of art and science, of intelligence and nature. For the Hopis and other American Indian tribes, the modern age is a time of *trial* and *purification*. Perhaps thirty or fewer Hopis still live by the teachings of their forefathers; the rest have succumbed to the pressures of a Faust who sets up his coal mine in their land. According to traditional Hopi teaching, this present period of purification marks the catastrophic end of the fourth world and the preparation for the emergence into the fifth, the world of expanded and illumined consciousness:

The Fourth World, the present one, is the full expression of man's ruthless materialism and imperialistic will; and man himself represents the gross appetites of the flesh. With this turn man rises upward, bringing into predominant function each of the higher centers. The door at the crown of the head then opens, and he merges into the wholeness of all Creation, whence he sprang. It is a Road of Life he has travelled by his own free will, exhausting every capacity for good or evil, that he may know himself at last as a finite part of infinity.[4]

Similarly this period of chaos, this dark age or Kali Yuga, was viewed by the ancient Mexicans as the Age of the Center, ruled by Quetzalcoatl's twin, Tezcatlipoca, the smoking mirror, who symbolizes the nocturnal sun, the *earth sun*, which is humanity itself, the matter through which the luminous sun becomes incarnate. Laurette Séjourné comments,

If this is so, then the many different facets of the god [Tezcatlipoca] would represent the reflections of this opaque and shifting mass in search of salvation. Only so understood does his chaotic personality become coherent: among the humans living in the Epoch of the Centre there could in fact be nothing more natural than that violence, discord and sin should be present together with the need for harmony and purification.[5]

The Age of the Center will end with a cataclysm—symbolized by the sign Ollin—in which an upheaval of matter will ravage and cleanse the earth. This event is paralleled in the human realm by the yearning for unity, and the purification and rebirth at the present time of persons in whom a luminous center—the new sun—has already come into existence. In them, vision, wholeness and reverence have been integrally restored.

In 1921 D. H. Lawrence wrote in the foreword to his *Fantasia of the Unconscious*,

Our vision, our belief, our metaphysics is wearing woefully thin, and the art is absolutely threadbare. We have no future; neither for our hopes, nor our aims, nor our art. It has all gone gray and opaque.

We've got to rip the old veil of a vision across, and find what the heart really believes in, after all: and what the heart really wants for the next future. And we've got to put it down in terms of belief and of knowledge. And then go forward again, to the fulfillment in life and art.[6]

The veil is torn, and the tear grows larger every day. "I do not believe in evolution," Lawrence wrote elsewhere, "but in the strangeness and rainbow change of ever-renewed creative civilizations."[7] Today this apocalyptic foreboding is not just one man's fantasy but a growing collective vision that expresses its fears and hopes in reports of flying saucers, of a resurgent Atlantis, of imminent technological breakdown, of global changes in climate, of earth shrugging her massive shoulders, of celestial rain falling like fiery snow upon the wanton and heaving seas. Whatever the outer truth these visions may attest to, the inner truth is that conscience and consciousness are in convulsion. We hear the word apocalypse and shudder. It is not a part of the technological or historical vocabulary. Yet in the mythic memory of all peoples is the recollection of earlier catastrophes. Just as the embryo recapitulates biological evolution, so the individual life recapitulates the history of civilization; at one point apocalypse is inevitable and natural. Apocalypse is precisely what the visionary or shaman must undergo in order to come into his own revelation of the integral wholeness of things, for *apocalypse is catharsis*. If we are indeed on the "edge of history," to use William Irwin Thompson's phrase, post-history will not be a utopia but a collectively altered state of consciousness, a radical shift in human perspective.

In order for us to transcend the combative dualism that is the very essence of our condition, there must be a unitive experience of the world that can be achieved only through a major collective catharsis. And it may well be that we are already in the throes of such an event. In making his case against the orthodox Darwinian interpretation of evolution, which tacitly subscribes to the notion of linear historical progress, Immanuel Velikovsky has put forward the thesis of "cataclysmic evolution":

Great catastrophes of the past accompanied by electrical discharges and followed by radioactivity could have produced sudden and multiple mutations of the kind achieved today by experimenters, but on an immense scale. The past of mankind, and of the plant and animal kingdoms, too, must now be viewed in the light of the experience of Hiroshima and no longer from the portholes of the *Beagle*. [8]

So we are already changing, mutating, whirling around the center, at the very least, of an apocalypse of consciousness. To pass through the center of this apocalypse is to embark on a new stage of growth. Once the test of personal and historical catharsis is met, true individuation becomes possible. The visionary experience now presents itself as a necessity for survival, as the purpose of life on earth inexorably unfolds. What else then, could be the purpose of three billion years of fitfully mutating spirit-and-matter? Surely the maintenance of gigantic freeway systems and highly policed airports is not the only purpose. The road is hard, and only those who are ready for individuation, the reunion of psyche and techne, will themselves become the path that must be traveled in order for humans to realize their full humanity. The vision-seed has already been planted in their fertile consciousness. Through these beings of transformed vision the earth and the heavens may experience reunion, and the world may be returned to a mythic space to be divined and explored by humanity in full consciousness.

In trying to treat the problem of art's relationship to life, I have ended with the most general observations on the future of the human race. Any further culture that may develop will do so only through the fully realized individual, and not through a collectivity based on race, religion, political affinity, or the like. It was the unique destiny of Europe and its chief descendant, the United States of America, to lead humanity through the path of materialism to the brink where it now finds itself. The resulting disequilibrium has exhausted European civilization and sapped the vitality of other living cultures and civilizations, or even eradicated them entirely. If there is to be a new flowering of European culture, it must derive from a psychotechnic cross-fertilization with the other cultures and peoples of the globe. But even this process would depend on the determined and imaginative efforts of a few fully individuated beings. Should such a process come to fruition, the result could be the creation of a global art-whole.

Various thinkers have suggested that once upon a time there existed such an art-whole, a great world previous to ours in which the same science and religion were taught and practiced in all lands of the earth. As D. H. Lawrence wrote,

In that world men lived and taught and knew, and were in complete correspondence over all the earth. . . . Then came the melting of glaciers, and the world flood. . . . And so it is that all the great symbols and myths which dominate the world when our history first begins are very much the same in every country. . . . And so besides myths, we find the same mathematical figures, cosmic graphs which remain among the aboriginal peoples of all continents, mystic figures and signs whose true cosmic or scientific significance is lost, yet which continue in use for purposes of conjuring and divining.[9]

If the history of our world is one at its beginning, at its end it regathers itself and is one again.

It seems appropriate to conclude with one of these "cosmic graphs," which has endured throughout time in both the Eastern and Western hemispheres. In the East, which symbolizes techne, the left cerebral hemisphere, this labyrinthine sign is called by the Tantrics of India, the Manas Chakra, or mind. It is interesting that the symbol bears a strong schematic resemblance to the cerebral structure. Mookerjee comments that "there are eight divisions of mind. *Manas*, or mind, is atomic in nature, has motion and velocity, but no elements. It cognizes objects instantaneously. It acts on all objects with equal force."[10] Among the Hopi Indians of the Western Hemisphere, which symbolizes psyche, the right cerebral hemisphere, this same "cosmic graph" is known as the Mother Earth Symbol. Of the two types of this symbol common among the Hopi, "the square type represents spiritual rebirth from one world to the succeeding one, as symbolized by the Emergence itself."[11] According to Frank Waters, the symbol is commonly known as Mother and Child, or Tapu'at. "The inside lines represent the fetal membranes which enfold the child within the womb, and the outside, the mother's arms which hold it later."[12] The circular type, which corresponds exactly to the Manas Chakra, represents the path of life unfolding from the center cross, which symbolizes the Sun Father, the giver of life. "All the lines and passages within the maze form the universal plan of the Creator which man must follow on his Road of Life. 'Double Security' or rebirth to one who follows the plan is guaranteed, as shown by the same enfoldment of the child by the mother."[13]

This symbol, which is also to be found in Crete and Egypt as well as in Central America, represents the wanderings of the soul and its point of origin and return, the Tree of Life. As the Tantric interpretation indicates, our wanderings are totally mind-created, yet in keeping with the Hopi teaching they relate to our life on this planet. The Indian leader Chief Joseph declared, "The earth and myself are of one mind." For ourselves, approaching a post-historical consciousness, the symbol expresses the emergence into a new world, a world of mind-in-earth and earth-in-mind, a planet no longer polluted by "industrial anarchy," and a mind purified of psychic anarchy. If we carefully follow the path of consciousness, which is the same as the process of individuation in which everything is brought to light, the Road of Life itself, our rebirth into this new world is inevitable.

To attain this rebirth only one thing is required—that we die to our frozen identities—scientist and artist alike. This is the true art, the art of transformation.

296

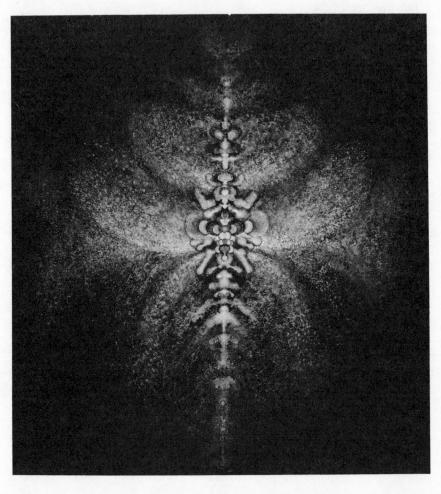

Helmut Zimmerman. *Presi casa à Roma*. [1962] Number 24 from a series of fifty paintings, *Individuationsprozess und Mandala-Symbolik, 1956–1969*.

The Development of the Holocene Era

According to the Four Ages

10,000 BC	*Key*
GOLDEN AGE	*Symbol*
Sat Yuga	
Undifferentiated	
Psychotechnical	FIRE
Continuum	
4,800 years	

5,200 BC	
SILVER AGE	
Dwarpara Yuga	SEED
Art-As-Ritual	
3,600 years	

1,600 BC	
BRONZE AGE	
Treta Yuga	SWORD
Art-As-Craft-Whole	
2,400 years	

800 AD	
IRON AGE	
Kali Yuga	MACHINE
Art-As-Technique	
1,200 years	

2,000 AD

APPENDIX B

The Ascent of the Jaguar

*A map of the later Kali Yuga * the Fourth World * the Iron Age * the Fifth Sun including correlations with Yeats, Mumford and assorted calendars*

		PHASE		Correlation with Yeats' TWENTY-EIGHT PHASES, including descriptions of Will and Body of Fate for phases after 1450 A.D.
PSYCHIC **PRE-TECHNOLOGICAL** **THESIS** (Yeat's Primary Tincture)	ca 800 A.D. 843 Beginning of last Mexican Heaven Cycle 1000 Development of mechanical clock 1027 Beginning of Tibetan Kalachakra system	26-27-28 1 2-3-4 5-6-7 8	1000 A.D. 1050 1100 1180 1250	
Primary *Cone:* Solar Feminine Religious	ca 1450 Height of Christian civilization Printing Press, One-point perspective Peak of Aztec, Inca empires 1519 Beginning of conquest of New World Fall of Mexico, Peru	9-10-11 12-13-14 15	1300 1380 1450	*No description except Complete Beauty* Peak of Christian European Civilization Peak of pre-technological aesthetic world-view and cultures
Hell I	Reformation, Protestantism Alchemical Renaissance (Paracelsus, Rosicrucians, Copernicus, Heliocentric Universe 1543) Council of Trent, Counter-Reformation, Birth of Catholic Church (1545+) Continuing flourishing of Islamic dynasties in Mid-East and India 1571 Hiawatha, Deganawida and Iroquois Confederacy Completion of Spanish-Portugese conquest of the New World Formation of Jesuit order, Catholic missionaries and Baroque culture	16 17 18 19	1550	*The Positive Man*—"The Fool is his own Body of Fate" Commencement of Faustian-European schizophrenic surge *The Daimonical Man*—"None except impersonal action" Triumph of Faust, elaboration of scientific world-view *The Emotional Man*—"The Hunchback is his own Body of Fate" Development of subjective individualist philosophies *The Assertive Man*—"Persecution" Ascendance of modern scientific and militaristic orthodoxy and fanaticism
Hell II **EOTECHNIC**	Marlowe's *Dr. Faustus*, Shakespeare, and beginnings of English imperialism Tycho Brahe, Kepler, Giordano Bruno, Galileo Perfection of telescope, microscope			

1623	Consolidation of North European Protestantism and development of money economy Slave trading in Africa	
Hell III	Descartes, scientific method, mechanistic world-view Incipient mechanization, standardization of commerce Peak of Catholic culture, Jesuit missions to China and Japan	
20	1680	*The Concrete Man*—"Objective action" Rise of rationalist/materialist personality Development of ability to maneuver mechanistic consciousness into industrial capacity and to order technical-material processes into stages of progressive refinement
1675	Peak of Islamic empires and civilization	
Hell IV	Enthronement of science over alchemy Newton's *Principia*, Law of Gravity, triumph of matter Foundation of modern chemistry, microscopy Puritan emigrations to North America Crystallization of academies of art and science	
1727	First coal mines in England "Age of Enlightenment," "Triumph of Reason," First modern encyclopaedias Decline of Catholic Baroque culture	
Hell V	Beginning of European-North American Indian wars Beginning of American Revolution (1776) Beginning of full-scale-industrialization in England End of Renaissance court culture	
1779	Discovery of Uranus, planet of revolution (1781) Tyranny of Reason begins Beginning of full-scale social upheavals William Blake, *Marriage of Heaven and Hell* (1793) French Revolution (1789–93)	
21		*The Acquisitive Man*—"Success" Ascendency of European materialist world domination World transformed into raw-goods market for European and American industrial consumption Doctrine of Progress formulated as law of success without end
Hell VI	Goya, Beethoven, Goethe—Romanticism Napoleonic Wars, Wars for Independence India under British control Industrialization spreads through Europe/America Museums, picture galleries, science societies	
PALEOTECHNIC	1831	Great period of industrialist/materialist expansion American-Indian Wars—"Manifest Destiny," Photography (1839), Telegraph (1844) Proclamation of the Bab (1844) Bahaullah, Bahai Discovery of Neptune (1846), pupulism, mass movements Communist Manifesto, Revolutions of 1848 Darwin, *Origin of Species* (1859) Fechner, *Psychophysics*, Hartmann, *Philosophy of the Unconscious* (1860)
Hell VII		

[continued]

TECHNOLOGICAL
ANTITHESIS
(Yeats' Antithetical
Tincture)

*Antithetical
Cone:*
Lunar
Masculine
Secular
Political

World Industrial Fairs and Exhibitions
Ramakrishna in India, Max Müller, Sacred Books of the East, Mme. Blavatsky and Theosophy (1875)
Beginning of Japanese industrialization
Construction of Suez Canal
Whitman's "Passage to India" (1871)
Electronic breakthroughs: telephone, phonograph, microphone, light bulb (1876–1883)

1883 Peak of European imperialism, consolidation of United States, beginning of US trans-Pacific imperialism
Electromagnetic theory (1880's), discovery of radium (1892), x-rays (1895), relativity theory (1906), quantum theory and particle physics (1920's)
Beginning of decomposition of materialism
First global convulsion (1914–18)
Russian Revolution, rise of Communism (1917+)
Mexican Revolution (1910+)

Hell VIII

European reactionaires, Hitler, Mussolini, rise of Japanese industrial imperialism
Rise of modern schools of psychology: Freud, Jung, Behavioralism
Avant-garde cultural explosion, rise of propaganda and advertising
Popularization of cinema, automobile, radio, airtravel
Discovery of Pluto (1931), planet of the underworld.
1935 Rise of Hitler, birth of present Dalai Lama (1935)
Second great global convulsion (1939–45)
Splitting of the atom (1939), atomic bombs (1945), hydrogen bombs (1953)

NEOTECHNIC
Pentagon and consolidation of US imperialist power
Cold War, rise of Communist China and spread of Communist world force
Fall of Tibet (1950–59), rise of capitalist Japan
Popularization of television, development of transistors, tape recorder, portable electronic media
Space Age: Sputnik (1957), man on moon (1969)
Third World liberation movements, Vietnamese War

Hell IX

---

22 1875 *Balance Between Ambition and Contemplation—*
"Temptation versus Strength"
Peak of European imperialist expansion, scientific optimism and belief that science can create heaven on earth
Period of great scientific breakthroughs and technological dominance
Build-up of great military powers and war industries

23 1927 *The Receptive Man*—"Enforced triumph of achievement"
Decline of Europe as world power, rise of fascism
Rise of Russia, United States
Planned and controlled economies
Scientific research subverted for war purposes

24 1945 *The End of Ambition*—"Enforced success of action"
Atomic warfare, cold war, world as communist/capitalist battlefield, armaments race, space race

Psychedelic revolution (1960's)
Anti-technocratic revolutions of 1968, triumph of technocracy
Consolidation of technocracy and ecological deterioration: fuel and food shortages, etc. (1970's–80's)
Techno-urban terrorism, disintegration of social values
Rise of spiritual movements and cults
Decline of avant-garde culture
Genesis of psycho-technic culture

POST-TECHNOLOGICAL SYNTHESIS

Psycho-technical Integration

1987 Climax of matter, conclusion of the 16th sixty year cycle of Tibetan Kalachakra system

INTERCHANGE OF TINCTURES

2012 Conclusion of Mayan 5,125 year Great Cycle

2039

25 1968 *The Conditional Man*—"Enforced failure of action"
Man on the moon
Technocratic stalemate and terrorism
Pollution and exhaustion of resources

26 1987 *The Multiple Man also called The Hunchback*—
"Enforced disillusionment"
Technocratic collapse and dissolution of international world civilization

27 *The Saint*—"Enforced loss"
Ascent of new religious forces, dispersal of old order

28 *The Fool*—"Enforced illusion"
Recommencement of cultural/civilizational cycle

Notes

INTRODUCTION

1. Wilhelm Worringer, *Form in Gothic*, trans. Sir Herbert Read (New York, 1964), pp. 12–13.

CHAPTER ONE

1. Sam Keen, "Sorcerer's Apprentice: Interview with Carlos Castaneda," *Psychology Today*, Dec. 1972, p. 95.

2. Robert Ornstein, *The Psychology of Consciousness* (San Francisco, 1972), pp. 51–53.

3. *Ibid.*, p. 53.

4. *Ibid.*, p. 54.

5. D. H. Lawrence, *Fantasia of the Unconscious* (New York, 1960), p. 188.

6. Arthur Koestler, *The Ghost in the Machine* (New York, 1967), p. 327.

7. Information regarding the ancient Mexican calendrical system and its prophecies is sketchy, and diffused through a number of generally incomplete indigenous texts. The precise working out of the thirteen heaven and nine hell cycles with the dates I have given is immediately derived from the work of Tony Shearer, and is further explained in his poetic study of Ce Acatl Topiltzin Quetzalcoatl, *Lord of the Dawn* (Naturegraph Press, Healdsburg, 1971). According to Shearer his realization and understanding of the present major cycles of heavens and hells developed from a conversation he had with the noted Mexican artist and art historian Miguel Covarrubias. Covarrubias in turn had received certain information from a *bruja*, a sorceress in the jungle hotlands of Tehuantepec. It is Shearer, however, who takes full responsibility for the correlation of the Mexican cycles with the European calendrical system. That is, though it is clear that the notion of the thirteen heavens and nine hells is a fundamental spatial and metaphysical concept common to all of the ancient Mexican cultures, it is Shearer who fully worked out this concept in the European time frame. According to Shearer the Aztecs used both the spatial and temporal aspects of this system, but we do not know how they received them, and it is not clear to what extent the Aztecs, who were "late comers," were aware of the system's far-reaching implications. One thing is obvious: April 21, 1519, was a critical date in the Mexican system, and considering the capitulation of the powerful Aztec empire, it is also obvious that the Aztecs were prepared for a major change occurring at precisely that time. Considering how things turned out, there seems little question that that date marks the shift from a period of heavens "of decreasing choice" to a period of hells of "increasing doom." Further research and work on the calendar by Tony Shearer will appear in his forthcoming book, *Beneath the Sun and Under the Moon*.

Somewhat less precise, though no less powerfully prophetic, is the information contained in the Mayan prophetic text, the *Book of Chilam Balam of Chumayel* (Vasquez Barrerra, Fondo de Cultura Economica, Mexico, 1948 and Ralph Roys,

University of Oklahoma Press, Norman, 1967). Though no dates are given, the entire concept of the thirteen heavens and nine hells as cycles of time following upon each other is expressed in a passage relating to the Mayan date, 11 *Ahau katun* (pp. 99ff.). Because of the peculiarities of the Mayan system, the date 11 *Ahau* is timeless and functions like a blueprint or an archetype of the way things are. Yet it also represents the *katun* or cycle when Spanish rule began in Yucatan. Very clearly the notion which Shearer develops is articulated in the following passage:

> *When* Oxlahun ti ku
> *Thirteen deity,*
> *was seized*
> *through the deeds of* bolon ti ku
> *Nine deity;*
> *then will descend ropes and fire*
> *and stone and stick*
> *and there will be smiting with stone and stick*
> *when* Oxlahun ti ku
> *Thirteen deity*
> *will be seized . . .*
> *Great nine begetter . . .*
> *will take hold*
> *of the thirteenth floor of the heavens*
> *and will scatter the dust*
> *which will fall off the seeds. . . .*

These lines clearly refer to the passage from a cycle of thirteen heavens (for the ancient Mexicans time was a deity, or series of deities; hence "thirteen deity" and "nine deity") to a cycle of nine hells. Then, referring to the end of the entire *katun*, presumably the nine hell periods, the particular text goes on to state:

> *The heavens will collapse*
> *and so will the earth collapse*
> *when the* katun *reaches its end. . . .*

Though *katun* specifically refers to a twenty-year period, since it is represented by a wheel or circle it may also mean more generally a cycle of time. The entire passage quoted refers to a theory of recurring apocalypse and regeneration. For following the collapse of heaven and earth—thirteen deity *and* nine deity—is a further devastation of the earth by the lord *Cantul ti ku*, Four-deity, who symbolizes the four cardinal directions or *bacabs*. Then

> *At the end of this devastation*
> *will rise* Chac imix Che
> *Primeval red ceiba*
> *the column of the heavens*
> *sign of the dawning of the world. . . .*

Following the rise of the tree of the east—the primeval red ceiba—with its holy bird, comes the rising of the trees of the other three directions plus the tree of the center and their holy birds. In other words, following a complete cycle of heavens and hells is a period of devastation, which in turn is followed by a mandalic recreation of the world. In the Hindu system the period corresponding to the Mayan Four-deity is *mahapralaya,* the great seed-time, that period of time which follows the Kali Yuga and precedes another *Sattya Yuga* or Golden Age. The translations of the *Chilam Balam of Chumayel* which I have given are from Miguel Leon Portilla, *Time and Reality in the Thought of the Maya* (Beacon Press, Boston, 1973), pp. 75–76.

One further observation. Although the Mexican hell cycle as worked out by Shearer comes to an end in 1987, this is a period of time based specifically on the 52-year cycle, the cycle which was commonly in use by the Aztecs at the time of the conquest, but it was not the only means of reckoning time known to the ancient Mexicans. Again, the Mayans had achieved an unparalleled sophistication in this realm, and attention should also be drawn to the fact that a larger 5,125-year cycle which began in 3113 B.C. will draw to an end in A.D. 2012. What this may signify in relation to the information given by Shearer and to other global calendrical systems is yet to be worked out. Obviously, time will tell!

CHAPTER TWO

1. Quoted in Gary Snyder, *Earth Household* (New York, 1969), p. 5.

2. Andrew Martindale, *The Rise of the Artist in the Middle Ages and Early Renaissance* (New York, 1972), p. 98.

3. *Ibid.*

4. William Blake, "The Laocoon," in the *Complete Writings* ed. Geoffrey Keynes (London 1969), p. 775.

5. Irma A. Richter, ed., *Selections from the Notebook of Leonardo da Vinci* (London, 1952), p. 108.

6. The dualizing interpretations of Plato and Pythagoras that occured in the Renaissance were the result of "breaks" in the Mediteranean tradition. In the actual teachings, especially of Pythagoras, there is clearly no body-mind dualism intended.

7. Richter, ed., *Notebooks of Leonardo*, pp. 110–111; italics mine.

8. René Descartes, *Discourse on Method* (New York, 1956), p. 21.

9. Kenneth Clark, *Leonardo da Vinci* (Baltimore, 1958), p. 159.

10. *Ibid.*

11. *Ibid.,* p. 160.

12. Lincoln Barnett, *The Universe and Dr. Einstein* (New York, 1957), pp. 20–21.

CHAPTER THREE

1. Arnold Hauser, *Social History of Art,* II (New York, 1957), 75.

2. Richard Wilhelm and Cary F. Baynes, trans., *The I Ching, or Book of Changes,* 3d ed. (Princeton, N.J., 1967), p. 447.

3. A. Reza Arasteh, *Rumi: The Persian, the Sufi* (Tuscon, Ariz., 1972), p. 4.

4. Hauser, *op. cit.,* p. 88.

5. Marshall McLuhan, *The Gutenberg Galaxy* (Toronto, 1962), p. 22.

6. Titus Burckhardt, *Sacred Art in East and West* (London, 1967), p. 147.

7. *Ibid.,* p. 155.

8. H. W. Janson, *History of Art* (New York, 1969), p. 294.

9. Lynn White, "The Historical Roots of Our Ecological Crisis," in *The Environmental Handbook* (New York, 1970), p. 24.

10. William Blake, "The Marriage of Heaven and Hell" in *op. cit.,* p. 154.

11. Lynn White, *op. cit.,* p. 17.

12. "The Writings of Kwang Sze," in James Legge, trans., *The Texts of Taoism* (New York, 1962), I. 286–87.

CHAPTER FOUR

1. José Clemente Orozco, *An Autobiography* (Austin, Tex., 1962), p. 20.

2. Burckhardt, *op. cit.,* p. 147.

3. Hauser, *op. cit.,* pp. 224–25.

4. Barnett, *op. cit.,* p. 22.

5. Siegfried Giedion, *Mechanization Takes Command* (Oxford, Eng., 1948), p. 30.

CHAPTER FIVE

1. Mircea Eliade, *Cosmos and History: The Myth of the Eternal Return* (New York, 1959), p. 141.

2. *Encyclopaedia Britannica* (Edinburgh, 1771), II, p. 778.

3. Eliade, *op. cit.,* p. 150.

4. Karl R. Popper, *The Poverty of Historicism* (New York, 1964), p. 161.

5. Mao Tse Tung, *Quotations* (Peking, 1966), p. 213.

6. "In Praise of Time (Kala): Hymn from the Atharva Veda," *Chakra: A Journal of Tantra and Yoga,* IV (1972), 169.

7. My use of the terms eotechnic, paleotechnic, and neotechnic to distinguish the three phases of technological civilization is derived from Lewis Mumford's classic study *Technics and Civilization* (New York, 1934). I have found this terminology

most helpful, and am indebted to Mumford's monumental effort in clarifying concepts regarding man as a tool-using animal. In a sense Mumford's work has laid the foundation for my own, but whereas he has focused more on techne, I have focused more on psyche. Though Mumford has been perhaps the most notable critic of technologism, neither his views nor mine are utterly antitechnological. As Mumford has stated, "Our capacity to go beyond the machine rests upon our power to assimilate the machine. Until we have absorbed the lessons of objectivity, impersonality, neutrality, the lessons of the mechanical realm, we cannot go further in our development toward the more richly organic, the more powerfully human." (*Ibid.*, p. 363.) The other key works in which Mumford develops his basic thesis are *Art and Technics* (New York, 1951) and *The Myth of the Machine*, Volume I, *Technics and Human Development*, and Vol. II, *The Pentagon of Power* (New York, 1967–70).

It should be noted that in my chart of the technocultural development of the Iron Age, the chronology I have developed for the three phases of technological civilization reflects my own intuitive assessment and not necessarily Mumford's work.

8. The terminology in the following paragraph—"dimming of the radiant light," etc., which I have applied to Mumford's three phases of technological civilization is derived from H. V. Guenther's explication of the Buddhist Tantric teachings and refers specifically to the passage from a highly awakened state of consciousness to one of sleep or total psychophysiological torpor. Such a state of torpor is equivalent to a complete mechanization of human functions, and a near-obsolesence of any organic sensibility. See H. V. Guenther, *The Tantric View of Life* (Berkeley, 1972), p. 27.

9. Jacques Ellul, *The Technological Society*, trans. John Wilkinson (New York, 1964), p. 44.

10. Quoted in Bernard Bosanquet, *A History of Aesthetic* (Cleveland, 1957), p. 240.

11. *Ibid.*, p. 242.

12. *Ibid.*

13. Gotthold Ephraim Lessing, *Laocoon: An Essay upon the Limits of Painting and Poetry* (New York, 1957), pp. 91–92.

CHAPTER SIX

1. Quoted in J. B. Bury, *The Idea of Progress* (London, 1924), p. 173. The anthropocentric and materialistic assumptions of this statement account for the acquisitive psychology of the warrior, like Napoleon, as well as the robber baron; the revolutionary as well as the capitalist.

2. Antonin Artaud, "No Divine Epic," a privately printed translation in the author's possession. This same piece in a different translation is published as "No Theogony . . . ," in *An Antonin Artaud Anthology*, ed. Jack Hirschman (San Francisco, 1965), pp. 65–67.

CHAPTER SEVEN

1. Irving Babbitt, *Rousseau and Romanticism* (Cleveland, 1955), p. 280. Babbitt was one of the first Western scholars (as distinct from poets and artists) to successfully integrate an Oriental view such as Buddhism into his general critique and philosophy of history.

2. Quoted in José A. Argüelles, *Charles Henry and the Formation of a Psychophysical Aesthetic* (Chicago, 1972), p. 49.

3. J. W. von Goethe, *Faust*, trans. Bagard Taylor (London, n.d.), p. 300.

4. Aldous Huxley, *Heaven and Hell* (New York, 1963), p. 182.

5. *Ibid.*

6. *Ibid.*

7. Etienne Louis Boullée, "To Newton," quoted in Elizabeth Gilmore Holt, *From the Classicists to the Impressionists* (New York, 1966), p. 269.

8. *Ibid.*, p. 270.

9. Friedrich Phillip von Hardenberg [Novalis] *Hymns to the Night and other Selected Writings* trans. Charles E. Passage (Indianapolis, Ind., 1960), p. 4.

CHAPTER EIGHT

1. Lewis Mumford, *The Myth of the Machine: The Pentagon of Power* (New York, 1970), pp. 157–58.

2. Friedrich Phillip von Hardenberg [Novalis], from "Pollen," in *op. cit.*, p. 66.

3. Peter and Linda Murray, *Dictionary of Art and Artists* (Baltimore, 1959), p. 28.

4. William Blake, "Annotations to Sir Joshua Reynolds's Discourses," in *Complete Writings*, p. 445.

5. Blake, "Jerusalem," in *Complete Writings*, p. 621.

6. Blake, "Songs of Experience," in *Complete Writings*, p. 210.

7. *Ibid.*, p. 216.

8. Blake, "Europe," in *Complete Writings*, p. 243.

9. Blake, "Jerusalem, *op. cit.*, p. 685.

10. Blake, "Jerusalem," *op. cit.*, p. 636.

11. S. Foster Damon, *A Blake Dictionary* (New York, 1971), p. 299.

12. Blake, "The Marriage of Heaven and Hell," in *Complete Writings*, p. 149.

13. *Ibid.*

14. *Ibid.*, p. 154.

15. Mircea Eliade, *Myths, Dreams and Mysteries* (New York, 1960), p. 97.

16. As one of the principle embodiments of Blake's mythic world view, Ulro appears in a number of the poetic sagas, including "Milton," "Jerusalem," and the "Four Zoas." The synthesized description of Ulro that I have used is adopted from Damon, *op. cit.*, pp. 416–17.

17. *Ibid.*, p. 417.

18. Blake, "Milton," in *Complete Writings*, p. 516.

19. Blake, "Jerusalem," *op. cit.*, p. 709.

20. *Ibid.*, p. 622.

21. *Ibid.*, p. 734.

22. Blake, "Milton," *op. cit.*, p. 498.

23. C. G. Jung, "Commentary" to Richard Wilhelm, *The Secret of the Golden Flower* (New York, 1962), p. 98.

24. Blake, "Jerusalem," *op. cit.*, pp. 623–33.

25. *Ibid.*, pp. 633–34.

26. *Ibid.*, p. 746.

27. *Ibid.*, p. 747.

28. Blake, "The Laocoon," *op. cit.*, p. 776.

29. *Ibid.*

30. *Ibid.*

31. *Ibid.*, p. 777.

32. *Ibid.*

CHAPTER NINE

1. Mumford, *op. cit.*, p. 39.

2. Idries Shah, *The Secret Lore of Magic* (New York, 1970), p. 12.

3. William Blake, "Annotations to Reynolds," *op. cit.*, p. 452.

4. Charles Baudelaire, "Some French Caricaturists," in Jonathon Mayne, trans. and ed., *The Mirror of Art* (New York, 1956), p. 168.

5. Colin Wilson, *The Outsider* (New York, 1956), p. 13.

6. Aldous Huxley, "Variiations on Goya," in *Collected Essays* (New York, 1960), p. 160.

7. Charles Baudelaire, "Some Foreign Caricaturists," in *op. cit.*, p. 185.

8. Quoted in Daniel Catton Rich, ed. *The Art of Goya* (Chicago, 1941), p. 24.

9. *Ibid.*, p. 26.

10. Lewis Mumford, *Technics and Civilizations*, p. 161.

11. Colin Wilson, *The Mind Parasites* (Oakland, Calif., 1972), p. 85.

12. Aldous Huxley, *op. cit.*, p. 159.

CHAPTER TEN

1. Jacob Boehme, *Dialogues on the Supersensual Life*, trans. William Law, et al. (New York, 1957), p. 60.

2. *Ibid.*, p. 61.

3. Blake, "To the Evening Star," in *Complete Writings*, p. 3.

4. Samuel Taylor Coleridge, "Lines Written in the Album at Elbingerode, in the Hartz Forest," in Donald A. Stauffer, ed., *Selected Poetry and Prose* (New York, 1951), p. 73.

5. Coleridge, "Essays from the Friend," XI: "The Meaning of Existence," in *Selected Poetry and Prose*, p. 527.

6. Coleridge, "Psyche," in *Selected Poetry and Prose*, p. 4.

7. William Wordsworth, "Ode: Intimations of Immortality from Recollection of Early Childhood," in *The Prelude: Selected Poems and Sonnets* (New York, 1954), p. 152.

8. C. R. Leslie, *Memoirs of the Life of John Constable* (London, 1951), p. 149.

9. *Ibid.*, p. 85.

10. *Ibid.*, p. 86.

11. *Ibid.*, p. 323.

12. *Ibid.*, p. 330.

13. Blake, "A Vision of the Last Judgement," in *Complete Writings*, p. 617.

14. Samuel Palmer, quoted in Geoffrey Grigson, *The Romantics* (Cleveland, Ohio, 1962), p. 263.

15. George Crabbe, "The Demons of Opium," in Grigson, *The Romantics*, p. 165.

CHAPTER ELEVEN

1. Helmut and Alison Gernsheim, *A Concise History of Photography* (New York, 1965), pp. 15–16.

2. Ananda Coomaraswamy, *Christian and Oriental Philosophy of Art* (New York, 1956), p. 46.

3. Charles Baudelaire, "The Salon of 1859: The Modern Public and Photography," in *The Mirror of Art* (New York, 1956), p. 230.

4. *Ibid.*, p. 233.

5. Baudelaire, *Intimate Journals*, trans. Christopher Isherwood (Boston, 1957), p. 29.

6. Baudelaire, "The Salon of 1859," p. 229.

7. Coomaraswamy, *op. cit.*, p. 18.

8. Jacob Boehme, *Six Theosophical Points*, trans. John Rolleston Earle (Ann Arbor, Mich., 1958), p. 6.

9. Baudelaire, *Intimate Journals*, p. 28.

10. *Ibid.*, p. 44.

CHAPTER TWELVE

1. Baudelaire, *Intimate Journals*, p. 44.

2. W. B. Yeats, *A Vision* (New York, 1971), pp. 202–3.

3. Thomas De Quincey, "The Opium Eater," quoted in Grigson, *The Romantics*, p. 228.

4. James Baird, *Ishmael* (Baltimore, 1956), p. 16. Baird's study is a very thorough investigation of the inherently religious symbolism of nineteenth-century primitivism, focusing especially on the work of Herman Melville.

5. Carl G. Jung, "Psychological Commentary" to *The Tibetan Book of the Great Liberation*, ed. W. Y. Evans-Wentz (London, 1954), p. xxxviii. Having observed the efforts of certain Westerners at aping oriental ways, Jung declared emphatically, "We must get at the Eastern values from within and not from without, seeking them in ourselves, in the unconscious. We shall then discover how great is our fear of the unconscious and how formidable are our resistances." These resistances, culturally built up over the last four centuries, make us doubt "the very thing that seems so obvious to the East, namely, the *self-liberating power of the introverted mind.*"

6. Jules Michelet, *The Bible of Humanity*, quoted in the title page to Romain Rolland, *The Life of Ramakrishna* (Calcutta, 1965).

7. Arthur Rimbaud, *Illuminations*, trans. Louise Varèse (New York, 1957), p. xxx.

8. *Ibid.*

9. *Ibid.*

10. *Ibid.*, pp. xxxii-xxxiii.

11. *Ibid.*, p. 29.

12. Arthur Rimbaud, *A Season in Hell*, trans. Louise Varèse (New York, 1961), p. 71.

13. *Ibid.*

14. *Ibid.*, p. 55.

15. *Ibid.*, pp. 29–30.

16. Walt Whitman, "Passage to India," in Mark Van Doren, ed., *The Portable Walt Whitman* (New York, 1945), p. 345.

17. *Ibid.*, p. 346.

18. *Ibid.*, p. 349.

19. *Ibid.*, p. 350.

20. *Ibid.*, pp. 351–52.

21. Carl Friederich Von Weizsäcker, "Introduction" to Gopi Krishna, *The Biological Basis of Religion and Genius* (New York, 1972), p. 6.

22. These little-known but remarkable aspects of nineteenth-century Chinese philosophy are well documented in Fung Yu-Lan's monumental work, *A History of Chinese Philosophy* (Princeton, N.J., 1953), Vol. 2, Chap. 16, pp. 673–721. What is most fascinating is the great awareness of historical change displayed by the so-called New Text School of the Ch'ing Dynasty—an awareness that seems immense compared with that of the contemporary positivist and progressive philosophers of Europe. The chart I have used is taken from the work of Tan Ssu T'ung, cited by Fung Yu-Lan, p. 699, n. 3.

23. Tan Ssu T'ung, quoted in *Ibid.*, p. 701.

24. *Ibid.*, pp. 701–2.

25. *Ibid.*, p. 702.

26. Arthur Rimbaud, *A Season in Hell*, p. 73.

27. Arnold Toynbee, "Aspects of Psycho-History," *Main Currents in Modern Thought*, Vol. 29, no. 2 (Nov.–Dec., 1972), p. 46.

CHAPTER THIRTEEN

1. Edgar Allan Poe, "Eureka: An Essay on the Material and Spiritual Universe," in *The Works of Edgar Allan Poe* (New York, 1904), IX, 48. Poe's unique essay was originally a lecture entitled "The Cosmogony of the Universe," delivered to the New York Library Society on February 3, 1848. Dedicated to the great German scientist Alexander von Humboldt, Poe's essay certainly supports the view that as long as what we call science and art proceed from the realm of the imagination, psyche, they are indistinguishable. Together they constitute a *gnosis*—a full, intuitive apprehension of the truth.

2. *Ibid.*, p. 40.

3. *Ibid.*, p. 44.

4. *Ibid.*, p. 47.

5. *Ibid.*, p. 52.

6. *Ibid.*, p. 60.

7. *Ibid.*, p. 88.

8. *Ibid.*, p. 127.

9. *Ibid.*, p. 151.

10. *Ibid.*

11. *Ibid.*, pp. 153–55.

12. Lama Anagarika Govinda, *The Psychological Attitude of Early Buddhist Philosophy* (London, 1961), p. 133. The entire question of the role of nineteenth-century psychophysics in relation to art, philosophy, and aesthetics has been treated in greater detail in my book *Charles Henry and the Formation of a Psychophysical Aesthetic* (Chicago, 1972), esp. chap. 2, "Psychophysics in Perspective," pp. 12–29.

CHAPTER FOURTEEN

1. Emile Zola, "The Realists in the Salon, May 11, 1866," in Elizabeth Gilmore Holt, *From The Classicists to The Romantics* (New York, 1966), p. 385.

2. Jules Laforgue, "Impressionism," in Linda Nochlin, ed., *Impressionism and Post-Impressionism, 1874–1904* (Englewood Cliffs, N.J., 1966), p. 18.

3. *Ibid.*, p. 19.

4. *Ibid.*

5. Quoted in Argüelles, *Charles Henry and the Formation of a Psychophysical Aesthetic*, p. 105.

6. Quoted in *Ibid.*, p. 113.

7. Prajnaparamita or Heart Sutra, translated as "The Sutra on the Essence of Transcendent Knowledge," by Francesca Fremantle in *Garuda III: Dharmas Without Blame* (Berkeley, Calif., 1973), p. 3. This sutra, which is really quite brief—scarcely more than a page long—is nevertheless one of the key texts of Mahayana Buddhism. Texts like this, which abound in paradox, are meant to demonstrate the impossibility of rationally comprehending the most basic (spiritual) facts. "Emptiness" (*shunyata*) does not mean a total void or a nihilistic state so much as a state devoid of preconception; that is, a state of openness and receptivity. It might be said that Western art and culture from the late nineteenth century to the present are continually flirting with, or more appropriately, skirmishing at the outskirts of *shunyata*.

8. Quoted in John Rewald, "Odilon Redon," in Rewald, et al., eds., *Odilon Redon, Gustave Moreau and Rodolphe Bresdin* (New York, 1961), p. 45.

CHAPTER FIFTEEN

1. Quoted in J. van Gogh-Bonger, "Memoir," in *The Letters of Vincent van Gogh*, ed. Mark Roskill (New York, 1963), p. 44.

2. Letter of mid-July 1888, in *Letters of van Gogh*, p. 272.

3. *Ibid.*, pp 272–73.

4. Letter of early Aug. 1888, in *Letters of van Gogh*, p. 275.

5. Paul Gauguin, *Intimate Journals*, trans. Van Wick Brooks (Bloomington, Ind., 1958), p. 28.

6. *Ibid.*

7. Quoted in Nochlin, *op. cit.*, pp. 158–59.

8. Paul Gauguin, *Noa Noa*, trans. O. F. Theis (New York, 1957), pp. 23–24.

9. *Ibid.*, pp. 50–51.

10. Gauguin, *Intimate Journals*, p. 184.

11. Gauguin, *Noa Noa*, p. 46.

12. *Ibid.*, p. 47.

CHAPTER SIXTEEN

1. Marshall McLuhan, *Understanding Media: The Extensions of Man* (New York, 1964), p. 179.

2. Rainer Maria Rilke, "Introduction" to *Duino Elegies*, trans. J. B. Leishman and Stephen Spender (New York, 1939), p. 14.

3. *Ibid.*

4. Paul Cézanne, "Letter to Joachim Gasquet and to a Young Friend," quoted in Nochlin, ed., *op. cit.*, p. 88.

5. Paul Cézanne, "Letter to Emile Bernard, Aix, 25th July, 1904," quoted in Nochlin, ed., *op. cit.*, p. 93.

6. William Morris, "Innate Socialism," in Asa Briggs, ed., *Selected Writings and Designs* (Baltimore, 1962), pp. 84–85.

7. *Ibid.*, p. 85.

8. Quoted in Peter Selz and Mildred Constantine, eds., *Art Nouveau: Art and Design at the Turn of the Century* (New York, 1959), p. 70.

9. The statement is taken from Henry's last major work, *Generalisation du theorie du rayonnement* (Paris, 1924), quoted in Argüelles, *Charles Henry*, p. 156.

10. Robert Delaunay, "La Lumière," in Pierre Francastel, ed., *Du Cubisme à l'art abstrait* (Paris, 1957), pp. 144–45.

11. Wassily Kandinsky, *Concerning the Spiritual in Art*, trans. Michael Sadleir (New York, 1947), p. 45.

12. *Ibid.*, p. 75.

13. *Ibid.*, pp. 74–75.

14. Charles Henry, from a magazine interview, 1891, quoted in Argüelles, *Charles Henry* p. 151.

15. Annie Besant and C. W. Leadbeater, *Thought Forms* (Madras, India, 1901), p. 19.

16. *Ibid.*, p. 20.

17. Kandinsky, *op. cit.*, p. 27.

CHAPTER SEVENTEEN

1. Paul Klee, quoted in Carl G. Jung, *Man and His Symbols* (New York, 1964), p. 265.

2. Kandinsky, *op. cit.*, pp. 28–29.

3. Robert Hughes, "Pablo Picasso: The Painter as Proteus," *Time*, April 30, 1973, p. 88.

4. Vaslav Nijinsky, *The Diary of Vaslav, Nijinsky*, Romola Nijinsky, ed. (Berkeley, Calif., 1968), pp. 185–87.

5. *Ibid.*, p. 32.

6. *Ibid.*, p. 13.

7. James Fadiman and Donald Kerwin, *Exploring Madness: Experience, Theory, Research* (Belmont, Calif., 1973), p. 6.

8. Herman Hesse, *Magister Ludi*, trans. Mervyn Savill (New York, 1919), p. 19.

9. Quoted in Henri-Pol Bouché, "Nomenclatures insurrectionnels," *L'Art brût*, II (Paris, 1964), p. 15. In 1921 there appeared a monograph by a Swiss physician, Dr. W. Morgenthaler, entitled *Ein Geisteskranker als Kunstler* (*A Madman Artist*). This little-known work was translated into French and published in Paris in 1964 under the title "Adolf Wölfli" by Henri-Pol Bouché, who also contributed the introductory essay, "Nomenclatures insurrectionnels," in *L'Art brût*, the publication of the Compagnie de L'Art Brût. This particular French journal was founded by the contemporary painter, Jean Dubuffet, with the aim of abolishing the strictly intellectual, elistist interpretation the word *art* has acquired in recent times. Since World War II Dubuffet has searched for art created by people scarcely conscious that their work might be considered art. A notable American example of *art brût* is the so-called Watts Towers made by Simon Rodia in Los Angeles. Like the Watts

Towers, Wölfli's work seriously calls into question the accepted, traditional canons of art as well as the rules of the art game as it has developed in the twentieth century.

10. *Ibid.*

11. Quoted in W. Morganthaler, "Adolf Wölfli," trans. Henri-Pol Bouché, *L'Art brût*, II (Paris, 1964), 22.

12. *Ibid.*

13. S. M. Schirokogorow, *Versuch einer Erforschung der Grundlagen des Schamanismus bei dem Zunghausen*, quoted in Andreas Lommel, *Shamanism: The Beginnings of Art* (New York, 1967), p. 37.

14. Mircea Eliade, *Rites and Symbols of Initiation: The Mysteries Of Birth And Rebirth*, trans. Willard R. Trask (New York, 1965), p. 89.

15. Morganthaler, *op. cit.*, p. 123. It may be noted that Morganthaler, whose essay on Wölfli was first published in 1921, was quick to acknowledge Jung's *Psychology of the Unconscious*, first published in 1917.

16. Morganthaler, *op. cit.*, p. 44.

17. *Ibid.*

18. Adolf Wölfli, "Autobiography," quoted in *ibid.*, pp. 56–59. My translation of a translation can hardly do credit to Wölfli's language, which is most idiosyncratic, often relying on subtle associations, puns, and so on, not unlike the technique of James Joyce in *Finnegan's Wake*. Accordingly, I have freely attempted to give the sense of Wölfli's prose rather than translate literally.

19. See W. Y. Evans-Wentz, *Tibet's Great Yogi, Milarepa* (London, 1951), for an extensive and detailed account of the life of this extraordinary mystic.

20. Hermann Hesse, *Magister Ludi* (New York, 1949), pp. 14–15.

21. Ramana Maharshi, *The Collected Works* (London, 1969), p. 32.

CHAPTER EIGHTEEN

1. Quoted in Joshua C. Taylor, *Futurism* (New York, 1961), pp. 124–25.

2. Blaise Cendrars, "The Prose of the Trans-Siberian and of the Little Jeanne of France," *Chicago Review*, XXIV, 3 (Winter 1972), 7–21.

3. W. B. Yeats, "The Second Coming," *Collected Poems* (New York, 1956).

4. Hans Arp, "Dadaland," quoted in Hans Richter, *Dada: Art and Anti-Art* (New York, 1965), p. 25. This passage also appears in a less forceful translation in Hans Arp, *On My Way: Poetry and Essays, 1912–1947*, trans. Ralph Manheim (New York, 1948), pp. 39–40.

5. Quoted in Richter, *op. cit.*, p. 55.

6. Quoted in *ibid.*, p. 89.

7. *Ibid.*

8. Quoted in Gene R. Swenson, *The Other Tradition* (Philadelphia, 1966). p. 21. Tatlins was a prominant artist in the new Russian Revolutionary movement.

9. Arp, *On My Way*, p. 76. Arp's organic sensitivity and realization of a need to go beyond civilized forms in a positive sense were expressed when he wrote, "Dada is for the senseless, which does not mean nonsense. Dada is senseless like nature. Dada is for nature and against art. Dada is direct like nature. Dada is for infinite sense and definite means."

10. Quoted in Richter, *op. cit.*, p. 203.

11. Arp, *On My Way*, p. 40.

12. *Ibid.*, p. 46.

13. André Breton, "First Surrealist Manifesto," quoted in Patrick Waldberg, *Surrealism* (New York, 1965), p. 72.

14. Quoted in Maurice Nadeau, *The History of Surrealism*, trans. Richard Howard (New York, 1965), p. 163, n. 11.

15. Antonin Artaud, "Van Gogh: The Man Suicided by Society," in *An Artaud Anthology*, ed. Jack Hirschman (San Francisco, 1965), p. 135.

16. *Ibid.*, p. 158.

17. Artaud, "Address to the Dalai Lama," in *Artaud Anthology*, p. 64.

18. Artaud, "Letter to the Buddhist Schools," quoted in Waldberg, *op. cit.*, p. 60.

19. Artaud, "Theater and Science," in *Artaud Anthology*, p. 169.

20. *Ibid.*, p. 172.

21. *Ibid.*, p. 173.

22. Artaud, "No Theogony . . .," in *Artaud Anthology*, p. 65.

23. *Ibid.*, pp. 67–68.

24. Artaud, "Concerning a Journey to the Land of the Tarahumaras," in *Artaud Anthology*, p. 82.

25. Artaud, "I Hate and Renounce as a Coward . . .," in *Artaud Anthology*, p. 233.

26. T. S. Eliot, "The Wasteland," in *The Wasteland and Other Poems* (New York, 1934, pp. 43–44.

27. For more information on LeSage (1876–1928) see "Le Mineur LeSage," *L'Art brût*, III (Paris, 1965), 5–45. Though LeSage's works were once exhibited at the Institut Metapsychique de Paris, few if any contemporary avant-gardistes seem to have taken an interest. Some other inscriptions that appear on LeSage's paintings

are the names Jesus Christ, Moses, John, Isaiah, Egypt, Israel, Krishna, Pytha-
gores, Plato, and Tut-Ank-Amen, and the phrases "Remember Yourself," "Enigma
of the Centuries," "Love of Humanity," "From the Most Ancient Past," "Ancient
Disappeared Religions," and on a single canvas, "Remember Yourself, Man—The
Thought of God Is the Source of the Highest and Most Healthy Inspirations."
Certainly the formal aspect of LeSage's work testifies to the fact that the archetypal
structures of man's past cultural efforts all reside within the human mind.

CHAPTER NINETEEN

1. Rainer Maria Rilke, *op. cit.*, p. 77.

2. From Abraham Lambsprinck, *The Museaum Hermeticum* (Frankfurt, 1678),
revised and enlarged by A. E. Waite (London, 1893). The Ouroboros (or Oroboros)
is the hermetic dragon that lives in the forest. Originally the evil serpent of
paradise, this dragon was transformed into beneficent Ouroboros by the early
Christian Gnostics. The fact that his body was said to be both light and dark also
inspired later alchemical interpretations.

3. C. G. Jung, *Memories, Dreams and Reflections*, trans. Richard and Clara
Winston (New York, 1965), p. 196.

4. *Ibid.*, pp. 196–97.

5. *Ibid.*, p. 199.

6. *Ibid.*, p. 198.

7. W. B. Yeats, *A Vision*, (New York, 1966), p. 8.

8. *Ibid.*, pp. 205–6.

9. "Hellucinations", Matta in Max Ernst, *Beyond Painting* (New York, 1948),
p. 193.

10. Dane Rudhyar, *Art as Release of Power* (Oceano, Calif. 1929), p. 1.

11. *Ibid.*, p. 5.

12. *Ibid.*

13. *Ibid.*, pp. 11–12.

14. *Ibid.*, p. 18.

15. *Ibid.*, pp. 30–31.

16. Dane Rudhyar, "The Artist as Avatar," *Occult Review* (London, 1939), p. 23.

17. *Ibid.*, p. 27.

18. Dane Rudhyar, *The Synthetic Drama as a Seed of Civilization* (Oceano[?],
1929[?]), p. 2. My copy of this text is an old pamphlet given me by Rudhyar.
Presumably it once formed a chapter of a book, *Art as Release of Power*, now long
out of print, from which the title of the earlier booklet I have cited is taken.

19. *Ibid.*, p. 5.

20. *Ibid.*, p. 29.

21. *Ibid.*, p. 30.

22. Dane Rudhyar, "Autumn," in *Of Vibrancy and Peace* (Wassenar, Netherlands 1967), p. 89.

CHAPTER TWENTY

1. Rudhyar, *Synthetic Drama as a Seed of Civilization*, p. 5.

2. Walt Whitman, "Democratic Vistas," in Mark van Doren, ed., *The Portable Walt Whitman*, (New York, 1945), p. 42.

3. *Ibid.*, p. 460.

4. *Ibid.*, p. 462.

5. *Ibid.*, p. 463.

6. As an example of an actual native American Book of the Dead, one may cite the remarkable text translated by Paul Radin from the Winnebago oration of Jasper Blowsnake and published as *The Road of Life and Death: A Ritual Drama Of The American Indians* (Princeton, N.J., 1973). This recounts the complete ritual of the Winnebago medicine society initiation into the most esoteric secrets of life-and-death. The beauty and mandalic perfection of this "ritual drama" are without parallel, and the work bears comparison with similar texts from other cultures. In the poem of death, death is integrated into life, and life into death.

7. D. H. Lawrence, "New Heaven and Earth," in *Selected Poems* (New York, 1959), pp. 75–79.

8. D. H. Lawrence, *The Plumed Serpent* (New York, 1926), pp. 193–94.

9. *Ibid.*, pp. 195–96.

10. *Ibid.*, p. 196.

11. *Ibid.*

12. *Ibid.*

13. *Ibid.*, p. 197.

14. *Ibid.n,*

15. *Ibid.*, p. 266.

16. D. H. Lawrence, "The Ship of Death," in *Selected Poems*, pp. 138–43.

17. Diego Rivera, *Portrait of America* (New York, 1934), p. 19.

18. *Ibid.*

19. José Clemente Orozco, *An Autobiography*, (Austin, 1962) p. 159.

CHAPTER TWENTY-ONE

1. James Joyce, *Finnegan's Wake* (New York, 1939), p. 1.

2. *Ibid.*, p. 221.

3. Marshall McLuhan and Quentin Fiore, *The Medium is the Massage* (New York, 1967), p. 120.

4. Joyce, *op. cit.* Joyce's book abounds with synaesthetic allusions to nonaesthetic illusions.

5. *Ibid.*, p. 349.

6. *Ibid.*, p. 593.

7. Quoted in Francis V. O'Connor, *Jackson Pollock* (New York, 1967), p. 40.

8. *Ibid.*, p. 73.

9. Quoted in Harold Rosenberg, "The Philadelphia Panel," *It Is*, Spring 1960, p. 35.

10. *Ibid.*, p. 37.

11. Harold Rosenberg, *The Anxious Object* (New York, 1966), p. 74.

12. Harold Rosenberg, *Artworks and Packages* (New York, 1969), pp. 13–14.

CHAPTER TWENTY-TWO

1. Max Ernst, *Beyond Painting* (New York, 1948), p. 7.

2. N. O. Brown, *Love's Body* (New York, 1966), p. 180.

3. Aldous Huxley, *The Perennial Philosophy* (New York, 1944), p. 189.

4. Aldous Huxley, *The Doors of Perception* (New York, 1954), p. 73.

5. *Ibid.*, pp. 74–75.

6. Aldous Huxley, "Drugs That Shape Men's Minds," in *Collected Essays*, p. 346.

7. The phrase is taken from Timothy Leary's "Homage to Huxley," in *The Politics of Ecstasy* (New York, 1965), p. 256.

8. Aldous Huxley, *Island* (New York, 1962), p. 265.

9. Quoted in Roger Cardinal and Robert Short, *Surrealism: Permanent Revelation* (London, 1970), p. 143.

10. Allen Ginsberg, *Howl and Other Poems* (San Francisco, 1956), p. 9.

11. *Ibid.*, p. 17.

12. *Ibid.*, p. 20.

13. Lawrence Ferlinghetti, "I Am Waiting," in *A Coney Island of the Mind* (New York, 1958), p. 49.

14. Quoted in R. Buckminster Fuller, *I Seem To Be A Verb* (New York, 1970), pp. 164–65a.

15. André Breton, *Nadja*, trans. Richard Howard (New York, 1960), p. 160.

16. Rainer Maria Rilke, *Duino Elegies*, p. 21.

17. Leary, *op. cit.*, p. 40.

18. Herbert Read, "God's Eye on Gandhi," *Gandalf's Garden*, no. 6 (1969), p. 22.

CHAPTER TWENTY-THREE

1. Mircea Eliade, *Shamanism: Archaic Techniques of Ecstacy*, trans. Willard R. Trask (Princeton, N.J., 1964), p. xiv.

2. Paul Laffoley, inscription on painting, *The Visionary Point*, 1972.

3. Pierre Teilhard de Chardin, *The Future of Man*, trans. Norman Denny (New York, 1964), p. 117.

4. Willard Van de Bogart, "Entropic Art," unpublished paper, 1973(?) p. 4.

5. *Ibid.*, p. 5.

6. Gene Youngblood, *Expanded Cinema* (New York, 1970), p. 163.

7. Quoted in Argüelles, *Charles Henry*, p. 128.

8. Willard Van de Bogart, "Environmental Media Art," unpublished paper, 1973(?).

CHAPTER TWENTY-FOUR

1. D. H. Lawrence, *Fantasia of the Unconscious*, p. 56.

2. Rainer Maria Rilke, *Sonnets to Orpheus*, trans. M. D. Herter-Norton (New York, 1942), p. 133.

3. Dan Katchongva, *From the Beginning of Life to the Day of Purification* (Los Angeles, 1972), pp. 1–2.

4. Frank Waters, *Book of the Hopi* (New York, 1963), p. 32.

5. Laurette Sejourné, *Burning Water: Thought and Religion in Ancient Mexico* (New York, 1960), p. 168.

6. Lawrence, *Fantasia of the Unconscious*, p. 57.

7. *Ibid.*

8. Immanuel Velikovsky, *Earth in Upheaval* (New York, 1955), p. 259.

9. Lawrence, *Fantasia of the Unconscious*, p. 55.

10. Ajit Mookerjee, *Tantra Art* (New Delhi, 1966), p. 80.

11. Waters, *op. cit.*, p. 30.

12. *Ibid.*

13. *Ibid.*

Bibliography

FOR PURPOSES of simplicity, the bibliography is divided into three parts: 1) visionary texts; 2) psychology and the philosophy and psychology of history and related texts; and 3) aesthetics and the history of art and culture. In some cases it was difficult to decide into which category to place a particular text, and I beg the reader's indulgence in the matter. All of the choices reflect either material directly utilized in the body of this work, or material which, though not necessarily referred to in my text, I have found helpful in the shaping of the *Transformative Vision*. A bibliography like this can only be suggestive of a certain approach to knowledge, and in no way pretends to be complete.

I. VISIONARY TEXTS.

Argüelles, José, and Miriam T. *Mandala*. Berkeley and London: Shambhala Publications, 1972.

Arp, Hans. *On My Way: Poetry and Essays 1912–1947*, trans. Ralph Manheim. New York: Wittenborn, Schultz, 1948.

Artaud, Antonin. *Artaud Anthology*, ed. Jack Hirschman. San Francisco: City Lights, 1965.

———. "No Divine Epic." Unpublished mss., translated and used by the Floating Lotus Opera Company. San Francisco, ca. 1970.

Baha'ullah. *Gleanings from the Writings of Baha'ullah*, trans. Shogi Effendi. Wilmette, Illinois: Bahai Publishing, 1952.

Baudelaire, Charles. *Flowers of Evil*, ed. Martha and Jackson Mathews. New York: New Directions, 1955. Oxford: Blackwell, 1942.

———. *Intimate Journals*, trans. Christopher Isherwood. Boston: Beacon Press, 1957. St. Albans: Granada Publications, 1969.

———. *Les Paradis Artificiels*. Paris: Gallimard, 1964.

———. *Spleen de Paris*. Paris: Gallimard, 1964.

Besant, Annie, and C. W. Leadbeater. *Life Visible and Invisible*. Madras, India and London: Theosophical Publishing House, 1901.

———. *Thought Forms*. Madras, India and London: Theosophical Publishing House, 1901.

Blake, William. *Complete Writings*, ed. Geoffrey Keynes. London: Oxford University Press, 1969.

Blavatsky, Helena Petrovna. *The Secret Doctrine*. 2 vols. Madras, India and London: Theosophical Publishing House, 1888.

Boehme, Jacob. *Dialogue on the Supersensual Life*, trans. William Law et al. New York: Frederick Ungar, 1957.

———. *Six Theosophic Points and Other Writings*, trans. John Bolleston Earle. Ann Arbor, Michigan: University of Michigan Press, 1966.

———. *Theologica Germanica*, trans. Susanna Winkworth. London: Stuart and Watkins, 1966.

Breton, Andre. *Manifests du Surréalisme*, Paris: Gallimard, 1963.

———. *Nadja*, trans. Richard Howard. New York: Grove Press, 1960.

Broch, Hermann. *The Sleepwalkers*, trans. W. E. Muir. New York: Grosset and Dunlap, 1964.

Bucke, Richard M. *Cosmic Consciousness*. New York: E. P. Dutton, 1969. London: Olympia Press, 1972.

Castaneda, Carlos. *Journey to Ixtlan*. New York: Simon and Schuster, 1972.

_____. *A Separate Reality*. New York: Simon and Schuster, 1971. London: The Bodley Head, 1971.

_____. *The Teachings of Don Juan, A Yaqui Way of Knowledge*. Berkeley: University of California Press, 1968. Harmondsworth, England: Penguin Books, 1970.

Cendrars, Blaise. *Selected Writings*, trans. Walter Albert. New York: New Directions, 1965.

Cocteau, Jean. *Opium*, trans. Margaret Crosland and Sinclair Road. New York: Grove Press, 1957. London: Peter Owen, 1968.

Coleridge, Samuel Taylor. *Selected Prose and Poetry*, ed. Donald A. Stauffer. New York: Random House, 1951. London: Nonesuch Library, 1933.

Damon, S. Foster. *A Blake Dictionary: The Ideas and Symbols of William Blake*. New York: E. P. Dutton, 1971. London: Oxford University Press, 1968.

Daumal, René. *Mount Analogue*, trans. Roger Shattuck. San Francisco: City Lights, 1959.

De Quincey, Thomas. *Confessions of an English Opium Eater*. London: J. M. Dent, 1960.

Ducasse, Isadore (Comte de Lautréamont). *Les Chants de Maldoror*. Paris: Librairie José Corti, 1961.

Eliot, T. S. *The Wasteland and Other Poems*. New York: Harcourt Brace, 1934. London: Faber and Faber, 1972.

Evans-Wentz, N. Y. *Tibetan Book of the Dead*. London and New York: Oxford University Press, 1927.

_____. *Tibetan Book of the Great Liberation*. London and New York: Oxford University Press, 1954.

Ferlinghetti, Lawrence. *A Coney Island of the Mind*. New York: New Directions, 1958.

Fuller, R. Buckminster. *I seem to Be a Verb*. New York: Bantam, 1970.

Gaddis, William. *The Recognitions*. Cleveland: World Publishing, 1955.

Gauguin, Paul. *Intimate Journals*, trans. Van Wyck Brooks. Bloomington: University of Indiana Press, 1958.

_____. *Noa Noa*, trans. O. F. Theis. New York: Noonday Press, 1957. Oxford: Bruno Cassirer, 1961.

Ginsberg, Allen. *The Fall of America*. San Francisco: City Lights, 1972.

_____. *Howl and Other Poems*. San Francisco: City Lights, 1956.

_____. *Indian Journals*. San Francisco: City Lights, 1970.

_____ and William Burroughs. *Yage Letters*. San Francisco: City Lights, 1965.

Goethe, Johann Wolfgang von. *Faust*, trans. Bayard Taylor. London: Oxford University Press, n.d.

Grigson, Geoffrey. *The Romantics: An Anthology of English Prose and Poetry*. Cleveland: Meridian Books, 1962.

Hall, Manley Palmer. *The Secret Teachings of All Ages*. Los Angeles: Philosophical Research Society, 1969.

Hardenberg, Friederich Philipp von(Novalis). *Hymns to the Night and Other Writings,* trans. Charles E. Passage. Indianapolis: Bobbs Merrill, 1960.

_____. *The Novices of Sais,* trans. Curt Valentin. New York: Curt Valentin, 19969.

Hesse, Herman. *The Journey to the East,* trans. Hilda Rosner. New York: Noonday, 1957. London: Peter Owen, 1970.

_____. *Magister Ludi,* trans. Mervyn Savill. New York: Frederick Ungar, 1957. London: Cape, 1970.

_____. *Siddhartha,* trans. Hilda Rosner. New York: New Directions, 1957. London: Peter Owen, 1970.

_____. *Steppenwolf,* trans. Basil Creighton. New York and London: Holt, Rinehart, Winston, 1963.

Hölderlin, Johann C. F. *Selected Verse,* trans. Michael Hamburger. Baltimore: Penguin Books, 1961.

Huxley, Aldous. *Brave New World.* New York: Harper and Row, 1932. London: Chatto, 1972.

_____. *Collected Essays.* New York: Bantam Books, 1960.

_____. *The Doors of Perception and Heaven and Hell.* New York: Harper and Row, 1963. London: Chatto, 1968.

_____. *Island.* New York: Bantam Books, 1963. Harmondsworth, England: Penguin Books, 1970.

_____. *The Perennial Philosophy.* Cleveland: Meridian Books, 1962. London: Chatto, 1969.

Jarry, Alfred. *Selected Writings,* trans. Roger Shattuck. New York: Grove Press, 1959. London: Cape, 1969.

Joyce, James. *Finnegans Wake.* New York: Viking Press, 1939. London: Faber and Faber, 1964.

Kerouac, Jack. *Mexico City Blues.* New York: Grove Press, 1959.

_____. *The Scripture of the Golden Eternity.* New York: Corinth Books, 1970.

Lama Foundation and Richard Alpert (Baba Ram Dass). *Be Here Now (From Bindu to Ojas).* San Cristobal, N.M.: The Lama Foundation, 1970.

Lawrence, D. H. *The Apocalypse.* New York: Viking Press, 1960.

_____. *The Later D. H. Lawrence,* ed. William Tindall. New York: Alfred Knopf, 1959.

_____. *The Plumed Serpent.* New York: Alfred Knopf, 1926. London: Heinemann, 1955.

_____. *Psychoanalysis and the Unconscious and Fantasia of the Unconscious.* New York: Viking Press, 1960. London: Penguin Books, 1971.

_____. *Selected Poems.* New York: The Viking Press, 1959. London: Heinemann, 1967.

Leary, Timothy. *High Priest.* Cleveland: World Publishing Co., 1968.

_____. *The Politics of Ecstasy.* London: Paladin Books, 1966.

_____. *Psychedelic Prayers after the Tao Teh Ching.* New Hyde Park, N.Y.: University Books, 1968.

_____, Ralph Metzner, and Richard Alpert. *The Psychedelic Experience.* New Hyde Park, N.Y. 1964. London: Academy Books, 1971.

_____, et al. *Psychedelic Theory*. Millbrook, N.Y.: Castalia Foundation, 1965.

Maharshi, Ramana. *Collected Works,* ed. Arthur Osborne. London: Rider, 1969.

Mann, Thomas. *Dr. Faustus: The Life of the German Composer, Adrian Leverkühn,* trans. H. T. Lowe-Porter. New York: Alfred Knopf, 1948. Harmondsworth, England; Penguin Books, 1971.

Marlowe, Christopher. *Dr. Faustus,* ed. Paul H. Kocher. New York: Crofts Classics, 1950.

Neihardt, John G. *Black Elk Speaks.* Lincoln: University of Nebraska Press, 1961.

Nerval, Gerard de. *Selected Writings,* trans. Geoffrey Wagner. New York: Grove Press, 1957. St. Albans: Granada, 1973.

Nijinsky, Vaslav. *The Diary of Vaslav Nijinsky,* ed. Romola Nijinsky. Berkeley: University of California Press, 1968.

Orwell, George. *1984.* New York: Harcourt Brace Jovanovich, 1948. London: Heinemann, 1965.

Poe, Edgar Allen. "Eureka," in *Complete Works,* vol. IX. New York: Funk and Wagnells, 1904.

Quasha, George and Jerome Rothenberg. *America: A Prophecy: A New Reading of American Poetry from Pre-Columbian Times to the Present.* New York: Random House, 1973.

Radin, Paul. *The Road of Life and Death: A Ritual Drama of the American Indians.* Princeton: Princeton University Press, 1973.

Redon, Odilon, *A Soi-même* Paris: Librairie Jose Corti, 1961.

Rilke, Rainer Maria. *Duino Elegies,* trans. J.B. Leishman and Stephen Spender. New York: W.W. Norton, 1939. London: The Hogarth Press, 1963.

_____. *Sonnets to Orpheus,* trans. M.D. Herter-Norton. New York. W.W. Norton, 1942. London: Hogarth Press, 1946.

Rimbaud, Arthur. *Illuminations,* trans. Louise Varese. New York: New Directions, 1957.

_____. *A Season in Hell and the Drunken Boat,* trans. Louise Varese. New York: New Directions, 1961.

Rothenberg, Jerome. *Technicians of the Sacred.* New York: Doubleday, 1968.

Rudhyar, Dane. *Of Vibrancy and Peace.* Wassenaar, The Netherlands: Servire, 1967.

_____. *The Pulse of Life.* Wassenaar, The Netherlands: Servire, 1963.

_____. *Return From No Return.* Palo Alto: The Seed Center, 1973.

_____. *Triptych.* Wassenaar, The Netherlands: Servire, 1968.

Shah, Idreis. *The Secret Lore of Magic and Books of the Sorcerors.* New York: Citadel Press, 1957. London: Muller, 1957.

Shearer, Tony. *Lord of the Dawn.* Healdsburg, Calif.: Naturegraph Press, 1971.

Shelley, Mary. *Frankenstein.* New York: Pyramid Books, 1957. London: Collier-Macmillan, 1961.

Snyder, Gary. *Earth Household: Technical Notes and Queries to Fellow Dharma Revolutionaries.* New York: New Directions, 1969. London: Cape, 1970.

Swedenborg, Emanuel. *Heaven and its Wonders and Hell.* New York: Citadel Press, 1965. London: The Swedenborg Society, 1937.

Thoreau, Henry David. *Walden, or a Life in the Woods and Civil Disobediance.*

New York: New American Library, 1960. London: Collier-Macmillan, 1962.

Valery, Paul. *Selected Writings*, trans. Malcolm Cowley. et al. New York: New Directions, 1950.

Van Gogh, Vincent. *Letters of Vincent van Gogh*, ed. Mark Roskill. New York: Atheneum, 1963. London: William Collins, 1963.

Whitman, Walt. *Portable Walt Whitman*, ed. Mark Van Doren. New York: Viking Press, 1945. London: Chatto, 1971.

Wilson, Colin. *The Mind Parasites*. Oakland: Oneiric Press, 1972.

_____. *The Philosopher's Stone*. New York: Warner Books, 1974.

Wordsworth, William. *The Prelude and Other Poems*, ed. Carlos Baker. New York: Holt, Rinehart and Winston, 1954.

Yeats, William Butler. *Collected Poems*. New York: Macmillan, 1956. London: Macmillan International, 1950.

_____. *A Vision*. New York: Macmillan, 1966. London: Macmillan International, 1962.

II. PSYCHOLOGY AND THE PHILOSOPHY AND PSYCHOLOGY OF HISTORY AND RELATED TEXTS.

Aaronson, Bernard and Humphrey Osmund. *Psychedelics: The Uses and Implications of Psychedelic Drugs*. New York: Doubleday, 1970. London: Hogarth Press, 1971.

Arasteh, A. Reza. *Rumi: The Persian, The Sufi*. Tucson, Ariz: Omen Press, 1972.

Barnett, Lincoln. *The Universe and Dr. Einstein*. New York: Bantam Books, 1957.

Brown, Norman O. *Life Against Death*. New York: Random House, 1959. London: Sphere Books, 1970.

_____. *Love's Body*. New York: Random House, 1966.

Burckhardt, Jacob. *The Civilization of the Renaissance in Italy*. 2 vols. New York and London: Harper and Row, 1958.

Burckhardt, Titus. *Alchemy: Science of the Cosmos, Science of the Soul*. London: Stuart and Watkins, 1967.

Butterfield, Henry. *Man on His Past: A Study of the History of Historical Scholarship*. Boston: Beacon Press, 1960.

Campbell, Joseph. *The Masks of God*. 4 vols. New York: Viking Press, 1959–68.

Dampier, W. C. *A History of Science and Its Relation to Philosophy and Religion*. Cambridge, England: Cambridge University Press, 1966.

De Bell, Garrett, ed. *The Environmental Handbook*. New York: Ballantine Books, 1970.

De Ropp, Robert S. *Drugs and The Mind*. New York: Grove Press, 1960.

_____. *The Master Game*. New York: Dell Publishing, 1968.

Descartes, Rene. *Discourse on Method*, trans. John Veitch Chicago: Open Court, 1962.

Eliade, Mircea. *Cosmos and History: The Myth of the Eternal Return*. New York: Harper and Row, 1959. London: Routledge and Kegan Paul, 1954.

_____. *The Forge and the Crucible: The Origins and Structure of Alchemy*, trans. Stephen Corrin. New York: Harper and Row, 1971.

_____. *Myths, Dreams and Mysteries: The Encounters Between Contemporary*

Faiths and Archaic Realities, trans. Philip Mairet. New York: Harper and Row, 1967.

———. *Rites and Symbols of Initiation: The Mysteries of Birth and Rebirth,* trans. Willard R. Trask. New York: Harper and Row, 1958.

———. *Shamanism: Archaic Techniques of Ecstasy,* trans. Willard R. Trask. Princeton: Princeton University Press, 1964. London: Routledge and Kegan Paul, 1964.

———. *Yoga: Immortality and Freedom,* trans. Willard R. Trask. Princeton: Princeton University Press, 1958. London: Routledge and Kegan Paul, 1958.

Ellul, Jacques. *The Technological Society,* trans. John Wilkinson. New York: Alfred Knopf, 1964. London: Duckworth, 1973.

Fadiman, James and Donald Kewman, eds. *Exploring Madness.* Monterey, Calif.: Brooks-Cole, 1973.

Freud, Sigmund. *Civilization and Its Discontents,* trans. James Strachey. New York: W.W. Norton, 1962. London: The Hogarth Press, 1963.

Fuller, R. Buckminster. *Operating Manual for Spaceship Earth.* Carbondale, Ill., Southern Illinois University Press, 1969.

Fung Yu-Lan, *A History of Chinese Philosophy,* trans. Derk Bodde. 2 vols. Princeton: Princeton University Press, 1952. London: Oxford University Press, 1969.

Giedion, Siegfried. *Mechanization Takes Command.* New York: W.W. Norton, 1969.

Gurdjieff, G. I. *Meetings with Remarkable Men,* trans. A.R. Orage. New York: E.P. Dutton, 1969.

Harold, Preston and Winifred Babcock. *The Single Reality.* New York: Harold Institute, 1971.

Heisenberg, Werner. *Physics and Philosophy: The Revolution in Modern Science.* New York: Harper and Row, 1958. London: Allen and Unwin, 1959.

Hobsbawn, E.J. *The Age of Revolution: 1789–1848.* New York: World Publishing Co., 1962. London: Weidenfeld and Nicholson, 1962.

Jung, Carl G. *Man and His Symbols.* London: Aldus Books, Ltd., 1964.

———. *Mandala Symbolism.* Princeton: Princeton University, 1972.

———. *Memories, Dreams and Reflections,* trans. Richard and Clara Winston. New York: Random House, 1963. London: William Collins Sons, 1967.

Koestler, Arthur. *The Act of Creation.* New York: Macmillan, 1956. London: Hutchinson Publishing Group, 1969.

———. *The Ghost in the Machine.* New York: Macmillan, 1968. London: Hutchinson Publishing Group, 1967.

Kovel, Joel. *White Racism: A Psychohistory.* New York: Random House, 1970. London: Allen Lane, 1970.

Krishna, Gopi. *The Psychological Basis of Religion and Genius.* New York: Harper and Row, 1972.

Kuhn, Thomas J. *The Structure of Scientific Revolutions.* Chicago and London: University of Chicago Press, 1962.

Laing, Ronald D. *The Politics of Experience.* New York: Ballantine Books, 1968. Harmondsworth, Mdx.: Penguin Books, 1970.

Leonard, George. *The Transformation.* New York: Dell Books, 1972.

Leon-Portilla, Miguel. *Time and Reality in the Thought of the Maya,* trans. Charles L. Boiles and Fernando Horcasitas. Boston: Beacon Press, 1973.

Maincurrents in Modern Thought, "Civilization as Psycho-History," (entire issue devoted to this theme), Volume 29, Number 2, November-December, 1972.

Mao Tse Tung, *Quotations.* Peking: Peoples Press, 1966.

Metzner, Ralph. "The Evolutionary Significance of Psychedelic Drugs." *Maincurrents in Modern Thought,* Sept.–Oct., 1968, Vol. 25, No. 1.

_____. *Maps of Consciousness.* New York: Macmillan, 1971. London: Collier-Macmillan, 1972.

McLuhan, Marshal. *The Gutenberg Galaxy.* Toronto: University of Toronto Press, 1962.

_____. *Understanding Media: The Extensions of Man.* New York: McGraw-Hill, 1964.

_____ and Quentin Fiore. *The Medium is the Massage.* New York: Bantam Books, 1967.

Michell, John. *The View Over Atlantis.* New York: Ballantine Books, 1972. London: Garnstone Press, 1972.

Mitcham, Carl and Robert Mackey. *Bibliography of the Philosophy of Technology.* Chicago and London: University of Chicago Press, 1973.

Mumford, Lewis. *The Myth of the Machine.* vol. I, *Technics and Human Development,* vol. II., *The Pentagon of Power.* New York: Harcourt Brace Jovanovich, 1967–70. London: Secker and Warburg, 1967, 1971.

_____. *Technics and Civilization.* New York: Harcourt, Brace, 1934. London: Routledge and Kegan Paul, 1934.

Needleman, Jacob. *The New Religions: The Meaning of the Spiritual Revolution and the Teachings of the East.* New York: Doubleday, 1970. London: Allen Lane, 1972.

Northrup, F.S.C. *The Meeting of East and West.* New York: Macmillan, 1946.

Ornstein, Robert. *The Psychology of Consciousness.* San Francisco: Freeman Co., 1972.

Ouspensky, Peter D. *In Search of the Miraculous: Fragments of an Unknown Teaching.* New York: Harcourt Brace and World, 1949. London: Routledge and Kegan Paul, 1950.

_____. *The Psychology of Man's Possible Evolution.* New York: Bantam Books, 1968. London: Hodder and Stoughton, 1951.

Pauli, Wolfgang. "The Influence of Archetypal Ideas on the Scientific Theories of Kepler," in Carl G. Jung and Wolfgang Pauli, *The Interpretation of Nature and the Psyche.* New York: Bollingen Books, 1955.

Pauwels, Louis and Jacques Bergier. *The Dawn of Magic,* trans. Rollo Myers. London: Panther Books, 1963.

Popper, Karl R. *The Poverty of Historicism.* New York: Harper and Row, 1964. London: Routledge and Kegan Paul, 1960.

Reiser, Oliver. *Cosmic Humanism.* Cambridge, Mass.: Schenkman, 1966.

Rolland, Romain. *The Life of Ramakrishna,* trans. E.F. Malcolm-Smith. Advaita Ashrama: Calcutta, 1970.

Roszak, Theodore. *The Making of a Counter-Culture: Reflections on the Technocratic Society and its Youthful Opposition.* New York: Doubleday, 1969. London: Faber and Faber, 1970.

————. *Where the Wasteland Ends.* New York: Doubleday, 1972. London: Faber and Faber, 1973.

Rudhyar, Dane. *The Astrology of America's Destiny.* New York: Random House, 1974.

————. *The Astrology of Personality.* New York: Doubleday, 1969.

————. *Astrological Timing: Transition to a New Age.* New York: Harper and Row, 1972.

————. *Directives for New Life.* San Francisco: Ecology Press, 1971.

————. *Modern Man's Conflicts.* New York: Philosophical Library, 1948.

————. *The Planetarization of Consciousness.* Wasenaar, The Netherlands: Servire, 1970.

Seidenberg, Roderick. *Post-Historic Man.* Boston: Beacon Press, 1957.

Seligman, Kurt. *Magic, The Supernatural and Religion.* New York: Grosset and Dunlap, 1968. London: Allen Lane, 1971.

Singer, Charles. *A Short History of Scientific Ideas to 1900.* London: Oxford University Press, 1959.

Siu, R. G. H. *The Tao of Science: An Essay on Western Knowledge and Eastern Wisdom.* Cambridge, Mass.: M.I.T. Press, 1957.

Smith, Preserved. *The Origins of Modern Culture, 1543–1687.* New York: Collier Books, 1962.

————. *The Reformation in Europe.* New York: Collier Books, 1962.

Spengler, Oswald. *The Decline of the West,* trans. Charles F. Atkinson. 2 vols. New York: Alfred Knopf, 1930–46. London: Allen and Unwin, 1932.

Tart, Charles, ed. *Altered States of Consciousness.* New York: Wiley, 1969.

Teilhard de Chardin, Pierre. *The Future of Man,* trans. Norman Denny. New York: Harper and Row, 1964. London: William Collins Sons, 1968.

————. *The Phenomenon of Man,* trans. Bernard Wall. New York: Harper and Row, 1959. London: William Collins Sons, n.d.

Thompson, William Irwin. *At the Edge of History: Speculations on the Transformation of Culture.* New York: Harper and Row, 1971.

————. *Passages About Earth: Explorations of the New Planetary Culture.* New York: Harper and Row, 1974.

Tibetan Nyingmapa Meditation Center. *Kalachakra, Tibetan Astrological Chart.* Berkeley, Calif.: Dharma Press, 1971.

Toynbee, Arnold. *A Study of History.* 10 vols. New York and London: Oxford University Press, 1934–61.

Velikovsky, Immanuel. *Earth in Upheaval.* New York: Dell Publishing, 1955. London: Gollancz, 1956.

————. *Worlds in Collision.* New York: Dell Publishing, 1950. London: Gollancz, 1950.

Watts, Alan. *The Joyous Cosmology: Adventures in the Chemistry of Consciousness.* New York: Random House, 1962.

Weber, Max. *The Protestant Ethic and the Spirit of Capitalism,* trans. Talcott Parsons. New York: Charles Scribners and Sons, 1958. London: Allen and Unwin, 1967.

Weizsäcker, Carl F. von. *The History of Nature,* trans. Fred D. Wieck. Chicago and London: University of Chicago Press, 1949.

Wilhelm, Richard. *I Ching or Book of Changes,* trans. Cary Baynes. Princeton:

Princeton University Press, 1967.

———. and Carl G. Jung. *The Secret of the Golden Flower*, trans. Cary Baynes. New York: Harcourt Brace and World, 1962.

Wilson, Colin. *The Occult*. New York: Random House, 1970. London: Hodder and Stoughton, 1971.

———. *The Outsider*. New York: Delta, 1967. London: Gollancz, 1956.

Yates, Frances. *Giordano Bruno and the Hermetic Tradition*. New York: Random House, 1964. London: Routledge and Kegan Paul, 1971.

———. *The Rosicrucian Enlightenment*. London: Routledge and Kegan Paul, 1972.

III. AESTHETICS AND THE HISTORY
OF ART AND CULTURE.

Aragon, Louis. *Les Collages*. Paris: Hermann & cie., 1965.

Argüelles, José A. *Charles Henry and the Formation of a Psychophysical Aesthetic*. Chicago and London: University of Chicago Press, 1972.

Arnason, H. H. *History of Modern Art*. Englewood Cliffs, N.J.: Prentice-Hall, 1968.

Arts Council of Great Britain. *The Romantic Movement*. London: Tate Gallery, 1959.

Babbit, Irving. *Rousseau and Romanticism*. Cleveland: Meridian Books, 1955.

Baird, James. *Ishmael*. Baltimore: Johns Hopkins University Press, 1956.

Balakian, A. *Surrealism, Road to the Absolute*. New York: Noonday, 1959. London: Allen and Unwin, 1972.

Banham, Regner. *Theory and Design in the First Machine Age*. London: The Architectural Press, 1960.

Bates, W. J. *From Classic to Romantic: Premises of Taste in Eighteenth Century England*. New York: Harper and Row, 1961.

Battock, Gregory. *The New Art*. New York: E.P. Dutton, 1966.

———. *Minimal Art: A Critical Anthology*. New York: E.P. Dutton, 1968.

Baudelaire, Charles. *The Mirror of Art*, trans. and ed. Jonathon Mayne. New York: Doubleday, 1956.

Beguin, Albert. *L'Âme Romantique et le Rêve*. Paris: Librairie José Corti, 1963.

Belz, Carl. *The Story of Rock*. New York: Harper and Row, 1969.

Blunt, Sir Anthony. *Artistic Theory in Italy: 1450–1600*. London: Oxford University Press, 1962.

Bodelsen, Merette. *Gauguin's Ceramics: A Study in the Development of His Art*. London: Faber and Faber, 1964.

Bosanquet, Bernard. *A History of Aesthetic*. Cleveland: Meridian Books, 1957. London: Allen and Unwin, 1904.

Bosse, Abraham. *Le Peintre Converty aux Règles de son Art*. Paris: Hermann & cie., 1964.

Breton, Andre. *Manifestes du Surréalisme*. Paris: Gallimard, 1964.

Burckhardt, Titus. *Sacred Art in East and West: Its Principles and Methods*. London: Perennial Books, 1967.

Cardinal, Roger. *Outsider Art.* New York: Frederick A. Praeger, 1973. London: Studio Vista, 1972.

Cassou, Jean, Emil Langui, and Nikolaus Pevsner. *Gateway to the Twentieth Century.* New York: McGraw-Hill, 1962.

Chicago, Art Institute of. *The Art of Goya,* ed. Daniel Catton Rich. Chicago: Art Institute of Chicago, 1941.

Clark, Kenneth. *Leonardo da Vinci.* Baltimore: Penguin Books, 1958. Harmondsworth, England: Penguin Books, 1968.

Compagnie de l'Art Brut. *Publications* (Paris), vol. II (special issue devoted to Adolf Wölfli). Paris: 1964; vol. III, "Le Mineur LeSage, pp. 5–45, Paris, 1965.

Coomaraswamy, Ananda. *Christian and Oriental Philosophy of Art.* New York: Dover Books, 1956.

Delacroix, Eugene. *Journal,* trans. Lucy Norton. London: Phaidon, 1951.

Delaunay, Robert. *Du Cubisme à l'Art Abstrait,* ed. Pierre Francastel. Paris: École Pratique des Hauts Etudes, 1957.

Ernst, Max. *Beyond Painting.* New York: George Wittenborn, 1948.

Fowlie, Wallace. *The Age of Surrealism.* Bloomington, Ind.: University of Indiana Press, 1960.

Francastel, Pierre. *Art et Technique aux XIXe XXe Siecles.* Paris: Editions Gonthiers, 1956.

Fry, Edward, ed. *Cubism.* New York: McGraw-Hill, 1966. London: Thames and Hudson, 1966.

Fry, Roger. *Last Lectures.* Cambridge, Eng.: Cambridge University Press, 1939.
_____. *Vision and Design.* Cleveland: Meridian Books, 1956.

Frye, Northrup. *Fearful Symmetry: A Study of William Blake.* Princeton: Princeton University Press, 1969. London: Oxford University Press, 1970.

Gardner, Louise. *Art Through the Ages,* revised and ed. Horst de la Croix and Richard G. Tansey. New York: Harcourt Brace Jovanovich, 1970.

Gernsheim, Helmut and Alison. *A Concise History of Photography.* New York: Grosset and Dunlap, 1965.

Giedion, Siegfried. *Space, Time and Architecture: The Growth of a New Tradition.* Cambridge, Mass.: Harvard University Press, 1942.

Goethe, Johann Wolfgang von. *Theory of Colors.* trans. Charles Eastlake. Cambridge, Mass: M.I.T. Press, 1970.

Goldwater, Robert. *Primitivism in Modern Art.* New York: Random House, 1966.

Gombrich, Ernest H. "Bosch's *Garden of Earthly Delights:* A Progress Report," *Journal of the Warburg and Courtauld Institute,* 1969, pp. 162–169.
_____. *The Story of Art.* New York and London: Phaidon Press, 1966.

Gray, Camilla. *The Great Experiment: Russian Art, 1863–1922.* New York: Harry N. Abrams, 1962.

Gray, Christopher. *Sculpture and Ceramics of Paul Gauguin.* Baltimore: Johns Hopkins University Press, 1963.

Greenberg, Clement. *Art and Culture: Critical Essays.* Boston: Beacon Press, 1961.

Grigson, Geoffrey. *Samuel Palmer's Valley of Vision.* London: Phoenix House, 1960.

_____. *Samuel Palmer: The Visionary Years.* London: Routledge and Kegan Paul, 1947.

Hauser, Arnold. *The Philosophy of Art History.* Cleveland: Meridian Books, 1963.

_____. *The Social History of Art.* 4 vols. New York: Random House, 1960. London: Routledge and Kegan Paul, 1969.

Hayes, Carl J. H. *A Generation of Materialism: 1871–1900.* New York: Harper and Row, 1941.

Henry, Charles. *Cercle Chromatique.* Paris: Charles Verdin, 1888.

Hofstätter, Hans H. *Symbolismus und die Kunst der Jahrhundertwende* Köln: Verlag Dumont, 1965.

Holt, Elizabeth. *A Documentary History of Art.* 3 vols. New York: Doubleday, 1957–66.

Hughes, Stuart. *Consciousness and Society: The Reorientation of European Thought, 1890–1930.* New York: Random House, 1958.

It Is, no. 5, Spring, 1960, New York.

Jacobs, Lewis. *The Movies: An Anthology of Ideas.* New York: Noonday Press, 1960.

Janson, Horst W. *History of Art.* Englewood Cliffs, N.J.: Prentice-Hall, 1969. London: Thames and Hudson, 1969.

Jeanneret, Jean(Le Corbusier). *Towards a New Architecture,* trans. Frederick Etchells. New York: Frederick A. Praeger, 1946. London: The Architectural Press, 1970.

Kandinsky, Wassily. *Concerning the Spiritual in Art,* trans. Michael Sadleir. New York: George Wittenborn, 1947.

Kirby, Michael, ed. *Happenings.* New York: E. P. Dutton, 1966.

Klee, Paul. *Diaries.* Berkeley, Calif.: University of California Press, 1964. London: Peter Owen, 1965.

_____. *Pedagogical Sketchbook,* trans. Sibyl Moholy-Nagy New York: Frederick A. Praeger, 1953. London: Faber and Faber, 1968.

Kracauer, Siegfried. *From Caligari to Hitler, A Psychological Study of the German Film.* New York: Noonday Press, 1959. London: Oxford University Press, 1967.

Leonardo da Vinci. *Notebooks,* ed. Irma Richter. London: Oxford University Press, 1952.

Leslie, Charles R. *Memoirs of the Life of John Constable.* London: Phaidon Press, 1951.

Lessing, Gotthold Ephraim. *Laocoon: An Essay on the Limits of Painting and Poetry,* trans. Ellen Frothingham. New York: Noonday Press, 1957.

Leverant, Robert. *Zen in the Art of Photography.* Berkeley, Calif.: Images Press, 1969.

Lippard, Lucy, ed. *Pop Art.* New York: Frederick A. Praeger, 1966. London: Thames and Hudson, 1967.

Lovgren, Sven. *The Genesis of Modernism: Seurat, Gauguin, Van Gogh and the French Symbolism of the 1880s.* Stockholm: Almqvist and Wicksell, 1959.

Mâle, Emile. *Religious Art from the Twelfth to the Eighteenth Century.* New York: Pantheon Books, 1959.

Malraux, Andre. *Saturn: An Essay on Goya,* trans. C.W. Chilton. New York and London: Phaidon Press, 1957.

Martindale, Andrew. *The Rise of the Artist in the Middle Ages and Early Renaissance.* New York: McGraw-Hill, 1972. London: Thames and Hudson, 1972.

Meier-Graeffe, Julius. *Entwicklungsgeschichte der Moderne Kunst.* 3 vols. München: R. Piper Verlag, 1927.

Moholy-Nagy, Laszlo. *The New Vision and Abstract of an Artist.* New York: George Wittenborn, 1947.

Morris, Williams. *Selected Writings and Designs,* ed. Asa Briggs. Baltimore: Penguin Books, 1962.

Mumford, Lewis. *Art and Technics.* New York: Columbia University Press, 1952.

Munro, Thomas. *The Arts and Their Interrelations.* New York: Liberal Arts Press, 1949.

Nadeau, Maurice. *The History of Surrealism,* trans. Richard Howard New York: Collier Books, 1968. London: Cape, 1968.

New York, Museum of Modern Art. *Art Nouveau,* ed. Peter Selz and Mildred Constantine. New York: Museum of Modern Art, 1959.

――――. *Cubism and Abstract Art,* ed. Alfred Barr. New York: Museum of Modern Art, 1934.

――――. *Jackson Pollock,* ed. Francis V. O'Connor. New York: Museum of Modern Art, 1967.

――――. *Odilon Redon, Gustave Moreau and Rodolphe Bresdin,* ed. John Rewald et al. New York: Museum of Modern Art, 1961.

Nochlin, Linda, ed. *Impressionism and Post-Impressionism.* Englewood Cliffs, N.J.: Prentice-Hall, 1966.

Orozco, Jose Clemente. *Autobiography.* Austin, Tex.: University of Texas Press, 1962.

Ortega y Gasset, José. *The Dehumanization of Art, and Other Writings on Art and Culture.* New York: Doubleday, 1956. London: Oxford University Press, 1969.

Ozenfant, Amadee. *Foundations of Modern Art,* trans. John Rodker. New York: Dover Books, 1952.

Paris, Musée de l'Art Moderne. *L'Ouevre de Kupka,* ed. Denise Fedit. Paris: Éditions Musées Nationaux, 1966.

Pelles, Geraldine. *Art, Artists and Society: Origins of a Modern Dilemma.* Englewood Cliffs, N.J.: Prentice-Hall, 1963.

Pevsner, Nikolaus. *Academies of Art, Past and Present.* Cambridge, Eng.: Cambridge University Press, 1940.

――――. *Pioneers of Modern Design.* Baltimore: Penguin Books, 1960.

Praz, Mario. *The Romantic Agony.* Cleveland: Meridian Books, 1956. London: Oxford University Press, 1970.

Raine, Kathleen. *William Blake.* New York: Frederick A. Praeger, 1971. London: Thames and Hudson, 1970.

――――. *William Blake and Tradition.* 2 vols. Princeton: Princeton University Press, 1969.

Raymond, Marcel. *De Baudelaire au Surréalisme*. Paris: Librairie José Corti, 1963.

Read, Sir Herbert. *Art and Alienation: The Role of the Artist in Society*. New York: Viking Press, 1969.

———. *Art and Industry*. Bloomington, Ind.: University of Indiana Press, 1961. London: Faber and Faber, 1966.

———. *Concise History of Modern Painting*. New York: Frederick A. Praeger, 1959. London: Thames and Hudson, 1968.

———. "God's Eye on Gandhi," *Gandalf's Garden*, No. 6, 1969, pp. 21–22.

———. *The Grass Roots of Art: Lectures on the Social Aspects of Art in an Industrial Age*. Cleveland: Meridian Books, 1961.

———. *The Philosophy of Modern Art*. Cleveland: Meridian Books, 1955. London: Faber and Faber, 1965.

Rewald, John. *History of Impressionism*. New York: Museum of Modern Art, 1962.

———. *History of Post-Impressionism*. New York: Museum of Modern Art, 1962.

Reynolds, Sir Joshua. *Discourses on Art*. New York: Collier Books, 1961. London: Collier-Macmillan, 1961.

Richter, Hans. *Dada: Art and Anti-art*. New York: McGraw-Hill, 1965. London: Thames and Hudson, 1966.

Roger-Marx, Claude. *Graphic Art of the Nineteenth Century*. New York: McGraw-Hill, 1962.

Rudhyar, Dane. *Art as Release of Power, and Other Writings on Art*. Oceana, Calif.: Harbison and Harbison, 1929.

———. "The Artist as Avatar," *Occult Review*, London, June 1939, pp. 23–27.

Ruskin, John. *Art Criticism*, ed. Robert L. Herbert. New York: Doubleday, 1964.

Scharf, Aaron. *Art and Photography*. Baltimore: Penguin Books, 1974. London: Allen Lane, 1968.

Schmutzler, Robert. *Art Nouveau*. New York: Harry N. Abrams, 1964. London: New English Library, 1970.

Seuphor, Michel. *L'Art Abstrait: Ses Origines, Ses Premières Maîtres*. Paris: Galerie Maeght, 1950.

———. *Dictionary of Abstract Art*, trans. Lionel Izod et al. New York: Paris Book Co., 1957.

Shattuck, Roger. *The Banquet Years: The Origins of the Avant-garde in France*. New York: Doubleday, 1961. London: Faber and Faber, 1959.

Stewart, Thomas C. *The City as an Image of Man*. London: Latimer Press, 1970.

Studio International, "Cybernetic Serendipity: The Computer and the Arts," London: 1968.

Swenson, Gene R. *The Other Tradition*. Phildelphia: Institute of Contemporary Art, 1966.

Talbot, Douglas, ed. *Film: An Anthology*. Berkeley, Calif.: University of California Press, 1966.

Tolstoy, Count Leo. *What is Art? and Essays on Art*, trans. Aylmer Maude. New York and London: Oxford University Press, 1962.

Vasari, Giorgio. *Lives of the Artists*, ed. Betty Burroughs. New York: Simon and Schuster, 1946. Harmondsworth, Mdx.: Penguin Books, 1970.

Venturi, Lionello. *History of Art Criticism.* New York: E.P. Dutton, 1964.

Waldberg, Patrick, ed. *Surrealism.* New York: McGraw-Hill, 1965. London: Thames and Hudson, 1966.

Willett, John. *Expressionism.* New York: McGraw-Hill, 1970. London: Weidenfelid and Nicholson, 1971.

Wolflin, Heinrich. *Principles of Art History,* trans. M.D. Hottinger. New York: Dover Books, 1932.

Worringer, Wilhelm. *Abstraction and Empathy.* London: Routledge and Kegan Paul, 1953.

————. *Form in Gothic,* trans. Herbert Read. New York: Schocken Books, 1964. London: Tiranti, 1964.

Youngblood, Gene. *Expanded Cinema.* New York: E. P. Dutton, 1970. London: Studio Vista, 1971.

Acknowledgements

THERE ARE many energies that go into a book like this, and in no way can I conceive of it as the effort of a single person. My gratitude and indebtedness extend to my wife Miriam who especially encouraged me to do this book in the first place; to my publisher Samuel Bercholz who had the vision and courage to accept the responsibility for backing up this book; to Michael Fagan and Vincent Stuart who kindly read the manuscript and offered their perceptive criticisms and encouragement; to the copy editor, Ellen Hershey, without whose keen critical abilities this book would not be what it now is; to Armando Busick for the splendid drawing of the hemispheres; to Ra Morris for some of the smaller diagrams; to my persevering typist Judith Tart; to Hal Hershey for the general design and coordination of the book; to Helmut Zimmerman for permission to reproduce a painting from his "Individuation" series; to Willard van de Bogart for permission to quote from his unpublished essays, "Entropic Art," and "Environmental Media Art," to my mentors who first set me on the particular path I have since followed; to my many students whose enthusiasm and interest encouraged me to pursue ideas and intuitions into realms where I might otherwise have been hesitant to tread; to all of my friends, colleagues and acquaintences who have borne with me through this long project; and finally, this book is a special tribute to all of those human beings of whatever time and place who have sincerely labored to express their vision of the inherent integrity of things.

I would also like to thank the following publishers for permission to reprint material copyrighted or controlled by them:

Excerpt from Blaise Cendrar's "Prose of The Trans-Siberian and The Little Jeanne of France." Translated by Roger Kaplan, copyright 1972 by *Chicago Review*.

City Lights for permission to quote from Jack Hirschman's edition of the *Antonin Artaud Anthology*, copyright 1965; and from Allen Ginsberg's *Howl and Other Poems*, copyright 1959.

E. P. Dutton & Co., Inc., for permission to quote from S. Foster Damon's *A Blake Dictionary*, and Gene Youngblood's *Expanded Cinema*.

Lawrence Ferlinghetti. *A Coney Island of the Mind*. Copyright 1958 by Lawrence Ferlinghetti, reprinted by permission of New Directions Publishing Corporation.

W. H. Freeman and Company for permission to quote from *The Psychology of Consciousness* by Robert E. Ornstein, copyright 1972.

Grove Press for permission to quote from Richard Howard's translation of Andre Breton's *Nadja*, copyright 1950.

Harcourt Brace Jovanovich and Faber and Faber, Ltd., for permission to quote from "The Wasteland," in *Collected Poems 1909–1962* by T. S. Eliot, copyright 1936 by Harcourt Brace Jovanovich Inc; copyright 1963, 1969 by T. S. Eliot, reprinted by permission of publisher; from Lewis Mumford's *Technics and Civilization*, copyright 1934 by Lewis Mumford and Harcourt Brace and Company and Routledge Kegan and Paul, Ltd.; and from Lewis Mumford's *Pentagon of Power*, copyright 1971 by Lewis Mumford and Harcourt Brace Jovanovich, Inc. and Secker and Wurburg, Ltd.

Harper and Row, Publishers, for permission to quote from *Myths, Dreams and Mysteries*, by Mircea Eliade; from *Collected Essays, The Doors of Perception & Heaven and Hell, Island*, and *The Perennial Philosophy*, by Aldous Huxley; and from Karl R. Popper, *The Poverty of Historicism*.

The Hutchinson Publishing Group for permission to quote from *The Collected Works of Ramana Maharshi*.

The Macmillan Company and A. P. Watt & Son Ltd., for permission to quote from W. B. Yeats' *Collected Poems*, copyright 1924, by the Macmillan Publishing Co., Inc. renewed by Bertha Georgia Yeats, 1952; from *A Vision* by W. B. Yeats, copyright 1937 by W. B. Yeats, renewed 1965 by Bertha Georgia Yeats and Anne Butler Yeats; from *The Ghost in the Machine* by Arthur Koestler, copyright 1968 by the Macmillan Company and A. D. Peters Ltd.

The McGraw Hill Book Company for permission to quote from the *Rise of the Artist* by Andrew Martindale, copyright 1972; and *Surrealism* by Patrick Waldberg, copyright 1964.

The Museum of Modern Art and Joshua C. Taylor for permission to quote from *Futurism* by Joshua C. Taylor, copyright 1959 by Museum of Modern Art and Joshua C. Taylor.

William Morrow and Company, Inc., for permission to quote from *The Universe and Dr. Einstein* by Lincoln Barnett, copyright 1948 by Harper & Brothers and Lincoln Barnett; copyright 1950 by Lincoln Barnett.

New Directions for permission to quote from *Illuminations* by Arthur Rimbaud, translated by Louise Varese, copyright 1957 by New Directions; and from *A Season in Hell*, by Arthur Rimbaud, translated by Louise Varese. Copyright 1961 by New Directions.

W. W. Norton & Co., and St. John's College, Oxford and Hogarth Press, Ltd., for permission to quote from *Duino Elegies* by Rainer Maria Rilke, translated by J. B. Leishman and Stephen Spender, copyright 1939 by

Random House, Inc., for permission to quote from *The Social History of Art, II,* by Arnold Hauser, translated by Stanley Godman, copyright 1957 by Alfred A. Knopf, Inc.

Simon and Schuster, Inc., for permission to quote from *The Diary of Vaslav Nijinsky,* edited and translated by Romola Nijinsky, copyright renewed © 1963 by Simon and Schuster, Inc.

Thames and Hudson, Ltd., for permission to quote from *The Concise History of Photography* by Helmut and Alison Gernsheim.

The University of Chicago Press for permission to quote from *Charles Henry and the Formation of a Psychological Aesthetic* by José A. Argüelles, copyright 1972 by the University of Chicago.

The University of Texas Press for permission to quote from the *Autobiography of José Clemente Orozco* by José Clemente Orozco, translated by Robert E. Stevenson, copyright 1962 by The University of Texas.

Viking Press, Inc., and Laurence Pollinger Ltd. for permission to quote from *The Complete Poems of D. H. Lawrence,* edited by Vivian de Sola Pinto and F. Warren Roberts, copyright © 1964, 1971 by Angelo Ravagli and C. M. Weekly, Executors of the Estate of Frieda Lawrence Ravagli, all rights reserved; and from *Fantasia of the Unconscious* by D. H. Lawrence, copyright 1922 by Thomas B. Seltzer, Inc., copyright renewed 1950 by Frieda Lawrence.

Viking Press, Inc., and the Society of Authors as the literary representative of the Estate of James Joyce for permission to quote from *Finnegan's Wake* by James Joyce, copyright 1939 by James Joyce, copyright renewed 1967 by James Joyce.

Viking Press, Inc., for permission to quote from *The Book of the Hopi* by Frank Waters, copyright 1963 by Frank Waters.

George Wittenborn, Inc., for permission to quote from *On My Way* by Hans Arp, translated by Ralph Mannheim, copyright 1948 by Wittenborn, Schultz, Inc.; and from *Concerning the Spiritual in Art,* by Wassily Kandinsky adopted from the Michael Sadleir translation, copyright, 1947 by Nina Kandinsky.

A major portion of Chapter 17 was originally published under the title, "Adolf Wölfli, St. Adolf II, and the Art of Transformation," in *Arts and Society,* Vol. 9, no. 2, Summer-Fall, 1972, pp. 308–324.

Index